JAMES REDDIE

RESEARCHES
HISTORICAL AND CRITICAL
IN
MARITIME
INTERNATIONAL LAW

VOLUME II

Elibron Classics
www.elibron.com

Elibron Classics series.

ISBN 1-4212-0055-4 (paperback)
ISBN 1-4212-0054-6 (hardcover)

This Elibron Classics Replica Edition is an unabridged facsimile of the edition published in 1845, Edinburgh.

RESEARCHES,

HISTORICAL AND CRITICAL,

IN

MARITIME

INTERNATIONAL LAW.

By JAMES REDDIE, ESQ.,

ADVOCATE,

AUTHOR OF "INQUIRIES IN THE SCIENCE OF LAW," AND OF "AN HISTORICAL VIEW OF THE LAW OF MARITIME COMMERCE."

VOL. II.

EDINBURGH:

THOMAS CLARK, LAW BOOKSELLER.

BENNING & CO., BIGG & SON,

WILLIAM BLACKWOOD & SONS, LONDON.

MILLIKEN, DUBLIN.

MDCCCXLV.

GLASGOW:—PRINTED BY GEORGE RICHARDSON.

CONTENTS.

VOL. I.

PRELIMINARY OBSERVATIONS.

SEVENTH PERIOD.

CHAPTER IX.

SECTION I.

EIGHTH PERIOD.

CHAPTER X.

SECTION I.

CONTENTS.

VOL. II.

PRELIMINARY OBSERVATIONS.

As formerly intimated, this second volume has been divided into two parts, embracing the two remaining periods of the history of Maritime international law, which elapsed —the one from the peace of Amiens in 1801, to the general peace in 1815; the other, from that happy event to the present times.

In the first of these periods, the chief object of investigation is, the actual administration of Maritime international law during war, unfortunately marked by too many deviations from the genuine principles of that law. And the multiplicity of events in the course of that period, has made it proper, for the sake of perspicuity, to divide it, although short, compared with the preceding periods of our historical sketch, into still shorter periods, such as from 1801 to 1803, from 1803 to Nov. 1806, from 1806 to 1812, and from 1812 to 1815.

In the course of these periods, there were great variations in the administration of the Common consuetudinary law; but we do not find much additional or different conventional maritime law, properly so called.

Several maritime states appear to have entered into treaties of commerce and navigation with other maritime states; some confirming, others modifying the common law of nations. And these treaties, which may be found in the Recueil des Traités by Martens, are, of course, to be consulted in the first instance, as constituting the Conventional law of nations, between the contracting parties, while the treaties lasted. But the treaties, into which the French Emperor, in a manner, compelled several of the other European governments to enter, in order to make them co-operate with him, in carrying into effect his continental system, appear to have terminated with the power of Napoleon. And neither the treaties concluded at the peace of Amiens, nor the treaties concluded at the general peace, in the years 1814 and 1815, contained any stipulations or engagements, with regard to the rule "free ship, free goods," or the other rules propounded in the scheme of the armed neutrality.

Although, however, the Common law of nations was not materially affected by any treaties or conventions during this period, reports of various important judicial determinations, various important systematic works and controversial pamphlets appeared, in the maritime department of that law. And, to the analytical review of the more important of these treatises, separate chapters or sections have been allotted, as well as to the shorter divisions of the period to be now surveyed.

In the concluding period, from the General Peace in 1815, to the present times, we have little additional, either new or renovated, Conventional maritime international law, peculiarly applicable to the state of war. Nor, happily, during this period, has there been occasion to resort to the administration of the Common consuetudinary law of nations, applicable to a state of war, so as to afford opportunities for the further illustration of pre-established principles, or for the determination of new cases, for the first time emergent. But during this period, there have appeared, as during the preceding more recent periods, especially on the continent, a considerable number of systematic works on international law. And, under the disadvantage of occasional, perhaps too frequent repetitions, we humbly conceived it might not be without its use, to give at some length, an analytical, and also a critical review of these works, in separate chapters or sections. For, in this way, it appeared we should have an opportunity of more fully unfolding the doctrines of Maritime international law, and of supplying in some measure, such defects in our first volume, as might have arisen from the brevity of our narrative of the state of the law, in so many successive ages. And in this way, it also appeared, we should have an opportunity of investigating the statements and doctrines of those more recent works, some of which appeared to us to require animadversion, both in point of fact, and in point of law.

At the same time, we are aware, that for the frequent repetitions just alluded to, we ought to request the indulgence of the reader. And our apology is, that, in reviewing in succession, the various systematic treatises on Maritime international law, we, of course, met again and again, with the same, or similar doctrines, which appeared to us to be erroneous. And that, for the sake of perspicuity, we found it necessary to repeat our objections or answers, on most of these occasions, rather than maké, merely a general reference to previous objections or answers, which would have left the argument incomplete and obscure. In our animadversions, likewise, when called upon in duty, to contradict statements which appeared to us to be groundless and fallacious, or to expose the looseness and inconsequential nature of the arguments on the opposite side, we may have occasionally been led, insensibly, to depart from our simple narrative, or the strictly philosophical language of scientific enquiry, and to adopt more of a controversial style than we could have wished. But, we trust, we have never exceeded the limits of fair criticism, or failed in the usual courtesy of authors, or on the duty imposed by the Comitas Gentium.

The most interesting new Conventional Maritime international law, which arose during this period, is happily applicable, not so much to a state of war, as to a state of peace. We allude to the International arrangements, made at, and since the congress of Vienna, among the nations of Christendom, for the more complete suppression of the African slave trade. Into the investigation of this subject, however, we do not propose to enter at present. There may, perhaps, in this department of the intercourse of nations, be rules of justice and equity, rights and obligations, independent of convention or treaty, as well as in war. The end must be such, as to justify the measures adopted. These measures must be regulated by their adaptation to the attainment of the end. But the subject is comparatively new, and formed no part of our original design. Although the abolition of this odious traffic, has long been familiar to the educated, and even to the labouring and less educated classes in Britain, the views and feelings of these classes among other nations, do not, on this subject, appear to have yet attained the same degree of maturity. In this situation of matters, there might be a risk of confusion of ideas, and consequent error, in mingling together, the principles of Maritime international law during war, and the rules of International co-operation, for the suppression of the African slave trade, which have hitherto rested very much, if not entirely, on convention alone. And there is now, happily, a fair prospect of any differences, between France and this country, on this subject, being settled, through the amicable negociation of the highly talented, accomplished, and philanthropic commissioners, nominated by the respective governments.

12, Blythswood Square,
Glasgow, *May*, 1845.

MARITIME INTERNATIONAL LAW.

PERIOD NINTH.

Of Maritime International law, chiefly during war, from the Peace of Amiens in 1801-2, *to the General Peace of Paris in* 1815.

THE peace of Amiens was, in fact, merely the truce which Napoleon Bonaparte found it for his interest to give to the European nations, that he might more effectually promote his own ambitious views, and consolidate the political power which he had by that time acquired in France. And, in the course of the war renewed in 1803, there occurred greater, or at least as great departures from, and violations of, the hitherto recognized maritime law of nations, as had ever taken place. As he was aware, that the government and people of Great Britain, presented the greatest obstacle to his ambitious schemes of personal and national aggrandizement, one of his first manœuvres was, to cultivate the good will of the smaller kingdoms and states of the north, by favouring their pretensions, to the entire, absolute and unlimited liberty of neutral navigation and commerce during war, in order to indispose them towards, or to convert them into enemies of Great Britain. It continued also to be his obvious interest to do so; because it was chiefly through the establishment of such neutral pretensions, and consequent neutral interposition, that he could in the meantime supply the commercial wants of the nation, and repair in some measure, the disasters which the French navy, and mercantile marine had sustained, from the uniform success of the British arms at sea. But, after he had taken advantage of the services of the neutral states, to assist him in prosecuting his victories by land, and after he had, through the errors committed in succession by the other great continental sovereigns, and through his own splendid talents and unprecedented power of availing himself of circumstances and events, extended his empire by land, from the Mediterranean and the Atlantic, to the Baltic, he laid aside his pretended regard for the neutral trade of the northern nations, and had nearly succeeded in seizing and appropriating the Danish naval force, and in employing it for the purpose of invading, and at least harassing and distressing Great Britain, as he had done the continental states.

CHAPTER I.

Of Maritime International law during the interval of Peace from 1801 *to* 1803.

WORKS OF INTERNATIONAL JURISTS.

Before, however, commencing our narrative of the various infringements of Maritime international law, which took place during the period we are now to survey, we must notice some important works, not of a mere controversial nature, which appeared during the interval of peace between the armistice of Amiens, and the rupture in 1803. And here first presents itself, in 1801, the second edition, entirely recast, of the, with a few exceptions, very excellent work of M. de Martens, entitled, Précis du Droit des Gens Moderne de l' Europe, in one vol. 8vo. This work was announced, as intended "pour servir d'introduction à un Cours Politique et Diplomatique." And there appeared during the same year, by the same author, in three vols. 8vo., the likewise very useful work, entitled, Cours Diplomatique, ou Tableau des Relations Extérieures des Puissances de l'Europe. During the same year, also, M. de Martens had completed the seventh vol. 8vo. of his Recueil des principaux Traités conclus par les Puissances de l'Europe, depuis 1761, jusqu' à présent; and this collection to which we generally refer, it may be mentioned has been continued down to the present time, in the shape of a Nouveau Recueil et Supplement. Of the first of these works, of course, only a part relates to the subject of these Researches; and as it has become a standard book in diplomacy, we shall postpone our detailed notice of that part of it, till we come to the appearance of the third edition of it, at Göttingen, in 1821, as corrected and enlarged by the author, a short time before his death.

Besides these works of Martens, however, there appeared during this interval, two other works in German, not altogether of a controversial nature. The first, entitled, Versuch einer kritischen Ubersicht, der Volker-Seerechte, by Ludolf Holst, Versteher des Handels-Instituts zu St. Georg, was published at Hamburgh, in 1802, and was dedicated to the late king of Prussia. The work is announced as only the first part of what the author intended; but it does not appear, from the German catalogues, that any second part was ever published; and we have not been able to procure any such. The work, so far as published, is divided into sections.

The first section contains a brief critical review of the principal writers who have treated of the laws of nations in general, and especially of the rights of navigation, from ancient times down to the present. To the nations of antiquity, he remarks, this branch of the science was unknown; they had not even an ordinary word to express the idea conveyed by the modern term, neutrality. On the revival of the arts and sciences, in the twelfth and thirteenth centuries, some traces of the ideas of neutrality and its rights, are to be found in the scholastic writers, who taught moral theology, as well as in the jurists and theologians who preceded Vasquez, Suarez,

Gentilis, and Grotius, in the fourteenth, fifteenth, and sixteenth centuries. The works of Albericus Gentilis, and Grotius, he notices at some length. Among the chief writers on the law of nature and nations, in the course of the seventeenth and first half of the eighteenth century, he, of course, reckons Hobbes, Selden, Zouch, Pufendorff, Henry and Samuel Cocceii, Thomasius, Heineccius, Bynkershoek, Wolf, Burlamaqui, Réal, and Mably. But, he says, he must, in his Review, pass over all these, because they have either merely repeated what Grotius said, or have omitted the rights of navigation, from the exigencies of the times not having called their attention to the subject. In this remark, we have seen the author is, in point of fact, so far mistaken. But it is true that none of the authors he enumerates, have treated solely and exclusively of maritime neutrality and its rights. And he therefore proceeds to the authors of the second half of the eighteenth century, who have done so; and gives a more full account of the writings of Hübner, Galiani, Lampredi, and Azuni. He then proceeds to give an account of the works of those writers, who have not, like the foregoing, endeavoured to unfold the subject systematically and profoundly, but who, he says, have expounded the common and general rules and maxims, which belong to the defence of the rights of neutrals, without allowing themselves to indulge or extravagate in theoretical investigations. Under this class, he gives an account of the Traité Juridico politico sur les Prises Maritimes, by D'Abreu, as translated from the Spanish, of the work of Schlegel Sur la visite des Vaisseaux Neutres sous Convoi, of the Collection by Eggers of state-papers, on the misunderstanding between Denmark and England, and the Northern Convention of neutrality; of Borneman on the customary visitation of neutral vessels, and on convoy. He next notices the writers on the empire of, or jurisdiction over the sea, and on the appropriation of the sea, such as Grotius, Selden, &c.; on the procedure of maritime courts and maritime police, such as Martens, Versuch über Kaper, feindliche Nehmungen, und Wiedernehmungen; D'Abreu, Traité des Prises, Valin, Traité des Prises; Code des Prises, 1784; Guischard, Code des Prises Maritimes, Paris an. VIII. 2 tom. 12mo. The author next treats of maritime law diplomacy, and of the politics of navigation and trade; and he concludes this section with an account of the history of the war between Denmark and England, by C. F. Primon, and of the work of Barrere, entitled, La Liberté des Mers, ou le Gouvernement Anglois devoilé, an. VI. de la Republique.

In this review of the works of previous writers on Maritime international law, Dr. Holst does not show much acuteness or extent of observation; and his views appear to be rather those of a merchant, bent on the accumulation of wealth by means of neutral commerce, than those of an impartial and enlightened lawyer, giving equal consideration to the rights and interests of all nations indiscriminately.

In the second section of this work, entitled, Geschichtliche Darstellung des ältern und des neuern Seerechts, Historical description of the older and of the more recent maritime law, Dr. Holst, if he does not misrepresent, at least does not state fully and correctly, the historical facts, and thereby leads others into error, and affords pretexts for propagating erroneous opinions.

He begins with what he denominates the old maritime law, and distinguishes it from the new, by stating the two contested principles of each; namely, of the old, neutral goods in a hostile vessel are free, hostile goods in a neutral vessel are unfree; and of the new, neutral goods in a hostile vessel are unfree, hostile goods in a neutral vessel are free. He goes on to give first, outlines for a practical history of maritime capture, as prize, its origin, progress and duration; secondly, a nearer historical view of the different epochs and steps, or progressive advancement of maritime law; thirdly, a short sketch of the system of privateering in all its principal parts and epochs; fourthly, a continuation of his historical description of the old maritime law. To this last he subjoins, what he calls an historico-critical examination of the Consolato del Mare. But in this, he does not show any of the critical discernment, or historical research and sagacity, previously displayed by Capmany, and subsequently in a still more eminent degree, by Pardessus. And he concludes this part of his work, with what he calls the wider extension, and farther advancement of the old maritime law, from the oldest treaties, to the middle of the seventeenth century. In the second division of this section of his work, Dr. Holst gives, what he calls, an historical description of the new maritime law, its origin, progress, and various fates or destinies. He first states its contents or substance to be, neutral goods in hostile vessels are unfree; hostile goods in neutral vessels are free; and then gives, what he calls the origin of this new maritime law, particularly with reference to what he makes the second half of it. He next gives, what he calls, the institution (establishment) of the new maritime law between Holland and Spain in 1650, in France, between that kingdom and Holland in 1651, particularly in 1662. He then gives, what he calls, the reception or adoption (aufnahme) of the new maritime law in England, between that kingdom and Holland in 1667.

But, in this account of the recognition and adoption of the alleged new maritime law in the course of the seventeenth century, Dr. Holst, if he does not misrepresent facts, at least sports with historic truth, or represents facts in such a way, and with such omissions, as to lead to erroneous inferences and conclusions. He does not pretend that the new maritime law is founded on the principles of the natural, or primary, or universal law of nations. He does not show that there is any reason or justice in the first half of this law, namely, in holding that the goods of a friend may be justly seized as prize and confiscated, merely because they happen to be found on board the vessel of his friend, who happens to be our enemy; or in holding, as in both the first and second parts of this new law, that the liability of goods to hostile capture should be determined, not by the character or property of the goods themselves, but by the character or property of the vessel, which accidentally happens to carry them. He does not show that this pretended new law was supported by universal practice, or even by general European usage. He omits to mention, that the maritime ordinances of France and Spain, during the sixteenth and seventeenth centuries, and particularly the celebrated Ordonnance de la Marine of Louis XIV. in 1681, established a rule quite the reverse of the second half of this new maritime law. He omits also to mention that the general practice of England and of Holland, as well as of Denmark and Sweden, was just the opposite of the second rule of this alleged new maritime law. And the fact turns out to be, that the whole foundation for this grand change, and new maritime law, is to be sought and found, merely in the treaties which several nations, chiefly through the urgency of Holland, in order to support her carrying trade, agreed to enter into pro tempore, and in consideration of the concession of reciprocal advantages. So far as those treaties went, so long as they lasted, they were obligatory on the contracting parties. And to this extent, as they were deviations from, and changes upon the old law, they may be said to have constituted a new law for the time. But this was merely a particular temporary law, a jus pactitium, not binding upon other nations, who were not parties to those special agreements, nor even upon those parties who were so, in relation to other nations.

The next division of his work, Dr. Holst entitles, progress of the new maritime law, down to the origin of the armed neutrality in 1780, and he embraces in his account, Spain, France, England and Holland. But after showing on what the new maritime law, so much lauded and magnified by Dr. Holst, is founded, and in what it consists; and after the narrative already given, of the actual general practice of the European nations, during the sixteenth, seventeenth and eighteenth centuries, independently of special paction, it does not appear necessary to follow this writer through this division. Still less does it appear necessary to do so through the last division of his work, entitled, Disputes, Controverted questions, on the right of navigation during the American war, and origin of the northern convention, and of the thence resulting armed neutrality of 1780. For here, he seems still more to lay aside the impartiality of the historian, or historical reviewer; and censures the conduct of Great Britain, because, while she proclaimed her willingness to abide by all her treaties, relative to neutral trade, she did not choose to alter the mode of administering the maritime law of nations, which she had followed for upwards of three hundred years, in order to please the despotic Empress of all the Russias.

The subsequent part of his treatise, as projected by him, and which was to be entitled, the Rights of navigation, and the contests respecting them, from the end of the American war, to the termination of the French revolutionary war, Dr. Holst does not appear to have published; probably in consequence of the events in the earlier part of the French imperial war.

BERNHARD SEBASTIAN NAU.

The other German work, before mentioned, as having appeared about the commencement of the present century, the Grundsätze des Völkerseerechts, by B. S. Nau, published at Hamburgh in 1802, is much more valuable. It is a short treatise, but it embraces all the principal doctrines of Maritime international law; is sytematically arranged; and is much more impartial.

In his introduction, he notices the different descriptions of international law; the necessary, original, and universal; the voluntary, modified, or natural social; the consuetudinary; the conventional; the European; and he gives also a brief history of Maritime international law, and a short account of its literature.

In chapter first, he treats of the sea. I. Of the appropriation of lands and seas generally, through original or derivative acquisition. II. How far the open and larger seas of the earth, or oceans, are susceptible of appropriation or dominion. III. Of the appropriation of, or dominion over, particular single smaller seas; and of the sea generally, adjacent to the coasts, or shores of the territories of nations.

In chapter second, he treats of the principles of international law, relative to maritime navigation, and other maritime affairs in time of peace. I. Of the freedom of navigation. II. Of the strand or shore right; Jus Littoris. III. Of the great fisheries in the European and other seas, and on the coasts. IV. Of the reciprocal treatment and management of vessels in the open seas. V. Of the maritime ceremonial.

In chapter third, he treats of the principles of Maritime international law applicable to powers at peace, during wars between or among other powers. I. Of neutrality generally. II. Of goods contraband of war. III. Of the right and mode of visitation and search. IV. Whether free ship makes free goods? or of the confiscation of hostile goods on board neutral vessels at sea. V. Whether the liability of a vessel to confiscation renders the cargo also liable to confiscation? or of neutral goods in hostile vessels. VI. Of the right of neutrals to carry on all kinds of traffic, to, and with, their own proper territories or possessions. VII. Can a trade, which is forbidden to neutrals during peace, be considered as permitted during war? VIII. The subjects of neutral powers are interdicted from entering blockaded ports. IX. Who is the competent judge in doubtful cases, of neutral vessels brought into port as prize. X. Of the right to remain neutral. XI. Of breaches, or infringements of neutrality.

In chapter fourth, he treats of the defence and prosecution of maritime international rights, via facti, by actual operations. I. Of retorsion and reprisal. II. Of maritime war, and the occurrences at the opening or commencement of it. Declaration not necessary in modern times. Manifesto. Embargo. III. Of the prosecution of hostilities by privateers, capture, and recapture. IV. Prosecution of hostilities by government, or state ships of war. V. Of the fleets of allies; of assistant or auxiliary, and subsidiary fleets. VI. Approximation to peace. Termination of hostilities by the conclusion of peace; treaties.

In chapter fifth, Mr. B. S. Nau treats, I. Of ambassadors, their power and privileges. II. Of commercial consuls. III. Of the balance of power among maritime states.

From the preceding detail, it is plain, M. Nau's

arrangement is good; and, that, although sufficiently zealous in supporting the claims of neutral traders, he is comparatively much more impartial, appears from his stating the chief disputed points, such as, "free ship, free goods," in the shape of questions; and from the following section of his work, § 185, "The preceding remarks prove, that, according to the positive law of nations, no general valid (generally prevailing) principle exists, which might prevent future mistakes. It is not to be denied, that the maxim, 'a free ship makes a free cargo,' would be a very advantageous maxim for neutrals: and the question comes to be, whether those nations, who do not adopt this maxim, act contrary to the natural law of nations, in cases where no treaty determines the matter otherwise. If it is permitted, it is argued, to capture and seize hostile goods, wheresoever they may be found, even on board neutral vessels at sea, to the manifest infringement of the freedom of neutral nations, and this upon the ground, that the belligerent has the right to weaken indefinitely the power of the enemy, in order to dispose him to pacific sentiments, why should it not also be permitted to seize neutral ships, and to prevent them from carrying their own proper goods to hostile places? The enemy, in the former way, does not receive so great an accession of strength, while it causes to the opposite party an irreparable loss. Why then, is the one allowed, and the other not allowed? Why does the necessity of defending ourselves permit an attack upon the freedom and independence of those who carry hostile goods; and why is it not permitted to do the same to neutral nations, who carry their own goods to our enemies? For this reason, answers Lampredi, because the losses arising from our capture of the hostile goods, fall almost wholly upon our enemies; and the little loss which thence arises to our neutral friends, may be easily compensated; while, on the other hand, the losses which neutral nations would sustain, if they were prevented from selling and conveying, even in the present way, their natural and industrial produce to nations involved in war, as they hitherto did, would fall wholly upon such neutral nations, and would, in no way, be compensated."

CHAPTER II.

Of the administration of Maritime International law from the commencement of the war in 1803, *to the General Peace of Paris in* 1815, *particularly by France and Great Britain;—French, Berlin and Milan Decrees, British orders in Council.*

So much for two of the more eminent, among others, of the German writers, whose works were expressly on the maritime law of nations, and appeared in the interval between the peace of Amiens, and the rupture in 1803. In the course of the war which ensued, and was only finally terminated in 1815, and which may be denominated the French imperial war, in contradistinction to its precursor, the French revolutionary war, there appeared several other writers on Maritime international law. But before giving any account of them, it may be proper to ascertain what was the actual practical administration of the maritime law of nations during this period, by the principal maritime states of Europe, particularly by Great Britain and France; and with a view to perspicuity, it may be right to divide this period into three shorter ones; the first, from the commencement of the war in 1803, to the Berlin decree of the Emperor Napoleon in November 1806; the second, from the Berlin decree in November 1806, to the revocation of the British orders in council, of January and November 1807, and of April 1809, in the year 1812; the third, from the revocation of the British orders in council of 1807, in the year 1812, to the general peace of Paris in 1815.

Section I.

Period 1803, *to November* 1806.

In Great Britain during this period, and prior to the extraordinary remedies, to which the boundless ambition and persevering animosity of the French Emperor, appear to have forced the British government to resort; Sir William Scott continued to administer the maritime law of nations according to the previously recognized equitable principles so luminously expounded by him, and still farther developed in their application to the new cases which emerged. These judgments, it is well known, continued to be ably recorded, and made known to the European public by Sir Chr. Robinson, in the fifth and sixth volumes of his reports, and afterwards by Dr. Edwards, Dr. Dodson, and Dr. Haggard. An abridgement of them was also given to the public in 1812, by Mr. Chitty, in his practical treatise "On the law of nations, relative to the effect of war on the commerce of belligerents and neutrals." To attempt a detailed review of these works, would be here superfluous, as they are pretty generally known to that portion of the British public who are interested, or take an interest in such matters. And, it may be sufficient here to remark, that the consistency, fairness, impartiality, and general equity of these judgments, made a very strong impression on those individuals among continental nations, whose views were not warped by national prejudice and temporary animosity, or by selfish personal interest; and that they formed a body of common or consuetudinary Maritime international law during war, which is much milder, on various leading principles, than the celebrated Ordonnance de la Marine of Louis XIV. in 1681, and is likely to have a greater, and more durable influence in future, on the administration of that department of international law among the European powers.

Even during this early period of the war, however, Britain has been accused of violating the law of nations, by extending the military operation of blockade from ports or harbours, to the mouths of rivers and whole coasts, by what has been designated a Paper, or Cabinet blockade, namely, a notification to neutral foreign powers, that certain ports, rivers, or coasts, from one port to another, will be held as in a state of blockade, although not actually blockaded by an adequate naval force. We shall therefore enquire, whether, and if so, to what extent, this charge is well founded. And in doing so, we must distinguish both the period to which the charge is applied, and the description of the operation, to which the appellation of blockade is given.

Now, according to the law of nations, as administered by Britain, in common with other maritime states, there is no such thing, properly speaking, as a Paper or Cabinet blockade; there is no legally effectual blockade, such as to warrant confiscation for a breach of it, unless it be an actual blockade, maintained by an adequate naval force, such as to render it dangerous to approach the place blockaded. In the case of the Betsey, 18th December 1798,[1] Sir William Scott thus laid down the law. "On the question of blockade, three things must be proved; first, the existence of an actual blockade; second, the

[1] Rob. Adm. Rep. I. p. 93.

knowledge of the party; third, some act of violation, either by going in, or coming out with a cargo, laden after the commencement of the blockade." And this judicial opinion was adhered to and confirmed in a number of subsequent cases, during the French revolutionary war; such as the Neptunus, 18th July 1799,[1] the Ocean, 16th May 1801.[2] Under such a declared state of the law, British ships of war or privateers, could have no inducement to capture any neutral vessel, on the ground of a breach of blockade, unless there was really a blockade de facto. Indeed, in the case of the Maria Schroeder, 15th July 1800,[3] where the blockade of Havre had not been strictly maintained, the neutral vessel was ordered to be restored. And such appears to have continued to be the administration of the law of blockade by Britain, from the renewal of the war in 1803, till after the Berlin decree of the French Emperor Napoleon in November 1806. The British orders in council, during that period, which notified the blockade to neutral powers, gave directions simultaneously for the preparation of the naval force requisite to commence and maintain it. And so far as regarded individual ports or harbours, there was no extension whatever of the old established right of blockade.

The only questionable points, were the blockade of rivers and the blockade of a whole coast. And there can be no doubt, the British government in the summer of 1803, ordered the blockade of the Elbe and the Weser, in consequence of the French having invaded and occupied the then Electorate of Hanover. But that the mouth of a river, which has its source and its whole course within the territory of the enemy, may, for the purpose of distressing and weakening the enemy, be lawfully blockaded, as well as a harbour or port, there

[1] Rob. II. p. 110. [2] Rob. III. p. 297. [3] Rob. III. p. 147.

seems to be no doubt; and, consequently, the blockade of the Elbe and the Weser was lawful, so far as directed against, and so far as it merely affected the enemy. The chief difficulty arises from these rivers running partly through neutral territories, either in the interior of the country, or towards the mouth of the river. And we apprehend belligerents are not entitled to blockade the mouths of rivers running through countries belonging to neutrals, although occupied by the military forces of the enemy, solely for the purpose, and without any other reason or object, than to prevent that enemy from having commercial intercourse with neutrals. Accordingly, in the blockade of the Elbe and the Weser, the British prize court held, that "such a description of blockade admitted of a greater latitude of interpretation, and entitled the neutral parties to all the indulgent considerations, that can fairly be applied to their case." The Spes and Irene, 10th July 1804,[1] the Maria, 20th November 1805.[2] And in this way, the objection to the blockade of a river may be, and was removed, by confining its effects to the enemy, and relieving neutrals from its operation.

There still remains the charge against Britain of having, even during the short period of the war we are now contemplating, blockaded not merely ports or harbours and rivers, but also whole coasts. And there can be no doubt, that by the order in council, of the 16th May 1805, the British government directed that the necessary measures should be taken for the blockade of the coasts, rivers, and ports from the river Elbe, to the port of Brest, both inclusive. Still, however, this was nothing but an actual blockade; the government simultaneously directed the measures necessary for an effectual blockade; and no neutral vessel was confiscated for the

[1] Rob. V. p. 76. [2] Rob. VI. p. 201.

breach of any thing less than an actual blockade. This was not a paper blockade, or by notification merely, without any adequate force to maintain it, like the subsequent prohibitory Orders in council of 1807. And there does not appear to be any valid ground in law, for holding that the blockade of a coast, or of a series or line of ports, situated near each other, is not an equally legitimate military operation, as the blockade of a single port, provided an adequate naval force be brought to bear upon the coast. If the ports be contiguous, or near each other, the force directed against each, will embrace and include the intervening coast. If the ports be distant from each other, the blockade will be an useless measure, in any point of view;—in fact, because neutral vessels are not likely either to land and deliver, or to ship and load goods on an open coast, without a harbour;—in law, as not being actual, or in reality, the military operation correctly designated a blockade.

Were it necessary to support the British blockade of May 1805 by precedent, reference might be made to the practice of the Dutch from the earlier part of the seventeenth century, as appearing from the resolutions of the States general in 1630, with regard to maritime blockade.[1] But this is unnecessary; because Britain hitherto claimed nothing but the ancient recognized right of actual blockade by a sufficient force. Nor is the distinction made in the order in council of May 1805, between the ports to the south, and the ports to the north of Ostend, liable to any valid legal objection. The former were the ports of the original territory of the enemy, or of countries annexed by conquest to that territory. The latter were the ports of countries merely under the temporary occupation of the

[1] Rob. III. p. 326.

enemy. And, in such circumstances, it was perfectly lawful for Great Britain as a belligerent, to relax her military operation of blockade in favour of the latter, in preference to the former ports.

The fact, then, seems to have been simply this, at least during the short period, we are here contemplating. While, on the one hand, the astonishing military successes of Napoleon had subjected a large portion of the continent to his dominion, or to his indirect influence; Britain had, on the other hand, by a series of naval victories greatly reduced, and almost annihilated the navies not only of France, but likewise of the other nations, over whom the influence of Napoleon then extended. And their thus increased naval establishment, the British government employed, not in extending the law of blockade, properly so called, as untruly alleged, but in extending de facto the legitimate exercise of the unquestionable right of blockade, by directing their increased naval power against a greater number of ports, and more extended line of sea coast.

With regard, again, to the practical administration of Maritime international law, by France, during the period we are now surveying, we have already seen, that, under Bonaparte, as First Consul, the jurisdiction in maritime prizes, was transferred from the ordinary courts of common law, to a Conseil des Prises, then instituted; and that under the direction of Portalis, and other able lawyers, a more correct administration succeeded, what the president of that council termed, "The previous insane (delirante) legislation of the Republic."

In addition to the Decisions du Conseil des Prises, established by Bonaparte when First Consul, pronounced chiefly under the direction of Portalis, as printed separately in sheets, with the Procés verbal of its installation, we have also an account of its proceedings, and of the other orders of the French government relative to maritime prize law, down to 1803-4, in the Code des Prises et du commerce, compiled by Dufriche Foulaines, published an. XIII, in 1804. Indeed, the last general body of prize regulations, established in France, excepting always the subsequent unwarrantably severe orders, to be afterwards noticed, which were promulgated in the Berlin and Milan decrees, and formed what was called the continental system of blockade, is contained in this work.[1] And so far at that time was France from recognizing the neutral doctrine of "free ship, free goods," that notwithstanding the favour otherwise shown to the neutral nations of the north of Europe, the captain of every neutral vessel destined for the ports of France, was required to have a formal certificate by the French commercial agent at the port of shipment, that he had not on board any produce of the British colonies, or any goods coming directly or indirectly from England; which, if found on board, were subjected to confiscation. And if, from omission, from forgetfulness, or from change of voyage, the neutral captain was not provided with such a certificate, he was admitted into the ports of the Republic, only upon condition of loading in return French produce and manufactures, equal in value to that of his cargo. Farther, so far was the French government from having given up, or being then disposed to give up, the exercise of the right of search, that by section 57 of this réglement of 1803, it was expressly declared, as in the Ordonnance de la Marine of 1681, "Tout navire, qui refusera d'amener ses voiles, après la sémonce, qui lui en aura été faite, pourra y être contraint; en cas de resistance, et de combat, il sera de bonne prise."

Soon after this, in 1804, 28 Flor. an XII, Napoleon

[1] No. 918, p. 1078.

Bonaparte was, by an Organic Senatus-consultum, declared Emperor of the French. And from this date, the chief departures from the ordinary administration of Maritime international law appear to have taken place. While Napoleon was guided by the advice of Portalis, France administered that law very much according to the principles of the Ordonnance de la Marine of 1681, modified, however, by the abandonment of the rules, the adoption of which had rendered the practice of France and Spain more severe than that of England and Holland, namely, the rules by which the hostile nature of the cargo was held to confiscate also the neutral vessel, and the hostile nature of the vessel to confiscate also the neutral cargo. To Portalis, likewise, Napoleon was greatly indebted, for his aid towards the accomplishment of his great measures, the Concordat, and the compilation and establishment of the Code Civil. But, towards the close of the short period now under consideration, Portalis died, and matters in France again changed for the worse. C' etoit en 1807, (says M. Hello, avocat general au cour de cassation, the eloquent biographer of Portalis) les voies du consulat etaient abandonnées; l' empire inclinait rapidement vers le despotisme; les usurpations du décret sur la loi, dataient de 1806. Pour un fondateur de l'ordre légal (Portalis) ennemi de l' intempérance dans le pouvoir, comme dans la liberté, il n' y avait, que la lutte, ou l'apostasie. Il fut dispensé de faire un choix. Il ne vit pas le gouvernement, qu' il avait aimé et servi, abuser de sa force, et dégénérer par la victoire. Il y avait eu de l 'opportunité dans son avênement aux affaires; il y eut de l' à propos jusque dans sa mort.

[1] Revue de Legislation, Tom. 9me. p. 41.

Section II.

Period from the Berlin Decree of the French Emperor Napoleon in November 1806, *to the Revocation of the British Orders in Council, of January and November* 1807, *and of April* 1809, *in the year* 1812.

The great charge against Great Britain, during this period, of deviation from the ordinary recognized administration of the maritime law of nations, is the British prohibitory orders in council, the general interdicts against all commercial communication with France and its dependencies, or the countries under its influence. Now, in point of historical fact, it appears, as formerly noticed, that England had once before, when persuaded by the Dutch, adopted, along with them, a similar mode of warfare, namely, in 1689, when these two nations were struggling to maintain the liberties of Europe against the overgrown power and aggressive policy of Louis XIV. But this general interdict England recalled, as soon as the neutral sovereigns of Denmark and Sweden remonstrated against it. And the answer of the British government, on the occasion we are now contemplating, was, that they had not commenced this mode of warfare; that a general interdict against all nations having any commercial intercourse with Great Britain, had been previously promulgated by the enemy; that they were compelled by necessity to resort to such an extraordinary remedy in self defence, against the unprecedented hostility of the French Emperor; and that they were disposed to recal their interdict, as soon as the enemy recalled his previous interdict.

To judge which belligerent was to blame, or was most to blame, for this acknowledged departure from the ordinary administration of international law, it is necessary to attend to their relative positions. By this time, Napoleon had, by his splendid military talents and indefatigable perseverance, and sagacity in availing himself of circumstances and events, succeeded in so wielding the extraordinary and almost supernatural energies, of a recently revolutionized and constitutionally warlike and pugnacious people, as to have not only completely subjugated Italy, Holland, and Flanders or Belgium, but also to have reduced almost all the other European nations to such a state of subjection, as not to have the power or hardihood to resist compliance with his demands. And the large extent of continental territory, over which his power or influence thus prevailed, he managed to render, if not absolutely hostile to Great Britain, at least so subservient to his wishes, as to exclude British commerce.

While occupied with the conquest of Italy, Holland, Belgium, and part of Germany, Napoleon, we have seen, rested satisfied with having removed the adjudication of maritime prizes from the ordinary tribunals to the Conseil des Prises, with establishing the reglement of 1803, resembling, in many respects, the ordonnance of 1681, and with confiscating all goods coming directly, or indirectly, from England. But, elevated beyond measure, by his unexampled series of successes against the other continental nations, particularly by his humiliation of Austria and Prussia, and provoked and irritated by the resistance of Great Britain by her naval victories, the reduction and almost annihilation of his naval force, and his consequent impotence at sea, Napoleon, in November 1806, issued from Berlin, his celebrated decree, subsequently known by that name, declaring the British islands in a state of blockade, and prohibiting all commerce or correspondence with them. In opposition to this Berlin decree, the British government first issued the order in council of the 7th January 1807, and finding it ineffectual, followed it up by the still more rigorous order in council, of the 11th November 1807, declaring that all the ports of France, or her allies, or of any other country at war with Great Britain, and also all the ports of Europe, from hich the sovereigns, without being at war, had excluded the British flag, and all the ports in the colonies belonging to the enemy, should, with reference to navigation and commerce, be subjected to the same restrictions, as if they were strictly blockaded; that commerce in the produce or manufactures of these countries should be deemed illegal, and that all vessels trading with these countries and colonies, should, with their cargoes, be deemed lawful prize. In consequence of this severe retaliation, the French Emperor in December 1807, issued from Milan, the decree which received that name, declaring, that every vessel, to whatever nation she might belong, whatever might be her cargo, to whomsoever it might belong, fitted out from, or going to England, or the British colonies, or any country occupied by British troops, should be captured and confiscated. In April 1809, the British government so far modified and relaxed the order in council of the 11th November 1807, as to limit the declaration of blockade, or rather general prohibition or interdict of maritime commerce, to France and its dependences, the north of Italy and Holland. In April 1812, the British government also declared its willingness to revoke the orders in council of 1807, as soon as the French Emperor should revoke the decrees of Berlin and Milan; and in June 1812, on the communication of an official report, that the French Emperor had revoked these decrees, actually issued an order in council, recalling the orders of 1807 and 1809.

The effects of such an unprecedented severe mode of warfare, could not fail to be most disastrous, not only to neutrals, but also to the subjects of the belligerent states. Indeed, so detrimental did it prove to the commerce and manufactures of Great Britain, by interrupting and impeding, if not preventing that neutral commerce which would so far have carried off the British colonial produce and manufactures, that the British government deemed it expedient, if not necessary, to have recourse to a great extension of the plan of granting licenses to individuals to trade with the enemy, so as to afford relief from the effects of the orders in council, and promote the introduction of British produce and manufacture into the continent, and at the same time preclude France from receiving any supplies through neutrals, unless the commodities had passed through, and paid a tribute to Great Britain.

There thus arose two questions: whether the British orders in council of 1807, as modified by the subsequent granting of licenses to trade with the enemy, were expedient or politic measures on the part of that government; and whether the general interdict of all commercial intercourse with the enemy, as relaxed by these licenses, could be justified, as consistent with the general principles of international law. And certainly, the policy or expediency of the general retaliatory interdict, even as modified by the licensing system, as it was called, was very much disputed at the time. It is questionable, whether the adoption of the exact counterpart of Napoleon's interdict against commerce with England, was the best mode of counteracting that unwarrantable measure. And it must be admitted, that the general interdict, and the concomitant licensing system, were attended with various bad consequences, as well as the exclusive continental system of Napoleon.

But the policy or impolicy of the British orders in council does not fall within the scope of this historical legal review. The long and keenly contested point of their national expediency, this is not the place to discuss. And it is to be hoped, that the extraordinary, but only conditional and temporary remedies resouted to, from necessity, just alluded to, will, like the Berlin and Milan decrees, and the continental system generally, never come to form any permanent part of the maritime consuetudinary law of nations during war.

With regard, again, to the justice or consistency with the principles of the natural common consuetudinary law of nations, of these orders in council, as establishing a declaratory general blockade of the ports and sea coasts of the enemy, and of the nations under his dominion, or rather as prohibiting all other nations from having any maritime commercial intercourse with these ports or sea coasts, except under the authority of licenses from the British government, under certification of confiscation as prize, Sir William Scott appears, in the case of the Fox and others, 30th May 1811,[1] to have thus expounded the law. "Their establishment," said that eminent judge, "was doubtless a great and signal departure from the ordinary administration of justice, in the ordinary state of the exercise of public hostility; but was justified by that extraordinary deviation (the Berlin and Milan decrees) from the common exercise of hostility, in the conduct of the enemy.[2] This blockade of France, if it is to be so characterized, is not an original independent act of blockade, to be governed by the common rules that belong simply to that operation of war. It is, in this instance, a counteracting reflex measure, compelled by the act of the enemy, and, as such, subject to other considerations, arising out of its peculiarly distinctive char-

[1] Edwards, Adm. Rep. p. 311. [2] p. 320.

acter. France declared, that the subjects of other states should have no access to England; on that account England declared, that the subjects of other states should have no access to France. So far this retaliatory blockade (if blockade it is to be called) is co-extensive with the principle; neutrals are prohibited to trade with France, because they are prohibited by France from trading with England. England acquires the right which it would not otherwise possess, to prohibit that intercourse by virtue of the act of France. Having so acquired it, it exercises it to its full extent, with entire competence of legal authority. And having so done, it is not for other countries to enquire, how far this country may be able to relieve itself farther from the aggressions of that enemy. The case is settled between them and itself, by the principle on which the intercourse is prohibited. If the convenience of this country, before the prohibition, required some occasional intercourse with the enemy, no justice that is due to other countries, requires that such an intercourse should be suspended, on account of any prohibition imposed upon them, on a ground so totally unconnected with the ordinary principles of a common measure of blockade, from which it is thus distinguished by its retaliatory character."

But while the conduct of the British, in issuing a retaliatory general interdict of commerce against France, may, as against the enemy, be thus legally justified, as necessary to counteract the similar interdict previously issued by the enemy, the effects of such an unprecedented mode of warfare could not fail to be very detrimental to the interests of neutrals. And the question comes to be, whether an unprecedented aggression by a belligerent, while it gives the opposite belligerent an equally extensive right of aggression against his enemy, gives him also a title to exercise that right of aggression against, or so as to damage the interests of third parties, bona fide and strictly impartial neutrals, who have had no accession whatever to the original act of aggression.

The proposition of Sir William Scott, that in consequence of the aggressive measure of Napoleon, the British government acquired a right which they had not before, namely, the right of retaliation against the aggressor, appears to be incontestable. It appears also to be clear, that those nations, who, though formerly neutral, entered into alliances with Napoleon for the promotion of his continental blockade, or who, although they did not enter into such alliances with him, or declare war, or dispatch fleets or cruizers against Britain, concurred or co-operated with the French Emperor, in the prosecution of his scheme, by excluding all British vessels from their ports, thereby legally and justly subjected themselves also to the consequences resulting from the British measure of retaliation. And such appears to have been the conduct and the actual state of many of the continental governments, before the more rigid British order in council of November 1807 was issued. It has, indeed, been argued, that this concurrence and co-operation of the other European continental states with the French Emperor, was not voluntary but compulsory. And, in an ethical point of view, this circumstance, so far as true, might give a claim to compassion, and to mild treatment in subsequent hostilities. But, in a legal point of view, their actual concurrence and aid in prosecuting the illegal aggression, although arising not from hostile intention, but from want of concert and judicious arrangements by these other governments among themselves, from intimidation, and the temporary dereliction of their national independence, sufficiently warranted the retaliation, even to the extent of affecting them.

If, on the other hand, there were nations, who, from a regard to their own welfare, cultivated, as they were entitled to cultivate, the friendship of the then powerful French Emperor, but who abstained from entering into any alliance with him against Britain, who, maintaining their national independence, did not in any respect aid, or become subservient to the promotion of the views of Napoleon, in excluding all British commerce with the European or other nations, and who bonâ fide observed a strict impartiality, the great characteristic and requisite of neutrality, such neutral nations, we humbly conceive, had a right to complain of the British retaliatory measures, so far as they interdicted and interrupted the ordinary commerce of these nations with the countries under the dominion of Napoleon, beyond the restrictions imposed by the established law of contraband of war, and of actual blockade. For, although, perhaps, in the majority of cases, retaliation, or the lex talionis, as it has been called, may be consistent with justice, it is not so invariably and indiscriminately. And at all events, the right of retaliation appears to be valid only against the aggressor, or those who side with and assist him. Accordingly, in expressing his disapprobation of certain international proceedings, such as the edict of Louis XIV. of 1672, and the Decrees of the States general of his own country of 1630 and 1666, Bynkershoek laid it down as clear doctrine, that the right of retaliation does not extend beyond the aggressor. Diceres id edictum, jure retorsionis subsistere. Sed retorsio non est, nisi adversus eum, qui ipse damni quid dedit; ac deinde patitur; non vero adversus communem amicum. * * Qui injuriam non fecit, non recté patitur.[1]

Nor, in the case here contemplated, of a third nation bonâ fide neutral, and acting with the strictest impar-

[1] Quaest. Jur. Pub. Lib. I. Cap. IV. p. 32, 33.

tiality between the belligerents, could the extension of the right of retaliation, so as to damage the interests of such a neutral, be much mitigated or altogether justified, by the subsequent measure of granting to the subjects of the neutral state, licenses to trade with the enemy, notwithstanding the general interdict. For a bonâ fide independent neutral, although equally well disposed towards either belligerent, might refuse, and certainly is not bound to trade under, such a license, though proffered. And so far as the licenses are confined to the subjects of the belligerent, who has imposed the retaliatory interdict, it seems rather an aggravation in the latter, to take in this way the benefit, to a certain extent, of a trade from which he had entirely excluded the neutral.

Farther, while differing on this rare occasion, with great deference and humility, from what appears to have been the opinion of Lord Stowell, we must also state our view with regard to another point intimately connected with the retaliatory interdict, and which Lord Stowell appears to have held as previously established, in his judgment in the case of the Fox before quoted, 30th May 1811.[1] We highly admire that part of the judgment, in which he thus expounds the jurisdiction and duties of British courts of prize. "This court is bound to administer the law of nations to the subjects of other countries, in the different relations in which they may be placed towards this country and its government. This is what other countries have a right to demand for their subjects; and to complain, if they receive it not. This is its unwritten law, evidenced in the course of its decisions, and collected from the common usage of civilized states." But we cannot equally admire, or approve of, what follows.

[1] Edwards, Adm. Rep. p. 312.

"At the same time," continues the eminently talented judge, "it is strictly true, that by the constitution of this country, the king in council possesses legislative rights over this court, and has power to issue orders and instructions, which it is bound to obey and enforce; and these constitute the written law of this court." These two propositions, "that this court is bound to administer the law of nations, and that it is bound to enforce the king's orders in council," are not at all inconsistent with each other; because these orders and instructions are presumed to conform themselves under the given circumstances to the principles of its unwritten law. They are either directory applications of those principles to the cases indicated in them—cases, which, with all the facts and circumstances belonging to them, and which constitute their legal character, could be but imperfectly known to the court itself; or they are positive regulations, consistent with those principles, applying to matters which require more exact and definite rules, than these general principles are capable of furnishing." Nor do we consider the following analogical comparison as strictly correct, or the subsequent reasoning as satisfactory. "The constitution of this court, relatively to the legislative power of the king in council, is analogous to that of the courts of common law, relatively to that of the parliament of this kingdom. Those courts have their unwritten law, the approved principles of natural reason and justice; they have likewise the written or statute law in acts of parliament, which are directory applications of the same principles, to particular subjects, or positive regulations consistent with them, upon matters which would remain too much at large if they were left to the imperfect information which the courts could extract from mere general speculations. What would be the duty of the individuals, who preside in those courts, if required to enforce an act of parliament, which contradicted those principles, is a question, which, I presume, they would not entertain a priori; because they will not entertain a priori, the supposition that any such will arise. In like manner, this court will not let itself loose into speculations, as to what would be its duty under such an emergency; because it cannot, without extreme indecency, presume that any such emergency will happen; and it is the less disposed to entertain them, because its own observation and experience attest the general conformity of such orders and instructions to its principles of unwritten law. In the particular case of the orders and instructions, which give rise to the present question, the court has not heard it at all maintained, in argument, that, as retaliatory orders, they are not conformable to such principles—for retaliatory orders they are. They are so declared in their own language, and in the uniform language of the government which has established them. I have no hesitation in saying, that they would cease to be just, if they ceased to be retaliatory; and they would cease to be retaliatory from the moment the enemy retracts, in a sincere manner, those measures of his, which they were intended to retaliate."

That, by the British constitution, the king in council possesses legislative rights over the British prize courts, it would be presumptuous in us to dispute, in opposition to such very high authority, as what we have just quoted. But we certainly did not previously understand, such to be the constitution: and we cannot help regretting it should be held to be so. For it necessarily follows, that the king in council may, in various important points, alter the law of nations, which the British prize courts are bound to obey. And the effect of such an admission or assumption, is obviously to strengthen the cause of the powers, who, in 1780 and 1800, confederated for the establishment of the doctrines of the armed neutrality, and to afford ground for the argument, that, upon the same assumption, the continental sovereigns, Louis XIV., the Empress Catherine, or the Emperor Napoleon, might have established a maritime code, such as the French code of 1681, according to which these prize courts would have been bound, and of course entitled, to administer law to the subjects of the other maritime states. That the king of Britain in council will so exercise his control over the British prize courts, as to make them deviate from the principles of the unwritten law described by Sir William Scott, according to which they are otherwise bound to decide, is certainly, as the learned judge observes, not to be presumed, and is very unlikely to happen. And the orders issued by the king in council may have always been, as here stated, directory applications of the principles of the unwritten law of nations, to the cases indicated in them, or positive regulations consistent with those principles. But, if the power of control and alteration be admitted generally, the result in future may be different from what it has been. And if the power of deviation from the law of nations is recognized as vested in the government of any state, it must be recognized as vested in the governments of all other independent states, to the prevention or destruction of any uniform consistent system of principles or rules, for the mutual intercourse of nations.

As little do we think the eminently talented judge fortunate, on this occasion, in his illustration of the unwritten law of nations bearing a relation to the orders of the king in council, similar or analogous, to what the unwritten or common law of England bears to the acts of parliament, the statute law of England. From the nature of the internal constitution of civilized states, the supreme legislative power necessarily controls and modifies by its acts or statutes, the unwritten or common consuetudinary and judiciary law of a nation. But among nations, there is no such supreme legislative power, except the Almighty Creator. The laws established by that all-wise Creator, are obviously either such as neither individual men nor nations can alter; or they are within the range of the delegated liberty and power conferred by the Creator on mankind, in their reciprocal intercourse, either as individuals and members of civil society, or as nations. And, with reference to separate civil societies or independent states, the common unwritten consuetudinary law of nations, is, as here described by Sir William Scott, "the approved principles of natural reason and justice, which assume the shape of, and become positive law, when adopted, recognized, and observed in practice by the governments of nations in their mutual intercourse."

Farther, without acquiescing, for the reason just stated, in the correctness of the comparison here instituted by the learned judge, even analogically, we do not see that the British constitution would be at all deteriorated by its being held or established, that the British international courts, original and appellate, are in war, as in peace, supreme; that these courts are, as propounded by Sir William Scott, bound to decide in conformity with the law of nations; and that the British government, as well as any other government, may make concessions, and pass from or relax their legal claims by treaty or otherwise, but cannot render the rules of the law of nations more rigid and severe.

Nor does it appear that any evil or even inconvenience would result from the practical recognition of this rule. For the executive branch of government being invested with the power of making war, from its very nature as agent, from its constitutional functions, from its natural desire, in the discharge of its duties, to employ the most efficient means of exercising the compulsory power of warfare, is naturally apt or disposed to adopt strong measures. And the constraint, which might thus be imposed on the executive, would be rather salutary as otherwise; inasmuch as the king and council would thus be merely put upon their guard, not to issue any orders in council, which the international prize courts would not have it in their power to sanction and enforce, in conformity with the law of nations. For we humbly conceive, that the British international courts in war, even the lords commissioners of appeal in prize causes, neither can, nor ought to be considered, as identical with the King in council, in his Majesty's executive capacity. And while we agree with the Emperor Napoleon, that the republican policy of France, which transferred the jurisdiction of the prize courts to the ordinary internal tribunals throughout the country, was a great error, we cannot, on the other hand, admit the justice, propriety, or general expediency of the prize jurisdiction being vested in the Executive branch of government, which has the power of making war; when, in the language of Napoleon's minister, "the question involves justice between nations, and the rights of war or their exercise; when treaties are to be weighed, and it is to be decided, whether other nations are friendly, or neutral; or that, when the interests of other states are to be dealt with, and managed with sagacity and prudence, no other authority ought to interfere, than that of the government." The obvious tendency of such doctrine, is to make the law of nations bend to the particular and temporary interests of belligerents and neutrals. It was, no doubt, admirably suited to the policy of Napoleon.

And he exemplified it exactly, in his conduct to neutrals from 1806 to 1812, the period, according to the biographer of Portalis, of "les usurpations du Decret, sur la Loi."

Section III.

Period from 1806 *to* 1812 *continued.*

But not only did the continental system of the French Emperor Napoleon induce, or rather impel the British government to resort to the extraordinary retaliatory measure of the prohibitory or non-intercourse orders in council, which bore so severely upon such as were real bonâ fide neutrals, and maintained their national independence; the prosecution of the scheme, inasmuch as its objects were not only the exclusion of Great Britain from the continent, but also the acquisition of more extended continental dominion and control, and of foreign ships of war for the long threatened invasion of that country, likewise, in a manner forced the British government in autumn 1807, into the much to be regretted hostilities with Denmark.

In the short space of four years, from the commencement of the war, Napoleon had not only firmly established himself as Emperor of the French, extended the boundaries of France by the annexation of Belgium and other adjacent territories, reduced Holland to dependency, and conquered and declared himself king of Italy, but had also, by a series of almost uniformly successful military operations, humbled Austria, deprived her of the Elective Imperial dignity, and established the confederation of the Rhine; had humbled Prussia, stripped her of some of her most valuable provinces, and converted her from an enemy into an ally, bound by treaty to support his continental system against Britain; and finally, had succeeded in persuading the Emperor of Austria, and the Emperor of Russia, to forego their amicable relations with Britain, and to join with him in enforcing that system within their respective territories.

By the peace of Tilsit, the ambitious projects then entertained by Napoleon, so far as regarded the continent, appeared to have been accomplished. By that peace, the large French army then in the north of Germany, ceased to have any grand operation to execute. But it is plain, that at this time, Napoleon might with much greater facility, and with equal justice, have invaded and occupied with his troops the adjacent kingdom of Denmark, as he had done the territories of Austria and Prussia. And, as his warlike operations against the latter comparatively strong nations, had been uniformly successful, there can be little or no doubt, they would have been equally so against the former comparatively small, and, consequently, less powerful kingdom. The English ministry in these circumstances, became apprehensive that Napoleon would not merely occupy Denmark with his troops, which was a measure comparatively of less consequence, after what had taken place, but would, by indirect influence or intimidation, or by direct force, obtain possession of the Danish fleet, and thereby supplying the deficiency in his military marine, occasioned by the British victories, would employ it for the long threatened invasion of Great Britain or Ireland. Under this apprehension, in order to anticipate what they believed to be the design of Napoleon, and in order to display greater energy, than their predecessors in office, who had been accused of inactivity, and of neglecting, if not of giving offence to, the Russian Emperor Alexander, the British ministers dispatched a fleet, with land forces on board, to Denmark, to request the removal for a time to Britain of the Danish navy, under the obligation of restoring it at the conclusion of the war. And this request being refused, the British government was reduced to the alternative, either of leaving the fleet to be taken possession of by Napoleon, or of enforcing the delivery of the fleet by the bombardment of Copenhagen. That the apprehension entertained by the British government was, in the then state of the continent, not only highly probable, after the expedition against Portugal, and the perfidious invasion of Spain, but was well founded, appears from various circumstances and events. A French bulletin, published after the battle of Friedland, contained the following expressions: "Bientôt le blocus du continent ne sera plus un vain nom!" At the same time that the decree of Berlin was intimated to Denmark, a demand was also made upon that government to withdraw its troops from Holstein, and to shut its ports against English and Swedish commerce. At an audience granted to the deputies of the city of Hamburgh, Napoleon did not refrain from menacing language against the Prince Royal. And finally, Murat proposed to the King of Sweden a reconciliation with France, at the expense of Denmark, from which kingdom he proposed to disjoin Norway, to be bestowed on Sweden. After such proceedings, little doubt could remain, that Napoleon would soon take possession of the Danish fleet; and this design is confirmed by the fact, that early in the following year, March 1808, Marshall Bernadotte passed the Belt, and arrived in Zeeland at the head of upwards of thirty thousand French troops, destined against Sweden.[1]

As the apprehension entertained by the British ministry was thus, to all appearance, well founded, the extreme

[1] Schoell Histoire des Traités, vol. IX. pp. 57—77.

necessity of self defence and of the prevention of invasion, might have justified the temporary and conditional seizure of the warlike implements and stores of a neutral, when on the eve of falling into the possession of an enemy, provided this could be effected without other hostile measures against the neutral. And this was probably what the British ministers expected; but upon this result they could not rely; and they ought not, in our humble opinion, to have authorized the commanders of the fleet and forces, to resort to the bombardment of Copenhagen; but rather to have incurred the risk of any invasion which Napoleon could effect by means of the Danish fleet. That such an invasion would have been attempted, and was prevented by the seizure of that fleet, there is every reason to believe. But although such an invasion had so far succeeded, and Napoleon might thus have inflicted distress and misery for a time upon a portion of the inhabitants of Great Britain and Ireland, the result would infallibly have been defeat. And the British government would have acted more correctly by incurring this risk, rather than resorting to a harsh measure of hostility against a neutral, exposing Great Britain to the charge of violating the law of nations, as Napoleon had done, and was then doing, in relation to all the surrounding countries in the west, east, and north of France. But the conduct of Napoleon could not justify similar illegal conduct on the part of the British government, towards other nations. If, indeed, there was evidence, that the Danish government was then acting in collusion with the French Emperor, and had commenced the negotiation for the alliance, which it immediately afterwards concluded with Napoleon, the seizure of the Danish fleet, though an extreme measure, might be justified as an act of hostility against those allied enemies. But if the Danish government was bonâ fide neutral, the only farther apology for the British government enforcing its demand for the temporary and conditional possession of the Danish fleet, is, that the Danish government might have, at least, sent its fleet on a cruize to its other territories or dependencies, instead of keeping it in a situation where it must inevitably fall into the possession of the French Emperor; and that the conduct of the Danish government towards Great Britain throughout the French revolutionary war, had been only ostensibly neutral, through the prudent policy of the shrewd and cautious Count Bernstorff, had been all along the reverse of amicable, and had ultimately terminated in hostilities and an alliance with Russia, for the purpose of compelling Great Britain to relinquish her treaties with that power itself, and to alter in favour of neutrals, and to the injury of Britain, the common law of nations, as it had been observed for centuries preceding.

Section IV.

Period from the Revocation in the year 1812, *of the British Orders in Council of* 1807 *and* 1809, *to the termination of the French Continental System.*

Not only did the prosecution of the continental system of Napoleon, in a manner compel the government of Great Britain, to resort to the extraordinary retaliatory measure of the orders in council of 1807, and reduce that government to the alternative of the forcible seizure of the Danish fleet, or of allowing it to fall into the hands of the enemy, and to be used for transporting the French troops to the British territories, but it ultimately also involved Great Britain in a war with the United States of America. For it does not appear, that even under the administration of the party then in power, the United States would have declared war against Great Britain, with the view of obtaining a settlement of the other points then in dispute between the countries. These points, it is well known, were the maintenance by Great Britain of the claim of right to search for, and seize native British seamen serving on board American vessels; and the maintenance by the United States of the neutral pretension, that "free ships make free goods," from the same, perhaps natural, but obviously interested motives, which induced the Hanse towns, the Dutch, the Danes, and the Swedes to do so.

The first of these claims was not, as by some falsely insinuated, an attempt to extend to, or exercise over other nations, the British severe law of impressment, for the purpose of manning the royal navy. This law of impressment, whether peculiar to Great Britain or not, is merely a municipal law, or an internal institution of the British nation—a power, which the government may exercise or not, over its own subjects, without any foreign government being entitled to complain. But the claim then maintained by Britain, and disputed by the United States, did not rest on any system of impressment peculiar to Britain. It rested upon a very general rule of practice or usage, which, if not strictly a principle of international law, has been recognized, and with different modifications, adopted, and observed in common, by almost all, if not all nations, who have made any progress in civilization; namely, that a natural born subject of a country, is not entitled, without permission, especially during war, to renounce his allegiance to his native sovereign, and to engage in the military or naval service of a foreign state, but may be reclaimed from that service.

This rule had been recognized in England, we have seen, from before the time of Sir Leoline Jenkins, who lived in the reign of Charles II. And proceeding upon this very generally and long established rule, while she tacitly admitted a breach of it was not to be presumed against the government of any state, to the effect of authorizing a search of the government or national vessels of that state, Great Britain maintained this rule might, upon just ground of suspicion, be enforced by a search of merchant vessels on the high seas. Between nations, in the ordinary case, the deserters from the service of their country may be easily and immediately distinguished. But from the great similarity in personal appearance, language, manners and customs, great difficulty existed in distinguishing British from American seamen; and the attempt to recover British seamen from the American service, may have been attended with great hardships in many instances. The accidental shot from the Leander frigate, while searching for British seamen off New York, and the subsequent attack of the Chesapeake by the Leopard frigate, were much to be regretted, as events too easily converted to the purpose of exciting popular national resentment. But for the latter unauthorized collision, the British government made ample apology and offer of reparation, so far as practicable. And there was a prospect of peace being still preserved between the two countries, had not the French, Berlin, and Milan decrees, and the consequent retaliatory British Orders in council stood in the way. Unfortunately, this claim of right was left undecided either way, even by the hastily concluded treaty of Ghent in 1814, which terminated this war between the parent state, and what were originally her colonies. And as the divergence in the personal appearance, language, habits, and manners of the inhabitants of the two countries, was not likely, for generations, to be such, as to facilitate the discrimination of the subjects of the two states, it is to be regretted, the question was not subsequently settled by the negociations in 1818, upon the equitable footing of regular authentic lists or registers of British and American seamen being made up, and kept, and of the nationality of the seamen being thereby determined.

With regard to the other main point in dispute, it does not appear that even the then government of the United States, would, in imitation of the Russian Empress Catherine, or Emperor Paul, have threatened, or declared war against Great Britain, for enforcing the adoption of the rule of "free ship, free goods," had not the continental victories of Napoleon, and his subjection of the other European powers to his influence, so excluded Great Britain from commercial intercourse with the continent, as to afford an apparently favourable opportunity for attack; and had not an alleged mistake taken place, with regard to the construction of the British retaliatory orders in council, as applicable to trade with the colonies of the enemy. Although it was manifestly inconsistent with the impartiality of neutrals, to carry on for the enemy the domestic trade between the parent state and its colonies, which it had been disabled from doing itself by the events of the war—the successes of its antagonist, the British government had, in 1803, announced that the same objection did not, and would not be held to apply to neutrals trading bonâ fide with the colonies of the enemy, by purchasing and importing the produce of those colonies into their country, for their own supply, or even to their afterwards exporting that produce to the mother country in Europe. And for some time this trade seems to have been bonâ fide carried on between the colonies of the enemy and the United

States, and between the United States and the hostile mother country in Europe. But, in time, this concession or liberal interpretation of the legal principle in favour of neutrals, came to be taken advantage of by American ship-owners and merchants, who contrived to convert this bonâ fide circuitous trade into a direct trade between the colonies and the hostile mother country, by merely calling at a port in the United States without unloading the colonial produce, and merely paying import duties, which were immediately drawn back in the shape of bounties on exportation. To such an evasion, the British courts of prize could not give their sanction; but declared, that such a mode of proceeding did not constitute a bonâ fide importation into the neutral country, and was, in reality, a trade between the hostile colonies and mother country. M. Shoell, on the supposition of there having been a change of principle, while he deems such a change quite justifiable in the prize courts, seems to think the government should have given intimation of it to the American traders. But there was in reality no change of principle; there was merely a refusal to sanction a perversion of the principle. And while it may be regretted, that previous intimation was not given, as a measure of courtesy and conciliation, legal justice does not require that parties knowingly and intentionally devising and concerting the means of evading a rule of law, should be put on their guard beforehand, that such a mode of evading the law will not be tolerated.[1]

In the months of March and May 1810, the Congress having resolved to resist vigorously both the French Berlin and Milan decrees, and the British orders in council, passed five acts, excluding both British and French vessels from the American ports, and pro-

[1] Schoell, Histoire des Traités, Tom. IX. pp. 407—443—471.

hibiting all commerce in goods from these countries and their respective dependencies. And such a law the American government was clearly entitled to pass. But it appears the minister of Napoleon, in August 1810, intimated in a note to the American Envoy, "that the Decrees of Berlin and Milan are revoked, and from the 1st November will cease to take effect, it being understood that in consequence of this declaration, the English shall revoke their orders in council, and renounce the new principles of blockade which they have wished to establish." And assuming as fact, the actual revocation of the French decrees, President Maddison, on the 2nd November 1810, announced by a proclamation, that the French decrees having been revoked, the restrictions imposed by the act of the 1st March, ceased to be in force with regard to France; and on the 18th November 1810, the order was renewed, for the confiscation of all English merchandize, which, having arrived in the ports of America, after the 2nd February, had been sequestrated, unless, before the 3rd March 1811, the court of London had recalled the orders in council complained of. The American ambassador at the court of London, communicated the declaration made by the French minister on the 6th August 1810, to the American government. But as no intelligence had been received of any such act on the part of the French government, although various channels of communication remained open, the British ministers merely replied, on the 31st August 1810, that as soon as the revocation of the French decrees should have actually taken place, and the commerce of neutrals should be restored to the situation in which it was prior to their promulgation, the British government would with pleasure renounce a system, to which it had been forced by the proceedings of the enemy. In this state of matters, the Congress, on the 27th February 1811, passed an act, bearing, that if the British government revoked its orders in council, or modified them in such a manner, as that they ceased to fetter the commerce of the United States, the President should announce to the public by a proclamation, that, from the date of the day of its promulgation, the restrictions on British commerce, prescribed by acts of Congress, shall cease to take place, but, that until this event, they should be maintained in all their force against Britain, her colonies and dependencies.

This act of Congress was manifestly a step decidedly directed against Great Britain; as it admitted French vessels into American ports, and excluded from them the English, while the former consisted almost entirely of privateers, who did a great deal of damage to British commerce. The year 1811 passed in preparations for war, and in fruitless negociations. From the commencement of the year 1812, the Congress of the United States passed a series of acts, which proved that it was the intention of that government to declare war against Great Britain. And on the 18th June 1812, upon the urgent message of President Maddison, the Congress, by a majority of seventy-nine against forty-nine, declared war against Britain, or rather formally declared the war with Great Britain, which had previously existed. The events of this distressing war, non est hujus loci to narrate. It was happily terminated in December 1814, by the treaty of peace of Ghent, which, however, left, as before remarked, the two most important points in dispute unsettled, and in statu quo, namely, the British claim of right to recover British seamen from the American service; and the American neutral pretension of "free ships and free goods." And we shall conclude our remarks on this unhappy war, which may be ranked among the bella nullos habitura triumphos, by quoting the observations of an independent and impartial German. "We shall leave," says M. Schoell, in his Histoire des Traités de Paix, 1817,[1] "We shall leave it to posterity to decide, whether circumstances forced the representatives of the Republic to a step which necessity alone can justify; or whether passion, the spirit of party, and the chimera of conquests to be effected, on the side of Canada, did not contribute to make a war be resolved upon, of which the uselessness and ill success have not contributed to augment the political consideration of the government of the Union. We say, the uselessness. In fact, five days after the senate of Washington had promulgated its hostile act, the British council gave an order, by which the object of the war ceased to exist. This council declared on the 23d June 1812, that, after having taken cognizance of a decree of the French government, bearing the date of the 28th April 1811, but which had not been communicated to the English government till the 20th May 1812, by the Chargé d'affaires of the United States in London, a decree bearing, that the decrees of Berlin and Milan have ceased to be in force, with regard to American vessels; the Prince Regent has ordered, that the orders in council of the 7th January 1807, and of the 26th April 1809, are recalled from the date of the 1st August 1812, in so far as they concern American vessels and their cargoes, upon the condition, well understood, that the United States shall revoke the acts, which exclude the English vessels from their ports."

"The English government has been accused of having feigned ignorance of this decree of Napoleon of the 28th April 1811, until the 20th May 1812. This reproach is unfounded. There probably does not exist a decree of Bonaparte of the 28th April 1811. That which the

[1] Tom. IX. p. 441–2.

minister of the United States at Paris succeeded in making Bonaparte sign, and by which the latter purely and simply revoked, in favour of the Americans, the decrees of Berlin and Milan, was given a short time before his departure for Russia, perhaps the 28th April 1812. We are ignorant whether, in the copy sent to London, the date was put by mistake, or whether Bonaparte caused it to be antedated, in order that his concession might have the semblance of having been dated a year sooner."

Section V.

Termination of the French Continental System.

In April 1809, the British government greatly modified and relaxed the order in council of November 1807. And in August 1810, the British minister declared to the minister of the United States in London, that as soon as the revocation of the French decrees should actually have taken place, and the commerce of neutrals should be restored to the situation in which it was, prior to their promulgation, the British government would, with pleasure, renounce a system, to which it had been forced by the proceedings of the enemy. But while the French Emperor professed his intention to recal those decrees, it does not appear from the collection of state papers of those times that he actually did so, as alleged, in August 1810, or until the alleged decree of the 18th April 1811; which decree, however, does not appear to be extant or on record, was probably not passed till the 28th April 1812, and antedated; and at all events, was communicated to the British government by the American minister, only on the 20th May 1812. Nay even, when he did revoke the Berlin and Milan decrees, in relation to the United States of America, in the year 1811, or more probably 1812, the French Emperor qualified this revocation, with the conditions that the British government should not only recal the orders in council of 1807 and blockade by notification; but should also abandon the administration of Maritime international law, which it had uniformly observed for ages, which France and Spain had likewise uniformly observed, with the exception of the conditional and temporary French réglement of 1778, and declaration of 1780, and which France had resumed during the Republic, and continued in 1803, under Napoleon, as First Consul and afterwards as Emperor; and should recognize the extravagant claims of the northern states, as contended for by Hübner, and now also urged by the United States of America, namely, that the neutral flag should be held to protect hostile property at sea; thus pretending, with singular inconsistency, to be the vindicator of the maritime rights of neutral states, while, by his victories by land, he had conquered, or at least reduced under his sway, and was oppressing almost all the continental nations, including those very maritime states. Soon after the recal however, by the British government of the orders in council, any mere formal and absolute revocation of the Berlin and Milan decrees became unnecessary. The still farther indulgence by Napoleon of his insatiable ambition of universal empire, ultimately led to his overthrow. The successive victories obtained over him and his generals by the Russians, Prussians, and Austrians in Germany, and by the British in the Peninsular, forced him from his Imperial throne. And ultimately the Berlin and Milan decrees were effectually revoked by the battle of Waterloo.

In June 1812, the British government, we have seen,

recalled the orders in council of 1807 and 1809, absolutely in favour of the United States of America. But that government had, a few days before, unfortunately declared war against Great Britain, chiefly on account of these orders, as alleged infringements of their neutral rights. And the war thus declared was only terminated by the treaty of Ghent in December 1814, after Napoleon had been placed in the island of Elba.

Before concluding this brief account of the aggressive continental system of the French Emperor, of the consequent retaliatory prohibitory orders of the British government, and of the seizure of the Danish fleet, and war with the American states, resulting from this conflict, we must here remark the device to which Napoleon had recourse through the medium of his ministers, after he had intimated the revocation of the Berlin and Milan decrees, so far as regarded the Americans. Although he had, by his unprecedented series of victories, subjected almost the whole continent of Europe to his dominion or his influence, he was unable to compete at sea with the naval force of Britain. The continental system had not succeeded to the extent he had anticipated. And the unexpected seizure of the Danish fleet, to which the British government conceived itself reduced by necessity, had disappointed the hopes he appears to have entertained of conveying, by means of it, an army to Ireland. In this situation he found it for his interest, to affect or pretend a great regard for the maritime rights of those very neutrals, whom he oppressed on land. And in March 1812, by his direction, his minister for foreign affairs made a formal report, promulgated in the Moniteur, in which it is held out, that the rights of maritime neutrality were solemnly regulated by the treaty of Utrecht, which had become the common law of nations; and that this law had been literally renewed in all the subsequent treaties. The allegation thus unscrupulously advanced by this minister, became, as M. Schoell informs us,[1] from that time, an article of faith, which it was not permitted to doubt, without being proclaimed an enemy of the great empire. But that this assertion was untrue, although the belief of it was thus enforced by all the power of Napoleon, we have formerly seen, and will see still more distinctly proved, when we come to notice the historical work of M. Schoell.

[1] Histoire des Traités, Tom. IV. p. 17.

CHAPTER III.

Of the Maritime Conventional Law of Nations during war, from 1801 *to* 1815.

Of additional maritime conventional law, properly so called, as remarked in our preliminary observations to this volume, we have not much, during the period we are now contemplating. Neither do such conventions regarding maritime commerce and navigation, as were concluded during this period, appear to have been held to extend beyond the contracting parties, or to have affected generally or materially, the practice or observance of the common consuetudinary law of nations.

The more important of the points which had been disputed from the time of Hübner, and the concoction of the armed neutrality in 1780, for which the Russian Empress Catherine was so long and so greatly lauded, but of which the origin has more recently, with some plausibility, been ascribed to the Prussian monarch Frederick II. and his minister Count Hertzberg, had been, after the brief revival of that scheme by the Emperor Paul in 1800, settled, in the meantime at least, and so far as Great Britain on the one side, and Russia, Denmark and Sweden on the other, were concerned, by the convention of June and October 1801, between the British government and the Russian Emperor Alexander; the other two governments afterwards acceding to that treaty, as thereby specially provided. By this convention, the rule of the common consuetudinary law of nations, hitherto observed from time immemorial, except in the case of special paction,—which subjected the property of the enemy at sea to capture and confiscation, although on board neutral vessels, and respected neutral property at sea, although on board hostile vessels—the only rule, consistent with truth in point of fact, or with justice and equality in point of legal right,—was recognized and confirmed. And, on the other hand, Great Britain, ex comitate gentium agreed, that, in the case of neutral merchant vessels sailing under their national convoy, the right of search should not be exercised by privateers, but only by state or government ships of war.

Whether this convention was annulled by the subsequent war between the contracting parties, or was renewed or kept in force by their subsequent treaties, is a matter which these nations solely have any interest or right to investigate or determine. The other nations took no part, and had no share in this convention. It preceded the treaty of Amiens between Great Britain and France, Spain, and the Batavian Republic. The treaty of Amiens contained no provisions whatever relative to maritime commerce and navigation; and renewed none of the treaties containing such provisions, which might have expired, like the treaty of Utrecht with Holland, or been expressly annulled as by the French Republic, or become void through supervening hostilities. The treaties, again, into which the French Emperor, after the peace of Tilsit, in a manner compelled some of the other European governments to enter, in order to make them co-operate with him in carrying into effect his continental system, appear to have terminated with the power of Napoleon. And the treaties which were concluded by the different governments at the general peace, in the years 1814 and 1815, neither contain any new provisions or arrangements with regard to maritime commerce and navigation, nor renewed any of the previous treaties relative to these matters, which might have ceased to be valid from supervening hostilities, without a distinct renewal.

In short, the only additional conventional maritime law, applicable to the state of war, which appeared during this period, seems to have been the few treaties of commerce and navigation, which several maritime states individually concluded with each other,—such as the treaty of commerce and navigation between Great Britain and the United States of America, in December 1806, between Great Britain and Portugal, in February 1810, &c. And these treaties, which may be found in the Recueil of M. Martens, are of course, to be consulted in the first instance, as constituting the conventional law of nations between the contracting parties, while the treaties lasted. But such particular treaties did not affect the common maritime law of nations, as pre-existing in general, if not universal usage, as recorded in the judicial determinations of international courts, and in the authoritative opinions of international lawyers, in questions, either between the parties to the treaties and other nations, or between these other nations.

CHAPTER IV.

Of the Common Consuetudinary Maritime Law of Nations during war, between 1803 *and* 1815, *as unfolded, expounded, and recorded in the Ordinances, and in the Judicial determinations of the International Courts of different civilized States.*

ALTHOUGH the common consuetudinary maritime law of nations was not materially affected by any particular treaties entered into during the period we are now surveying, it received considerable accessions and development from the successive judgments of the maritime prize tribunals; to the reports, however, of these cases and judgments, all we can do, in this historical sketch, is merely to refer.

In Britain, Sir William Scott continued, as formerly stated, to expound the law, with such learning and fairness, and soundness of reasoning, as, in almost all cases, to carry conviction to the minds of intelligent foreigners. These luminous judgments, it is well known, are easily accessible, as recorded in the fifth and sixth volumes of Sir Chr. Robinson's Admiralty Reports, in Dr. Edwards' Admiralty Reports, one volume, and in Dr. Dodson's Admiralty Reports, two volumes. They are also abridged in the practical treatise by Mr. Chitty on the law of nations, published in 1812.

In Britain, too, the supreme Court of appeal in prize causes, continued, as formerly, to be assisted by eminent English judges of the courts of common law and equity; was guided by the profound judicial talents of Sir Wm. Grant, and also of Sir Wm. Scott, in such causes as were brought by appeal from the vice-admiralty courts; and discharged its judicial functions throughout, with great deliberation, impartiality and dignity. But for the judgments of this supreme tribunal, it is to be regretted, that, with the exception of occasional notices of them in their admiralty reports, by Sir Chr. Robinson, Drs. Edwards and Dodson, and of Mr. Harman Acton's two thin volumes of prize appeal reports, we should be obliged to resort to the collections of printed cases for the parties, and the written records of court.

The learning, talents, and correctness of procedure, with which questions of maritime prize law were adjudicated during this period, in the vice-admiralty courts, in the British colonies and dependencies, may be seen from Mr. Stewart's reports of the cases decided by Dr. Alexander Croke, judge of the vice-admiralty court, at Halifax in Nova Scotia, and from Judge Hinchcliffe's Rules of Practice for the vice-admiralty court of Jamaica.

In France, we formerly saw, that, at the close of the eighteenth century, the administration of the maritime law of nations during war, underwent a favourable change under the Consular government, by the re-establishment of a Conseil des Prises; when Bonaparte, as First Consul, was guided by the advice of the estimable Portalis. And this improved administration continued for a short time after the recommencement of the war. Upon that event, the government of the Republic passed a law (arrêté) portant réglement sur les armemens en course. Tit. I. Armemens en Course.

Chap. 1. Des Sociétés pour la Course. Chap. 2. Equipages. Chap. 3. Lettres de Marque et Cautionnemens. Chap. 4. Encouragemens. Chap. 5. Police de la Course, et Rançons. Tit. II. Prises. Chap. 1. Captures. Chap. 2. Procédures des Prises. Chap. 3. Déchargemens, Manutention Vente, et Liquidation particulière des Prises. Chap. 4. Liquidations Generales. Chap. 5. Repartition. Tit. III. Des Armemens en Course et des Prises dans les Colonies, et dans les Ports étrangers. Tit. IV. Dispositions Générales. This réglement forms No. 918 of the Code des Prises, by M. Dufriche-Foulaines, formerly mentioned, published in 1804, and dedicated to Cambacérés, Arch-Chancellor of the empire, extending from p. 1078 to p. 1098, 4to. It resembles much the prize practice of France in 1744 and 1778; and it seems to be the most recent *piece of French legislation* on the subject. For the Code de Commerce of Napoleon, although it treats of maritime commerce, does not embrace the French administration of Maritime international law during war. And in his excellent Cours de Droit Commercial, M. Pardessus treats even less of maritime prize law, than M. Emérigon had done, and merely so far as the interests of individuals engaged in maritime commerce are affected by it. But this arrêté, or réglement of 1803–4, did not continue to be adhered to. Severe laws were soon passed against hostile colonial produce, and hostile manufactures, although they had ceased to be the property of the enemy. And these severities, the animosity of Napoleon against Britain induced him to continue to increase, until, as we have seen, they terminated in the Berlin decree of 1806, and the Milan decree of 1807. With regard to the more recent French Maritime international law, after the cessation of these decrees, we are not aware we can do better than refer to the Repertoire Universel de Jurisprudence, by M.

Merlin, voce Prise, and to the Exposition de la Législation Commerciale of M. Vincens, 1821, part of which we shall afterwards have occasion to review.

In the supreme and admiralty courts of the United States of America, likewise, the common maritime law of nations underwent, during the period we are contemplating, considerable discussion, and received considerable development and illustration, as will be found by consulting the reports of the judgments of these courts, by Judge Cranch, Dr. Wheaton, Mr. Mason, and Mr. Peters. But in this historical sketch we can merely refer to these reports; concurring in the observation of Dr. Hoffman, that during the period embraced by Judge Cranch's reports, from 1801 to 1815, the principles of their admiralty and maritime jurisdiction were, in a great measure, defined, and those of their neutral and belligerent rights and duties, pointed out and vindicated. And we may perhaps have an opportunity of tracing the principles recognized in these judgments, when we come to review Dr. Wheaton's digest of the law of maritime captures.

CHAPTER V.

Of the Common Consuetudinary Maritime Law of Nations from 1803 *to* 1815, *as investigated, discussed, and illustrated in particular departments, in the contemporary and usually controversial writings of Jurists and other authors.*

The works of the writers on Maritime international law, during this period, may be divided into two classes; first, controversial pamphlets or treatises discussing particular points, and maintaining particular propositions, usually of a polemical description, but written with great talent; secondly, systematic treatises on Maritime international law generally, arranging, or attempting to arrange, scientifically, the different doctrines of that branch of law, and to trace them to the primary principles on which they rest. To give any lengthened review of the whole of the pamphlets, which fall under the first class, would be superfluous, as they are still accessible to the professional or curious general reader; and it will be sufficient, briefly to notice the more important of them.

In 1805, there appeared the very able pamphlet of the late Mr. Stephens, entitled, "War in disguise, or the frauds of neutral flags;" and in 1806, the professed answer to it in English, and La Paix en apparence. There appeared also in 1806, a pamphlet, entitled, an Examination of the British doctrine, which subjects to capture a neutral trade, not open in time of peace; and an answer to it, entitled, Belligerent rights asserted and vindicated against neutral encroachments. Besides these professed answers to it, the merits of the pamphlet of Mr. Stephens are ably discussed in Article XV. of the Edinburgh Review for April 1806. And we refer to the Review, as containing a very acute investigation of some of the leading principles of Maritime international law. On some points we agree with the talented reviewer, in others not.

We, of course, inquire not, whether it was good or bad policy in the British government in 1806, to enforce what has been called, the Rule of the war of 1756; we inquire merely into the justice and legality of the rule. With regard to its foundation in mere usage, the rule certainly pre-supposes the pre-existence of parent states, and distant colonies or dependencies separated by oceans or seas, and the abandonment by one or more of these parent states during war, of the exclusive colonial policy observed, and strictly maintained by the European nations during peace. And although the case rather seems to have occurred, or been considered, earlier than the war of 1756, the question does not appear to have been much discussed till about the middle of the eighteenth century. By his reasoning, we think the reviewer has established, that the restriction involved in this rule is not applicable to the direct trade of the neutral with the colony, any more than with the other territory of the mother country, either according to legal principle, or analogous usage in other neutral trade, and does not prevent the neutral from thus supplying himself with the colonial produce, which he used to procure through the mother country. Accordingly, in the more correct administration of the common law, this direct trade of neutrals with the colony of the enemy has been sustained as legal, not merely for their supply with colonial produce, but in all innocent commodities, and even to the extent of supplying the mother country with the produce of her own colonies, provided this neutral trade be carried on circuitously bonâ fide, by means of neutral capital embarked in the enterprise or adventure.

But we do not think the reasoning of the talented Reviewer affects the rule, which renders it illegal for a neutral, whether upon the invitation of a distressed belligerent, or ultroneously with a view to profit, not merely to trade *with* the parent State or its colonies, but to trade *for* the parent State and its colonies, by interposing his services between the two, and carrying on for the belligerent that traffic, which the latter has been disabled from carrying on himself, through the military operations of his antagonist. For the rule, thus restricted and explained, does not rest on usage since 1756, or anterior; but flows from the essential duty of neutrality, by which a neutral, if he desires to maintain that character, is not entitled to afford such assistance to the one belligerent, as causes direct damage to the other, by counteracting, or doing away the effect of his military operations. It rests upon the same principle of the law of nations, as the prohibition to trade in articles contraband of war, or with a blockaded port.

In urging the rights of neutrals, too, the distinction between the trade of the neutral and the trade of the belligerent, has not been sufficiently attended to. In many cases it may be difficult to draw the line of demarcation. But no such difficulty occurs in the coasting and colonial trades. Each of these is peculiar, and belongs entirely to each country or state. No foreigner can legally claim a share in either of these trades, or complain of his exclusion as an injury. No neutral nation can legally demand permission to carry on the colonial trade of another nation that happens to be a belligerent. In being prevented from doing so, the neutral nation sustains no loss of what is really its own.

As little do we consider the state or condition of neutral nations during the peace, immediately before the rupture, as precisely the *legal measure* of their rights, when the war has taken place. Neutral nations derive certain benefits from wars, which they have not during peace, necessarily and inevitably, without either belligerent being able to prevent it. And to such benefits they are clearly entitled. On the other hand, there are certain disadvantages and inconveniences to which neutrals are necessarily subjected, when wars take place among other nations, by whose territories they are surrounded, or with whom they have commercial intercourse, obviously from their forming a part of the great society of nations. And to such disadvantages, neutrals appear, in reason and equity, bound to submit, in consideration of the advantages which necessarily accrue to them from wars among other states.

But it would be quite inconsistent with distributive justice, to add to the benefits which a neutral nation necessarily derives from the war, by reverting to the preceding state of peace, and mixing up its share of the trade formerly carried on between it and another nation now belligerent, with the share of the latter in that trade, and combining the two into a whole, to maintain that the neutral state is likewise entitled, during the succeeding war, to the whole of the benefit of that trade. In justice, these portions must be discriminated. In war, the neutral is entitled to carry on the whole of his own share of the former trade between him and the belligerent. But he is not entitled to any share of the trade which properly belonged to the other nation, now belligerent.

The proper trade of the neutral during the preceding peace, was, what was carried on by means of his own ships, goods, and other capital. The proper trade of the other nation formerly at peace, now belligerent, was likewise what was carried on by means of its own ships, goods, and other capital. The neutral state is entitled to retain, during the war, its own share of the trade during peace, in addition to the other advantages necessarily arising to it from the war. But it is not entitled to retain what never belonged to it, or to receive credit for the part of the mutual traffic, which belonged to the other state now belligerent. That part of the traffic, the opposed belligerent has a right to interrupt or destroy, without the neutral having any right to complain.

To illustrate the preceding observations; if, as generally happens, a maritime war reduces much the shipping or mercantile navy of one of the belligerents, a neutral ship-owner is entitled to lease out in freight his vessels, to carry innocent goods to or from the ports of the enemy, at the ordinary or current rates of freight; and the opposed belligerent has no right to object to this prosecution of what was, and is clearly, the neutral's accustomed trade. But during peace, the part of the trade between the one country, now neutral, and the other country, now belligerent, carried on by means of the ships, goods, or other capital of the latter, formed no part of the proper trade of the neutral. And the latter is not entitled to have, what did not belong to him, exempted from, or protected against legal capture, jure belli, or to indemnification for the want of such exemption or protection, by being now allowed to carry it on himself.

Under these limitations, and with these distinctions, which appear to us to be founded on fact and legal principle, we are glad to find, we come to nearly the same conclusion, at which the talented Reviewer himself arrives. For he thus concludes,[1] "Although the view which we have been led to take of the general privileges of the neutral traffic, have forced us to condemn the whole principle of the Rule of 1756, and to conclude in favour of an unlimited trade with the colonies of the enemy, we are by no means prepared to say, that in practice there should be no limitation. The facts and cases detailed by the author before us, have satisfied us completely, that a great part of the produce exported from these settlements is truly the property of the enemy, and is carried to market under a false neutral name, on their account. This property is, therefore, a fair object of hostility; and we are not only entitled to enquire very narrowly, into the evidence of neutrality by which it is guarded, but also, as it appears to us, to proceed, in many cases, upon the general presumption arising from the nature of the voyage undertaken. The direct trade, for instance, between the colony and the mother country, to which it belongs—that trade which comes in place of the supplies and remittances, interchanged in time of peace between the proprietors and their agents or factors—can scarcely be presumed to be converted all at once into a genuine neutral trade of foreign adventurers, buying and selling upon the mere chance of a market, and in a department, where it seems impossible to dispute, that a great deal of simulation and fraud is admitted, no great injustice will be done, probably, by disallowing one whole class of transactions, that stand, in other respects, in a very suspicious predicament. In this view of the matter, indeed, we do not see that the neutrals would have any cause to complain, although the subsisting instructions should be retained, and their commerce with the hostile colonies restricted

[1] Vol. VIII. pp. 33, 34.

to their direct trade with their respective mother countries. It is an argument of some weight, that in the most favourable times of peace, all the produce of these colonies which they exported, were first landed in their own territories; and considering the vast amount of the hostile trade, which they unquestionably carry on under false and fraudulent pretences, it is probably no more than a fair compensation, to limit their neutral traffic a little more, than might be justifiable upon strict principle, in the case of unsuspected persons."

In 1806, likewise, there appeared a republication of the letters of Phocion, or American arguments for British rights; and the speech of Mr. Randolph, representative of the State of Virginia, with an introduction by the author of War in disguise. In 1807, there appeared a second edition of a pamphlet, by Macall Medford, entitled, "Dignity without pride, or British, American, and West India interests considered;" and a letter entitled, "the Policy of the blockading system refuted." Two of these pamphlets were at the time ably criticised in the Edinburgh Review for October 1807.[1] And, agreeing that the search of ships of war for British seamen deserters, is not the generally expedient mode, in which such otherwise valid right of recovery ought to be exercised, because it has manifestly a direct tendency to violence and to involve in hostilities; we concur in the following conclusion at which the talented Reviewer arrives: "The inference which is suggested by this dry and tedious discussion now brought to a close, is, that there are no points now in dispute between England and America, so important in themselves, as to justify a war. The claim of searching ships of war, must, both in justice and in prudence, be abandoned:— it is at once unfounded and unprofitable. The right of

[1] Vol. XI. p. 1. No. XXI.

searching merchant ships is clearly ours; it is of some value, and should be insisted upon in the manner formerly pointed out. It is neither our right, nor our interest to destroy the American carrying trade. And in our endeavours to limit the benefit which our enemies derive from it, we should be satisfied with such regulations, as may increase the obstacles already thrown in the way of fraudulent transactions, and perhaps augment the expenses of the circuitous voyage."

In 1808, Mr. Roscoe published a pamphlet, entitled, Considerations on the causes, objects, and consequences of the present war; and Sir Frederick Morton Eden published an address to the people on the maritime rights of Great Britain. In 1808, there appeared a pamphlet, entitled, Orders in council, or an examination of the justice, legality, and policy of the new system of Colonial regulations. In 1808, also, Mr. A. Baring, now Lord Ashburton, published a third edition of his Inquiry into the orders in council, containing an answer to the arguments in War in disguise. And during the same year there were published, the speech of Lord Erskine against the legality of the orders in council, and the speech of Mr. Brougham in support of the petitions to the House of Commons against the orders in council. The last three of these pamphlets are likewise ably discussed in the Edinburgh Review for April 1808.[1] But the object of these productions is less to investigate and evolve the principles of international law, than to show the impolicy of these orders, in the existing circumstances.

In 1809, there was published the speech of Mr. James Stephens on Mr. Whitbread's motion, relative to the late overtures of the American government.

In 1811, there was published an address by Mr. Robert

[1] No. XXIII. Art. 13.

Smith, late Secretary of state to the people of the United States. In 1811, there appeared a pamphlet, entitled, the Crisis of the dispute with America; and this last pamphlet is discussed at considerable length in the Edinburgh Review for February 1812.[1] But the chief object of this discussion is to prove the illegality of the orders in council, as a general system of blockade by notification merely, without an adequate naval force to render the blockade effectual. And that this objection is well founded, we have already seen.

In 1812, Dr. Phillimore published a very able letter respecting the orders in council and the licensing system, reviewed in the New Quarterly Review for July 1812.[2] In the same year, there were published an abstract of the evidence taken in the House of Commons against the Orders in council; and the powerful speech of Mr. Brougham in the House of Commons, on the 16th June 1812, on the present state of commerce and manufactures, also discussed in the New Quarterly Review.[3]

During the period from 1803 to 1815, there also appeared in the northern kingdoms and states, a good many pamphlets on Maritime international law, chiefly of a controversial description; and among others, the work of August Wilhelm Schlegel, in 1813, über das Continental System, and that of Georgius, in 1814, entituled, Versuch einer Darstellung der Licenzen-Geschichten, addressed to the sovereigns allied for the welfare of Europe, and urging the abolition of maritime capture by privateers.

[1] No. XXXVIII. [2] No. III. [3] No. III. p. 121.

CHAPTER VI.

Of the Common Consuetudinary Maritime Law of Nations during war, from 1803 *to* 1815, *as scientifically investigated and discussed, and methodically arranged in the systematic works of International Jurists.*

So much for the principal contemporary controversial pamphlets on Maritime international law during the French imperial war, from 1803 to 1815. But besides these controversial pamphlets of the day, there appeared also during that period, several larger works, which, although to a certain extent controversial, may be entitled to the appellation of systems of Maritime international law, inasmuch as their authors, like the Jurists of former ages, have investigated and expounded the principles of the science, and their foundation in nature. Of these larger systematic works, we shall now give some account. And as they differ considerably in their doctrines, we shall contrast them; and consider first the Milanese advocate, Piantanida, as so far opposed by the Nice commercial judge, Azuni; and the French lawyer and statesman, Rayneval, as opposed by the Danish Conseiller de conférence, Tetens; thus endeavouring to ascertain, whether the practice of England in the administration of Maritime international law be not justified, not only as shown by Mr. Chitty, by the usage of the English prize courts from time immemorial, and by the impartial and enlightened reasoning of Sir William Scott, but also by the disinterested views, and profound reasoning of fair and judicious foreigners, still more recent than Lampredi, whom we formerly contrasted with Hübner.

SECTION I.

Review of the work of Luigi Piantanida.

In the years 1806, 1807, and 1808, Piantanida published, in four vols., 4to, his large work, entitled, Della Giurisprudenza Maritima-Commerciale Antica, e Moderna Trattato. The work is voluminous, from its embracing the private or internal maritime law of states, which from the general and common nature and similarity of its rules, among all civilized states, has frequently received the appellation of the Jus Gentium, or law of nations, as well as the Public External, or international maritime law, Jus Gentium Publicum Maritimum inter Civitates. The first two volumes are chiefly devoted to the former, the other two, to the latter department of law. As his ancestor, Pietro Piantanida, a valorous naval commander, the author informs us, had rendered faithful services to his sovereign, the Emperor Charles V., so the author himself, Luigi Piantanida, dedicates his work, in testimony of his hereditary fidelity, to the invincible and immortal Emperor, Napoleon I. The work is very learned; but it is more learned than acute or profound; the style is verbose, and what is worse, the matters are ill arranged, being brought out under a list of separate titles, frequently unconnected, and not following each other in natural order.

On the other hand, Piantanida distinguishes pretty accurately, the general natural primary law of nations, consisting of the legal or juridical relations of communities or states to each other, as arising from the nature and constitution of these civil societies, and the circumstances in which they are placed, and as gradually unfolded and recognized by consuetude; from the particular and transient conventional law of nations, founded on the special treaties or pactions of nations with each other. Thus,[1] "Questo Diritto può essere desunto, dal gius primitivo della natura; ed allora è permanente, immutabile ed universale; e può anco procedere dal consenso attuale delle nazioni in tali casi, ed in tali circonstanze; ed allora, non è che consensuale, accidentale e particulare. Se nasce dalla prima fonte, commune a tutte gli esseri del Globo, dicesi Jus naturale, e per eccellenza, fra i popoli civilizati, Jus delle Genti assoluto, universale. Il secondo constituisce ancora il gius commune, o delle Genti, se adottato appare, dalla Generalità delle nazioni. Questo, però, assume più propriamente la sua qualità de convenzionale; se non comprende, che i trattati, e le convenzioni dei popoli fra di loro. Dove un tal Diritto partecipa dei primi elementi del Jus naturale, della general costumanza di popoli, e dei Trattati delle nazioni confermata dall' uso, e dalla Ragione, assume allora la solenne qualità di Diritto universale delle Genti, assoluto e convenzionale." Of the last description, or division of Maritime international law, Piantanida expounds the doctrines in the ten titles of his third volume, and in the first eight titles of his fourth volume. Of the former description of Maritime international law, il Diritto conventionale, or Jus Pactitium, he expounds the rules in the ninth and last title of his fourth volume; in other words, details

[1] Vol. IV. p. 315.

the substance of the treaties or conventions, which the European nations have entered into with each other, in the course of the three preceding centuries.

Thus, in the third volume, he treats of the arrest by princes, and of embargo; of maritime capture as prize; of recapture; of ransom and hostages; of reprisals; of contraband of war, and the confiscation thereof; of privateers or corsairs; of war; of peace; of neutrality. And in the fourth volume, he treats of the sea-coasts, harbours and roadsteads; of the dominion of the sea, or rather of maritime rights; of the national colours or flag; of blockade; of free ports; of lazzarettos; of convoy, and sailing in company for mutual protection; of fisheries; and, in the last title, of conventional law.

In the title on prizes,[1] Piantanida recognizes the legality of the capture as prizes, not only of vessels belonging to the enemy, but of vessels belonging to neutrals, if armed for war, or loaded with arms, ammunition, or other articles contraband of war. He admits, also, the necessity of self-defence may justify the act of intercepting innocent goods, upon condition of restitution, or payment of the current price of the commodities. He admits, also, the right of the belligerents to capture as prize, neutral goods on their passage to blockaded ports. Maritime prizes, he says, have been recognized by all nations, cultivated or barbarous, as the inevitable consequence della ragione di guerra. But to prevent abuse in the exercise of this right, certain rules have been established. All vessels are held good prize in which there are found a hostile super-cargo, master, or other marine officers, or crews. Want of the ordinary ships' papers is a ground of condemnation, unless the want be explained to have arisen from necessity. Refusal to answer the ordinary invitation at sea, or to suffer visit-

[1] Tom. III. p. 44—48—62.

ation, followed by combat, is a ground of condemnation. The right to invite or summons is not competent to merchant vessels, but only to government vessels or privateers. Rules are established for the practice of visitation. Goods belonging to the enemy, or impledged to him, or destined in fulfilment of his engagements, found in neutral vessels on the high seas, are good prize. Hostile vessels are good prize; but the neutral cargo is to be restored to the proprietor. Neutral vessels carrying contraband goods, if for immediate use in war, are liable to confiscation. If the goods be of the second class, not of immediate use in war, as grain or other provisions, the neutral vessels carrying them are not liable to confiscation, but may be stopped, and the cargo either released or retained, on condition of the price being paid to the lawful owner.[1]

The maritime law of nations on some of the more recently disputed points, is thus expounded by Piantanida in 1807.[2] "All' effetto pertanto di verificare la neutralità delle navi, che si affacciano in mare, e l' innocuità delle cose, che vi sono a bordo, è indispensabile, ch' esse soffrano di essere visitate dai vascelli a guerra. Ma la fede, che si dee ai certificati, alle patenti ed ai ricapiti nautici, che vengono esibiti a vedere dal capitano del bastimento, basta per togliere ogni dubbio sulla neutralità della nave, e del carico; a meno che vi fossero urgenti indizi di frode, e simulazione, nel qual caso, si possono prendere più rigidi misure, non esclusa quella di una provvisoria catturazione.

"Trovandosi delle merci nemiche su d' una nave neutra, quelle si confiscano; e di questa, col loro prezzo, ricavato dalla vendita, se ne paga il nolo, e la condotta. Ma se gli effetti sono neutri, e nemico il vascello, questo è preso, e quelli si restituiscono ai proprietarii; senza

[1] Tom. III. p. 62—136. [2] Tom. III. Tit. X. p. 470.

però loro fare abbuonamento alcuno per i retardi, e danni, ch' essi possono avere sofferti. Il vascello prenditore, se usando della forza per diritto di guerra, avesse a colpi di cannone per arrestare, il vascello nemico, non solo fatte perire le merci, ma, ben anche uccise delle persone neutre, che come passeggiere si trovassero a bordo, non sarebbe per tali tristi avenimenti responsabile verso di alcuno."

But while he thus correctly expounds some of the principal rules of Maritime international law, as founded on the constitution and natural relations of nations to each other, Piantanida had various inducements to incline him to approve of the recent doctrines of the neutral nations of the north. He was a great admirer and supporter of Napoleon; who, although, as we have seen, he retained the former French prize law, in the regulations established in 1803-4, had subsequently found it for his interest rather to favour the pretensions of the neutrals against England. And so far as he was influenced by patriotic considerations, as a native of one of the small states into which Italy was divided, it was natural for Piantanida to favour those new neutral doctrines; because the smaller maritime states in the south, as well as in the north of Europe, have neither quantity of population nor extent of territory, sufficient to enable them to aim at conquest, or universal empire, like Charles V, Louis XIV, and Napoleon; or to come forward like Britain in support of the independence of the continental nations, but have an obvious interest to remain at peace during the contests of their more powerful neighbours, and to profit in point of commerce, by these very contests. Still, however, Piantanida marks distinctly the difference between the rules which are founded on the natural juridical relations of states, and those which are introduced between particular states, by paction or treaty. Thus, after observing that neutrality may be conventional or natural, independently of convention, he thus points out the advantage of declarations and treaties of neutrality at the commencement of wars: "Ma quantunque non sia necessario, per conservarsi, ed usare i diritti della neutralita, di fare un manifesto, una dichiarazione, e meno una stipulazione di essa pure questa sarebbe utile e prudente, tanto rispetto alle altre Potenze neutre, quanto alle guerreggianti. Un atto di solenne convenzione sebbene non potesse obligare gli altri neutrali, che non vi hanno parte (res inter alios acta) pure renderebbe piu fissi e securi i diritti della guerra, e della neutralità."[1]

And, while he immediately afterwards displays his feelings of philanthropy, by lauding the neutral doctrine of "free ship, free goods," he does not represent this indulgent mode of procedure, as resulting from the natural legal, or juridical relations of states; but describes it as only attainable by stipulation, or special treaty. Thus, "a queste regole generali appartengono le savie e giuste stipulazione o massime speciali, dei principi grandi e liberali (a higher tone of morality, generosity, above strict law,) di non turbare la libera navigazione dei vascelli neutri, di un porto all' altro, sulle coste delle nazioni in guerra; di non attentare alla sicurezza degli effetti delle potenze belligeranti, i quali sieno a bordo di qualunque vascello neutro, ad eccezione di quelli, che sono di bellico contrabando; di non osare i neutri di far introdurre merci o derrate in luoghi assediati od investiti, e di non retenere communemente blocati, che quei porte, soltanto, che si trovano in tal guisa guardati, od attorniati dai vascelli delle potenze, che lo attacano, ed investono, che ne sia pericolosa l'entrata."[2]

[1] Tom. III. p. 487, § 109. [2] Tom. III. p. 487-8, § 111.

In the third title, however, of his fourth volume,[1] Delle bandiere, 1808, Piantanida, not very consistently with the passages before recited or referred to, adopts, and endeavours to justify the rule of the neutral flag covering the hostile cargo; indulges, like a good many other continental controversial writers, in incorrect and untrue statements; accuses the English of altering the maritime law of nations, because they would not agree to the new fangled doctrine, so convenient for neutrals, and their now great and warlike continental ally; breaks out into a furious tirade against the English government, and absurdly enough attempts to prove them to be in the wrong, by citing the unjust and illegal Berlin and Milan decrees of Napoleon, of whom he proclaims himself to be "umilis obsequios, fedelis servo e suddito." But the groundless and abusive declamation, in which Piantanida thus occasionally indulges, apparently to please his despotic master, can only be regarded by a nation like the British as unworthy of notice.

Finally, Piantanida devotes more than a fourth part of his fourth volume, to what he designates conventional law of nations; and this he rather obscurely divides into absolute and relative; giving the following definitions or descriptions of these two kinds. "Di questo primo diritto, convenzionale assoluto, che è il resulto della volonta generale dei popoli del mondo, se n' è già fatta l' applicazione nello svilluppo delle materie che nei varii titoli, ed in tutto il complesso di quest' opera, formano il soggètto della maritima giurisprudenza. Del secondo, cioè, del convenzionale relativo, io non posso meglio farne discorso, che col citare i trattati, le convenzioni, i concordati delle varie potenze maritime, che sottoposero a certe leggi le comuni o particulari loro ragioni, e modificarono coi patti, quelle regole generali

[1] Tom. IV. p. 80.

di Diritto, che render lo dovrebbero eguale per tutto il mondo."[1]

What is here described as absolute conventional law, seems to approach very near to what has been usually denominated the natural, modified natural, voluntary, or common and consuetudinary law of nations. What is described as relative conventional law, seems to be conventional law properly so called, constituted by express and special treaty, or convention; Jus Pactitium. And Piantanida proceeds, as he has here proposed, to examine at considerable length, the substance of these particular treaties, and the points established by them between the contracting parties. But into this detail we shall not follow the author, partly because the task appears to have been better executed by Martens, in his Cours Diplomatique; partly because Piantanida does not appear like Martens, in his Précis du Droit des Gens de l' Europe moderne, and like Klüber, to attempt to extract out of treaties, temporary in point of duration, and limited to certain nations, as parties, a conventional law, which is not temporary, but of permanent duration, and which extends beyond the contracting parties, and binds nations who never entered into such treaties at all, or only for a definite time, with particular nations, and for certain special considerations.

SECTION II.

Review of the work of Azuni.

While the work of Piantanida was in the course of publication at Milan, there appeared at Paris, in 1805, the improved work of Azuni, a judge in the commercial

[1] Tom. IV. p. 316.

court of Nice. Azuni had originally published his work in 1795, in Italian, under the title Sistema universale dei Principii del Diritto Maritimo dell' Europa; and it was translated into French in 1798. But subsequently, Azuni revised and enlarged his work, and published it in 1805, under the title of Droit Maritime de l' Europe, two vols., octavo. And a considerable portion of the first volume of this enlarged work, namely, the fourth chapter, for which, M. Pardessus informs us, he was verbatim indebted to the unpublished work of Michele di Jorio, Azuni again published at Paris, in 1810, under the title of Origine et progrés du Droit et de la Legislation Maritime. The first part of the larger work thus republished, relates chiefly to the history of the common and general, but private law of maritime commerce, not to the history of Maritime international law; is rather vague and unsatisfactory; and has been in a great measure superseded by the more judicious and profound researches of M. Pardessus, in his Collection de Lois Maritimes. The second part of the revised and enlarged work of Azuni, relates to Maritime international law, properly so called.

In chapter first of the first part, Azuni discusses the empire of the sea, and gives an account of the nations of antiquity, and of the modern nations, prior and subsequent to the discovery of America, who made pretensions to that empire, concluding with a parallel in this respect, between England and France; in which, adopting the spirit of the worthless republican Barrēre, De la liberté des mers, and apparently also to gratify his patron, Napoleon, by that time Emperor of the French, and King of Italy, he, like Piantanida, breaks out into a violent and abusive tirade against Great Britain, making statements in point of fact, which, were it worth while, it might be very easy to prove are untrue, and indulging in predictions, lugubrious for England, which can now only provoke a smile, since, happily for humanity, they have not been, and are not likely to be realized.

In chapter second, Azuni having recovered from the phrenzy into which he had wrought himself, while indulging his hatred of the maritime ambition of England, without once reflecting upon the still greater and more oppressive continental ambition of France, especially when directed by the energy of his master, Napoleon, proceeds coolly to discuss the empire of the territorial sea; the extent of that sea; and the opinions of international Jurists with regard to that extent. In chapter third, he treats of the effects of the empire of the sea; of the property of the territorial sea and its dependencies; of narrow straits of the sea; of harbours, bays, gulfs; of anchorage; of fisheries. The fourth chapter we have already described.

The second volume and second part of the work of Azuni, has for its object the maritime law of Europe in time of war.

In chapter first, he treats of the rights of nations in a state of war, or in a state of neutrality. In art. I. of this chapter, of the origin and causes of maritime wars. In art. II. of neutrality, and of the pretended law of nations on that subject, differing from most of his predecessors. In art. III. of neutrality, as being the exact continuation of the pacific state of a power, which, when a war breaks out between or among two or more other nations, abstains absolutely from taking any part in their disputes. In art. IV. of the different kinds of neutrality. In art. V. of the declaration of neutrality. In art. VI. of the rights and duties attached to neutrality; maintaining, agreeably to the preceding definition, (which, however, appears to be incomplete, if not otherwise erroneous,) that a neutral nation preserves in all its extent, the right of commerce, which it had before the war; that the belligerent power cannot impose upon it obligations, to which it was not subject before the rupture; that it is, therefore, only treaties and express conventions, which can limit the natural right of nations; and that, if sometimes inexorable necessity puts a belligerent power in the situation of preventing the transportation to the enemy, of the goods of a neutral, and of seizing them, it contracts naturally the obligation of repairing all the damage which the seizure may have occasioned.

In chapter second, Azuni treats of the liberty of maritime commerce in time of war. In art. I. of the commerce of neutrals in general. In art. II. of the right which belligerents have to limit the active commerce of neutrals; maintaining that belligerents have no right to issue threatening orders, assigning to pacific and neutral states certain rules, as the limits of their navigation on the high seas; and that the only exception is the case of a blockaded port, sanctioned by the necessity of a just defence. In art. III. of the right which belligerents may have to limit the passive commerce of neutrals; maintaining that impartiality in commerce is the sole duty of neutrals towards belligerents; namely, that they may continue it upon the same footing as before the war; and consequently, that the restrictions which have been imposed upon the independence and liberty of mercantile relations, depend solely on conventions, express or tacit, which form the conventional law of Europe.

In art. IV. of this second chapter, Azuni treats of the conventional law of Europe, touching the commerce of neutrals in time of war. And, as he here seems to lay aside the impartiality, otherwise exhibited by him, and to become the advocate of the extreme neutral doctrine, not very consistently with the legal principles expounded by him in the other parts of his work, we must here stop to ascertain the exact meaning of the term conventional, as to which a good deal of vagueness and confusion have prevailed among the more recent international Jurists, and have been unwarrantably employed to support the extreme doctrine just alluded to.

At the commencement of this article,[1] Azuni so far justly, observes in correction of the error of Galiani, and as a deduction from a series of successive treaties among the European nations, that the restrictions which the conventional law of Europe has prescribed for the commerce of neutrals, never had for their object, solely, the quality of the merchandise, now-a-days called contraband of war, but rather the concurrence of two circumstances, as giving them that character. Of these, says Azuni, the one results from the positive fact of the importation of these goods into the territory of the enemy, with partiality on the part of the neutrals, or of direct measures taken for securing the conveyance of them into that territory; the other is found in the exportation of these goods out of the neutral territory, with all the specific directions of destination for the enemy; then, only, if they were encountered on the point of entering into the possessions of the enemy, do they become the subject of contraband, and good prize; not because they are instruments or provisions for war, but by reason of their belonging to the enemy, or of their being manifestly enough destined to pass into his hands, and to increase his forces. The flag, whatever it may be, cannot serve as a safeguard. Never, he continues, did nations, even the most powerful, namely, those who could with impunity avail themselves of the right of the strongest, dare, in their declarations

[1] p. 137.

of war—always dictated by the most ardent animosity —to interdict to neutrals the impartial sale of any commodity upon their own territory. Hitherto they have confined themselves to threatening with confiscation, those contraband goods, which should be found evidently destined for the enemy.[1]

Azuni goes on to state, it has sometimes happened, that a nation has chosen to sacrifice the incontestable rights of its commerce, by prohibiting in whole or in part, within its territory, the sale of warlike stores, whether from political prudence, or from the dread of displeasing one of the belligerent powers, whose insults it was not in a condition to resist. But, he justly adds, the example of some feeble and unarmed states, whom necessity forced to yield, and to prefer to a greater evil, the temporary sacrifice of their commerce, proves nothing against the constant and universal practice followed by Europe for so many ages.[2]

So far the observations here made by Azuni, are correct. But it is equally clear, on the other hand, that besides the two circumstances noticed by him, as constituting conventional (or rather consuetudinary) contraband of war, namely, the partial furnishing, and the exportation and direct destination to the enemy, the quality or description of the merchandise behoved also to concur, namely, their natural aptitude, or artificial preparation for the purposes of war; otherwise the neutral might have freely exported the goods, and destined them directly to the coasts of the enemy, if they did not tend directly to aid his military enterprises, or marine equipments.

Farther, Azuni proceeds in this article, erroneously, and to all appearance, designedly, for the purpose of deducing the conclusion, that, by the conventional law of

[1] Vol. II. p. 171. [2] Vol. II. p. 172.

Europe, at least, the neutral vessel protects the hostile cargo—to mix up together, and to confound the confiscation of neutral property, as being contraband, and the confiscation of goods at sea, although on board neutral vessels, as being the property of the enemy. Thus,[1] referring to the Ordonnance de l' Espagne, and the commentary of D'Abreu, he concludes, that goods belonging to friends or allies, found on board hostile vessels, were not held good prize. But, admitting the conclusion to be well founded, this is no more than the general rule of practice, observed from the ages preceding the Consolato del Mare downwards, and all along by England. And it obviously does not show, that hostile goods on board neutral vessels, were not held good prize.

Proceeding to the maritime law of France, Azuni admits, what he could not deny, that the ordonnance of 1681 declared good prize every vessel loaded with goods belonging to the enemy, as well as the goods of Frenchmen or allies; but observes, that the règlement of 1704 declared those goods only liable to confiscation, which were of hostile growth or manufacture, and excepted neutral vessels; and that the règlement of 1744 introduced a farther modification in favour of Denmark, Sweden and Holland, permitting their respective subjects to trade from one hostile port to another hostile port, and to transport goods of the growth of the enemy, with the exception of those denominated contraband of war. He adds, the règlement of 1778 extended this faculty or permission to all neutrals in general, provided the reciprocity was accorded by England, the other belligerent power. "Le gouvernement Anglois," he continues, "fort de son Droit des Gens particulier, et exclusif du Droit des autres nations, refusa positivement d'accéder à cet acte généreux de la France, sous le prétexte

[1] p. 175.

(que M. Pitt n'eut pas honte de proclamer,) que l'Angleterre pouvant se passer des neutres en tems de guerre, elle auroit continué à les saisir.[1]

Now, although England, strong in the justice of her conduct, may despise this attack, as probably made by the Italian Judge to please the Emperor Napoleon, it cannot be denied to be a partial, unfair, and so far untrue statement of the fact. England claimed for herself no peculiar law of nations, exclusive of the rights of other nations. She merely adhered to the right to seize the goods of her enemy, found on the high seas, which had been recognized in the practice of nations for four or five centuries preceding, and had never been departed from, except by special treaty. And, so far from there being any generosity on the part of France in this conditional proposal, the fact is, that France having taken advantage of the unfortunate struggle between Great Britain and her American colonies, and thus involved herself in war with the mother country, found her mercantile navy so reduced, as to render it necessary for her to employ neutrals, to carry on her coasting and colonial trade. But, because France found it convenient, to employ neutrals in her trade, it did not follow, that England was bound to do so. There was no reciprocity in the case. And no belligerent in the situation of England, would have been so foolish, as by such a concession, and departure from recognized law and usage, to throw away the advantage she previously possessed, or might have obtained during the war, over her enemy. Spain, as well as Great Britain, declined the proposed alteration in the established law of nations. And the conditional proposal by France being only for a very limited time, the old law was, after the lapse of that period, resumed by that government.

[1] Vol. II. p. 178.

The refusal of England to give up the long established right belonging to all nations, to capture the property of the enemy on the open seas, although in neutral vessels, Azuni proceeds to observe, was the motive or cause which induced the Empress of Russia to proclaim, as a fundamental law, that, inter alia, neutral vessels should be held to determine the character of their cargoes, and should protect hostile goods. But without here diverging into what has been given to the public, as the secret history of this measure, the political motive and object of the ambitious Princess, it is well known, was not to protect the weak, or vindicate the rights of feeble neutrals, beyond the consequent popularity which flattered her vanity, but to promote the commerce of her own country with the southern nations of Europe, who required its produce, by means of neutral vessels. And she had just as much right to proclaim a fundamental law, contrary to the rules recognized and practised for centuries, as the smallest independent state in christendom. From similar interested motives, Denmark and Sweden, we have seen, joined with Russia in the convention, for establishing what was quaintly, and not very consistently, termed the armed neutrality. And Prussia, Austria, and the Neapolitan kingdom afterwards acceded to the treaty. But Great Britain chose, as she had clearly a right to do, to abide by the ancient rule, except as modified by the particular treaties, into which she had entered with other powers, and which she, of course, declared her resolution faithfully to observe. France agreed only conditionally, for a short period, and thereafter returned to her former practice, more rigid than that of England. Spain never acceded to the convention. The Empress Catherine herself lived to relinquish her system. And the attempt of her son, the Emperor Paul, to revive it, was, we have seen, still more unfortunate and unsuccessful.

Azuni is next forced to admit, that the French courts, upon which the cognizance of prizes was devolved by the laws of the 14th February, and 1st October 1793—until the government, as we have also already seen, again centralized the prize jurisdiction—saw every where nothing but disguised enemies; there were no ships' papers on board, in which they did not find faults; no merchandise, which was not reported to be of English growth or manufacture, and the loading of which did not entail the confiscation of both vessel and cargo. He is also forced to admit, that, although the règlement of 1778 permitted, not explicitly or absolutely, as he says, but conditionally, and for a short period, the carriage of hostile goods by neutral vessels, nevertheless, even the Conseil des Prises, established by Bonaparte as First Consul, an. IX, declared such hostile goods on board neutral vessels to be good prize, agreeably to the Ordonnance de la Marine of 1681.

Yet, upon such a narrative, telling the story in his own way, and glossing over every thing adverse to the cause he here advocates, Azuni does not scruple to found, with much self complacency, the following conclusion: "Il résulte donc en principe, qu' il doit être libre aux nations neutres de continuer leur commerce avec les belligérans, comme avant le guerre, à l' exception des marchandises réputées de contrabande; que le transport de la propriété ennemie sur les navires neutres, ne blesse en rien les droits des belligérans; que ce principe est reconnu par les nations les moins civilisées, comme on peut le voir, par les traités du 19 Septembre 1689 entre la France et l' empire Ottoman, renouvellé depuis, par ceux de 1719, 1764, et celui de 29 Mar. 1790. "Il résulte enfin du tableau historique des lois,' disait le savant M. Portalis, dans ses conclusions au Conseil des Prises, du 5 thermidor an. 8, relatives à la prise du

Navire la Statira, qu' elles ont varié selon les mœurs et les circonstances; que la politique du moment a presque toujours modifié les principes du droit politique; que dans nos tems modernes, les règlemens ont paru constamment incliner vers l' équité générale; et que la nation Française peut s' honorer d' avoir eu, dans la dernière guerre, l' initiative des maximes douces et généreuses, qui ont prévalu et d'avoir donné des exemples utiles à tous les peuples."[1]

Now this may be a fine story, a beautiful theory, and plausible argument, to show that the rule by which the neutral flag protects the hostile cargo, has been adopted into what has been called the conventional law of Europe. At the time Azuni wrote, a doctrine so conducive to the advantage and profits of neutral states, and so convenient for France, when the reduction by her enemy of her mercantile marine, rendered the aid of neutrals absolutely necessary for carrying on her colonial, and even her coasting trade, must have been very agreeable to the First Consul and Emperor. And the able M. Portalis may have oratorically availed himself of the règlement of Louis XVI. in 1778, although only conditional and temporary, as affording him a favourable opportunity for lauding and congratulating the French nation, on having shown the example during the last war (1776—1783), of introducing into the laws of war, mild and generous maxims. But, in fact, did not the adoption by France of this gentle and generous maxim, in favour of neutrals, originate in the French nation requiring at sea the aid of these neutrals? And does not M. Portalis, in 1801, confine his compliment to the then last war, which terminated in 1783, because, prior to 1778, both the French and Spanish administration of Maritime international law, was much more

[1] Vol. II. p. 181—183.

severe against neutral nations than the English or Dutch, in as much as the former nations held hostile vessels to confiscate neutral goods, and hostile goods to confiscate neutral vessels; which the latter nations never did.

To return to M. Azuni, his theory on this article will not bear investigation. His tableau may be an agreeable picture to those whom he wished to please; but it is not a tableau historique, or a true picture. And his conclusion is not a deduction from facts; but an assumption without facts to support it. If, indeed, by the conventional law of Europe, Azuni meant merely the contents of the conventions, or treaties entered into from time to time by the different nations of Europe, or of the globe generally; merely the stipulations, counter stipulations, declarations, and provisions comprehended in these treaties, either separately in detail, or arranged in a somewhat systematic order, then, of course, the different treaties, which contain such stipulations, are part of, or rather constitute, the conventional law of nations, binding upon the parties who have entered into such treaties, and for the period of endurance, which these parties may have assigned to them. But Azuni, and the other inventors of what is called the conventional law of Europe, or of nations, obviously mean something more than the mere contents of the treaties, limited to the contracting parties, and of temporary, or at least of indefinite and doubtful duration. They mean a law not merely founded upon treaties, and partaking of their limitations in point of extent, or number and duration. They mean some law derived from, or extracted out of treaties, but of a higher and more exalted nature than the treaties themselves; not of a temporary or doubtful duration, but perpetual; not limited to the contracting parties, the makers of the law, but embracing all civilized nations. And the historical deduction by which it is endeavoured to rear up this legal edifice, appears to be the following. In search of a foundation for this new law, they go back to about the middle of the seventeenth century; and from about that period they find a certain number of treaties, entered into by different nations with each other, by which one nation, for certain valuable considerations, or suppose, from no other considerations than pure friendship, agreed to relinquish the right of seizing the property of its enemy, in the open sea, if found on board the vessels of the other contracting party. They farther find, that in the latter part of the seventeenth, and in the earlier part of the eighteenth century, treaties containing such a stipulation continued to be entered into, or were renewed. The reason or cause of this is obvious. The concession thus obtained by stipulation, was very desirable for all neutrals, in as much as it enabled them, not only to carry on their accustomed commerce during peace, but to extend that commerce, and to reap profits from the disputes of their neighbours; and from the recourse had by the latter to forcible measures, although these measures were unavoidably resorted to in self defence, for the preservation of their national independence, or at least, in prosecution and vindication of their just and undoubted rights. The concession thus obtained by treaty, was peculiarly advantageous to small states, whose weak ness in point of population and territory, prescribed the prudence of pacific conduct; or who had raised themselves by, and depended very much upon, the carrying trade. It was also peculiarly advantageous for certain states possessed of larger territories, but whose particular remote position, exempted them from being so frequently involved in continental European disputes; or whose prosperity depended very much on the exportation of their comparatively rude produce, so necessary for the navigation and commerce of the southern nations of Europe. In progress of time, too, this concession, obtained by stipulation, became acceptable to one, at least, of the great continental nations of Europe, whose strength and military power by land are so great, as to have twice, at least, enabled its rulers to aim at, and nearly accomplish, universal empire, in subversion of the independence and liberties of the other continental nations; but whose maritime force, military and mercantile, has more than once, been so reduced by the victories of its adversary, as to induce it to resort to the assistance of neutrals, for the purpose of carrying on its maritime trade, coasting and colonial.

From the operation of these causes, and so far as guided by political considerations, apparently for the purpose of promoting the exportation, in neutral vessels, of the rude produce of the northern parts of her vast empire, the Empress Catherine, accustomed to rule despotically by land, conceived she might, for the accomplishment of this interested object, prescribe a new code of laws for the sea, under the pretence of maintaining its liberties, and exact by force, as a right, what nations had formerly been accustomed to solicit, stipulate for, and acquire by treaty. She accordingly promulgated her system of an armed neutrality. In this scheme, Denmark and Sweden joined, from similar interested views. Great Britain, of course, resisted this innovation, as an uncalled for and unwarranted requisition, to surrender and sacrifice the superiority she derived from her naval strength, in self defence and in enforcing her just rights against her enemies; excepting, always, any obligations under particular treaties, by which she declared her willingness and determination, at all times, to abide. Spain also declined adopting the innovation, and continued to capture hostile property on board neutral vessels. France gave a conditional acquiescence for a limited period; but the condition annexed, not having been complied with by other nations, she, after the lapse of that period, resumed her former practice. The accession of Prussia, Holland, Austria, and Naples, was afterwards obtained to the Russian convention. But in 1793, the Empress Catherine herself, no longer urged the adoption of her system. And although the scheme was subsequently revived in 1800, the last attempt to enforce it, appears to have expired with her son, the Emperor Paul.

Such is, in a few words, the Tableau Historique, the historical deduction in point of fact, on which the system of the armed neutrality, or the rule of the neutral flag protecting hostile goods, is founded; and we shall now examine more minutely, the reasoning, if such it can be called, by which it is attempted to be supported. One nation, A, has long ago entered into a treaty with another nation, B, by which it consents and agrees, for certain valuable considerations, or suppose, from no such considerations, but from pure friendship, not to seize the property of its eventual enemy, X, in the open sea, if found on board vessels belonging to B. Therefore A ought to enter, or ought to be held to have entered, into a similar agreement with another nation, C, with reference to another eventual hostile nation, Z. Here the non sequitur, the inconsequential nature of the reasoning is so apparent, as to require no farther exposure. But it is farther argued, on the other side, such agreements have not been confined to two or three nations; they have been entered into by a variety of the European nations, at different times; they increased in number and frequency, from the middle of the seventeenth, to the middle of the eighteenth century; and a custom has thus grown up. Towards the end of the eighteenth, or last century, such an agreement or convention was entered into by three nations, and was acceded to by all the other European nations, except two or three, or suppose except only one, so as to constitute at least a great majority. Therefore this general convention or custom is binding on all the European nations, as conventional law. But here the same fallacy exists, as in the more simple case; though not quite so apparent, from the multiplicity of objects, and the consequent obscurity or mystification. The number, the repetition, and the increased frequency of such treaties, doubtless prove a custom. But what custom do they prove?

They do not certainly prove the custom of conceding to neutrals the faculty of protecting hostile property from hostile seizure, in the open seas, without any such treaties. They merely prove the custom of granting such a concession by treaty, and by treaty only. For where no consent is proved to be given, except by treaty, it is manifest that no consent is given beyond that treaty; and that the nation entering into the treaty, reserves to itself the power of otherwise withholding the concession thereby made. The entering into the treaty is optional. The grant made, and obligation thereby undertaken, can never, consistently with legal principle, be extended from the opposite contracting nations to another, or other contracting nations, however numerous. And the British nation, acknowledging, like all other independent states, no superior on earth, is not bound to submit to the dictation of any other nation, even although the rule prescribed should, as Azuni says, be proclaimed as a fundamental law, by an Empress Catherine, by an Emperor Paul, or even by an Emperor Napoleon.

So much for the factitious, or rather fictitious maritime conventional law of Europe; which, in reality, has no foundation, but the particular treaties concluded between, or among different nations; and obviously does not extend beyond the particular stipulations and concessions, or beyond the original contracting parties, and the other nations who may accede to such treaties.

In article V. of this second chapter of his second volume or part, Azuni specifies the different goods which have been declared contraband of war, in the different treaties concluded between the different European nations. And, as usual, he declaims against England; exhibiting the British enumeration, as much more extensive and severe than the French; although in consistency with the principles previously laid down by himself, the British administration of the law in this department, beyond the goods, which are directly prepared and adopted for the purposes of war, considers chiefly, not so much the quantity or description of the goods, as their exportation and direct destination to the enemy for military purposes.

In chapter third of his second volume or part, Azuni treats of the collision of rights between belligerents and neutrals. In art. I. he treats of the conventional law of Europe, touching the capture of hostile goods under a neutral flag; recites the different treaties, which from the peace of Westphalia, or from about the middle of the seventeenth century, have regulated this matter, and shows, "que ces conventions offraient en dernière analyse, les contradictions suivantes; 1. Le Pavillon ami sauve la propriété des ennemis. 2. Le Pavillon ami ne sauve point la propriété des ennemis. 3. La propriété des amis trouvée sur des vaisseaux ennemis est de bonne prise. 4. La propriété des amis trouvée sur des vaisseaux ennemis n' est point de bonne prise."[1]

[1] Vol. II. p. 218.

In this article, too, Azuni is not over scrupulously correct in his narrative, and shows his usual partiality to France, and enmity to England. In particular, he states, without any distinction, that the opinion, that every vessel loaded with merchandise belonging to the enemy, might be confiscated by belligerents, though under a neutral flag, prevailed for a long time. But this practice of confiscating neutral vessels, on account of having on board hostile goods, appears to have prevailed only in France and Spain, and does not appear to have ever prevailed in England and Holland; such confiscation being then inflicted only on account of the goods being contraband of war, and directly destined to the enemy. He also states, that when the right claimed by England, to search neutral vessels under convoy, had, during the French revolutionary war, given rise to the hostile preparations by the powers of the north, "l'Angleterre voyant, que ses forces navales n'en imposaient guères aux coalisés, sollicita une convention avec Russie;" whereas, the Emperor Alexander required no such solicitation, merely complied with the wishes of his subjects, and lived cordially to unite with Britain in the glorious struggle for the maintenance of the liberties of the European nations, against the stern tyranny of Napoleon. But these petty misrepresentations are perhaps below notice. And it is sufficient to state the conclusion, to which Azuni here comes; that the conventional law of Europe furnishes no fundamental uniform and constant maxim, which can settle or determine all the subjects of complaint, which, in all wars, the collision of rights, both natural and conventional, occasions.

In art. II. of this third chapter, Azuni proceeds to treat of the primitive and universal law of nations, touching the capture of hostile goods on board neutral vessels; and here, after so much censure, we trust not undeserved, for partiality and unfair representations, we are happy to have it in our power to express our approbation of this part of his work; not because he here takes the side favourable to Britain, but because he has the good sense to adopt the legally correct and enlightened views of his able and excellent countryman, Lampredi; and because, laying aside his usual servility to French interest, he has the independence and manliness to state his opinion, although not perhaps altogether consistent with some of the doctrines to which he had previously given his sanction. "We must therefore," says Azuni, "since the conventional law of nations affords no fundamental maxim, examine whether the pretended privilege of the neutral flag, to guarantee or protect the goods of the enemy, is conformable to the principles of the primitive and universal law of nations, or, in other words, whether belligerents commit an injustice, in seizing hostile goods on board the vessels of neutrals, when the latter have not renounced the privilege of their flag by a special treaty, or tacit convention."

There appears to be an error in the mode of putting the question, here proposed for enquiry, inasmuch as it supposes a privilege originating solely in convention to require a convention to take it away; whereas, in the absence of convention, the privilege has no existence, as Azuni proceeds to show on the following grounds. 1. The imperative law of necessity, founded on self preservation, authorizes and entitles a belligerent to take from his enemy every means of becoming stronger, and more fitted or better prepared for attack; and to weaken him in all possible ways, in order to prevent him from increasing his military force, and from prolonging the war, and in order to constrain him to peace. 2. The open sea is a space subject to no one. The belligerent may therefore take possession there of the property of his enemy, in whatever way chance may afford him the opportunity of doing so, even although the property should be on board a neutral vessel, provided that, in exercising this right, he do not exceed the limits of a just moderation. 3. At first sight, this principle seems to place the right of the belligerent to seize wheresoever they are found, the goods of the enemy, in collision with that, which neutrals, on their side have, not to be troubled in their peaceful and lawful navigation. But straightforward justice and public reason will not pronounce that judgment. There is in nature, a sacred and inviolable law, which, in the conflict of two equal rights, authorizes the suspension of that one of which the obstruction produces a less damage, in some measure reparable, either more easily, or at less expense. Thence this general theory of the law of nations, which no one has ever contradicted; when the perfect right of a people comes in collision with that of another, reason, justice, and humanity will, or command, that the one shall yield and renounce his right, who will thereby experience the least damage. 4. It may be argued, the commerce of neutrals in time of war, is confessedly free, so far as regards their own goods, with the exception of contraband of war. But the goods of neutrals, which they are thus not prohibited from transporting and conveying to the enemy, likewise augment the strength of the enemy, as much as his own goods, and give him the power of causing irreparable damage. If, therefore, it is permitted to seize the latter, it should also be permitted to seize the former. But the non-sequitur, the inconsequential nature of this objection becomes obvious, if one attends that the capture, on board a neutral vessel, of goods belonging to the enemy, damages and affects him alone, by taking from him an aid upon which he relied; and that the little damage which neutrals may experience therefrom, is immediately compensated by the payment of freight, and indemnification for the delay; that on the contrary, the interruption of the commerce which neutrals were accustomed to carry on with the belligerent nations before the rupture, would throw upon them an irreparable damage. There is not more solidity in the opinion of Hübner, who pretends gratuitously, and without proof, that a ship in the open sea, ought to be considered as a part of the territory of the sovereign whose flag it bears; that it ought, consequently, to be inviolable; and that to take possession of goods which are on board of it, is the same thing as pillaging in neutral territory. This is a false principle—unfounded in fact. If this opinion were founded in reason, it would carry along with it also, and necessarily involve the unlawfulness of the capture of arms and ammunition, and other articles contraband of war; or of provisions destined for blockaded ports, when carried by neutral vessels; whereas all writers on public law, and Hübner himself, are of the opposite opinion.

As an apology for his independence in expressing the preceding opinion, which rests upon the grounds stated by Lampredi, and apparently in order to please neutrals, and the then existing government of France, Azuni next observes, that it is not to be inferred from what he has said, that nations have not the faculty of renouncing, by their treaties of navigation and commerce, their right to the goods of the enemy found on board neutral vessels; because it is lawful for every one to dispose of, and to desist from, the exercise of his rights, as it may seem good to him. On the contrary, he says, he cannot too much laud the moderation, which in our days, has led many powers to renounce this right. And he adds, that it will always be his earnest desire, that all the nations of the universe should, in time of war, make this sacrifice to the liberty of navigation and commerce. But whether the ostensible moderation, here lauded by Azuni, has not its origin in selfish considerations, national and individual, and whether the privilege contended for by neutrals, be not partial and unjust, may form the subject of future enquiry. Azuni concludes this article, with pointing out, how the attempt should be made to establish the neutral rule; abounding, as usual, in clamour and unfounded declamation.

In art. III. of this chapter, Azuni admits, as a consequence of the preceding principles, the right of belligerents, by the universal law of nations, to capture hostile goods on board neutral vessels, if in the open seas; but not otherwise. And, of course, he explains, at the same time, that neutral goods are not liable to confiscation, although found on board hostile vessels.

In art. IV. of this chapter, Azuni, in treating of the visitation of neutral vessels in the open seas, observes, that the primitive and universal law of nations, as well as the conventional law of Europe, permitting belligerents to prevent neutrals from transporting to the enemy goods contraband of war, to capture hostile vessels, and to stop and seize even those which are under a neutral flag, must also necessarily give them the faculty of employing all the means most proper for facilitating the exercise of these rights. And for that purpose, there are no means more efficacious, than the stoppage and visitation of the vessel in the open sea. He proceeds to detail how the summons to stop, and the visitation and inspection of papers, ought to be conducted. The mode of doing so, he says, was first regulated by the treaty of the Pyrenees, in 1659; and as so regulated, it affords the neutral no excuse for disobedience or resistance. He next specifies the ship's papers, which ought to be found on board;

and observes, that the proof of neutrality lies on the captured.

In chapter fourth, Azuni treats of the right of belligerents upon the sea, and of its effects. In art. I. of prizes. In art. II. of the acquisition and transference of lawful property in the prize. In art. III. of the judge competent, and capable of pronouncing judgment on the lawfulness, as prizes, of captured neutral vessels. All publicists, he says, before Hübner, ascribed this power to the tribunals of the belligerents. Hübner maintained the opposite; and Galiani went farther on that side. Lampredi, we have seen, decided against both, with two exceptions. Azuni here makes farther distinctions. Neither belligerent can make prizes within the territorial sea of neutral nations; but may, when beyond the reach of cannon shot, and may carry the prize into the adjacent port of the neutral sovereign, without the risk of losing it. If the captain of the captured vessel have recourse to the tribunal of the neutral country, to declare the prize unlawful, the captor is entitled to oppose the want of jurisdiction. On the other hand, in all such cases as the preceding, the neutral sovereign may enquire into the fact, whether the capture was made within his territorial sea, as his proper domain. And the prerogative of a ship of war can have effect, only when the prize belonged to the enemy, not to the sovereign of the port, into which she has been brought, or to other neutrals. If the prize has been taken from the enemy, the captor may carry her from the neutral port, into which he had first conducted her, to his own country for condemnation. But if the captured vessel or cargo, have belonged to neutrals, and the captor has brought the vessel into a neutral port, and the vessel or cargo are reclaimed by the captain of the captured vessel, or others, the captor cannot refuse the jurisdiction of the neutral sovereign in all that concerns the interest, which the subjects of neutral powers had, or may have, in the vessel or cargo, and still more the subjects of the neutral sovereign, into whose port the vessel has been brought. This right, says Azuni, has been rendered vain in Europe, by express treaty; but such a stipulation would have been superfluous, if the sovereign of the port had not the right of cognizance. And this opinion, he adds, is fortified by the practice of several nations, not bound by such conventions. When a prize, continues Azuni, has been conducted into the port of a neighbouring neutral sovereign, the captain of the prize accuses the captor of not being a lawful privateer, or of being a pirate, or of atrocious conduct, like that of a pirate, the government of the place may decide the question; and also, if the privateer has violated the law of neutrality of the country, into whose port she has come. A neutral sovereign, continues Azuni, may also have jurisdiction, if the captor brings into port a neutral vessel containing goods of the enemy, and also goods belonging to the subjects of the neutral power, into whose port the captor has brought his prize, namely, the hostile goods in the neutral vessel. Into the accuracy of these distinctions we shall not enquire farther, than to remark, that Azuni has not shown in a satisfactory manner, the ground upon which a neutral sovereign can claim jurisdiction, or set himself up as a judge, between a belligerent, and another neutral sovereign.

In art. IV. of this fourth chapter, of prize courts, Azuni observes, that agreeably to the principles which he has established in the preceding article, and the constant usage of the maritime powers, there is no doubt each belligerent power has the right of establishing within itself, tribunals to judge of the validity of the prizes made by their privateers, and brought into their ports, or into a neutral port. These are tribunals of exception, instituted to judge nations and foreigners, agreeably to treaties and the maritime laws. We see also, every where, that the discussion of prizes is regulated administratively, and subjected to the immediate action of the governments; whether to direct the fitting out of privateers, or to regulate their operations, or to modify their effects.

In art. V. of the same chapter, Azuni treats of recapture and its effects. In art. VI. of the ransom of prizes.

In chapter fifth, Azuni treats of several other rights, which nations may exercise at sea. In art. I. of the right of asylum in favour of belligerents in the ports and seas of neutrals. In art. II. of reprisals in time of peace. In art. III. of privateers—of pirates.

Section III.

Notice of the works of Jouffroy and Saalfeld.

JOUFFROY.

In the year 1806, there appeared at Berlin, an able work by M. Jouffroy, privy councillor to his Prussian Majesty. Of this book we have not been able to procure a copy, at Paris, Hamburgh, or Berlin, in consequence, it is believed, of the work having been composed at the request of the late King of Prussia, and only a few copies thrown off, without any publication through booksellers, in the usual way. The general object of the treatise, however, appears from the detailed title, as given by Von Kamptz in his Neue Literatur des Volkerrechts; le droit des Gens Maritime universel, ou Essai d' un systême général, des obligations réciproques de toutes les

Puissances, relativement à la navigation, et au commerce maritime; systême fondé sur les seuls principes du droit naturel, et abstraction faite des traités existans, ou des usages établis; on y a joint un projet de traité, tendant à concilier les droits du commerce neutre, avec ceux d'une nation en guerre, d' après les principes developpés dans ce systeme. And we may add, on the authority of M. Jacobsen, on the laws of the sea, that M. Jouffroy supports the maxim of "free ship, free goods," only so far, as concerns the direct trade of neutral countries, with their natural products to any enemy's country, or from an enemy's country to neutral ports.

SAALFELD.

In 1809, Professor Saalfeld of Göttingen published a neat text book, entitled, Grundniss eines systems des Europäischen Volkerrechts, zum gebrauche Academischer Vorlesungen, a sketch or outline of a system of the European law of nations, for the use of academical lectures. In this sketch Saalfeld has obviously benefitted by the works of his more recent predecessors, Martens, B. S. Nau, and Azuni; and his arrangement is an improvement on that of Martens. In the first part, he treats of the law of nations during peace; of Europe in general, considered as a great body or corporation of states; of the property of nations; of the rights and obligations of nations, with reference to the maintenance of the friendly relations existing among them; ambassadors, negotiation, commercial councils. In the second part, he treats of the law of nations in time of war; with regard to the belligerent powers in relation to each other; with regard to allied and auxiliary powers; and with regard to neutrals. Under the last division, he distinguishes neutrality by land and neutrality by sea; giving an account of the leading counter claims of belligerents and neutrals, and of the discussion of the contested points during the last two centuries, particularly during the latter part of the eighteenth century. But in a mere outline for a course of lectures, we are not to expect details; and we do not perceive in it any indications of profound or enlarged views. Although obviously under the influence in favour of neutrals, so prevalent in the north of Germany, as if their cause were that of genuine liberty, our author does not go so far as to maintain with Professor Cobald Totze, that conventions entered into by a majority of the European nations, for their own advantage or profit, are binding on the minority of these nations, although manifestly to their disadvantage, and deterioration of their national strength. He does not maintain that the mutual stipulation and concession of a privilege, in a treaty between two nations, is binding on them in favour of all and sundry other nations, although not parties to that treaty. But he seems to entertain, like Martens, some vague indefinite idea of treaties altering or new moulding the common maritime law of nations, beyond the extent and duration of their stipulations or provisions, so as to create modified obligations in perpetuity, after the treaties themselves have expired, been annulled, or ceased to exist. He seems to consider the rule of "free ship, free goods," though not supported by the practice of the European nations, independently of express treaty, as consistent with the natural law of nations, from analogy to the recognised rights of neutrals on land. But this analogy can only be discovered by Hübner's absurd assumption of a vessel or flag in the open sea or ocean, being equivalent in physical fact and law, to those solid and stable parts of the globe, continental or insular, which form the territories of nations. And, while Professor B. S. Nau admits, that the rule "free ship, free goods," is extremely favourable for neutrals, obviously implying more favourable than they can reasonably ask or expect, Professor Saalfeld, on the other hand, admits that this rule is unequal and partial, in relation to the belligerents, because it enables the one belligerent, although defeated at sea, still to carry on at a moderate increase of expense, its accustomed commerce, and thereby to protract the war, while it deprives the opposite belligerent government of a great portion of the naval strength, which it naturally derives from its territory and the industry of its people.

Section IV.

Review of the work of M. de Rayneval.

There still remain two eminent writers on Maritime international law, whose works appeared during the period we are now surveying, from the peace of Amiens in 1801, to that of Paris in 1815; M. de. Rayneval, a Frenchman, and M. Tetens, a Dane. And as the former supports throughout, upon general principle, the new neutral doctrine, and the latter upholds, also upon general principle, the doctrine so long and so universally prevalent, as the genuine law of nations in this department, we shall conclude our account of this period, by contrasting the views and arguments of the one, with those of the other.

M. de Rayneval distinguished himself in 1803, by the publication of his useful work, entitled, Institutions du Droit de la Nature et des Gens; in speaking of which work, M. Dupin observes, "C'est un grand avantage, de pouvoir jouir des méditations d' un homme, qu' une longue pratique a éclairé. On a cet avantage, dans la possession du livre de M. Gerard de Rayneval. Il a toujours été attaché aux affaires étrangères, et à la Diplomatique Françoise." From his knowledge of the law and practice of his country for centuries, and from the moderation of his former work, we should have expected from M. de Rayneval, a more impartial exposition of the principles of Maritime international law. But he appears to have forgot, or rather intentionally to have kept out of view, the French administration of that law, as exhibited in the ordonnances of 1543, 1584, and 1681, and in the works of Valin and Pothier. He appears to have become enamoured of the new fangled doctrines, which Hübner and Galiani were employed to devise and support. And he perhaps felt himself called upon to attempt to vindicate the altered policy towards neutrals, which Louis XVI, and subsequently the Emperor Napoleon, for a short time, found it convenient to adopt, for the purpose of carrying on, by means of neutrals, the otherwise almost ruined maritime commerce of France, and of annoying England. Accordingly, he gave to his treatise, published in 1811, the same title nearly, as the worthless republican Barrère had done —De La Liberté des mers—apparently with the view of obtaining popular favour in neutral countries; and he devoted about the half of his work, almost all the second volume, to an examination of the works of Selden and Grotius, the Mare Clausum, and the Mare Liberum. This revived discussion in the nineteenth century, of the exploded doctrines of Selden, in the earlier part of the seventeenth century, cannot easily be ascribed to any other motive, than a desire to exhibit England as still persisting in certain extravagant pretensions, which, in fact, she never actually put forth in practice. For, we have seen, the Swedish lawyer, Loccenius, who wrote so far back as 1651, mentions that these disputes about the pretended empire and appropriation of the sea, were even at that time considered settled, and had ceased to excite any interest. Indeed, so out of time and place was the revival of this discussion, except for some collateral and indirect, if not sinister purpose, that the American lawyer, Dr. Hoffman, in his late course of legal study, recommended only the first volume of this work, as the student can reap but little useful instruction from a discussion on the long agitated, and we may now add, exploded doctrines of Mare Clausum. And we shall follow this advice, by confining our attention to the first volume, or rather to the second part of that volume, the first part being devoted to the same exploded doctrines.

In the second part of his first volume, De Rayneval certainly adduces many ingenious arguments in support of the novel doctrines maintained by neutrals. But in the words of Dr. Hoffman, the work "has many defects, and some opinions to which we cannot subscribe." It is to be regretted, that on this occasion De Rayneval should have laid aside the character of an impartial man of science, maintained by him in his former work, and should have carried the exhibition of his animosity against England, to such an almost ludicrous height. The Treatise appears to have been composed while the Berlin and Milan decrees of Napoleon were in force—while the French Emperor, then invincible by land, was prosecuting with unabated success, his progress towards universal empire, and while Great Britain presented the chief obstacle to the ultimate gratification of his insatiable ambition. And as M. de Rayneval seems to have been then a French minister, in the department of foreign affairs, this work is perhaps to be considered, not so much a scientific treatise, by an impartial spectator, as a controversial pamphlet, or political brochure, such as frequently appeared during the revolutionary war.

Not being able to find any support for his comparatively novel theory, in the mode in which the maritime law of nations had been practically administered for centuries by the different European states, and particularly by his own country and Spain, Rayneval not only treats with contempt, as barbarous, the Consolato del Mare, the record of the usages of the first civilized maritime states of the Mediterranean, but endeavours, though unsuccessfully, as could easily be shown, to convict of error, and to throw discredit upon his own countryman, M. Valin, whom all Europe has respected, and will still continue to respect, for his veracity and fairness, as well as for his learning and acuteness.[1] Aware, that, with the exception of Hübner, Galiani, Totze, and some other German controversialists, he could find no support for his theory, in the more eminent continental international jurists, such as Grotius, Pufendorff, Cocceii, Thomasius, Wolff, Barbeyrac, Bynkershoek, Vattel, and Lampredi, Rayneval, thus boldly, and not very ceremoniously, dispenses with any reference to preceding writers on international law. "On remarquera sûrement, que, je ne cite pas d'auteurs, à l'appui de ma doctrine; la raison en est que la verité, ou la fausseté des principes est en eux-mêmes, si je puis m'exprimer ainsi, et que, dès que cela n'est pas, ils ne peuvent être considérés, que, comme des maximes, ou des hypothèses, qui rentrent dans le cercle des opinions, qu' on peut admettre ou contester, et sur lesquelles on peut disputer mille ans, sans s' entendre, et s'accorder. J' ai donc dû exposer ma doctrine, sans le cortège des auteurs, qui ont écrit avant moi, c' est à dire, sans étaler une érudition, dont le lecteur n'a pas

[1] Vol. I. pp. 89, 90, 91.

besoin, pour adopter des vérités, qui se présentent d'elles-mêmes, à tout homme, qui réfléchit, qu'aucun prejugé ne pre-occupe, et qui a le courage d'analyser les principes; mais j'ai jugé devoir signaler, et combattre, quelques ecrivains contraires à cette liberté, ou qui, du moins, en restreignent les consequénces, tels que Bynkershoek, Vattel, Jenkinson, &c. Si j'ai cité Valin, Commentateur de notre Ordonnance de 1681, c'est uniquement pour rélever l'erreur, dans laquelle il est tombé. Je passe sous silence plusieurs écrivains étrangers, très estimables, parce que là, où ils s'écartent, des principes, que J'ai posés, ils rentrent dans les opinions des auteurs, que je viens de citer."[1]

Upon this mode of proceeding we may, en passant, remark, that if certain general principles be conceded, certain consequences will follow; but that all depends upon the formation of the principles; that if they are deduced from a correct, comprehensive and complete view of the whole circumstanccs, relations and events, they may be well founded; but that, if they be deduced from an incorrect, incomplete and uni-lateral view of the circumstances, relations and facts, leaving out of consideration, the interests and consequent rights of a number of the parties whom we ought to contemplate, the conclusions or principles deduced from our observation, will be partial and incomplete, and likely to lead into error.

In the same assumed high tone, Rayneval says in a note,[2] "Pour éviter les répétitions, Je me borne ici, à indiquer les bases de ce premier moyen, parce que je l'examine plus bas, où je refute les opinions de M. Jenkinson, de Bynkershoek, de Barbeyrac, de Lampredi, &c." And in page 102, on the subject of contraband of war, he scruples not thus to accuse Vattel of bias and

[1] Avant Propos, p. 21, 22, 23. [2] p. 103.

partiality. "En un mot, La Terre est susceptible de propriété, et la Mer non, Vattel s' est laissé égarer par sa predilection pour l' Angleterre, et c' est à Londres, qu' il a composé, et publié son ouvrage!!" With régard to the true state of the fact, Vattel's work, according to Von Ompteda, Literatur des Volkerrechts, was published at Leyden in 1758, at Neufchâtel in 1773, at Amsterdam in 1775, and again at Neufchâtel in 1777.

Farther, finding that his new doctrines were not even supported in a satisfactory manner, by the treaties which the different maritime European powers had concluded with each other in the course of the last three centuries, so as to give them the obligatory force of special compact beyond the contracting parties, Rayneval thus throws aside these treaties, as not containing the true principles of international law, any more than the works of the most eminent international jurists who preceded him, or the practice and usages of nations, or the judicial determinations of their tribunals. "Si dans l'état actuel des choses, la jurisprudence maritime est plus incertaine, plus embrouillée, plus arbitraire, qu'elle l' ait jamais été, et s' il paroit difficile de la ramener vers sa source, c' est du moins une enterprise louable, que de fixer les veritables principes, et de les dégager, de l' alteration, qu' ils éprouvent, par leur alliage avec les usages, les conventions, les circonstances, les passions des gouvernemens; car les usages peuvent être vicieux; ils peuvent avoir pour fondement une maxime erronée; quant aux conventions, elles ne sont, que des dispositions partielles, émanées de la volonté des contractans, et elles ne sont, que trop souvent, le produit de la superiorité d' une part, et de la faiblesse de l' autre."[1] * * * * * "Comme Je l'ai remarqué plus haut, J' ai mis a l' écart, les traités, les coutûmes, les proclamations, la

[1] Avant Propos, p. 17, 18.

pratique; Je me suis renfermé dans les principes du droit de la nature, et des gens, applicables à la mer. C' est là, selon moi, la source, à laquelle, il faut nécessairement rémonter, pour pouvoir juger les droits, et les procédés des nations; car le droit des gens est à cet égard, ce que l' arithmétique, est à la géometrie.

Proceding on the plan thus announced by him, Rayneval, after some general observations in chapter I, propounds, in chapter II, the reciprocal independence of nations, to be the foundation of international law. And applying, in chapter III, the principles of the law of nations to the sea, he propounds this doctrine. The independence which each nation enjoys within its own boundaries, it preserves upon the ocean, because that element is free; and the effect of that liberty is, that the sea is not the domain of any one; that it is common to all nations; that all have in it an equal right; that all may use it with full and absolute freedom; and that this liberty cannot be placed within limits, abridged or restricted, without making an attack upon, or giving a blow to, their independence. This doctrine, he says, founded on the first notions of natural reason, which constitute the natural code, has full observance and execution in time of peace. The first exception, he says in chapter IV, is in time of war, with reference to belligerents, from the sea presenting to them a field of battle. The second exception, he says in chapter V, relates to neutrals. Equality of rights and reciprocity are the basis of proceedings between or among nations; they cannot be permitted to do any thing which they would not be obliged to tolerate against themselves. In time of war, a neutral nation, which wishes not to take part in it, must abstain from every act offensive to either of the belligerents. In chapter VI, he treats of the impartiality to be observed by neutrals. And in chapter VII, he enquires, what articles are to be considered as dangerous?

In chapter VIII, he admits, that arms and ammunition are contraband of war, but contends that naval stores are not to be held contraband, because they are not dangerous. And it is here he accuses Vattel of mistaking the obvious rules and rights of war,[1] and argues thus: "When a city is besieged, all the surrounding country, occupied by the besieger, is under his control; it is his conquest, at least transient; and he has a right to prevent any person whatever, from penetrating or passing through it, and having communication with the besieged; the neutral neither has, nor can have a contrary right; he can allege nothing but mere convenience. It is quite otherwise with regard to the sea; the right of navigation is independent of the will of others; it depends upon and arises from the nature of the element; nations exercise it by a right their own, and not acquired, not by tolerance; and the restrictions must be consented to, or result from the same principles of the law of nations. Without one or other of these two conditions, they are merely acts of violence."

In chap. IX, Rayneval states, as the third exception or restriction, which powers at war pretend to impose on neutrals, the seizure by the former, of the goods of the enemy on board neutral vessels. And he seems to add in § 2, that if the neutral ventures to carry such goods, he is punished by confiscation. But this last statement is incorrect, in as much as it has not been the practice of almost any nation, since the age of the Consolato del Mare, except France and Spain, to confiscate neutral vessels on that account. For the seizure of the hostile cargo, he states the assigned grounds to be, that a state at war, may take possession of the property of the

[1] Vol. I. p. 101, 102.

enemy, wheresoever it is found; that by carrying his goods, a neutral favours the enemy, and that this favour is hurtful, because it procures resources for continuing the war. This, however, he argues, is inconsistent with the former exception of goods contraband of war. For the latter description, he says, is applicable, and only applicable to articles subservient to war, because these are the only goods considered dangerous, and the exception, therefore, cannot comprehend anything beyond these, without the consent of neutrals. Against this pretended extension he argues farther, by stating a somewhat similar case on land, and puts a tirade in the mouth of a neutral, founded chiefly on the alleged inconsistency of allowing a neutral to carry his own innocent goods to the enemy, and capturing those belonging to the enemy, when carried by him; since the neutral might more effectually have aided the enemy and injured the opposite belligerent, by merely purchasing the goods, paying the price in cash, and then carrying them to the enemy.

But the case here put by Rayneval is by no means parallel; and the alleged extension of the description of contraband articles, and alleged inconsistency, are quite imaginary. For, besides dangerous articles, belligerents are manifestly entitled to seize even innocent articles, if belonging to the enemy. The requisite of being dangerous or subservient to war, is only necessary to warrant the seizure of neutral goods. The respect shown to goods, as being the property of a neutral, affords no ground whatever, for not seizing the property of the enemy, whatever may be the description of the goods, if they tend to increase his resources for carrying on the war.

Apparently distrustful of the reasoning here employed by him, Rayneval thus concludes the chapter, by resorting to his favourite principle.[1] "Pour juger, si une doctrine quelconque, est ou un principe positif, ou seulement une exception, il faut nécessairement rémonter au droit naturel; or, ce droit établit la plus parfaite égalité, de nation, à nation; et le fondement de cette égalité c' est l' indépendance. Voilà le principe; tout ce qui y est contraire, ou qui le restreint, n' est peut être considéré, que comme une exception. Les unes ont pour objet des sacrifices arrachés pour le maintien de la paix, les autres ne sont fondées, que sur des conventions particulières, sur des intérêts privés, ou sur la prepotence." But it is very easy thus to assume, gratuitously, vague general positions as principles; and to call rules of action, acknowledged as right by all nations for ages, exceptions from the principle thus assumed, as being more definite, and less general. Does it form, in reality, any part of the independence of a nation, to be allowed to screen and protect, throughout the navigable globe, the property of another nation, although otherwise justly liable to seizure by the enemy of that other nation, in self defence, or in vindication of its violated rights? If such a plea had been at all tenable, upon general legal principle, the European nations would not have resorted to special treaties, for the purpose of obtaining this profitable privilege; and the carrying neutral nations in particular, from the Hanse towns, downwards, would not have left the plea to be discovered for the first time, in the nineteenth century, by the subject of a noted belligerent state. The Hanse towns, we have seen, while their confederacy was powerful, contrived to exercise this privilege de facto in their own favour; but they never recognised it de jure in favour of other states; and were ultimately content to obtain it by special stipulation.

[1] Vol. I. p. 111.

In chapter X. Rayneval discusses the question, whether neutral goods on board hostile vessels are liable to confiscation. But it is needless to enter into this discussion, as none of the European nations, since the age of the Consolato del Mare, appear to have adopted such a rule, except the native country of M. de Rayneval, and Spain. That writer, however, naturally enough wished to sink, or keep out of view, the former harsh administration of the maritime law of war by France, and to cover it over with the comparative liberality to neutrals exhibited by Louis XVI. in 1778.

In chapter XI. Rayneval alleges, that belligerents, and particularly Great Britain, have denounced as illegal, any new commerce on the part of neutrals during war. But this charge is unfounded. Belligerents do not object to neutrals discovering and carrying on new branches, or descriptions of commerce, during war, provided they do not directly arise out of, and counteract the objects of, that war. But they do object to neutrals reaping profits directly from the disputes of their neighbours, and officiously, or by invitation, interposing themselves to carry on, for the behoof of a reduced belligerent, his coasting or colonial trade, from which neutrals have been uniformly excluded during peace, and thereby counteracting and doing away the effects, which the naval victories of the opposite belligerent would have had in the restoration of peace.

In chapter XII. Rayneval argues against a presumption said to be recognized against goods found on board a neutral vessel. But it is not believed that any such presumption is really recognized by European courts of law. And it is believed such goods are always adjudged to be neutral, unless the contrary appear from the want of the ordinary regular documents, which would accompany such goods, if the transaction was a bonâ fide one, or from the manifest fabrication and falsehood of these documents.

In chapter XIII. Rayneval argues against any presumption being recognized against goods under a hostile flag. But from the ordinary course of events, there obviously arises a presumption, that a hostile vessel is carrying hostile, not neutral, goods. And the rule, which, in such a case, throws the onus probandi on the neutral, is manifestly just, since he wilfully brings the burden upon himself.

In chapter XIV. the author inveighs against the condemnation of neutral vessels, on the ground of a deviation from the route or voyage, indicated by the ships' papers. But prize courts uniformly admit proof in justification of such deviation. And the farther argument proceeds upon dangerous articles only warranting such a confiscation.

In chapter XV. the author inveighs against the declarations and proclamations issued by the belligerent governments, so far as they are held to impose any obligations on other nations to obey them. And it is quite true, that the mere proclamation of one nation, cannot, as such, bind other nations. But it is equally true, that such declarations are valid and obligatory, so far as they merely go to enforce the generally recognized law of nations; and are of advantage, inasmuch as they usually contain information, of which it is of service to neutrals to be early put in possession. Indeed, the author himself admits, that in modern Europe such declarations have been introduced from necessity, and consecrated by usage.

In chapter XVI. the author inveighs against visitation and search; and the substance of the chapter may be gathered from the following sentence. "Sans doute, nombre de traités et l'usage ont consacré cette pratique; mais, faute de précautions suffisantes, il en est résulté une jurisprudence arbitraire, vexatoire, subversive de la liberté des mers, et directement contraire aux véritables principes du droit des nations."[1] Such groundless invective, while it may provoke a smile at the boldness, if not intemperance of the expression, may perhaps be excused, in so far as the practice he condemns is inconsistent with the principles of the author's favourite theory. But, it is obvious, he here forgets altogether, that visitation and search are indispensable for ascertaining, whether neutral vessels are carrying to the enemy, not merely hostile goods, but those dangerous articles, which the author himself admits, it is illegal for neutrals to carry. And it is rather amusing to observe a French author declaiming against such a necessary mode of proceeding, which has been practised by the government of his own country for centuries, both prior and subsequent to the celebrated ordonnance of Louis XIV. in 1681, with the exception of the merely conditional and temporary relaxation by Louis XVI. in 1778 and 1780; which was continued during the Republic with aggravated severity; and was sanctioned under Napoleon by the latest French reglement sur les Armemens en course.

In chapter XVII. the author next inveighs against, what he calls the punishment of neutrals, for resistance to the right of visitation and search; and the following is the substance of his argument. "La nécessité n'existe, que dans le cas, où votre conservation serait en danger; et alors, moi neutre, je conviens, que je dois m'abstenir de tout ce qui pourrait maintenir, ou augmenter le danger; c'est par cette raison, que je suis d'accord, que je ne dois fournir ni troupes, ni armes, ni munitions de

[1] Vol. I. p. 154.

guerre. Hors de là, je ne vous dois plus rien; et ce que vous exigeriez de plus, vons ne pourriez l'obtenir, que par la force; c'est-à-dire, en me faisant injure. Voilà, je pense, les véritables principes du droit des gens relativement à la guerre, aux visites, et à la resistance. La visite présuppose la preuve de la fraude, contraire à une obligation reconnue; la résistance repousse un injuste soupçon, ou un acte de violence. Dans le premier cas le neutre est coupable; dans le second, c'est le croiseur; et cependant, dans l'un, comme dans l'autre, on prétend punir le neutre. Quelle jurisprudence!"[1]

Now, although certainly a bad enough picture of international law, as practised by the European nations—this is fortunately not a true picture. A neutral, who carries goods through the open seas to a hostile country, may carry goods confessedly dangerous and contraband, or lawfully liable to seizure as hostile property. Experience proves, that with a view to gain a profit, neutrals very often carry such goods. The conclusion thus warranted by experience, justifies reasonable enquiry, for the purpose of ascertaining the fact. If, upon investigation, it appears no such goods are on board, the neutral, after the short delay, unavoidably requisite for such ascertainment of the fact, proceeds on his destined voyage. If, upon investigation, it appears, that such goods are on board, the neutral is justly detained, to the effect of these goods being captured as prize; but upon payment of his stipulated freight, if the goods be not contraband of war. There is thus, no punishment whatever inflicted on the neutral. He is merely subjected to the loss of the time, unavoidably requisite for ascertaining the fact—a risk to which he voluntarily exposes himself by traversing the open seas. And if a longer stoppage takes place, to admit of the enforcement

[1] Vol. I. p. 195.

of the belligerent's right, he is compensated for that stoppage by the payment of the freight, or profit which he would have earned in the meantime, except when he has knowingly and culpably undertaken the unlawful conveyance of goods dangerous or contraband of war.

In chapter XVIII. Rayneval treats of military escorts and convoys; and thus expounds the state of the question. "S'il existe un traité, il est la loi commune des deux commandans. S'il n'en existe pas, il s'agit de savoir s'il y a eu des déclarations, ou des réglemens, communiqués et adoptés officiellement. Dans ce second cas, le croiseur, et le neutre, ont également une loi commune. S'il n'y a ni traité, ni déclaration, le droit des gens prend tout son empire; c'est d'après ses principes, que les deux parties doivent se conduire; et celle, qui s'en ecarte, commet une injustice, que la force a le droit de repousser. On ne saurait point invoquer d'usage générale, parce qu'il n'en existe point; la preuve en est dans la variété des traités et de la politique. D'ailleurs il n'existe pour une nation indépendante d'autre usage que celui, qu'elle a reconnu."[1] We shall afterwards see, whether M. Tetens does not propound the state of the question more correctly and fairly, and investigate the grounds of the decision to be pronounced more acutely and profoundly.

In chapter XIX. the author treats of sieges and blockades, and here expounds the universally admitted doctrine, that in order to be respected, a maritime blockade must exist in fact, not merely in thought or words—must be an actual and real, not a fictitious and nominal blockade; and that a simple declaration of blockade is not sufficient, because one cannot rule over, or conquer a country without occupying it, without being able to defend it. All this is quite true. But is it quite

[1] Vol. I. p. 206–7.

consistent with the doctrine maintained by Rayneval elsewhere, that a flag, a piece of coloured cloth, hoisted in a vessel or boat in the middle of the Atlantic ocean, is, if not a part of the territory of a European nation, at least as actual and real a seat of sovereignty and independence, as practically exclusive of the intrusion or interference of foreigners, as the territories of Russia, France or Spain? Fictions, according to the ablest jurists, are inadmissible in international law.

In chapter XX. Rayneval treats of the competent judge of prizes. And here his views are comparatively, less extravagant, and more practical. But before giving these views, he renews his deplorable description of the multifarious wrongs, injuries, losses, and miseries, inflicted by belligerent cruizers on poor neutral ship owners and merchants. And there can be no doubt many abuses have taken place under the system of Armemens en course, or of privateering, adopted by the European nations; many unnecessary acts of arrogance and violence on the part of belligerent cruizers; many selfish, avaricious, fraudulent, and highly culpable acts on the part of neutral ship owners, ship masters, mariners, merchants and dealers. But such abuses and evils are not confined to maritime warfare. War on land is attended with similar, and equal, if not greater abuses and evils. Why a higher standard of morality should be set up, and a greater regard, not merely to justice, but to all the other virtues and ethical duties, should be expected or required of maritime, than of continental belligerents, it is not easy to see. And were not the subject too grave for a smile, it would be amusing to find a Frenchman, like Rayneval, under Napoleon, deploring in the sentimental spirit of universal philanthropy, the hardships inflicted chiefly, of course, by British cruizers, on that small portion of the population of neutral nations who engage in maritime and mercantile adventure with a view to gain, and bewailing the disappointment of France, in not having her languishing coasting and colonial trade carried on by these neutral adventurers; while he forgets, or at least places entirely out of view, the miseries inflicted on all classes of the population by land or continental warfare, not merely by greater destruction of human life, but by arrogant and cruel military exactions, and forced contributions; not to particularise the forcible division of the kingdom of Poland by Russia, Prussia, and Austria, in the course of last century, and the twice repeated attempts by France to subjugate the European nations, and establish an universal empire, the last attempt by his imperial master, Napoleon, nearly successful, and spreading death, devastation, want and misery, throughout these other nations, from Cadiz to Moscow. The horrors of warfare by land, it is quite true, will not justify abuses by maritime cruizers. But, if the truth be adhered to, the latter, though they certainly merit decided reprobation, and ought to be checked and prevented by every practicable means, will be found, upon comparison, to constitute but a very small proportion, of the evils of humanity, arising from warfare.

In this chapter, too, Rayneval resorts to his favourite fundamental principle, that the idea expressed by the independence of nations, embraces, not merely the exclusion of all foreign interference, the integrity and self government of each nation, within its own territory—the portion of the earth which it has acquired by occupation; but also the integrity and inaccessibility to others, of every vessel or boat which can hoist a national flag, although in the midst of any of the great oceans. Thus, "Un bâtiment neutre, en pleine mer, est hors de toute juridiction étrangère; et la plus légère atteinte à son immunité est une offense. Tel est le principe général, positif, incontestable, du droit des gens!!"[1]

But Rayneval here goes on to reason more practically and soundly on the competent tribunals for prizes. "Mais, comme je l' ai exposé ailleurs, il (le droit des gens) éprouve en temps de guerre, des modifications, à l' égard des gouvernemens, qui veulent se maintenir dans l' état de paix. Il en est une, d' où derivent toutes les autres; elle a pour objet les choses, qui, par leur usage sont considérées comme dangereuses pour l' une des parties belligérantes. Il est convenu, que les états neutres ne sauraient les fournir, sans violer la neutralité, elles doivent donc s' en abstenir; et de là résulte une modification de l' absolue indépendance des navires neutres. Les objets, dont il s' agit sont les armes de toute espèce, et les munitions de guerre."[2] "Il est certain, que c' est exercer une voie de fait, que d' arrêter un bâtiment neutre en pleine mer, et de le forcer d' entrer dans un port, autre que celui de sa destination; c' est une violation manifeste de l' immunité de son pavillon. Toutefois, dès que le droit de visite est réconnu par des traités, dans certains cas, et qu'il peut exister une fraude, il doit aussi exister, un moyen de la réprimer; car l'indépendance et l'immunité, qui en résultent, ne sauraient servir d' égide à l' impunité. D'un autre côté il n' arrive que trop souvent, que le capteur est coupable d' un acte de violence, d' une infraction aux traités, ou au moins d'une arrestation illégale; et dans l' un et l' autre cas, il doit être puni."[3]

"Entre nations, il n'y a, que deux moyens, répressifs de la fraude ou de la violence; c'est la guerre, ou la conciliation. Personne ne soutiendra, que le premier doive être préféré; car dans ce cas, la moindre querelle serait le signal de la guerre. On a supplée à ce rémède ex-

[1] Vol. I. p. 216. [2] Vol. I. § III. p. 217. [3] § V. p. 219.

trême, par un mode plus doux; c' est d' un coté, la confiscation de la propriété du neutre coupable; de l' autre, le châtiment du capteur, qui a excédé sa commission."[1]

"Mais pour appliquer cette double peine, il faut nécessairement, que quelqu' un la prononce; que par conséquent, le delit soit constaté. Sera-ce le gouvernement du maître du bâtiment marchand, ou bien celui du capteur, qui doit être chargé de cette double fonction?"[2]

"La saisie a lieu en pleine mer, ou dans les eaux du souverain du bâtiment en croisière, ou enfin dans des parages dépendans d' un état neutre. Dans le premier, cas elle a lieu hors de toute juridiction humaine, et, (abstraction faite des traités) elle est en elle-même un acte vexatoire. Dans le second cas, la juridiction du souverain du capteur est incontestable, parce que la mer est censée faire partie de son domaine, par conséquent de sa juridiction. Dans le troisième cas, la juridiction appartient à l' état, dont le territoire a été violé. Il ne peut donc être ici question, que de la prémière hypothèse." "Selon la pratique et les traités, un vaisseau armé ayant commission ad hoc, est autorisé à visiter en pleine mer, un bâtiment justement soupçonné, et à le saisir, s' il est réellement en fraude. Le croiseur, conformément à ses instructions, doit chercher à mettre sa prise en sûreté, en la conduisant dans un port de son propre pays, ou, en cas de necessité dans un port neutre. Mais la saisie ne suffit point pour le rendre maître de sa capture, parce qu' elle peut être injuste, illégale, vexatoire; elle doit donc être jugée. Il ne faut point perdre de vue, que le croiseur est seul acteur, ou, si l'on aime mieux, agresseur, au moment de la capture; que c' est lui-même, qui exerce un fait, une action; qu' il en est responsable envers son gouvernement, comme envers

[1] Vol. I. § VI. p. 220. [2] § VII. p. 220-1.

le patron marchand; que celui-ci ne joue qu' un rôle passif; qu' il est sur la defensive. Or, qui peut prononcer sur la responsabilité du premier? C' est sans contredit, son propre gouvernement. Car c' est lui, qui la lui a imposée en lui traçant la règle de sa conduite. C' est donc lui seul, qui est compétent, pour juger des transgressions, et pour les punir. Il faut aussi observer que, dans la poursuite du jugement de la prise, c' est le propriétaire du navire saisi, qui est demandeur en restitution, et que le capteur est défendeur, comme dans le cas précedent. Ainsi, le premier se trouve dans le cas de l' axiome de droit, puisé dans la raison naturelle, actor forum rei sequitur. Ce serait donc intervertir, l' ordre naturel des choses, que de proposer au capteur d' aller dans un pays étranger pour être jugé, dans un pays dont il n' est point justiciable, pour un fait, qui ne s' est pas passé, dans ses limites. * * * * Dira-t-on, que le bâtiment saisi doit être ramené dans son propre pays? Mais où est le droit, où sont les moyens d' y contraindre le capteur? à quel titre peut-on exiger de lui, qu' il se dessaisisse de sa prise, qui fait sa garantie et qu'il présuppose être sa propriété; qu'il quitte son juge naturel pour aller se défendre devant un tribunal etranger? * * * On peut, sans doute, objecter que le gouvernement du capteur, en prononçant, est en même tems juge et partie, et que sa partialité dictera le jugement. Il est certain, qu' en matière de prises, le gouvernement seul est juge; et que les commissions, ou conseils, qu' il établit pour le remplacer ne sont, que ses agens, ses organes; qu' ils n' ont aucuns des caractères, qui constituent un juge ordinaire, parce qu'ils n' existent point en vertu de la loi, mais en vertu d' un simple mandat, revocable à volonté; qu' ils ne prononcent point d' après une loi, mais seulement d' après des réglemens, des ordonnances, des déclarations, des traités; en un mot, qu' ils ne jugent, qu' en administration. Mais, enfin, le caractère, qu' a la forme des procédures devant le gouvernement du capteur, serait le même, s'il s'agissait de plaider devant le gouvernement du neutre arrêté; ainsi l' objection faite sur ce point ne mérite aucune considération. Quant à la partialité, si elle existe d'un côté, elle peut exister de l'autre; mais il faut regarder comme une inculpation aussi gratuite que grave, le soupçon de corruption et de prevarication. Quant à la prévention, elle est malheureuserment inhérente aux affections humaines. * * * "Mais enfin, dans une matière aussi serieuse, et où tout est hors de l' ordre ordinaire des choses, où il faut, en quelque sorte débrouiller un chaos, on doit s' attacher à ce point essentiel: c' est qu' il ne suffit point, que les delits soient constatés; il faut aussi un moyen certain pour les punir; or, le seul gouvernement du capteur le peut; donc lui seul peut être établi juge. Au surplus, on ne saurait trop le répéter, c' est en grande partie la faute des puissances neutres, s' il existe un si grand nombre de prises et de procès. Elles réclament, comme de raison, la liberté de leur navigation et de leur commerce; et les états en guerre entendent la restreindre. Dans ce conflit, les abus, les voies de fait, les dommages, les injustices, les plaintes sont inévitables. Le seul moyen de prevenir, ou au moins de diminuer tous ces désagrémens, serait de se concerter, et d' adopter des principes uniformes, qui servissent de règle commune, et surtout des môyens de les rendre efficaces."[1]

Farther, "Ici se présente la question de savoir qui est le juge compétent d'une prise conduite dans un port neutre. Est-ce le souverain du port, ou bien le juge naturel du capteur? Il me semble, que cette question doit être décidée, d'apres le principe; qu'en matière

[1] Vol. I. § VIII. pp. 223 24, 25, 26, 27, 28, 29, 30, 31.

personnelle, la compétence appartient au juge dans le ressort duquel s' est passé le fait. Si donc la prise a eu lieu dans les eaux d' un état neutre dans le port duquel elle a été conduite, c' est à lui seul qu' appartient le droit de la juger; et il doit en prononcer l' illégitimité. * * * Mais si la saisie a été exercée en pleine mer, elle ne peut être jugée, comme il a été observé plus haut, que par le souverain du preneur; et celui du port de retraite, n' a aucune qualité pour intervenir. La raison en est, que le fait s' est passé hors de sa juridiction, et que l' asile, qu' il accorde, ne saurait le denaturer."

In chapter XXI. Rayneval treats of reciprocity and reprisals. And under the former article, he justifies France and Spain for not acceding, unconditionally, to the system of the armed neutrality in 1780; because England refused to adopt the rule in favour of neutrals, which gave them the privilege of protecting hostile goods.

In chapter XXII. the author examines at length, the arguments of Mr. Jenkinson, the first Lord Liverpool, against the claim of neutrals to protect at sea the property of the enemy; and appears satisfied he has succeeded in refuting these arguments. But that he has not so succeeded, we shall take an opportunity of showing, by our review of the more acute and profound observations of M. Tetens on that subject, as being less liable to the charge of partiality, and more free from national bias, than any remarks we could offer.

In chapter XXIII. entitled, "Du Mérite des faits," Rayneval seems almost to deny the existence of what has been denominated the consuetudinary law of nations, and to refuse any legal effect to the usage or practice of nations, although it may have been uniformly observed for centuries. Thus, "Je ne conteste aucun des faits, aucune des ordonnances, qu' il, (M. Jenkinson) rapporte; mais, je dis, que les faits, quelque multipliés, qu' ils soient, s' ils ne sont pas généralement, et surtout librement adoptés pour règle, n' établissent point le droit des gens; qu' au contraire, le droit des gens est la loi, d' après laquelle, ils doivent être approuvés, ou condamnés. Le droit de naufrage était, aussi jadis, à peu près, généralement, établi. Soutiendra-t-on pour cela, qu' il était juste, qu' il était fondé sur la raison naturelle? L' usage, chez les peuples anciens, avoit consacré l' esclavage des prisonniers de guerre; et cet usage, n' est-il pas, généralement réprouvé aujourd' hui?"[1] "Cependant, je conviens, que les faits peuvent établir un préjugé, et même ce qu' on nomme droit coutumier; mais pour qu' ils acquièrent ce dernier caractère, ils doivent être avoués de toutes les parties intéressées; hors de-là, ils n' imposent que des obligations partielles, à l' instar des traités, qui ne lient, que ceux, qui les ont souscrits. Ainsi, les souverains, qui ont pour système de gêner le commerce des neutres, ont beau réclamer leur intérèt à cet égard, et citer à l' appui, tous les réglemens anciens et modernes; ils ne trouveront de la docilité, qu' en raison du plus ou moins de foiblesse des neutres. Mais ni le silence de ceux-ci, ni leur inaction, ne légitiment la pretension."[2]

But although it is quite true that there exist in nature certain legal or juridical relations, between, or among nations, whether rude or civilized, independent of all human regulations, enactments or observances, constituting what has been called the natural law of nations, it is equally true, that the rules composing this natural law of nations, may, in the present condition of mankind, be carried into operation or execution, or become positive law, by the adoption thereof by nations, in their mutual intercourse; and that this adop-

[1] Vol. I. § I. p. 284. [2] Vol. I. § II. p. 285.

tion may be as substantially effected, rebus et factis, by uniform observance for ages, as by express bargains or treaties, binding on the contracting parties. Indeed, the doctrine here propounded by Rayneval, is quite contrary to the mode, in which human laws of any description have come to be established and enforced, either internally among the associated inhabitants of a country composing a civil society or state, in relation to each other individually, and between the government and the subjects of that state, or externally between or among such states; and it is obviously brought forward in support of his new theory in favour of neutrals.

In chapter XXIV. entitled, Des Règlemens, et des Traités, Rayneval seems to deny all effect to the former of these arrangements, as constituting any part of, or contributing to, the formation of international law. Thus,[1] "Les règlemens particuliers, ne comptent pour rien dans le droit des gens; parce qu' ils ne peuvent par leur nature même, avoir d' effet, au-delà des limites de la juridiction du souverain, qui les a donnés; et s' il arrive, qu' on les respecte au dehors, ce n' est nullement par obligations; la nécessité seule, ou quelqu' autre cause, peuvent produire cet effet passager; en un mot, les nations étrangères les adoptent, ou ne les adoptent pas, selon leur position, leur convenance ou leur intérêt. Mais quelle jurisprudence peut on tirer, d' un genre d' actes contradictoires et constamment variables?" Now, while it is quite true, that regulations established by one state with regard to matters of international interest, cannot bind other states, if contrary to, or inconsistent with, the natural law of nations, it is equally true, that, when in conformity with that law, such regulations are an actual adoption and enforcement of it; and as such, binding on other states. And

[1] Vol. I. p. 287.

in this view, the prize codes of France and Spain, while they departed from, and were more severe than, the common and general maritime law of nations, in several important particulars, before pointed out, at the same time recognized and enforced that law, in the great majority of instances. Upon the legal principle of reciprocity, also, it appears clear, that a government, which establishes a particular regulation, with regard to maritime captures, gives other governments a right to require from it compliance with that rule, when it is directed, or bears against itself. Farther, the comparison which the author here introduces between the conduct of Great Britain, and that of France, towards neutrals, merits no other remark, than that it is unfair, because it proceeds on what is untrue.

With regard to treaties, Rayneval seems here to give them a preference over particular ordinances or reglemens; and so far correctly, inasmuch as the former constitute the conventional law of nations, properly so called. And while he enumerates certain treaties, as showing that the neutral flag was thereby held to protect the property of the enemy at sea, and that naval stores were thereby held not contraband of war, he repeats his caution, that such treaties do not constitute the general law of nations. "Les seuls traités peuvent être cités, comme des exemples, parce qu' ils sont des actes publics du nombre de ceux, qui constituent, le droit des gens conventionnel. Or, si nous considérons les traités, en ne remontant plus haut, que celui des Pyrénées (between France and Spain) la plupart stipulent la liberté des munitions navales, et des effets ennemis chargés sous pavillon neutre. Une partie de ces traités a été conclue par l' Angleterre elle-même; et tous ceux, qui ont étés signés, depuis une vingtaine d' années, (sauf celui conclu en 1796, entre la Grande Bretagne, et les

Etats Unis, de l'Amerique,) renferment ces mêmes clauses. Si donc, les traités doivent nous servir de règle, s'ils doivent fonder le droit commun, il est à peu près démontré, qu'il est, sur les deux points en question, conforme au principes, que j'ai établis. Mais je ne puis cesser, de le répéter, les traités, n'importe leur contenu, ne constituent point le droit des gens; ils sont l'expression de la volonté particulière des contractans; et le droit des gens, est indépendant de cette volonté; ils ont la même nature, que les contrats entre particuliers; mais à defaut de contrat, c'est la loi commune qui décide; et entre nations, la loi commune, c'est le droit des gens."[1]

In chap. XXV. Rayneval gives an account of the convention of 1780, called the armed neutrality; and in chap. XXVI. of the conventions of 1800, as of similar import, but somewhat different from the former. But of both these unsuccessful attempts to establish by treaty or by force, the new rule of maritime international law, in favour of neutrals and certain belligerents, and against other belligerents, we have already given, or will in the sequel give, a sufficiently detailed narrative.

In chap. XXVII. Rayneval treats of the right of preemption, and seems to consider it as having no foundation, except in stipulation by treaty, and even then, as an act of partiality, and not consistent with neutrality; apparently because the treaty to which he refers, was an impediment to France obtaining naval stores from Sweden.

In chap. XXVIII. Rayneval treats of the rights and duties of privateers. But the general principles of the doctrine here maintained by him, have been already sufficiently noticed.

[1] Vol. I. p. 288.

Section V.

Analytical abridgement of the work of M. N. Tetens.

The other eminent writer on Maritime international law, during the period we are now surveying, from 1803 to 1815, is M. Nicol Tetens, Conseiller de conference to his Danish majesty, whose work appeared first in German, and afterwards in French at Copenhagen, in 1805, entitled "Considérations sur les Droits réciproques des Puissances Belligérantes, et des Puissances Neutres sur mer." And we deem it right in our historical review, to give a full analysis, or almost abridgement of this valuable work, apparently little known in this country, not merely as answering, and we think refuting the arguments and doctrines of Hübner, Totze, Galiani, and Rayneval, but as the most free from national bias, and most impartial exposition of the general principles of Maritime international law, which has appeared in recent times; distinguished alike by practical knowledge of business, acuteness of discernment, and views extensive and profound. This memoir, the author informs us, was not originally intended for publication, but was composed for the use of an illustrious and highly estimable man.

The first section of the work is devoted to the general principles of Maritime international law, and the author sets out with an enumeration of the subjects, which, in the application of these principles, are to be discussed in the subsequent sections.

Primarily.

1. The capture as prize, of vessels and cargoes at sea; privateers.

2. Articles contraband during war.
3. Rights in the case of blockade.

Consequentially.

4. The visitation of vessels, particularly under convoy.
5. The organization of courts of admiralty, to act as judges in prize causes.

In No. 2, he lays down the following fundamental propositions as a sort of axioms, of which the truth is incontestable and self-evident, or at least, has never been contested or called in question in the conventional law of Europe; and as embracing the natural rights of belligerent powers in relation to other nations, and the natural rights of neutrals in relation to belligerents.

Belligerent powers.

1. They may lawfully prevent all aid or supply (secours) being carried to their enemy by other nations, and thus oppose the augmentation of the warlike forces of that enemy, either in numbers or quality.

2. They have, in the same way, a right to weaken the warlike forces of their enemy, by taking from him the means of augmenting and multiplying them. They have, therefore, a right to seize the effects and treasures of that enemy. Commerce, and in particular, maritime commerce and navigation, are among the most powerful means by which a state can procure both money and men fit for marine service, as the history of all times, and still more of our days, proves. It is, therefore, evident, the rights to impede or obstruct, to diminish, and even to destroy the commerce and navigation of the enemy, are to be ranked among those primeval or original titles, which constitute the right of making war.

3. They have a right to watch, and cause their people to take care, that their rights be respected by neutrals during war.

4. Each belligerent may also itself judge, whether its rights have been respected or violated, in the cases in which circumstances give rise to an inquiry into that subject.

Neutral powers.

1. They may lawfully prevent the property of the state, and also the private property of their individual subjects, from being invaded or violated by belligerents; supposing always, that the conduct of their subjects is legal, and conformable to the rules of neutrality.
2. They are entitled to prevent the commerce and navigation of their subjects from being disturbed, fettered, or destroyed.
3. It is the duty as well as the right of neutral governments, in behalf of their subjects, to watch over the maintenance of the free exercise of their rights of commerce and navigation during war.
4. Neutral governments are entitled themselves to judge in the cases which occur, whether the rights of neutrality, with regard to their mercantile and seafaring subjects, are respected, or not, by belligerents.

No. 3. Such are the fundamental propositions, from which we must set out, in order to reason soundly on the points at issue. Simple good sense is sufficient for understanding them; they need not the speculations of philosophy. They are recognised as just, both by belligerents and neutrals, however much reason the latter may have to complain of the mode in which belligerents have applied them. The ancient teachers of natural law, as well as Grotius, and those who have followed him, have never called these propositions in question.

The author next treats, as a chimerical hypothesis of the day, a theory then prevalent, that war is only legitimate between state and state, not between the inhabitants of the countries at war, so as to exempt the property of individuals. But while he does so, he distinguishes between the war of savage tribes, in which each individual of the one tribe acts in a hostile manner when he can, against every individual of the other; and the war of civilized nations, which is only between states, independent and separately constituted, that is, between nations united under different sovereigns and governments, and in which no individual of the one nation is entitled to attack an individual of the other nation, without the authority of his sovereign or government. From this idea of civilized war, he observes, may be deduced several consequences, tending to determine and modify the natural right inherent in war, of doing evil to an enemy, which in general, is sufficiently indefinite; jus in hostem infinitum. And to these consequences, he adds another proposition of natural law, that neither war in itself, nor any particular hostile operation, can be considered as legitimate, except when rendered necessary by circumstances, which gives a new principle, very fertile in salutary conclusions.

In No. 4, the author next treats of the collision of rights. The reciprocal rights of belligerents and neutrals before expounded, being incontestable, the only object is to determine the means of conciliation between them, in the cases in which there may occur collisions in their exercise. It is evident, that if there was no neutrality, or if belligerents combated each other in an isolated world, there would be no question about such collisions. It is from the connections and intercourse of different countries and nations, from their physical and moral, or juridical relations, and from the commercial relations of belligerents and neutrals, that the rights of war of the former, interfere, and come in collision with the rights of peace of the latter. Where such collision takes place among such rights, or, as they have been called, moral faculties, the same happens, as in the case of opposing physical forces in the material world. Knowing the laws and magnitude of the latter, we may calculate upon effects and results; but this only so far as no opposite force destroys or weakens these effects, by a contrary action. All rights, all obligations with regard to actions, and particular external objects, says our author, are liable to be struck by, or to come in collision with, other opposite rights and obligations; excepting only the small number of absolute rights, such as that to existence, which form a class of moral or legal forces, as generally irresistible as in physics, the impenetrability of bodies. Thus, to take another familiar example, no one can contest with me the right to move at will, and according to my good pleasure, my arms and limbs in my chamber, if I am there alone. But I can no longer pretend to this liberty if I am in a crowd, or in a company, or in any place where the exercise of my rights may hurt others.

Setting out, then, from the general rights already enunciated, we must proceed from them to the questions, which form the problem we have to solve. Thus, supposing the rights of belligerents and those of neutrals, are found in opposition in practice, we must consider the causes, and the conditions or circumstances which give birth to this contrariety. Perhaps there may be modifications, by which rights in their generality may be defined more precisely, and thereby become reconcilable with each other. Where there are direct collisions, without any compromise or accommodation being practicable, we have to determine the moral or juridical preference, justly due to the stronger and more urgent rights, and to fix the extent and limits of this preference.

Finally, in the particular and complicated cases, where what is right and just cannot be exactly carried into effect or executed, as but too often happens; and where there must be concessions on both sides, the question will be as to the rule which ought to be followed, in order that the reciprocal deferences or concessions may balance each other, and be equitably compensated. The solution of these problems, generally considered, must be sought in the principles of the law of nature, or of the natural law of nations, and in those of the conventional law of nations. If the question regards the rights of a particular state, as opposed, or with reference to another state, it is to the conventions or treaties which subsist between them, that recourse must then be had.

In Nos. 5 and 6, the author treats of the distinction between the commerce and navigation of the enemy, and of neutrals.

It is necessary to consider first, the nature of commerce, in order to distinguish the commerce which belongs to the enemy, from that which belongs to neutrals; since belligerents have a right to attack the first, and ought to respect the second. There are writers, who have zealously declared themselves in favour of the absolute liberty of all commerce during war, upon the sole ground, that to invade the commerce of the enemy, is always to attack the commerce of neutrals. All commerce, say they, consists in mutual relations between the trading parties, which are of the same nature, and of the same importance, for the one and for the other. If the hostile country has commercial relations with the neutral country, say they, the latter has the same relations with the former; so that damage cannot be done to the commerce of the enemy by constraint or interruption, without the same damage being done to the commerce of neutrals. There is thus, continue they, an alternative which cannot be avoided. It is absolutely necessary, either that the right which neutrals have to maintain their commerce during the war, be sacrificed, or that the entire liberty of all commerce, without exception, be granted to enemies as to neutrals. Now, the first proposition is not admissible; it would violate the most incontestable rights of neutrality. It is the second, therefore, which must constitute the law. It would, they still add, be infinitely more conducive to the interests of nations, to admit this liberty without restriction, into the conventional law of Europe. It appears to them evidently more advantageous for the general good of humanity, to allow commerce to be carried on during war without any restriction, although the right of war of belligerents may suffer from it, than to leave to this last right, its natural extent and vigour, and to derogate from the right of neutrals to free commerce. We speak elsewhere of this pretended interest for the general good of humanity; we know sufficiently the disastrous consequences of those compassionate sentiments, and of those vague principles of a partially enlightened philosophy. Let us rather examine here, the supposition from which we set out—the pretended identity of the commerce of the enemy, with the commerce of neutrals.

Is it, then, in fact, one and the same thing, to have commercial relations with a country, and to carry on the commerce of importation and exportation of that country? The farmer, who carries his grain to the city in order to sell it, and provide himself with the articles of which he has need, is not, on that account, a trader or merchant, although he sells, and employs the proceeds of his sales in making purchases. He who purchases only to use, and who sells only to procure articles of necessity or convenience, does not carry on the trade of a merchant. The merchant is he, who purchases in order to sell, and who sells in order to purchase new merchandise, that he may sell it again, in order to obtain benefit or profit, both upon his sales and his purchases. A country, which draws or receives the produce of another country, whether rude or manufactured, and which delivers to it its own, has undoubtedly relations of commerce with that country. Nay, we may even say that it carries on commerce there; for in grave and important matters, we should not be too scrupulous about words. If, however, we give the name of commerce to such relations, it becomes necessary to distinguish two modes of participating in it; which may be designated by the denominations, passive commerce and active commerce. If the merchants of the one country send merchandise to the other, and bring back from the latter its raw produce and manufactured articles, the latter makes only a passive exchange. It permits the importation of foreign articles of commerce, and the exportation of these which, belong to it, without any active traffic on its part. There may be merchants in this country who traffic in foreign wares—who purchase what is imported, and re-sell it in the same country; they then trade in foreign articles, without having commerce with the foreign country. But if merchants out of the country, transport to it merchandise, at their risk, and on their account; and if they draw, or receive back from it, in the same manner, they carry on the active commerce of this country—commerce properly so called. There exists, then, a very essential difference between neutral commerce and hostile commerce, totally independent of the country, whence the commodities come, and to which they are carried. This difference is founded on the neutrality, or the non-neutrality of the merchants, who are the proprietors of the transported articles. The simple and passive exchange of the raw produce and manufactures of a country, with those of other countries, is of very great importance; and sometimes necessary for the subsistence of this country. The latter gives what it has too much of, or what it can do without, and receives what it has need of. If, in consequence of its industry, it has more to sell than to purchase, it may apply this surplus to its enjoyment and conveniences, or it may convert it into money; and it is then to its labour or industry, but not to its commerce, that it owes its wealth.

The effects of commerce, properly so called, go much farther. Even when the ungrateful soil refuses their subsistence to the industry of nations, not only can commerce supply it, but it can also give them superfluity, abundance, and riches. This effect, especially, is rapidly produced, when the country is itself provided with articles of commerce. The trading country, while it gains by the mere exchange of commodities, gains also by the freight, and the workmanship in the construction of carriages for conveyance, or vessels. These profits form a considerable part of the value of the commodities. The trading country, then, gains, separately and independently of its own proper products, a part of the products of others; and it receives it in money. Such is the source of the riches and pecuniary strength, which a nation derives from its commerce.

Let us see the consequences which flow from the distinction we have explained. The simple commercial relations between a neutral and a hostile country; or the simple exchange of their produce, cannot be interrupted, fettered, or destroyed, without the consequences falling upon both parties. At least, that is true, if the neutral country cannot immediately replace these relations, by similar relations with another neutral country; which is indeed very difficult. Belligerents, therefore, do a wrong, more or less great, but real, to the interests of neutrals, if they interrupt these connections. It is not the same, if the point at issue be the prevention of active commerce; the question then totally changes its nature. The commerce of the enemy alone is attacked, if the belligerent seize the goods of hostile merchants, without directing this attack against the neutral merchant, giving always perfect liberty to the property of the latter. The exchange of the merchandise of one country with the other, may continue with the same activity. Neutrals usually gain by it, by rendering themselves masters of the active commerce, which was previously carried on by the enemy. Experience has also proved, that in maritime wars, the commerce of neutrals takes a higher flight, and is enlarged in the same proportion, as that of the belligerents is diminished or destroyed.

The same observation may be made with regard to navigation. To interrupt, molest, or annihilate the navigation of a hostile country, is quite a different thing from interrupting, molesting, or annihilating the navigation of the subjects of the hostile country. In the last case, the neutral navigators may go to, and come from it. The communication by sea with this country, may be the same during the war, as it was during the peace, provided the political or national character of the navigators be changed. There, then, accrues to the navigation of neutrals, the same advantage as to their commerce; it gains in extent during maritime wars.

No. 6. From the difference we have just explained, continues the author, between the commerce and navigation of enemies, and the commerce and navigation of neutrals, it again follows, that the belligerent powers, in seizing the goods and vessels of their enemies, at sea as by land, do not attack by that merely, the commerce and navigation of neutrals. It is the hostile government and hostile subjects who are deprived of their property, and whose commerce and navigation are hurt; but neutrals do not suffer from it, at least from the nature of the thing; for it is possible they may be accidentally interested in it. It may also happen, that neutral individuals, and even a whole neutral country, may suffer much from another country being in a state of war, and particularly from the consequent ruin of the merchants and ship owners of that country. The misfortunes of a war are never confined to the country solely, which is at war. There result from it evils or benefits, even to those who are not directly interested as parties. This prospect of accidental advantages or inconveniences, may make neutrals desire there should be no war; but it does not furnish them with any just reasons for taking part in it, unless under some rare cases of necessity, from singular connection. As long as the neutral continues to be such with regard to belligerents, the hostile operations of the latter against each other, although detrimental in their consequences to neutrals, cannot be regarded as directed against them.

In No. 7, the author treats of the seizure of the property of private individuals in maritime war. It is a peculiarity of maritime wars, that the attacks upon the navigation and commerce of the enemy, are immediately and equally directed against the individual subjects of the hostile state, as against the military forces. Vessels and merchandise are captured at sea, which are private property; while in wars on land, this conduct would be regarded as robbery. For although such seizure on land be not forbidden by the natural law of nations, the positive (consuetudinary?) law of Europe has proscribed it, as dishonourable and barbarous.

With regard to this positive received law of cultivated nations, it doubtless ought to be respected; and special regard ought to be had to its rules, which relate to the mode of making war—as rules which, with regard to civilized states, appertain to the law of nature, in its application to the wars of such civilized states. It is in this respect, that it may be called the positive law, the secondary law of nature, or rather, the natural law of nations, applied to civilized states; which in their wars, admit the principle, that we must not do any more mischief or evil to our enemies, than what is absolutely necessary, for the attainment of the object of the war. This is the positive (consuetudinary?) law, which forbids the massacre of prisoners and such of the enemy, as in the action, throw down their arms, and surrender themselves; which forbids the use of poisoned arms; which does not permit the poisoning of victuals, or springs of water; and which proscribes many other similar acts. The reason of these prohibitory laws is self-evident. Indeed, why kill men who are not in a state to act in a hostile manner? and why kill, when the same end can be attained by merely wounding? Supposing, then, the authority of this positive (consuetudinary) law, to be clearly recognized and well established, it remains to examine, whether the seizure of effects, belonging to private individuals, be contrary to it. In wars by land, no doubt, the belligerents who have invaded the territory of an enemy, do not allow themselves to take possession of effects, the property of private individuals. Whatever violates this rule of honourable warfare, whether committed by soldiers or by officers, is designated pillage. Nevertheless, the object of military operations, namely, that of weakening the enemy, of depriving him of his resources, and of appropriating them to one's own use, is not neglected in this species of warfare. There are exacted from the inhabitants of the conquered provinces, collectively and in mass, in the shape of contributions and requisitions, all that is needed for war; and which they are in a condition to furnish; money, provisions, clothes, ammunition, and other articles. Commands are issued to magistrates, prefects, and other chiefs of villages, cities, communities, districts and provinces, to furnish these articles, leaving only to these chiefs the power of distributing the quota to be furnished by each, among those liable, or subjected to contributions. There is no abstinence, then, from the effects of the subjects of the hostile state, in war by land. Far from it, very often in this respect, the limits of the principle of civilized wars, just noticed, are transgressed. The contributions are levied upon the mass of the citizens, instead of being wrested from individuals; but this manner of seizing collectively the hostile property, whether public or private, has nevertheless, very severe consequences.

Oppressive and ruinous, however, for the inhabitants who are compelled to contribute, as this mode of proceeding may be, however barbarous and unjust it may be, when it is extended beyond what is necessary, it is yet infinitely preferable to the pillage of individuals exercised by common soldiers. These facts prove clearly, that the positive (consuetudinary?) law of nations does not prohibit belligerents from seizing the property of hostile individuals. It is rather the mode of exercising this rigorous right which it regulates and modifies. It is manifest, at first sight, that in maritime wars, there is no room for the application of these rules; since in them the system of contributions is impracticable. It is only in the case of the invasion of hostile coasts or islands, that naval forces can exact contributions, and that failing the discharge thereof, they have the right of seizing directly the property of individuals.

In No. 8, the author treats of the rights of war, and

of necessity, as its basis. In general, the right of war is derived from necessity. This right is, that of doing evil to others, of plundering them, of taking or destroying the effects belonging to them, of wounding them, of killing them. All this, doubtless, presents a series of actions very bad, and very unjust, considered abstractly, or apart from all other relations, and which can never become legitimate, unless they be rendered necessary and unavoidable. Now, the necessity of hostilities in wars, can only be founded, in the ultimate analysis, upon the right of conservation of the state. And as the end or object of war, is thus, in general, determined by the motive, cause, or reason of necessity, so in the same way, military operations, and all kinds of hostilities, must also be necessary, and in connection with the end, in order to be regarded as just. This necessity may be judged of by this criterion that the means employed to produce the effect, be in proportion to the end for which they are employed. To obtain the object to be effectuated, we must not do more mischief, than what is unavoidable, in order to obtain it. This is an universal rule, applicable not only to the plan of operations against the enemy, but also to each single operation.

But this necessity relative to the end of the war, may be more or less strong. There are degrees, from the most absolute necessity, to that which ceases to be such, and which, properly speaking, is no more than an advantage or convenience, in relation to the same end.

Farther, we must never confound the necessity with regard to the total of military operations, with that which exists with reference to such or such a particular operation. The enemy must be absolutely forced or coerced; but the doing so in one such manner, rather than in another—the attacking precisely on this side or that, is not equally necessary There may be many routes to arrive at the same goal. * * * There are thus, real differences in the necessity for operations in war.

In considering hostilities in general, it is very clear, there are some which hold the first rank in comparing their necessity. Military operations, to the effect of combating the armed forces of the enemy, to diminish them, to destroy them, if practicable; those by which it is proposed to prevent re-inforcements or supplies reaching the enemy, or to take them from him—to seize his magazines or stores, his ammunition, his vessels, his forts; to cut off his resources; and the other operations of this kind, must be put in the first class, among those which war renders necessary. It is not the same with attacks upon the commerce and navigation of the enemy. There are cases in which, for belligerents, it is of as much importance to make these attacks with success, as to gain battles on land, and take fortresses; but there are other circumstances in which that interest is very inconsiderable. If the hostile government carries on the commerce itself, the belligerent, who captures his vessels and merchandise, does precisely the same thing as he who invades a hostile country, and takes possession of the public property. With regard to the commercial affairs of private individuals, it may, no doubt, also be of more or less consequence to embarrass and to ruin them, according to the relations which they have to the armed forces. But in general, whatever may be the advantages to be derived from this class of hostilities, for the attainment of the object of the war, their necessity is of an inferior order to that of the other military operations, directed immediately against the armed forces.

In particular cases, doubtless, the belligerent government must judge of, and appreciate the necessity of a hostile enterprise. In virtue of its independence, this judgment cannot be submitted to any foreign tribunal. There is no other judge upon earth, but a moral judge, —the good sense of the public, and history. When, however, the rights of neutral nations are involved—when there are collisions between the respective rights of neutrals and belligerents, the latter cannot be altogether the parties and the judges. Neutrals have also a right to examine and to judge. Even this right of necessity, which belligerents might allege, is then submitted to the examination of the reason of others.

In No. 9, the author treats of the rights of neutrality. Having propounded, says he, necessity, as the basis of the right of war, let us see whât is the basis of the right of peace, in behalf of neutrals. The first right of neutrals is, doubtless, that of preserving their neutrality. The necessity of maintaining the condition of peace, and of defending itself from the calamities of war, is the same as that of preserving the state, or at least immediately connected with the latter. The neutral, then, is entitled to prevent whatever may be done on the part of the belligerents, to drag him into the quarrel. He has a right to refuse to the parties at war, the use of his territory, of his armed forces, of his fortresses, and of his warlike stores. It is, indeed, one of his duties, to exercise this right as much as he can, if he wishes to maintain his neutrality.

We may place in the second rank, the right of preserving the well-being of the state, such as it was enjoyed before the war. This welfare of a state may be considered as the assemblage, the collection of the conveniences, of the advantages, and of the facility of procuring them, which are enjoyed collectively by all classes of the citizens, and by all the individuals who compose the state. Among the particular rights, comprehended under the general right of preserving the national welfare, is that of maintaining the commerce and navigation of the country, and of defending them against whatever may diminish their extent and importance. If the foreign war incidentally fetters or impedes either, it is a misfortune which must be submitted to, as derangements produced by physical calamities. But if there were direct attacks against the commerce or manufactures of the country, they would be considered as hostilities, which there is a right to repel by force.

In the third place, there cannot be refused to neutrals the right of augmenting their welfare, of ameliorating their condition during the war. Why should they not avail themselves of the opportunities which arise from the misfortunes, even of the other states, in order to derive advantage from them, to extend their national industry, and to augment the number of their merchant vessels? The events of war often cause them losses and disadvantages, of which they cannot complain; it is therefore allowable for them to seize the occasions of profit which present themselves. Qui jure suo utitur, neminem laedit.

In Nos. 10, 11, 12, and 13, the author discusses the rules for determining the preference of the rights of belligerents and neutrals, respectively, when they come in collision. On the supposition, he says, of the justice of the observations he has just made, it will not be difficult to fix the rules to be followed, in the case of collision between these respective rights.

Rule first. If the rights of belligerents to execute their plan of operations against the armed forces of the enemy, that is to say, if their rights, relative to the special measures to be taken, are in opposition to the rights, which neutrals have to preserve their neutrality, the preference must be given to the rights of neutrals. Supposing that neutrality may take place, that it exists, and that in whatsoever manner it may be, it is recognized by the belligerents, it is very clear, that the necessity for neutrals to preserve this relation, is more absolute and more urgent, than it can be for those at war, to act in such or such a particular manner. It is quite another question, if by the concurrence of circumstances, the power at war finds itself necessitated to refuse neutrality to another power, or to concede it, only with restrictions, which may compromise the neutral in relation to the opposite power. * * * It is clear, however, that the right to force another to take part in a war, can have no other foundation, than the right itself to make war. It cannot be disputed, that by singular circumstances, the same reason which necessitated the war, may require, with the same force, the refusal of neutrality to another state. Under this general rule, it is recognized in practice, that a belligerent cannot enter a neutral territory with armed forces, to take there military positions against the enemy, nor occupy neutral fortresses, nor carry off neutral warlike stores, nor use effects belonging to neutrals, in order to derive advantage from them, for offensive or defensive operations. And the positive (common consuetudinary) law, which here, as in almost all the points of the natural law of nations, supplies what cannot be fixed by general notions, ought never to depart from the principle, which emanates from supreme reason, and which is very clear, that belligerents cannot lawfully dispose by force, of what is neutral, either with regard to persons or things, in order to make them instruments of their hostilities. If they act differently, in cases of extreme necessity, they have then an excuse; provided they make restitution, as soon as the urgency has ceased, and indemnify the parties interested.

Second rule. With regard to the rights of belligerents

to prosecute their operations against the armed forces of the enemy, when they come in collision with the interests of neutrals, their commerce and navigation are naturally more powerful, and they are those to which the preference must be given. This proposition is very evident, according to the natural law of nations. Indeed, if we suppose several states, independent and co-existent, in the neighbourhood of each other, it is clear, the first necessity for each of them, is that of existence. The one to whom this necessity is refused, has no social duties or obligations in relation to the others. It is from it, that is derived, the other necessity of preserving the state, and of defending it by force against him who attacks it; and also that, in making war, of acting in a military capacity—of resorting to military force, to weaken and destroy the armed forces of the enemy. If, then, by social relations between the states at war, and those which remain at peace, the former cannot exercise their rights and their duties, without affecting and hurting the interests of the latter, provided they attack neither their safety or conservation, nor consequently their right of neutrality, there can remain no doubt that the inconveniences on the part of the neutrals, ought to yield to the reasons of war, on the part of the belligerents. It is very true, that this modifies the rights of neutrals during war; but it is a natural consequence of the relations of states to each other, in their general society. We have seen above, that on the other side, the rights of belligerents are modified by those of neutrals.

This ground of preference of the rights of belligerents is of general application, and extends to all the opposite interests of neutrals, so far as the latter relate only to advantages and profits, and the question with neutrals does not involve the conservation of the state. Military operations are for the belligerents, of such a nature, that the smallest circumstances and obstructions, or impediments, very slight or trivial in appearance, may have consequences indefinite and extreme. A vessel loaded, more or less, with provisions and ammunition for the succour of a blockaded city, may decide the issue of the blockade undertaken, and perhaps the fate of a whole campaign. It would be the same, if the enemy were furnished with the materials and stores necessary for the armament of a squadron, or of some body of troops. The consequences might be indefinite, and of a nature not to admit of reparation. Such acts, then, affect immediately the state at war, and the welfare of all its subjects; while the restraints upon neutrals, in their commerce and navigation, are merely temporary; sometimes only for a very short time, as usually happens in the case of a blockaded place. Almost always, too, these restraints ought rather to be considered as an interruption of profit, (lucrum cessans), than as positive losses. They do not directly affect the existence of the neutral state; although in affecting individual merchants and shipowners, they may be of consequence with reference to the public prosperity. But, in fine, whatever may be the advantages of commerce for neutrals, in balancing them with the importance of military operations on the part of the belligerents, there is too much inequality in the comparison, to admit of any dispute, on what side is the natural preference of rights?

It is upon the principle of the natural law of nations, established in this second proposition, that the distinction of commerce and navigation into legitimate and illicit, during war, is founded. It is evident that it is not permitted to neutrals, to send, or to carry, to places besieged or blockaded, either materials or provisions, or warlike stores, or to furnish to hostile armies or fleets, any of the articles which they need for acting in a hostile manner, and for combating or fighting. These transmissions or furnishings are forbidden, by land as by sea, and in all the places, where the enemy might take advantage of them for that purpose. The positive (consuetudinary) law of nations recognizes universally this distinction; and even during the last contests, the neutral governments have not denied either the legality of contraband during war, or the illegality of communication with blockaded places.

Yet certain modern authors, in defending the rights of neutrals, have been led, in the excess of their zeal, to wish to annihilate this principle; and have advanced the following doctrine. Neutrals are totally strangers to war; whence it follows, that with regard to them, there does not exist any war. They are, therefore, entitled to act, and to conduct themselves, with regard to each of the belligerents, in the same manner, as they might do during peace. Their commercial relations with the country at war are not changed. In a word, every thing ought to be allowed them, as if there was no war. This reasoning is very rash. The principle that neutrals are strangers to the war, although rather vaguely expressed, is very true, on the supposition that the neutral states are entirely insulated, and separated from those at war. But, when we consider the former, in their social connections with the latter, and in the reciprocal relations, which result from their co-existence on the same part of the globe, where the war takes place, it is a little singular to wish to establish their right of acting by the supposition, that there is no war, in the very place, where a war actually and really exists.

Third rule. The question here regards the kind of hostilities, which belligerents may exercise against each other, but which are not operations against the armed forces of the enemy, or in direct connection with them.

The rights of neutrals, attached to their commercial relations with the countries at war, when they come in collision with the rights of belligerents, relative to the sort of hostilities now under consideration, are then the strongest, and ought to be preferred in the order of justice. If, however, the question merely involves a simple privation of profit on the part of the neutrals, or merely an obstruction or constraint, or impediment in the possibility of augmenting and giving greater extent to their commercial relations, then neutrals can no longer pretend to demand the same preference.

This principle may be regarded as the line of demarcation to be drawn in these researches. It is chiefly on this point that the opinions of learned jurists have varied and differ from each other; without alluding to some modern authors, who have plunged into vague and obscure theories. We must, therefore, expound this principle a little more distinctly, in order to fix its import. Besides military operations conducted directly against the armed force of the enemy, there are a vast number of other hostile acts, and of other modes of doing damage to the enemy, whether with regard to the government or its subjects. There may be taken from the enemy, by all possible means, his resources, whether consisting of money, or of other articles necessary for war; and they may be turned to profit, or may be destroyed. The necessity of operating in conformity to the object of the war, does not annihilate the essential difference between military operations against the armed forces, and the other hostilities in wars. It is absolutely necessary to defeat the hostile armies and fleets, for the preservation and security of the state. But, when that end is accomplished, there is nothing more to be dreaded, either for its own existence, or with regard to ravages, which can only be perpetrated by armed people. It is permitted by the law of war to do more; it may even be necessary to put the enemy out of the condition of re-establishing his forces, so as if not to procure an immediate peace, at least to obtain a peace more promptly, more advantageous, more honourable, more secure for the future. But it is evident that the necessity which exists for aiming at this last end, is of a different nature from the primary and more absolute necessity, namely, that of self-preservation against the attacks which the enemy may make by armed forces. The preference, therefore, which is due to the rights of war, relative to military operations, which are in opposition to the rights of neutrals, ought not to be extended to all sorts of hostilities, which the belligerent has the right of exercising, but only to those, in favour of which there can be alleged, what is called la Raison de Guerre.

It is an universal law of society, that each member having secured what is necessary for his own existence, cannot, in order to procure a surplus, deprive others of what belongs to them. In applying this law to hostilities against commerce and navigation, the right of belligerents is there incontestable. This right is in many cases of great importance. There cannot manifestly be denied to belligerents, the right of restraining and annihilating the connections of commerce, which the enemy carries on with neutrals; or which, on the part of the enemy, are in the class of passive relations. The question is, whether the belligerent may exercise this right, in the cases in which he cannot do so, without hurting the rights of neutrals, attached to their relations with hostile countries? With regard to attacks upon the active commerce and the navigation of the enemy, it has already been shown, that really there is not in these cases, any opposition or collision between the rights of war, and those of neutrality. This active commerce and navigation of the enemy may be totally destroyed, without the neutral being entitled to complain, or having more than a fortuitous interest. Indeed, if the neutral himself has not an active commerce, or a navigation of his own, his commercial relations with a hostile country may cease entirely, by the ruin of the commerce and of the navigation of the enemy. In that case, the neutral must exert himself to create it, or apply to other neutrals who possess it, in order thus to procure the commodities of the belligerent country, of which he has need. If he cannot do either, he may be deprived of these commodities during the continuance of the war. But then, this is one of the unfortunate consequences, which wars never fail to spread over the different states of the European society.

On the other hand, the simple relations of commerce of one country with another, (or what has been termed passive commerce) cannot be attacked, without damaging both at the same time. It follows, that the right of belligerents in this case, cannot be exercised without doing wrong to neutrals, and without exciting their just complaints; excepting, however, the cases of contraband, and all that regards military operations. Although then, a belligerent may have a great interest in insulating, to use the expression, his enemy, in the commercial world, nay, although he may not have any other means of arresting or obstructing the commerce of that enemy, protected by superior naval force, than that of forcing neutrals to abstain from all commercial intercourse with him; still, nevertheless, this is not the case in which a power at war, can allege an urgent necessity for believing itself entitled to exact from neutrals such a renunciation. In order merely to do some additional mischief to one's enemy, one ought not to infringe the rights of others.

Farther, some authors refuse to neutrals, the right of augmenting their commerce and navigation during the war. Others, on the contrary, pretend, that except military operations, and the case of contraband, belligerents, in all other hostilities of any kind, can do nothing which may be adverse to the interests of the commerce and navigation of neutrals. The first of these propositions refuses too much; the latter grants too much to the rights of neutrals. According to the rules of general justice, the truth will be found in the medium, between these two extreme opinions. Belligerents, doubtless, ought not to interrupt the commercial intercourse of neutrals, with the countries at war, except in the cases of their military operations; since that could not be done without affecting the right, of which the latter were in possession. If, then, by the ruin of what commerce was active on the part of the enemy, the neutrals cannot preserve the same relations of commerce, without augmenting their active business, and increasing the number of their vessels, they cannot be denied the right of doing either or both. And as the preservation of what existed in the state before the war, with regard to connections with the hostile countries, may be claimed by all neutrals, even by those who have no navigation nor active share or part in the commerce, it is clear, that so far as the totality of relations between the neutral countries and those at war, does not become greater and more extensive than it was before the war, the belligerent cannot justly interrupt or restrict it, although it should be a real increase of business for the one or other of the neutrals; especially when it involves only some disadvantages, or some particular evils, which would result from it to the enemy. The right of belligerents, however, to fetter and diminish even the simple commercial relations of the hostile countries, is not thereby, or on that account, annulled. It remains entire, and it may be lawfully exercised in the cases where it can be done, without depriving neutrals of what they possessed before the war. Governments at war prohibit their own subjects from continuing their communications with the enemy. They cannot do so with regard to neutral subjects. But if the latter wished to extend the sphere of their relations, beyond what it was before the war, there would be a collision of interests between the coveted profits on the one side, and the right of acting in a hostile manner against the enemy on the other. There the rights of belligerents preponderate. Those at war may lawfully prosecute their right to press the enemy, to do him damage, although neutrals may be thereby deprived of the advantages which they might have reaped from the circumstances. To this occurrence may be applied the rule of the common law, and of good sense, that no one ought to enrich himself at the expense of others; Damno alterius, nemo debet fieri locupletior. It is, doubtless, a disadvantage for the belligerents, not to be able to attack their enemies in all possible modes. It is a restriction upon their rights, caused by the opposition of the right which neutrals have, to preserve the connections of which they were in possession. But, if neutrals should pretend to increase these advantages, it would only be at the expense of the belligerents, whose rights of war would thereby be still more limited.

In these particular cases, however, it will be very difficult to judge, whether such or such a cargo, transported from hostile to neutral countries, or reciprocally, from the latter to the former, be contained within the limits of the exchanges, which have existed before the war, or whether it be a surplus, a new branch of neutral commerce in favour of the enemy. This is so much the more difficult to determine, that the war, as has been already remarked, substitutes the neutral in the active part of the commercial relations, which the enemy had previously. Yet there are cases in which the application of the principle is practicable; for example, in the coasting trade, and in the commerce of the colonies. With regard to these branches of trade, the state of matters before the war can be ascertained, and compared with the business carried on by neutrals during its continuance. In the colonial trade, neutrals are entitled to draw directly from the colonies of the enemy, the same commodities which they received from them indirectly, before the war. They could not, then, be reproached with the increase of their commerce and navigation, which would be a natural consequence of it, if this commerce was really confined to what is necessary for them, and to what the country at war had previously furnished to them, and which they would want, if they did not go to provide themselves with them.

Such are the limits of this increase, traced by the rules of law. Farther, in order to be legal, it is understood, that this commerce of neutrals with the colonies of belligerents during war, be such in reality, and not a fictitious neutral commerce, while it is really a hostile commerce, having nothing but the appearance of neutrality. With regard to the navigation of neutrals to the colonies of the enemy, without any direct commerce, it can have for its object, only a simple transportation for the profit of freight, and serving the enemy. The belligerents would be fully entitled to oppose it, and to place it under constraint.

In No. 14, the author adds the following remark. When the question regards the rights of neutrality, it is, of course, assumed, that the neutrality is exact and perfect. It is independence, indeed, which constitutes equality of right among states. Physical inequality of strength may lead nations, as it does individuals, to form mutual connections of protection on one side, and of deference and regard on the other. The situation of countries and other relations may be such, that the weaker state is in a kind of moral dependence, and can, with difficulty, separate its interests from those of the stronger. Yet such a state, though small, may be completely independent in point of right, and support that independence in political affairs.

There is another view or sense of the term neutrality, often put in practice; being the basis of a right, found in the code of merchants, although the law of nations, and that of reason know it not, or disavow it; according to this view or meaning of the term, in order to be neutral, it is sufficient to take no more particular interest in the welfare of the one of the parties at war, then in that of the other, preserving, in other respects, with regard to each of them, the faculty of serving them equally. Neutrals are, therefore, it is pretended, at liberty to supply the wants of the latter; provided this is not done without partiality—solely in the relation of payment. But it would, indeed, be an abuse of reason, to employ it in the investigation of such a right, of which the basis is duplicity. * * * The governments of maritime and commercial states, however, particularly the smaller states of that class, ought to be so much the more attentive in checking the illicit traffic of their merchants, as the liberty of lawful commerce is comparatively of greater consequence to them.

In No. 15, the author treats of the liberty of the sea. The sea, (out of the limits, within which it is regarded as dependent on the adjacent coasts, and as part of the territory of a state,) is not the property of any power. It is not a territory; it belongs to no one, neither to enemy, nor to ally, nor to neutral. It may be called a solum or space, upon which people may go and come; but not a territory, from which one power is entitled to exclude another, or to limit his use of it. The most powerful nation on the sea, has no more territorial jurisdiction over the sea, than the weakest, or than even the state which has absolutely no naval forces at all. We must, therefore, carefully distinguish the superority in force, of a nation at sea, from the right of sovereignty or dominion which has no existence.

We leave to others, says the author, the task of disputing about the origin of this law; of inquiring whether it may be deduced from the general principles of natural law, or whether it is solely positive, and dependent on a convention among nations expressed in treaties; whether it has been adopted tacitly by usage, or expressly recognized? It is sufficient for us, that now-a-days, no government in Europe disputes this liberty of the sea, except the cases in which, by convention or usage, a portion of the sea is recognized in some measure to be shut.

Supposing, then, the authority of the principle just enunciated, to be established, it is clear, that the conduct of a state or of individuals, relatively to other states or individuals, cannot be reputed just or unjust, lawful or illicit, because it has taken place at sea. This circumstance cannot change the moral quality of an action, nor render it legal or illegal, if it is not so otherwise, from its nature and relations to other rights

Some explain the liberty of the sea in this sense, that people may go and come upon it according to their good pleasure—may convey or transport upon it what they choose, without any regard to the relations which such conduct may have to the interests of others, or to the rules of law, which pronounce what is permitted and not permitted. Doubtless, in this sense, the sea is not free. This would indeed, be licentiousness at sea, rather than liberty. At sea every one is free; that is, totally independent of all territorial jurisdiction; but the sea gives no privilege to do what is unlawful. For example, to carry arms and other succours to blockaded places, to provide hostile countries with articles of contraband during war, are acts which are not permitted on land, and which do not become indifferent or lawful, by being performed at sea.

The true and genuine liberty of the sea, or independence of territorial superiority, on the part of any power whatever, has consequences, which will be considered in the sequel. On land, a government may prohibit any foreigner from entering the country, or setting foot on a public road. The foreigner, if he is advertised of the prohibition, must conform to it. The law obliges every one to observe it; and the foreigner is justly punishable if he disobeys it. At sea, on the contrary, there is no power which can justly proclaim such an interdict. Every navigator may take the course which suits him best, provided he does nothing adverse to the rights and interests of others.

In Nos. 16 and 17, the author shows, that a neutral vessel at sea is not a neutral territory. A vessel, says he, sailing on the sea, is certainly an article of property; and of course, a neutral vessel, is neutral property. This has given rise to the question, whether a vessel may not be considered as a territory, belonging to the state whose flag it bears; and this state being neutral, whether its government might not claim for the vessel, bearing its flag, the rights of a neutral territory.

We have nothing to do here, with either mere words, or fictions. Let us allow a captain to consider his vessel on the sea, as the territory which he commands, and imagine himself to be the sovereign lord of a floating island. That is of no avail here. The question is concerning real actual rights, concerning that inviolability, which the law of nations, in Europe, accords in wars to the neutral territory. By that inviolability, it is not permitted to any of the belligerents to commit hostilities against each other, on the territory of neutrals. The reason of the inviolability of the neutral territory is very obvious. The neutral, by permitting enemies to attack each other, and to fight on his territory, would not only expose his soil to damage or ruin, but also the inhabitants to wrongs, which are inseparable from military operations. He would compromise his neutrality.

This reciprocal security against hostile attacks on the neutral territory, is also of a common interest, even for the belligerents. Each party may profit by the certainty of being sheltered, and safe from any hostility on that side. * * * The neutral territory forms an asylum, or place of safety for persons not armed, as well as for effects belonging to one or other of the parties at war. The persons and goods which are conveyed thither, are no longer exposed to the violence of the enemy. It is, in this sense, that the neutral territory neutralizes the objects which are found in it. Another reason for this last conclusion is, that the persons and things which are on the neutral territory, are, by that very position, out of the power of the state, to which they belong.

From these reflections, it is evident, the first characteristic of a territory is being determinate, or definite, that is, fixed, within known, and not variable, limits. It is thus, only, it can be known whether there be such a neutral territory, where it is situated, and on which side, consequently, people can neither attack the enemy, nor have cause to dread being attacked. How then can a vessel at sea be considered as a territory? It would be a moveable and floating territory; which might go hither and thither to such a part of the world, or to such another part; interpose its inviolability between the floating isles of the belligerents, to prevent their attacks; offer a place of safety to persons and effects, in order to withdraw them from hostile pursuit, and convey them to such place as the hostile proprietor might desire! Even although there existed floating islands, they would be only a moveable territory, that is, such, that there could not be claimed for them, the rights of a fixed and immoveable soil, as a territory, properly so called, must be.

With regard to merchant ships, it is then very clear, they ought not to be considered as territories, any more than a waggon of merchandise, the trunk or the portmanteau of a traveller. It would be an excessive abuse of the analogy, which may exist between the rights of property in a moveable object, and the rights of a territorial domain, to attempt to deduce from it the conclusion, that such a vessel can enjoy the rights of territory. A ship of war can still less be regarded as a territory belonging to the public. Such a vessel has rights which merchant vessels have not; and with regard to the power of preventing every stranger or foreigner from coming on board, the commander may lawfully act in the same manner, as a commander of a fortress. Such a neutral vessel, however, has not in war, the right before mentioned, of an asylum or place of refuge against the pursuit of the enemy, in the same sense, as belongs to a neutral territory. A vessel chased by a hostile vessel, and seeking refuge under the protection of the cannons of a neutral ship, could not there be lawfully received; nor even could the persons or goods.

Having thus ably expounded the general principles of Maritime international law, the author concludes this section with observing, it still remains to make a just application of these principles, in order to find their consequences, in the determination of the particular points which occur in practice. And he proceeds to do so in the subsequent sections.

In section second, the author treats of the seizure or capture at sea, of the property of enemies; and of cruizers and privateers.

In No. 1, the author shows that the seizure of the goods of individuals at sea, has different characteristics, from those of their seizure on land. The right of seizing the property of enemies during war, has never been contested with regard to articles of public property; nor has any exception been made of the effects of private individuals, either by land or by sea. The governments which have maintained that the goods of individuals, when placed under the protection of a neutral flag, could not be subjected to capture, thereby admitted they were so liable, without that alleged safeguard.

In wars by land, these effects are seized in mass, or collectively, by requisitions and contributions; because it would be held barbarous to take them individually by pillage. But at sea, where the collective mode is not practicable, this hostile operation is conducted by cruizers and privateers; and it takes place against the vessels and goods of the enemy, whether they belong to individuals or to the public. The difference in the mode of capture, by land and by sea, is obviously founded on the nature of things, and may be a little more unfolded. 1. In wars by land, the immoveable property of individuals cannot, of course, be carried off by the enemy. Their houses, buildings, and other cultivated possessions, might be destroyed by fire and otherwise. But this is only held pardonable in rare cases, when it may be the means of extorting from the enemy concealed specie, and other valuable articles. In wars by land, even moveable effects, if of great bulk, cannot be easily removed, sold, or used; and, if of small bulk, are easily concealed. On the contrary, the articles of property captured at sea, are cargoes of merchandise, which may be realized immediately, though frequently below their value. The belligerent who captures them, increases his pecuniary resources;—that great instrument of military operations. 2. On land, private property consists chiefly of articles destined for the habitation, subsistence, entertainment, or enjoyment of the possessors. On the other hand, the goods conveyed by sea are articles of commerce, exposed voluntarily to the violence of the winds and waves, and during war, also to the attacks of the enemy, with the view of deriving a profit from them, since without this motive, the goods would be kept in safety at home. 3. The cargoes of vessels which may be captured at sea, are great masses of effects of very considerable value. They form treasures, which, in fleets of merchant vessels, amount to millions. Their seizure, therefore, is of great consequence to the hostile state. The capture of even a single vessel, affects the revenue of the state, to which it belongs; the capture of a merchant fleet is felt as a national disaster. In wars by land, there are also to be found, magazines of grain, and of other merchandise of great value. But, on comparing the articles, which may be seized on land, in bulk, and all at once, with those which may be captured at sea, we shall find there is an immense difference between the loss which the state may sustain in the former, and in the latter case. 4. The cargoes rarely belong to one single individual; several merchants usually are interested in them. If they are insured against war-risk, the loss is scattered over a number of insurance companies and individual underwriters. In this respect, captures by sea resemble contributions by land, which fall heavily on communities, and bodies corporate. 5. Beside these differences in the seizure of goods upon the two elements, there is another essential difference in the mode of carrying these seizures into execution. On land, if single soldiers, or companies of soldiers, were ordered, or permitted to pillage indivi duals, this could not be executed without the latter experiencing hardships, injuries, bad treatment, and personal violence. The victims would seek to conceal all, they thought they could withhold from their plunderers; and the latter, not content with what might be presented or abandoned to them, would exert themselves to extort still more. At sea, again, the capture may take place without any of these hardships. The hostile vessel is summoned by the cruizer; and if no resistance is made, if the conduct on either side does not give rise to the bad treatment of the crew or mariners, the vessel is brought peacefully into the port, where the captor places his prize in safety, and where the legality of the seizure may be ascertained by a court. At least, it is thus the statutes and ordinances of civilized nations provide. In this there may still be, as there have been, many abuses. But these abuses are not intimately, or necessarily, connected with seizure at sea, any more than they are with military execution by land; which is here the main point. There are not at sea, any fraudulent devices for the withdrawal of articles, unless it may be with regard to some papers, which the captain may, and ought, to avoid delivering. A private cruizer is neither a pirate, nor a Barbary corsair. He has neither the right nor the power to touch the cargo, until the law has declared the prize legal.

In No. 2, the author treats of capture at sea by privateers. The capture of the property of the enemy at sea, is made either by the ships of war of the state, or by privateers. The difficulty at sea, of following the traces of the enemy, and of overtaking and encountering him, renders the last means very fit for the attainment of the end proposed, to destroy his commerce, and take possession of his property. When it is wished to make war by sea with energy, there is a necessity for augmenting the number of cruizers. Permission is therefore given by governments, to individuals, to fit out and arm privateers, it being understood, that they do so at their own expense, on their own account, and at their own risk; but under certain conditions, conformably to what is prescribed by the statutes or ordinances for privateers, and after having obtained special commissions from government. Privateers may be compared to light troops by land, with this difference, that they are simply volunteers, having the power to continue the business, or give it up, and to choose freely the stations which they believe most suitable for the attainment of their object in capturing; not being responsible to any one for the issue of their expeditions, while they exactly observe the rules prescribed to them.

Not to confound lawful privateering at sea, with that kind of privileged piracy, which the Barbary corsairs practice, as some modern declaimers are pleased to do—who, from the want of precise ideas of what they treat, merely utter verbiage—we must mark the following requisites in the organization of the system of privateering, as justified by the jus gentium, among civilized nations. 1. The owners and commander of every privateer must be authorized by their government, and have a special commission to that effect. 2. As the commanders of privateers cannot be under immediate inspection, governments take precautions to ensure the legality of their proceedings, by prescribing regulations, and holding the owners responsible. 3. The effects lawfully seizable at sea, are distinctly defined, namely, the vessels and goods of the enemy, and the goods of neutrals, which are contraband of war. 4. The commander of a privateer, after having captured hostile property at sea, cannot regard it as his own, nor dispose of it at his pleasure, until it has been adjudged by the prize court. The captured vessel must be taken to a port, where there are competent judges, before whom, the master of the captured vessel may put in his claims, if there be any grounds for them. Attempts have been made to put an end to privateering, by reciprocal stipulations in treaties of commerce. It was during a short period of the last century, that the friends of humanity began to entertain great hopes, from the pretended progress of illumination, that it was considered possible to extract or remove from wars, the evils occasioned to individuals by privateering. Although it was then seriously regarded as an operation indifferent to the object of war, it may yet be doubted, whether such a convention would have been observed, if war had taken place between these contracting parties. Indeed, people have now-a-days come back to be of this opinion. It may happen that a state cannot be attacked, except on the side of its commerce and navigation. An enemy, then, by renouncing privateering, would, by that alone, renounce the only means of acting against that state. If both the contracting parties were in the same predicament, the convention not to employ private cruizers in their wars, would be tantamount to an agreement, not to make war during their wars. The proscription, too, of lawful privateering, would perhaps afford an encouragement to piracy; at least the latter would have more opportunity during wars. It is, indeed, very probable, that the damage caused by pirates to one of the belligerent parties, might not be disagreeable to the other; because evil done to an adversary, although one would not do it himself, may not be displeasing, where another is the author of it; so difficult is it to be just towards an enemy. It is upon the form of the regulations by governments, in that behalf, and on the mode of causing them to be observed, that the question depends, whether privateering is, or is not, really within the laws of war. It is incontestable, that a government is entitled and bound, not to allow to be seized with impunity, property which the law of war does not permit to be attacked; and that when privateering degenerates so far, as not to observe this principle, it becomes an unjust hostility.

In No. 3, the author treats of hostile property, whether vessels, or cargoes, as solely liable to seizure at sea. Holding then, says he, to be established in principle, the legality of the capture of hostile property, and the illegality of the capture of neutral property; we may deduce from it the following consequences. 1. If the vessel and cargo belong to the enemy, both are legally captured, it being understood that the capture is made in the open sea, not in a neutral port, nor on the sea, so near the neutral land, as to be deemed territorial. 2. If the cargo is hostile in a neutral vessel, the cargo alone can be captured. The owner of the neutral vessel who avails himself of his right, hurts no one, and cannot be punished. The captor who has carried the vessel into a port, and placed the cargo in safety, is bound to pay the freight and other expenses. Perhaps the neutral captain may experience damage, from his being constrained to repair to a place for which he was not destined; but this loss is to be placed to his own account, or to that of the owner of the vessel, since he might have foreseen such an accident in the transportation of goods, which he behoved to know were hostile property. If a part of the cargo only is hostile, and the rest neutral, it is plain the former only is subject to condemnation. 3. When the cargo is neutral, and the ship hostile, the latter only is subject to capture. As the neutral proprietors, however, would suffer by the arrangement, by which the captor, after having seized the vessel, should throw the goods into the sea, which would as little be of any benefit to himself, it is natural that the cargo should be brought with the vessel to a port, and there delivered to the owners. The latter, moreover, could not exact any indemnification for the loss and damage, which that mode of proceeding may occasion to them, because it is a consequence of their own imprudence, in having trusted their goods to a hostile vessel. It is by following these rules, with regard to prizes made at sea, that we separate with equity, hostile from neutral property; that the first, whether vessel or cargo, is legally seized and confiscated; and that the latter is justly restored to the owners.

In Nos. 4 and 5, the author states the difficulties in the application of the general principle just expounded. The rules we have just explained, says he, are very simple, and very conformable to the laws of war, since they attack only hostile property. By a natural consequence, they permit hostile operations against the commerce and navigation of enemies; but they are not, on that account, the less consistent with the law of nations. These rules, says the author, were admitted as fundamental, in the ancient Consolato del Mare, compiled in the twelfth century, or even at a more early period. It is very true, that under the times in which these rules were so expressly established, the maritime commerce of Europe was not of the importance, which it has since attained, and which it now especially possesses. But there is no ground for concluding, that, by the increase in the magnitude and extent of the interests of merchants, ship-owners, and other sea-faring people, the nature of justice and law has been changed. Yet, however evident may be the justice of these rules, relative to hostile property found at sea, contemplating them generally and theoretically, according to universal principles, it cannot be denied, that in practice, and in their actual application, they present great inconveniences to neutrals, partly depending on the thing itself, and in a greater measure, caused by the frauds attempted on the one side, and suspected on the other. This is what has made it be doubted, whether rules, so simple in speculation, can be exacted, observed, and put in practice. Neutrals have complained of them in all maritime wars. Let us consider these difficulties more nearly, in order to appreciate them.

1. When the cargo of a neutral vessel is mixed, composed partly of hostile property, and partly of neutral property, the vessel is carefully brought into a port by the captor. The indemnity of the captain is easily regulated on equitable principles. The hostile goods are confiscated, and the neutral are sold. But, when the neutral proprietor has not been able to prevent a part of the cargo being hostile, as may often happen, either from his ignorance, or in spite of him, and he claims to be indemnified, whether for the carriage of his goods, to a place to which they should not have gone, or for the delay of their arrival at their destination, which has made him lose his profit, how are his losses to be estimated? This is, doubtless, an important point for a neutral merchant. But this difficulty does not appear to be insurmountable; and a great deal may be done, when people wish sincerely to do so.

On the part of neutrals, this connection in the conveyance of hostile goods, may be obviated, or avoided. On the other side, when goods liable to seizure have been slipped into a neutral vessel, without the knowledge of the captain, regard may be had to it, in fixing an indemnity for the neutral merchant. As in the case of the vessel being hostile, the latter, as we have already remarked, could not complain of the wrong conveyance of his goods; his losses would then be a consequence of his having employed such a vessel for their transportation.

2. Another source of inconvenience arises from the difficulty of fixing, with precision, the characters of neutral vessels. That the captors may not give for an excuse, that they took them for enemies, the rules on this subject ought to be clear and well defined, in the orders and instructions. There are cases, in which, from want of this clearness, vessels have been seized without any bad intention on the part of the captors. When this happens, the indemnity for the vessel is well regulated; but that for the owners of the neutral cargo, remains to be examined.

3. The most important, and the most difficult point in these matters, is the destination of neutral cargoes. If the papers on board are regular, the charter-parties, the bills of lading, the invoices, and the other documents, if they are not fictitious, show every thing. There are found on board, the names of the persons, who cause the merchandise to be transported, on their account, and at their risk; the quantity and quality of the latter are designated; and these papers would be decisive on the question of property, if there were no other reasons to doubt their verity, their true and genuine nature. They always, indeed, afford primâ facie evidence. But there may happen in them, as experience has demonstrated, circumstances which give rise to just suspicions;

and too often the documents on board, produced by the captain, are found to be false and fabricated, solely to cloak or conceal the abuses.

In Nos. 6, 7, and 8, the author treats of factitious neutralizations. Such are the inconveniences which prevent the strict application of the rules of justice. In the public differences of nations, as in private affairs, there are cases, in which it is very difficult to be exactly just. Never were there maritime wars, in which there have not been seen embarrassments, occasioned to the commerce and navigation of neutrals, by this difficult separation of effects really neutral, from hostile effects. But to these natural difficulties, which, however, are not altogether insurmountable, there are added factitious neutralities, which have infinitely increased the embarrassment. Self-interest has strenuously exerted itself to devise suitable means for eluding justice. We must consider a little more nearly, this masquerade of neutrality. During last war it has been systematically arranged, and it will, in all probability, be rendered more perfect, if such fraud be not repressed by enlightened and firm justice, which may surely put forth as great efforts to trace its windings and tortuous proceedings, as it shows finesse and cunning in concealing itself. There are chiefly two modes of imposition, by assuming the appearance of neutrality. 1. Proprietors who are really hostile subjects, get themselves admitted as naturalized neutral subjects, during the war. 2. For the names of hostile proprietors, there are substituted the names of neutral proprietors; which thereby change the political or national quality or character of the goods, so far as appearance goes. There are thus, the neutralization of proprietors, and the neutralization of properties, including both vessels and cargoes. And frequently the two modes are combined; and use made of the first chiefly, with regard to vessels, and of the second, with regard to cargoes; the whole, as suits best, for supporting the fiction.

The neutralization of proprietors cannot have very extensive effects, from the obstacles, difficulties, and inconveniences which the author shows attend it. The second kind of simulated neutralization, that of properties, is much more important, as it embraces both vessels and cargoes. And it is not difficult to perceive the cause. If we reflect on the nature of property in an external moveable object, on the modifications and restrictions of which the right of disposing of a thing at one's pleasure—the characteristic mark of property—is susceptible, we easily see what a vast field the contracts of appropriation offer in practice, constructed in such an equivocal manner, that the true proprietor is confounded with another individual, who is not so; and who is, properly speaking, merely an administrator, or a commissioner, factor, or agent, bearing the title of owner. Accordingly, the advocates of chicanery have found no difficulty in fabricating in abundance, marks of neutrality, with regard to goods transported by sea. And if these artifices do not escape a clear sighted and assiduous judge, they may dazzle those who have not the same habit of detecting the plots of fraud, and always cause embarrassment and delay in the suits of this kind, brought before the courts of prize.

But most frequently, people do not take the trouble attending these simulated neutralities. They prefer acting more directly by the way of corruption. The neutral, in the ship's papers, is directly named as being the owner, both of the vessel and of the merchandise; and he acts throughout, as if he were such. To guarantee, however, the true proprietor, against the abuse by the neutral of his title, the latter gives the former a declaration, by which he acknowledges, that the transaction between them has been entered into merely for form sake; or the substitute acknowledges himself to be debtor, and binds himself to pay to his constitutent, a value proportional to the goods intrusted to him; and in this manner, the goods captured at sea, are claimed by the neutral, as belonging to him in property. The constituent, no doubt, runs very considerable risks, from the confidence reposed by him; but the profits of the neutral, as simple commissioner, are usually of sufficiently great importance, to prevent his being tempted to abuse his ostensible title.

In No. 9, the author treats of the voluntary cession, of the commerce and navigation, of hostile countries to neutrals. That these simulated, or fictitious neutralities are illicit, is beyond doubt. Even neutral governments disapprove of them on the part of their subjects; at least to judge by their public declarations. But there is also a real or actual neutralization, of which the illegality is not so evident.

In prolonged maritime wars, the commerce, or a branch of the commerce of a country at war, as well as a part of its navigation, are spontaneously ceded to neutral merchants, ship-owners, and navigators. We do not here allude to the changes in commerce and navigation, referred to in Section I. No. 13, which are a natural consequence of the war, especially maritime war, and by which the commerce of neutrals is increased and extended, almost in the same proportion as that of the country at war, is limited. This last effect operates of itself, depends on circumstances, and has no need of any stipulation to regulate it, and define its limits and duration. We are here contemplating these voluntary transactions, by which merchants individually, or united in co-partnership, or commercial companies, perceiving the necessity of either absolutely renouncing their mercantile business, since they can no longer be protected by the naval forces of their country, or of substituting in their place, neutral individuals or companies, for conducting these affairs, until they are in a condition to resume them—really and actually transfer their navigation and commerce to neutrals. Such transferences, the author shows, besides being the result of pressure and necessity, are attended with difficulties which prevent their being general, or embracing many of the branches of maritime traffic. To transfer a large and extensive trade to others, it is not sufficient to substitute new names, or new forms of proceeding. Merchants must furnish these substitutes with the requisite funds and credit; and thus risk their own money. Or, if these substitutes have themselves the necessary capital, there is a great risk that the business, once passed into their hands, may be lost for ever. For it is doubtful whether the commerce, diverted by the war, and once fixed elsewhere, may at the peace soon resume its ancient course. And in this case, is it not far more expedient for countries at war, to see their commerce cease for some time, than to incur the risk of being entirely deprived of it? For these reasons, it does not appear, that such a cession of commerce can well take place, except in the colonial trade; since it is of that trade only, the mother country has the monopoly, and can resume it at the peace. There are similar risks for navigation; except where navigation at the peace, is exclusively secured to a country by a navigation act, which may then, without risk, be suspended during the war.

To judge of the legality of this neutralization, to which we have just referred, we must revert to the general principles, and particularly to that of the fourth proposition of No. 13, Section I. But in the mode of applying the law to each particular case, there are many things to distinguish and to unravel. When the neutrals substituted, are in reality merely commissioners, with regard to the essential points; when, for instance, they are placed by the agreement out of all risk, they are not really any longer merchants, nor entitled to claim the rights of neutrals. Where there is, on the contrary, a regular contract, there are two opposite aspects, under which the transaction may be contemplated. On the one side, there is an increase of business for the neutrals, arising from the diminution of that of the countries at war, and of which neutrals cannot be denied the right of availing themselves. On the other side, there cannot be refused to a power at war, if it has succeeded in destroying the colonial commerce of its enemy, the right of preventing this commerce from being re-established, through the interposition and substitution of neutrals. When the belligerent has lost, through war, its relations with its colonies, it can no longer dispute, as their master, nor make contracts with neutral individuals, nor specially designate those to whom it should be allowed to carry on commerce, nor who are those who ought to be excluded from it. It is quite another thing, to relinquish this business to neutrals, when in possession of the free disposal of it.

In comparing these opposite sides of the question, we are led to the following results. The country at war may declare free, its colonial commerce, by renouncing its right of monopoly during the war; and then neutrals are entitled to carry on this commerce directly themselves, in such a manner as to preserve the same commercial relations, which they possessed before the war, through the medium of the mother country. There is here a limitation, explained before, which the power at war has a right to cause to be observed. It may lawfully prevent the relations of the commerce of neutrals with the hostile countries, from exceeding those which existed prior to the war. This limitation, however, does not imply that one of the neutral countries may not specially increase its commerce with the enemy, since that may be necessary to maintain the totality of the relations, which the neutrals previously enjoyed.

Indeed, as the produce of the colonies, which, during the peace, were carried to neutrals by the mother country, could not reach them by that way; would it be just, that on that account, they should want them? And, if they ought not to be deprived of them, they must be allowed to go themselves in search of these commodities. It is, therefore, also necessary, that those neutrals, who have themselves neither navigation, nor commerce, suitable for procuring such articles, should have them imported by other neutrals. But the part of this colonial commerce, which, before the war, was carried on by the mother country, is that which neutrals have no right to exercise. Thus, on the one side as on the other, we see that the stipulations, by which the merchants of the mother country substitute other persons in their place, in their commercial business—this neutralization—cannot be considered as lawful by the powers at war. How grant to the enemy the right of disposing of what he is compelled to abandon? even although he should not be suspected of acting under secret articles, by which the neutrals who take his place, are merely his agents in the business.

In Nos. 10 and 11, the author discusses the question, whether the neutral vessel covers the merchandise. Let us now see, whether the maxim of the separation of the goods belonging to the enemy, and of the goods belonging to neutrals, naturally just in itself, may serve as a rule, and be practised, without leading to, or involving any injustice. To judge of it hitherto from experience, this may certainly be doubted. But, if we reflect upon the causes, which have led to the proceedings of belligerent powers, of which people have had reason to complain, we see, that they must be attributed, in part, to the dishonesty of neutrals, and particularly to the conduct of merchants, who, from the thirst of gain, have allowed themselves to engage in illicit transactions. There are, then, faults on both sides; on the part of neutrals, as well as of belligerents. But it is alleged that the tribunals of the latter have acted unjustly;—that those courts have been partial, beyond what can be excused from the weakness of men, entrusted with the power of judging, is demonstrated by a number of sentences, evidently contrary to reason and justice. How can it be expected, that the same causes will not produce the same effects in future wars?

This is what has been alleged, and may still be alleged, in order to establish in the positive law, with regard to privateering, other maxims than those of the separation of goods, into hostile and neutral. These maxims have been called a "new maritime law," in opposition to the natural principles before expounded. But there is a preliminary enquiry to be made, namely, whether the abuses complained of on both sides, are the necessary consequences of the ancient principle of separation, and whether they are absolutely unavoidable in practice, in the event of exertions being made to oppose to them, means calculated to prevent illicit acts on the one side, and injuries on the other. This question, no doubt a little difficult, has been passed over; and it has been proposed to follow other rules, particularly certain conventions, which being already established among some states, appear more conducive to the interests of neutrals, and more fit to be recognized as general laws.

The rule which has been principally proposed, is, that the vessel ought to cover the merchandise; that is to say, that the neutrality of the vessel being ascertained, the goods on board shall be thereby neutralized; or, as it is still expressed, that the free vessel renders the cargo free. It is clear, that if this law were universally established, there would be no longer any questions or processes on the legality of captures, except ascertaining the political or national quality or character of the vessels. The most difficult question, that of the neutrality, or of the non-neutrality of the cargoes, and of the separation of the latter into their different classes, would be absolutely done away in all cases, when the vessel belonged to neutrals. The difficulty is still more diminished, if we add to this rule for neutral vessels, another rule with regard to hostile vessels, namely, that if the vessel is hostile, the cargo ought to be liable to confiscation, without distinction. There are authors, who, in insisting upon the former rule, do not hesitate to acquiesce in the latter. This would, without doubt, be the most simple and the most uniform mode of distinguishing what is liable to capture, and what is not. It is the law which the Barbary states generally follow, in their cruizing expeditions. They thus cut short, or dispense with the formalities of justice. Others, however, who find this appendage, that the hostile vessel confiscates the cargo, without distinction, too unfavourable for neutrals, have rejected it entirely. The separation of what belongs to enemies, and of what is neutral, ought, according to their opinion in this case, to take place. When, then, the vessel is hostile, all the difficulties with which the rule of the ancient laws is reproached, remain in full force.

To judge whether this pretended new law, which since 1780, has been too much celebrated, and too much magnified, is of a nature to be substituted for that of the separation of the properties; and whether it is calculated to conciliate the rights of belligerents and neutrals, by avoiding the embarrassments connected with this separation, it is necessary, to develope the consequences which necessarily follow from its execution.

1. It is very true, that this maxim cuts short much of the procedure in the adjudication of prizes, that it facilitates and abridges the judgment of others, without, however, preventing them all. In general, it is more easy to put in evidence, the political or national quality or character of vessels, than that of the goods on board them; then, the fewer the processes before the prize courts, the fewer complaints on the part of neutrals, the fewer the representations on the part of their governments. These are all certainly objects of importance. But the end is only half accomplished, if the whole is not left to depend on the quality or character of the vessel. In fact, although the neutral vessel rendered the cargo neutral, if the hostile vessel did not also render her cargo liable to confiscation, it would still always remain, in these cases, to distinguish between the merchandise on board, those which belong to the enemy, and those which are neutral property.

2. If the neutral vessel neutralizes the cargo, the navigation of the countries at war will remain exposed to hostile attacks; but not their commerce, nor the private properties of their subjects, provided they use the precaution of not employing other vessels, than those of neutrals. In the case, therefore, of the navigation of a country at war, being embarrassed by the naval force of the enemy, the object will be, to secure neutral vessels. It may then continue its commerce, in all other respects, as during full peace.

3. In considering the interest of neutrals, we see, that

their shipping would be augmented, and have additional advantages during the war, but that it would not be so, with regard to their commerce. There would for them be no hope, no prospect of extending their trade and commercial relations, since each country at war would continue its own trade, without any other restrictions, than those, to which we have just referred. Neutrals, therefore, would gain nothing in this respect. According to the ancient law of the separation of properties, it follows very naturally, that, as often as the one or the other of the belligerent powers has the superiority at sea, not only the ships of neutrals are in demand, but their commerce also must prosper, and be extended. In following the new principle, which it is wished to substitute, they will perhaps profit a little more in the carrying trade, or in freights; but the profits to be expected from the extension of their commerce, would elude their grasp; and doubtless, that would not be for their advantage.

What has just been said shows, that the interest of neutrals, well understood, cannot lead them to maintain the maxim, that the neutrality of vessels neutralizes the cargoes. Individual merchants, also, who might believe it in their power to avail themselves of this prerogative of neutral vessels, in order to transport more easily articles of contraband, might perhaps be deceived in their expectations, if the cargoes were to be carefully visited at sea; and doubtless, the powers at war would not fail to authorize their cruizers to do so.

But the new principle would compromise greatly the interest of the powers at war. Their natural right of war, which allows them to take from the enemy his property, his treasures, and to attack his commerce, to deprive him of his resources, would be infinitely restricted, and confined within very narrow limits, by the law which would put every thing in safety, that was under the flag of a neutral. Of what service, then, would be the naval force of a state; and what would be its importance in maritime wars? This force might indeed conquer the fleets of the enemy, and capture his vessels, if it pleased the latter to send them to sea; it might transport troops and warlike stores, to act upon land, to make incursions upon the coasts, and to blockade ports and bombard maritime cities; but it could operate or effect nothing against the commerce and the property of the enemy at sea; being obliged to allow to flow freely that source, so abundant for the enemy, of prosperity, profits, and pecuniary force. All property of any value would be put by the latter out of reach and attack, on board neutral vessels at sea. Thus, the armed force by land, might invade the provinces and cities of the enemy, and weaken him by requisitions and contributions, and draw from them resources for himself; while, on the contrary, the naval forces, with the means of acting in a similar manner, would, in this respect, be reduced to impotence.

Such is the cause of the difficulty, and this difficulty is equivalent to a moral impossibility. This is the reason why maritime powers, of which the principal force consists in their marine, have constantly refused a conventional law, which would place them so far behind, with regard to a point of the greatest importance. This is the reason why none of the maritime powers, who in their treaties had consented, agreeably to the new rule, that the neutral vessel should cover the merchandise, conformed to it, on the actual occurrence of war. This law has never been exactly observed in modern wars. In fact, it cannot be imposed as a duty on continental powers, never to occupy the provinces of their enemy, nor to draw from them resources for the war. There cannot be conferred on neutrals the right of opposing such proceedings, by sending to these provinces their colours or flags. In the same way, there cannot be demanded of the maritime powers, such a renunciation of the right of war; and this is what would be done, by taking from them the power of attacking and capturing from their enemy, the goods of the latter, transported under the neutral flag. There ought to be introduced into the wars of civilized nations, all the moderation possible; abstinence from all hostilities, which are not necessary for the attainment of the end, and especially from those, which are suggested by animosity. To decline making use of one's forces, to enfeeble those of the enemy, is an act which belongs to magnanimity, when circumstances admit of a people doing so; but in general, it would be too dangerous for a people to allow itself to be constrained to do so. Such an obligation is by no means fit to become a law of nations in the positive code.

In No. 12, the author discusses the possible application of the rule just considered, to some particular branches of trade. The principle just investigated, although little calculated to become a general law, might perhaps be suitable for a good many particular cases. And if so, might there not be made of it a special rule for those cases, so as thus to become a general law for some branches of the particular commerce? This well merits consideration. It is, indeed, important to find the means of diminishing the number of prize causes or questions, at least of those which are the most intricate and perplexing, and which, notwithstanding the strongest desire to have no rule but justice, seldom fail to excite jealousies and quarrels.

In running over the different branches of commerce, with the view of marking those in which the rule, that the vessel covers the cargo, might suit in practice, without doing prejudice to any of the parties, we are led to instances, in which, to appearance, this might take place. This would be a kind of conciliation between the old and the new rule. And although such projects may have more appearance than reality, they deserve, from the interest of the subject, to be a little more developed.

One of the branches of commerce to which the rule appears to be applicable, is the commerce of importation made from without, with commodities destined for internal consumption, with the exception always of articles of contraband. In the second place, fisheries, but limited to the use of the country which carries on the trade. With regard to all other branches of traffic, it would be too great an encroachment on the right of war, to admit the rule; still more, if it were wished to establish only the part of the proposed law favourable to neutrals, namely, to allow the cargo to be covered by the neutral vessel, without the neutral cargo being held reciprocally liable to confiscation, on board a hostile vessel. The author proceeds, with his usual acuteness, to examine the result of the application of the new rule, in the cases of the commerce of importation, and of the trade of fishing. And the conclusion of his reasoning is, that the conventional establishment, by treaties, of this new rule, in these cases, would not terminate in any essential advantages to neutrals.

In No. 13, with regard to the conciliatory propositions, and those which might be added, or substituted for the same end, the author makes a remark, which will not escape those who consider the subject in a more general point of view, namely, that in these cases, the question is not concerning what is just, or not, or what the law authorizes. The natural law, indeed, orders the most exact separation of what belongs to the enemy, and of what does not belong to him; and it does not permit the seizure of the latter part. Such a separation, although embarrassing and tedious, in many cases, is not impracticable, as experience has proved. Fraud knows well how to create obstacles to it; but judicial wisdom knows how to obviate or remove them. We have here, then, only measures of prudence, to avoid the embarrassment of the execution of the law. It is a very important subject for neutrals, and still more so, perhaps, for the belligerents, of whom we must presume a desire on their part, to obviate the just and well founded complaints of neutrals. But, if it is wished to substitute for the principles of natural law, other principles, which do not belong to it, solely with the view of obviating the difficulties of its application, this is, to wish to traffic and negotiate with the law, from motives of interest and convenience; which enlightened justice will never permit. It would avail more, to revert to what is practised on each side, to the proceedings of neutrals and belligerents, to those of their merchants and their ship-captains, and to their respective modes of managing affairs; and it is there, also, we must search for the remedies. * * * It is clear, that it is chiefly fraud which creates the difficulties in the separation of hostile from neutral merchandise. Let the illicit compacts of individuals be narrowly watched, and let them not be protected either publicly or secretly, without, however, passing over in silence, or tolerating the acts of violence which may be committed on either side, and there will be no necessity for derogating in any way, either from the natural law of war, or that of neutrality.

In section third, the author treats of contraband in war. And in Nos. 1 and 2, he gives a general idea of contraband, and of the principles of law applicable to that subject. Here we have to do only with those articles of contraband, which, by the natural law of nations, ought not to be carried either to the one, or the other of the states at war. The state which, during war, makes levies of soldiers from among its subjects, to furnish them as auxiliary troops to one of the belligerents, although it does not thereby range itself as one of his party, acts, however, in such a manner, that the hostile state is entitled to employ force to prevent it from doing so. It is the same with regard to furnishing of arms, ammunition, and other articles, which are subservient to the operations of war. He who carries them to one hostile state, exposes himself to the attack of the other; at least, so far as shall be necessary to constrain him to renounce or withdraw his services. It is quite different, when neutrals merely allow these articles, when in their own country, to be delivered to, or taken possession of by, the belligerents, who wish there to purchase them, and to transport them at their own expense and risk, in their own vessels or waggons. The neutral does not compromise his neutrality by such permission, provided he grants this liberty of commerce without partiality, and in the same manner, to each of the opposite parties.

Belligerents, then, in order to prevent the enemy from being supplied with the articles necessary for war, are, doubtless, entitled to seize these articles at sea as on land, and in neutral as in hostile vessels. The only question to be discussed is, whether these articles are liable to confiscation, even when they belong to neutrals. The belligerent may lawfully keep them for his use; but ought he, in that case, to pay their value? If he does not wish to keep them, ought he to send them to the neutral country, from which they have been brought? With regard to the vessel, which was in the course of transporting them to the enemy, although neutral, it may be asked whether, in consequence of that very act, it is liable to be lawfully condemned? There are persons, who, limiting the right of war relative to articles of contraband, to the single point, that the enemy be deprived of them, pretend that belligerents are not entitled to confiscate them, since there are other means of attaining that end. These articles, say they, may be kept till the end of the war; they may be sent back, or they may be purchased. This, however, is not reasoning according to the rules of common justice. The belligerents are entitled to expect, that neutrals shall not furnish such articles to their enemy. And is it not very clear, that it is the duty of neutrals to abstain from such furnishings? The neutral merchant, then, who transports to a belligerent the means of war, acts illegally; and by a natural consequence, he may be punished for it, by the confiscation of the merchandise.

With regard to the vessel, it may happen that the owners or (charterers) freighters, may not really know the quality of the goods which the captain may have undertaken to convey; it is even possible, that without the knowledge of the latter, some contraband articles may be slipped on board. But as it is the duty of the captain, to observe carefully what is put on board his vessel, and the duty of the owners to assure themselves beforehand, of the conduct of the captain, for whom they are responsible, as being their mandatory, it is right, that the vessel carrying articles of contraband should be confiscated. If there has been fraud on the part of the shippers of the cargo, the captain may have his recourse upon them; and in the same manner, the owners upon the captain, if the latter, from negligence or fraud, is the cause of the confiscation of the vessel. It is not here, as in the case where the hostile cargo, not contraband, is alone liable to confiscation; and where the neutral vessel is released, although the merchandise be condemned. The reason of this difference is, that the hostile merchant does nothing illicit, in transporting his goods by sea during war, although he thereby exposes them to the danger of capture, and that the neutral captain, on his side, does not act unlawfully in freighting his vessel to a merchant, in what is a legal trade. There are, however, differences in the treaties of nations in this point. In the greatest number of conventions, the vessel is declared confiscated, as well as the cargo; at least, when the principal part of the cargo is found to be illicit. But there are other conventions, by which the neutral vessel remains free, after the confiscation of the articles of contraband, which she carried. Farther, it is not generally illegal for neutral vessels to have on board warlike stores; but they ought not to have more than is necessary for their defence against pirates; which quantity may be greater or smaller, according to the size of the vessel, and length of the intended voyage. And if there should be on board a surplus, evidently beyond the quantity which there ought to be, it is consistent with principle, that the vessel and the contraband should be confiscated, although the other part of the cargo should remain free.

In Nos. 3 and 4, the author treats of the characteristics of the absolute contraband of war. It is not the general principles which create difficulties in this matter; but the greater diversities in treaties, the greater is the embarrassment with regard to the particular articles, which ought to be reputed contraband during war. On comparing the different enumerations which we find in conventions, we easily see, that certain general notions have been laid down as the basis of these determinations; but we see also, that other considerations have entered into them. There are neutral countries, of which the commerce with foreigners depends, for the greatest part, on the exportation of articles, which are principally destined for the use of military forces. These countries are, therefore, greatly interested in not giving too great extension to the article of contraband, since that would cause, at least, many embarrassments in their commercial relations. On the other hand, it is advantageous for the belligerents, who have the preponderance at sea, that the class of articles of contraband, should be extended over whatever is requisite for war, that their enemies may be deprived of them. It must be admitted, that the condition by which goods, destined for countries at war, could be captured on board neutral vessels, only under the burden of paying their value to the neutral proprietor, would be a condition quite unfavourable for the power at war, which should have acquired the superiority at sea; and that, not so much from this obligation, to pay for the articles, instead of confiscating them, as because, neutrals having thus no longer any thing to risk, might send them in such quantities, that in spite of the vigilance of cruizers, the enemy could not fail to receive them. On the contrary, if these articles were regarded as illicit, and declared liable to confiscation, as such, it must be admitted, that neutral merchants, no longer venturing to convey them in their vessels, the enemy being unable to procure them directly himself, would be no longer supplied with them, and would soon be without them entirely. There is here, then, an opposition between the interests of neutrals, and those of belligerents. And with regard to the latter, although it seems that there may always be a compensation, or reciprocity of advantages between the parties, so far as each of them can protect their navigation, yet it will never be indifferent to them, to see the enemy able to draw with facility from neutrals, all he requires for war. It follows, that we must designate the articles of contraband, according to the principles of natural justice, save the exceptions which the particular conventions of states may introduce.

In the first place, all articles adapted exclusively for armaments and equipments, are absolute contraband during war; and form contraband of the first order. Their destination for hostile ports is evident, and ascertained by their very nature, and by the sole use, to which they are applicable. This class comprehends cannons, balls or bullets, muskets, bayonets, sabres, pikes, gunpowder, ships of war, and whatever is fit only for similar uses.

Whether the articles be already constructed or prepared, and of immediate application to military uses, or be still rude materials, which require a new manufacture or operation to become such; this circumstance does not change their quality, when their destination for war is manifest. Among these rude substances, there are found some inserted in all the lists of contraband, such as sulphur, saltpetre, and pitch. Saltpetre or nitre in particular, it is true, is fit for so many purposes, and employed in so many manufactures, that its destination might sometimes appear doubtful. But if it is imported in great quantities, and if this transportation takes place during war, the object of converting it into gunpowder is so highly probable, that it is considered with reason, to be a certainty. It is the same with pitch and tar. With hemp, and with timber for building ships, the scantling of the pieces of which marks its exclusive employment, for the construction of ships of war. It follows, then, in the second place, that materials fit for making instruments of war, and of which the destination for this use is not doubtful, are to be placed among the absolute objects of contraband.

In No. 5, the author treats of contraband of the

second order. There are other materials, such as iron and leather, and also manufactured articles, such as masts, which, though essential to the exigencies of war, are nevertheless, not by their nature, exclusively destined to that end. Horses are also in the same situation. Some treaties of commerce prohibit the conveyance of these articles, as illicit; others authorize it. In consulting general principles, we reason thus. There are articles of which the qualities do not form a sufficient proof of their destination for war; but this destination may become manifest, from the quantity of these articles imported. We may justly range, then, among articles of contraband, those which, although they be not such absolutely by their nature, become such from their number and their quantity. These are articles of contraband of the second order.

But if, notwithstanding the quantity, the destination of the articles remain still doubtful, as may happen with regard to leather, linen, woollen cloth, canvass for sails, &c., if no preponderating cause can justly fix the opinion, it is not permitted to class these articles among contraband, either of the first or second order; and neither cargoes, nor vessels, can be legally confiscated. These objects, however, being of great utility for war, being often even wants of the first necessity for armaments, belligerents preserve the right of preventing them from passing to their enemies. It follows, then, in the third place, that when the destination of the articles is not manifestly for war, but that they may nevertheless be important, or necessary for military use, the right of war is limited to that of preventing their importation, into the country of the enemy. They may be taken by the belligerent for himself, on paying their just value; or sent into other countries, or diverted, in some other manner, from the hands of the enemy; but neither cargoes, nor vessels, are liable to confiscation.

In No. 6, the author treats of contraband by accident. Finally, as the destination of articles for war, gives the basis of the right of belligerents in this respect, there cannot be denied the latter, the right of confiscating, as illicit, whatever is destined to the military service of their enemy, not merely the articles of contraband of the first and second order, but generally all things, when their destination for military armaments, is manifest. This forms a fourth rule. Supposing, then, that a fleet is to be equipped, or an army to be supplied with provisions, and that magazines or stores are in the course of being prepared, with these views, all kinds of commodities, in the course of being brought to these places by neutrals, are justly considered as contraband, even although they should not be so, by their nature. They become illicit by the circumstances solely; and may be called contraband by accident. Even grain and money are prohibited articles in this case, as in that of blockade, of which in the sequel. There is, then, room for the confiscation of vessels, as well as cargoes; saving, however, the modifications and exceptions, to which the proud ignorance of the neutral furnishers, or the constraint of the enemy, may give a right.

In No. 7, the author shows the necessity for special designations of the articles of contraband, The articles, then, which are contraband during war, are such solely, because they are useful, or necessary for military service; they are so, by their destination for the enemy, whether manifest, or indicated by their nature, or by their quality, or by a quantity, which would not suit any other purpose. It is, however, a condition precedent, that they are constituent parts of the wants, or requisites for war. All articles, then, which are not of this kind, have no relation with armed forces; and all those commodities, which are subservient merely, to the comfort and conveniences of life, cannot be prohibited in any way, in the commerce of neutrals with the countries at war. But there is an infinite number of things, which are at once, both the one and the other; which may be regarded on one side, as requisites for war, as necessary for the subsistence of men; and on the other, as articles of simple convenience, which, by themselves, by their qualities, or even by their quantity, do not mark or characterize any destination. It is with regard to this class, that there may be good reasons for declaring such articles contraband in certain treaties, while in others, they are declared free; and with good reason; one and the same state may consider them under these two opposite points of view, in relation to two other states, with whom it treats. What is not determined by the natural law, may be differently modified by the diversity of other relations, whether commercial, or political. It is, therefore, absolutely necessary, that the articles which are to be considered as contraband, be specially named in treaties, and publicly designated at the commencement of wars. Merchants and captors may easily distinguish absolute contraband articles; but the same facility of distinction is not to be expected, with regard to all articles, which are contraband by natural law, and still less those, which are so, solely from positive conventions.

In section fourth, the author treats of the law concerning blockades. In No. 1, he considers the right of blockade, in its relation to the liberty of navigation in general. The law relative to contraband, prescribes limits to the commerce and navigation of neutrals in general, by designating the articles, which, during war, ought not to be transported by them to belligerents. But there are still other restrictions. The communications of neutrals with one or other of the parties, may be totally interdicted for some time, with regard to a place, a port, or country, or a particular district; and this occurs specially in the case of blockade. The entry to, as well as the departure from such blockaded places, are legally prevented or repressed by force. Here we are to consider particularly, maritime blockades executed by naval forces. But in general, what is law here with regard to neutrals, is equally applicable in maritime wars, as in those by land; with the exception of the accessary modifications, which arise from the difference of the elements, on which the operations take place.

In No. 2, the author enquires, whether the blockade be effective and complete, and on the contrary, whether it be neither the one nor the other. There are here two opposite cases, but very simple, in which, what is just, and what is not so, is evident, and can never be called in question. If the blockade of a place, whether by land or sea, be effective and complete—undertaken for the purpose of compelling the enemy to surrender; if all the avenues to this place are shut by military forces, it is evident that, while this situation exists, it is not permitted to any neutral to introduce himself into this place, or to carry to it any provisions. The attempt to enter it, without the knowledge and permission of the besiegers, is illicit. The belligerent, in this case, may not only prevent the communication, and send back those who present themselves, but is even authorized to punish the attempts made to elude the blockade, unless ignorance of the fact, or some other circumstances render them excusable. In analyzing this case, it is to be remarked; first, that there are here military operations, which the prosecution of the war has rendered necessary, as being proper for the end proposed, at least in the opinion of those who order them, and who are alone competent to judge of them. If, then, the rights of neutrals to trade and to make voyages, are opposed for the time the blockade lasts, they must yield to the preponderating rights of the belligerents, as generally enunciated in the second fundamental proposition, in section first. In the second place, we see that there is here an action against the enemy, effectively commenced and continued, which, according to the principles of the law of war, neutrals ought not to impede or prevent in any manner, by their interposition.

Let us take the other simple and opposite case—let us suppose a belligerent power without really blockading, declares as blockaded, ports, places, isles, or provinces of his enemy, in the view of depriving these places of all commercial relations with neutrals; it is evident, that this arbitrary arrangement of the commerce and navigation of others would, in no view, deserve to be respected as lawful. It would be a manifest infringement of the law of neutrality. See No. 12 of section first.

In No. 3, the author considers the intermediate cases of blockade between the two extremes. In comparing these two extreme examples, we shall find, that in all the intermediate cases, where the just and the unjust are less striking, we may have the means of deciding them by the application of these two questions. 1. Is there a military operation required for the purpose of the war, or is there merely an intention to do some mischief to the enemy, or to embarrass his commercial relations, at the expense of the commerce and navigation of neutrals? 2. Is this military operation really and actually existing? With regard to the first question, it is necessary that the verity of the allegation—the reality of the alleged blockade—be manifest from facts and circumstances, and established by the means employed by the belligerent, for attaining the end which he has announced. With regard to the second question, the will solely,—the absolute determination to act, even the preparations, not being yet the action, can, at most, in the view of the approaching blockade, merely authorize the prevention of the introduction of necessaries into the menaced place; but as long as the blockade is not really commenced, the belligerent cannot have the right of punishing, as culpable, those who have wished to introduce necessaries into it.

In No. 4, the author marks the differences between blockade by sea and by land. The ports and cities situated on the continent, are seldom in a condition to be blockaded by naval forces only, so as to be reduced by famine; unless other forces by land, act in combination with the fleet. And in this respect, blockade by land, with regard to places situated on the main land, has a great superiority over blockade by sea. At the same time, there are cases of cities, ports, and even large districts of country, which, although not physically separated from the continent, are nevertheless, in a situation similar to that of islands, with regard to the conveyance to them of necessaries. And in such circumstances, the blockade by sea is very similar to that by land. Again, blockades by sea, supposing always the same object to force or concuss the enemy, by depriving him of subsistence, may have more extent than those by land. Not only mere sea-ports, but islands even of large circumference, if they have not the means of subsisting themselves, are liable to be wholly blockaded. The so easy mobility of naval forces, enlarges the field of their operations. But this advantage in maritime blockades is diminished, by their more frequent discontinuance. The winds and tempests interrupt and make them cease, which does not take place on land, except in consequence of military events. Farther, the occasions, the causes, the views which belligerents may have in these kinds of military operations, are much more numerous and more varied in maritime wars, than in those by land. It is the multiplicity of objects which may be proposed in maritime blockades, which renders them more frequent than blockades by land, and which occasions more collisions of rights, and more complaints and contests between belligerents and neutrals. From the diversity of projects, which may be had in view in these maritime blockades, may be deduced different modifications in these operations; and also with regard to the degree of rigour of the blockade. If it is wished merely to prevent the armaments, which the enemy is preparing in a sea port, it should seem that neutral vessels might be permitted to enter it, if they carried nothing contraband. But while the proposed operations may not require an absolute and complete blockade, it may be disadvantageous, and even dangerous for the blockades, that the people in the blockaded place should be informed of the forces and other means employed against them. In this case, neutral vessels cannot be allowed either to enter or to depart freely, although their doing so, may in other respects be indifferent, and their cargoes legal. This is the reason why, in general, blockades are considered as absolute and rigorous, and extending universally to all vessels.

In Nos. 5 and 6, the author lays down the rules of law in blockade. From the premises, it will not be difficult to deduce general rules, for the determination of the essential points of law. 1. It is a principle, that belligerents, in cases of blockade, as in all their other military operations, which may be crossed or thwarted by the commerce and navigation of neutrals, may legally repel these obstacles, and interrupt the commercial relations with the places or ports of the enemy. 2. On the contrary, when the commercial relations of neutrals with the hostile countries cannot hurt belligerents, the latter cannot lawfully interfere with them, nor shut up any place or port, for the sole purpose of breaking these connections.

In the cases of the coasting, and of the colonial trade, of which we treated in Section I. No. 13, and where the opposition to neutrals becomes lawful, it will be very rare, that such a subject can authorize the formation of a blockade. It is also thus, with regard to the conveyance of contraband. Certainly the belligerent has the right to prevent it by force; but why would he blockade places, for this object? If the belligerent shuts up the mouths of rivers, the entrances to straits, or gulfs, which are under the dominion of the enemy, without any other reason than to prevent that enemy from having commerce with neutrals, it is doubtless an hostility directed against the latter; and it will not cease to be such, even if the belligerent should then be dispossessed on his side, of the right of navigating, which he formerly exercised in these narrow seas. The ports of neutrals forcibly invaded by the enemy, must be considered as ports of the hostile country; and if, then, the navigation of neutrals ought to be free in the latter, it cannot be interdicted in the former. The action, therefore, of shutting them up, can be justified only in the circumstances, where it is an act of reprisal, in part directed against the enemy, who, not respecting the rights of neutrality, abuses the neutral possessions in his attacks, and partly directed against neutrals, who, in relation to the enemy, do not maintain their rights of neutrality. So far as neutrals, in reality, are no longer such, or so far, as against their will, they can no longer remain such, they are doubtless exposed to hostile treatment, on the part of the belligerent, whose interests are invaded, because they have ceased to be in a neutral situation.

Although, in general, the wrongs committed by one of the parties, do not excuse the acts of violence of the other, if the injustice which one of the belligerents commits against neutrals becomes, for him, an additional means of warfare against his enemy, the latter may be under the necessity of having recourse to the natural law of reprisals. 3. The blockade must, at all times, be real and effective, to enable a party to claim its rights. While it is still incomplete, although already prepared, the right derived from it with regard to neutrals, cannot be legally executed with all its rigour. The belligerent, in this case, may prevent imports and exports, and cause the vessel, sailing towards the places, to which he is going to shut the avenues, to return; but he cannot punish, by confiscation, those who have sought a passage still open. Still less, in cases, in which a complete blockade is absolutely impracticable, can a belligerent interdict neutrals from the use of roads, which cannot be shut, whether that impossibility be the effect of physical causes, or be produced by the opposite forces of the enemy. 4. Where the blockade is complete, it is just, that in the case of contravention, the vessels and cargoes be liable to confiscation. It is the same, if the navigators are seized in the adjacent narrow seas, which are actually shut.

In No. 7, the author concludes with the remark, that to apply the general rules of the law of blockade, to individual cases, it is necessary to consider well the circumstances, particularly the probability of the knowledge of the blockade, which the navigators may have acquired at sea.

In section fifth, the author treats of the visitation at sea, of vessels generally, and under convoy. In No. 1, he shows the importance of the question. What has been expounded in the preceding sections, regards the rights themselves, relative to commerce and navigation, in maritime wars. What remains to be here treated of, belongs to the execution or enforcement of these rights, or the mode of exercising them at sea. It might be presumed, that, upon this last point, there would be very little difference, if people were at one upon the principles. For where the rights themselves are no longer doubtful, either for the one party or the other, it is not difficult, according to the rules of common justice, to judge of the legality of the means for their enforcement. Such, then, would be the case, if each party could be assured, reciprocally, of the free exercise of his rights; and the disputes about the visitation of vessels at sea, would be without importance, on the supposition, that there would never be any acts of violence on the part of belligerents, or of fraud on the part of neutrals; or, if one could expect, on the part of governments, that they should see the misconduct and wrongs, done by their subjects, constantly punished and repressed. But the experience of all past maritime wars, demonstrates the chimerical nature of such a hope for wars to come. Merchants will constantly pursue the principles of the counter, in contradiction to the principles of the law; and the governments at war, notwithstanding their willingness, and even desire to do so, have it not in their power, to prevent, or make reparation, for all the wrongs committed by their subjects. There is here another point of view, from which we must regard the differences, on the visitation of vessels at sea. If, on the one side, be alleged, the necessity of the visit, because without it, the rights of belligerents would be evaded; on the other side, it is denied, because, through it, the liberty of the commerce and navigation of neutrals, recognized and admitted, as having a legal basis, becomes actually insecure in practice. This difficulty must be explained.

In No. 2, the author treats of the right of visitation of vessels in general. The right of belligerents to visit merchant vessels at sea, in order to discover their quality, and that of their cargoes; to ascertain whether they are hostile property, or contain articles of contraband during war, flows naturally and obviously from first principles. In general, also, it is not called in question; and really, without the right of visitation, the right of seizure would be quite ineffectual. Such a search may be made in two ways. The belligerent may be content with inspecting the papers on board the vessels he visits; or the examination may extend farther. The documents of property, the charter parties, the bills of lading, the certificates by magistrates, which attest the property of the vessel and of the cargo, which designate the places where the deliveries must be made, which specify the persons to whom the goods are consigned, are pieces subjected to examination, as well as the other papers; such as, orders given to the captain, his letters of credit; and, so far as they regard the political quality, the national character of the vessel and cargo. None of these pieces can be withheld from the examination of the belligerents, when they require them to be presented; and that is usually sufficient. If there be no fraud—if the necessary precautions have been taken—if the requisite documents have been provided, the truth of the declaration of the captain is soon manifest; and in this case, the person who visits, if he be not an unreasonable and troublesome man, avoids the task of ulterior search. But when these conditions are not fulfilled, the belligerent thereby acquires a well founded reason for pushing his search farther. He may visit the vessel himself, see the goods which are contained in it, and if this examination cannot conveniently take place in the open sea, he may conduct the vessel into a port, to proceed there, to the verification of all the suspicious points.

Although, however, this right of visitation is generally accorded to belligerents, there are differences about it in some particular cases. It is asked, whether the belligerents can insist on the right of visitation, when merchant vessels are escorted by a naval force? We stop not here to consider the pretension, that a local visit of neutral vessels is an invasion of the neutral territory; we have already said enough, not to revert to this chimerical idea of a moveable and sailing territory, and to the comparison of vessels under convoy, to floating islands under the command of a chief. In general, it is evident that the legality of the right of visit, involves the obligation of making it, in the manner which may attain the object in view; and on the contrary, what is not necessary in the search, and may affect the interest of neutrals, ought to be considered as vexatious and illicit acts, for which the searchers are responsible.

In Nos. 3 and 4, the author treats of the obligation on neutral governments, to interdict their subjects from whatever is illicit. To judge, whether there be cases and circumstances, which may annul the right of visit, particularly when the vessels are escorted by neutral vessels of war, it becomes necessary to consider the facts, such as they occur in our actual wars. We are going to submit some preliminary remarks. If they be just, the conclusion which will result from them, will be equally decisive, as evident. 1. It is a wise foresight for neutral governments to obviate, during war, as far as possible, all illegal conduct on the part of their subjects, for the double advantage of preserving them from risks, and of preventing the suspicions of belligerents against the traders, who sail under neutral flags. The conduct exhibited by several individuals in a neutral nation, produces naturally a presumption for, or against their fellow countrymen; which seldom fails to have consequences favourable or unfavourable to the vessels of that nation, which the belligerents encounter. There is also a political reason, for neutral governments watching their subjects in this respect. They cannot, indeed, manifest more authentically, their perfect neutrality, than by clear and precise ordinances for their commerce and navigation during war; and by a rigorous police, severely directed against those who contravene them. The more they exert themselves to restrain fraud, the more they are in a state to protect their loyal subjects, and to interpose with success, in the cases of just claims made by the latter against the cruizers of the belligerent powers.

What neutrals, however, may do, in this respect, does not arise from any right, which imposes on them the obligation of maintaining a more special surveillance, over their subjects during war, than they are in the habit of doing during peace; nor to exercise a more extensive inspection over the legality of their conduct towards belligerents, than that which is prescribed by law. In even allowing them to act entirely as they choose, they in no manner infringe the rights of the belligerents, provided they do not pretend otherwise to protect their contraventions. But such indifference may inspire belligerents with unfavourable opinions, which it may be as well to prevent, especially if it be preponderating powers who are at war.

From neutral governments, not being under an obligation to obviate the abuses of their subjects, it follows, that belligerents, whatever condescension they may have to expect from them, for that purpose, cannot reasonably require them to extend their measures, beyond what is in practice in these same neutral countries, for preventing frauds being committed on their own customs, and for checking the other deceitful contrivances for evading payment of the revenues of the state. The maximum of precaution, in this case, is to maintain and enforce the observance of neutrality in vessels and cargoes, with the same diligence and exactness, as are exercised in inquiries and other proceedings, relative to taxes, or imposts, and customs. He who does as much, to prevent a wrong meditated against another, as he does for his own protection, satisfies every just and reasonable expectation on the part of that other. Perhaps, however, more might be done, if it were wished, completely to attain the object. In time of war, special inspections might be ordered; tribunals of inquiry might be established against the frauds of merchants and ship-owners; and more rigour might be shown in the punishment of their delinquencies. But this cannot be demanded on the one side; and on the other, it might be difficult to grant it, because there might result from it consequences inconsistent with the general spirit of the prohibitory laws of the state. At least, this care must be left to the neutral governments, to whom alone it belongs, to judge what it may be proper for them to do, with reference to the circumstances of the war.

2. It is not really in the power of neutral governments, to prevent fraudulent navigation and commerce during wars. It may even be said, that it is physically impossible to prevent them absolutely or completely. All that can be done, is so far to restrain them. It is notorious that the practice of fraud, excited by the thirst of gain, is too strong, too extended, and too ingenious, to be stopped by ordinary vigilance. What police, in the most exact arrangements of the customs, has ever been able, completely to shut the channels of contraband? And if this be so, where there may be had persons to keep a constant surveillance—roused to vigilance by their own profits—how expect this advantage, where

the interests of foreigners only are concerned? Let us consider some special circumstances a little more nearly. It has already been often remarked, that the neutrality of vessels was much more easily ascertained, than that of cargoes. This neutrality is usually certified in the ports; yet experience shows, how often the magistrates, who give these certificates, are deceived by the false allegations of those, who declare themselves proprietors, and are in reality, merely lent names. It is still more difficult to ascertain the truth, with regard to cargoes of goods. Fraud, armed with innumerable artifices, strengthened by the power of money, that irresistible source of corruption, knows well how to open a road amidst all the obstacles which the ordinances of government oppose to it. Let us suppose, that in the ports, where the superintendance of superiors presses more upon subalterns, the searches necessary for certifying the quality of the goods to be shipped, may be exact, would it be the same, if these vessels took on board their cargoes in more distant ports? In fine, to what would the probability be reduced, that neither contraband, nor hostile goods, should be slipped into the neutral vessels, which load in the ports of the countries at war,—in those ports, where it is deemed a duty to deceive, as far as possible, the cruizers of the enemy. Then it is, upon the vigilance of the consuls, or commercial commissioners of the neutral governments, established in the countries at war, that the observance of the rules prescribed for neutral navigators, depends; that is, it depends upon the vigilance of people, born in the country, or domiciliated there, who are connected by many relations with the other inhabitants of these places, and who, even for the execution of their duty, are obliged to employ persons, who belong to the enemy. How, then, venture to guarantee the exactness of their surveillance?

In Nos. 5 and 6, the author treats of the effect of convoy. To the ordinary precautions for preventing contraventions of the rules of neutrality, there have been added others, as in the case of the convoy to neutral vessels. The commander of this convoy is specially directed, in his instructions, to prevent any vessel joining the fleet, whose papers are not completely in order. But it is easy to see, after what has been said on the means of fraud, that this form scarcely augments the probability in favour of exactness; or, really and substantially, even when he takes under his safeguard, only the vessels of the state which furnishes the convoy. Indeed, it must be admitted, on the subject of convoys, that there is very little probability of the commander being able to discover the fraud, when once it has known how to disguise and conceal itself from the eyes of those who are appointed to watch the loading of the vessels.

3. Such is the real state of matters. But whatever may be the guarantee, which neutral governments may be willing to offer, for the honesty of their subjects during war, the belligerents are not under any obligation, to trust to it entirely, and to neglect their own surveillance. Rights, and very important rights, are at stake. The government at war, is even, from duty, jealous that these rights be not invaded by any one. It ought, therefore, as far as it is possible for it, to endeavour, by its own proper agents, to prevent this happening. At least, to it alone, it belongs to judge, whether the arrangements made by neutrals, are of such a nature as to give sufficient security.

In No. 7, the author treats of the right to visit vessels under convoy. Such are the premises, let us come to the consequences. 1. It is evident that in general, the right of visiting at sea cannot be denied to belligerents.

Whatever may be the papers, with which the master and crew are furnished, to attest the lawfulness of the goods they transport, it is necessary that the former may see them, examine them, and according to occasion, extend still farther their searches. 2. The right does not cease by the convoy or escort, which neutral powers resolve to give to their merchant vessels. The superintendance of the commander of the convoy, cannot guarantee to the belligerents their rights against the frauds of individuals. The escort given to neutral vessels, ought not then to have any other object, than to protect them against vexatious proceedings. It can never have that of taking from the belligerents the exercise of their rights, at least as long as the neutrality subsists, and as long as there is no design to have recourse to reprisals, against wrongs experienced, and for which reparation has not been made.

In No. 8, the author enquires, whether the right of visitation may be exercised against merchant vessels, under convoy by privateers. A distinction, however, may be here made, with reference to the right of visiting merchant vessels under convoy, between vessels armed by the state, and those armed by private individuals. These last are authorized by letters of marque, to search for goods that are contraband, or the property of the enemy, and to seize illicit articles, but all this at their own expenses, for their own account, and at their own risk. Such a permission includes, without doubt, the right of visiting neutral vessels, in order to see and ascertain whether there are in them, goods liable to seizure; but they are not ordered to do so; and they do not thus act immediately for the public good, and the profit of the state. If, then, it is said, the commander of a convoy, refuse to allow private cruizers to visit the vessels, which are under his escort, he does not refuse this right to the government itself, but he refuses the exercise of it to people, who are not directly appointed by the state for that purpose. It is in this difference of service between the ships of war of the state, and the cruizers fitted out by individuals, and in the diversity of their connections with the government, in this respect, that we must look for the reason of the desire, that the authority given to cruizers should be limited. There is granted them freely, the right of visiting neutral vessels; since without that, letters of marque would, in a great measure, be ineffectual: but with regard to those vessels which sail under convoy, it is thought the service of privateers is no longer applicable, and that their government ought, in this case, to dispense with it. Indeed, the convoy given by a neutral government is a public attestation that all is regular in the vessels convoyed. And although that does not oblige the belligerents to trust to it entirely, it is, however, decorous, or courteous, that such an attestation should be considered sufficient for individuals, who have armed and fitted out privateers of their own accord, and at their own option. This restriction, however, with regard to privateers, is rather a point of convenience, belonging more in reality to positive, than to natural international law. The reservation of the visit to the vessels of the state solely, may be sufficient for belli gerents; and perhaps they might, without inconvenience, renounce the right of visiting vessels under convoy by their privateers. But, if the first proved insufficient for the exercise of their rights, must they then absolutely renounce these rights, rather than employ privateers? And how deny to a government, which may not have a sufficiency of naval forces, to employ the right of making use of armed volunteers, that is, private cruizers? The almost indubitable result would be, except in the case of treaties, which might be contrary to it, that governments would be under the necessity of changing the form of letters of marque, and would give to privateers, commissions similar to those of the ships of war of the state.

In No. 9, the author enquires, whether the visit is prejudicial to the honour of the flag of the nation, which gives the convoy? There are authors, who, in reasoning on the right of visit, particularly with regard to vessels under convoy, have alleged the principle of honour, as adverse to it. Reason, however, cannot recognize such a principle of opinion, and of vanity, in questions of law. It has been said, that it was prejudicial to the respect due to the flag of a nation, that vessels ranged under its protection, should be held bound to admit on board, people of another nation, who come to make searches there. Usually, when these armed convoys encounter each other, it is the smallest vessels which proceed to the visit, such as cutters, corvettes, small frigates, most frequently of an inferior rank to the vessels which convoy. Privateers, of which the greatest part are only small vessels, present a still greater difference, between the force of the one, who wishes to visit, and of the one which escorts. Now it is singular, say they, that a petty privateer, of a petty state, at war, may examine the vessels belonging to great powers, and even carry them into port by force, in presence, and in the face of ships of war, of which the commander has orders to protect them.

The answer to such arguments, which can scarcely be stated, without employing the language of vanity, is otherwise very easy. Certainly, it is necessary and right, to respect, and to cause to be respected, the honour of the state. It is the shield of its safety; and still more for weak states, than for those which are powerful;

since the latter can more easily be indifferent to the opinions of others. It is, therefore, the duty of a government not to allow its flag to be in any manner insulted at sea. But how can it be degrading to be just and honest? If the injuries of the weak towards the strong, are ridiculous; those of the strong towards the weak, are detestable. The sole question of any importance here, is, whether the visit of neutral vessels, even of those sailing under convoy, is a right natural to nations at war? If the government is persuaded, that it cannot be exacted as a right, it ought to refuse it; if it has been recognized as lawful, the difference of forces is nothing, provided, on each side, they belong to states independent, and thereby equal in rights. Alas, in practice, between nations, as between individuals, how often are the pretensions of force made to prevail over the claims of right! Before the tribunal of reason, it is not so. The right of visit is steady and consistent, and always reciprocal; to be exercised and executed by the weak against the strong, as by the strong against the weak. It is thus by land. If large convoys by waggons, belonging to neutrals, meet military detachments during war, no one is hurt or offended by a visit, of which the object is to discover, whether there be any contraband goods destined for the enemy; and in these cases, it has never entered into consideration, what was the civil dignity of the chief entrusted with the charge of the conveyance of these goods. Convoys at sea are not given, in order to fight against the belligerent powers; their object is to repel pirates, and the violent acts of privateers; and it is quite consistent with such an object, not to resist the visit which the belligerents claim. Besides, the point here is, not to assimilate the convoy of neutrals, to the escort which belligerents send to protect their merchant vessels against the enemy. But whatever may be the relations between the forces of those who visit, and the force of those who are visited, it is here of no importance. Civility is always very convenient and agreeable in itself, and is often even a duty; but it must not derogate from the natural rights of war.

In No. 10, the author treats of the consequences of the visit, with regard to neutral commerce and navigation. The question, then, as to the visit, is decided so far, as we put in thesis, merely the simple right. But it must also be considered under another aspect. It is first asked, if the right of visiting neutral vessels, whether under convoy or not, can be actually executed or enforced, without violating in practice, the rights of neutrality? Doubtless, a right which cannot be used without doing an injury, or without being prejudicial to others, ceases to be a right; and would no more be such in the actual circumstances. But one may also ask at the outset, what are, then, the disadvantages which result to neutral navigators, from the visit made by belligerents? If every thing is regular; if neither the vessels nor the cargoes are legally liable to seizure, the little delays or retardations in navigation, which are the consequence of it, are inconveniences; but they are not, after all, of great importance. Along with these inconveniences, inseparable from the state of war, we must consider the advantages which come to compensate them. The nations which fight are much more to be pitied; while those who remain at peace, are the more enriched, often, from those foreign misfortunes. Supposing, then, that every thing is regular on the part of the neutrals, the visit must be for them, an act almost absolutely indifferent; provided, on the part of the belligerents, there be conformity also to the rules of moderation and equity. There must not, on either side, be any excess in pretensions; the conduct of cruizers in their acts of visitation, must be distinctly specified and well regulated; there must be indemnification secured to neutrals, who may have been harassed or subjected to vexatious treatment. In short, let there be honesty on the one side, and justice on the other; and the differences in visits vanish. But there is the difficulty. These last conditions are necessary; and may we not, with some probability, suppose them possible? To judge from the facts which have taken place hitherto, from the multiplied vexations which neutrals have experienced in maritime wars, particularly on the part of privateers and in distant seas, it might perhaps be presumed, that, as long as there shall be letters of marque and visits, there will be wrongs and acts of injustice. We shall not stop to notice unreasonable complaints; and of this number, is the complaint, that the right of visit is the death of mercantile speculations, which is true only of illicit commerce. But there remain enough of other complaints; we have voluminous collections of them.

In Nos. 11, 12, and 13, the author treats of the wrongs committed by the parties respectively at sea, and of their connection with the right of visit. We must, then, says he, return to this question. Do the vexations which neutrals experience, in the visitation of their vessels at sea, belong to it from the nature of the thing, and because they are inseparable from it; or do they depend solely on accidental causes, and which may be made to cease? If we reason according to the idea which may be formed of the manner of making these visits, and of introducing into them suitable forms, the dispute will be at an end. In founding our conclusion, on the contrary, on past events, and on experience, we must consider these facts more nearly, in order to distinguish those which really touch or affect the subject in question, from those which do not belong to it, and which have been improperly mixed up with it.

In the great number of disorders at sea, committed to the prejudice of neutrals, it is necessary first to separate those which the belligerents permit upon false principles, namely, all those committed by the order or authority of the government. Let us not forget what passed in the war of the revolution; when the laws of nations, so far as regarded neutrals, were no longer respected, nor recognized, no more by land than by sea; and when cruizers were permitted to act almost entirely as robbers. Wrongs of this kind have nothing to do, in discussions concerning what is right and just. To prevent them, it is to arms recourse must be had, and not to reasonings. The same answer might be made with regard to all the other points of law, to which the passions and force refuse submission. This reply, however, would often be unreasonable; because we must suppose, that, for the most part, the good will or disposition to be just, is not wanting, provided people know how to conduct themselves, in order to be so. In general, we must not reason upon law or right according to facts. It was for this, that Rousseau reproached Grotius: but without reason. The censor, absolutely, had not seized the spirit of the system of the latter. For although there be some passages in the work, De Jure Belli et Pacis, which might lead the reader to suppose the author has sometimes conceded a little too much to authorities, to opinions, and to facts, and even that, in reality, Grotius has not always profoundly enough, investigated principles, he was nevertheless well aware that facts show merely the maxims which have been followed, but do not demonstrate their justness. Moreover, if it be permitted to add another word with respect to this great author, some defects may well be pardoned in a first essay on natural law. It was, then, a voyage of reason on an ocean of moral ideas, upon which no one had yet navigated. Grotius has, in reality, drawn his precepts from the source from which they ought to be drawn, from the nature of man and of human society, such as it truly exists, and exhibits itself in history and experience; which is quite a different thing from taking facts, to make of them the basis of law.

Setting aside those wrongs which are committed at sea against neutrals, from false principles, there remain many other, which, contrary to the wish of governments during war, accompany the mode of proceeding of their subjects. It is not difficult to find the causes of them; but to understand distinctly their multiplicity and their importance in maritime wars, while wars by land present few examples of them, we must observe how much more frequently the military forces of the belligerents, and the subjects of neutral powers, encounter each other at sea, than they do on land. In wars by land, the people of neutral countries, who travel, or who carry on trade, and the transportation of merchandise, pass very rarely by places where the soldiers of the belligerents are stationed; and if that happens, it is still more rare, in these cases, that the property of the commodities transported is examined, and that these commodities are articles of contraband during war. By sea, again, the commerce and navigation of neutrals, being usually much more active during war, give rise daily to meetings, rencounters, and debates, between the neutral vessels which carry merchandise in mass, and the vessels of belligerents commissioned to observe the conduct of these neutrals. It is, therefore, to be expected, that the more opportunity there is for the military people to employ force, the more temptations there will be to abuse that force, and particularly for the cruizers who find their advantage in it. This is the reason, why neutrals are infinitely interested in the conduct of the belligerents, with respect to their private cruizers, and the military discipline to which they are subjected. The establishment of tribunals of admiralty, and their proper organization for the purpose of repressing the visitations of private cruizers, are, doubtless, one of the most essential points in the maritime law of nations.

Another cause of wrongs done at sea, to neutrals by belligerents, arises from the difficulty of keeping a sufficiently strict surveillance over the conduct of privateers, and especially that of some cruizers, who, under the title of authorized privateers, conceal their national character, and act and rob like pirates. These are, doubtless, misfortunes for neutrals; but they are not wrongs, which can be imputed to the people engaged in war. With regard, however, to authorized cruizers, there are, indeed, too many instances, when they have no opportunity of making lawful prizes, of their determining to make prizes, which are not lawful. Regarding themselves in the open sea, as in a solitude or desert, the hope of escaping justice, leads them to disorders, in which they find their advantage. If these excesses cannot be prevented, their authors at least ought to be severely punished. Finally, it is very evident, that the disorders which arise from this source, have no connection with the visitation of vessels here in question. These people seize neutral property contrary to the tenor of their ordinances, and they would do the same, whether visitation were permitted, or not. If it be absolutely impossible to repress entirely, these disorders, they must be regarded as evils attached to the nature of maritime wars; but the fact is, they might be ascribed to any other right of war, as well as to that of visiting neutral vessels.

There exists another cause of complaint against the right of visitation; and, in truth, it is, perhaps, the greatest; but it is to neutrals themselves that it belongs to foresee and to prevent it. This cause is the neglect of neutral merchants, ship-owners, and ship masters, to take the precautions necessary for putting in evidence the legality of their transactions. More frequently still, fraud, systematically arranged, has excited a general distrust of the operations of neutrals, and has given to belligerents probable reasons for commencing always by presuming something illicit. Hence the increase in the rigour shown to neutrals in their searches; hence more seizures, more stoppages of vessels, occasioned by suspicion alone.

The result of these considerations is clear. If facts and events be traced and referred to their causes, it is plain, that from the abuses, which their passions lead men to commit, in the exercise of their rights, no legitimate conclusion can be drawn against the rights themselves. Neither the right of visitation, nor that of seizure, have other consequences for neutral subjects, than those which they might reasonably expect, and which may be remedied. Even in cases in which neutral governments believe it their duty to cause their merchant vessels to be escorted against the dangers, to which they are exposed from the pursuit of cruizers, this is not an inconvenience which can be imputed to the right. There are cases, in which, in the same way, it is necessary to escort, by land, the transportation of considerable quantities of specie, and other valuable articles; and even the season of peace does not dispense with this. At sea, convoys are rarely necessary, in the seas adjacent to the mother country, where piracy may be more easily repressed. But, in other seas, they may not be neglected. There, perhaps, acts of violence might be still more to be dreaded, if there were neither private cruizers, nor legal visits of vessels. It must not be forgotten, that the cargoes of vessels are treasures, and consequently, allurements for the passions.

In No. 14, the author explains how visitation may be refused under the right of reprisal. There are, however, says he, circumstances in which the visitation of vessels which sail under convoy, may be refused by neutral governments. It is so where there is ground for the right of reprisals. It is so, when on the part of belligerents, their cruizers are neither sufficiently watched and looked after, nor punished for their vexatious proceedings, and when the just remonstrances of neutral subjects against such acts of violence, remain without effect. Neutral powers have been seen even to unite to form an armed neutrality, in order to obtain the respect due to their loyal, honest subjects. In such circumstances, it may be proper to send convoys, and to admit no visitation of the vessels so convoyed. But it is plain, this is not the question we are discussing here. It is always, besides, a critical situation to come to reprisals; which are in effect, hostilities, if not direct, at least circuitous; and which are most frequently the precursors of an open rupture. Yet even when governments have come that length, reason and moderation may still terminate the differences, provided other political passions are not mixed up with them.

The sixth and last section of the work, is upon the tribunals for the adjudication of prizes. In Nos. 1 and 2, the author shows, that the organization of prize courts is an essential point in the maritime law of the European nations. It is by this measure, and almost solely by this measure, that the powers at war can make the rights of neutrals at sea be respected. The less a proper police and surveillance, in order to prevent acts of violence, are practicable, the more exact ought the discipline to be, in order to punish offenders, and to make reparation for damage done. This duty of governments at war, flows from their very rights, and from the equity of their claims in relation to neutrals. If, in this matter, belligerents had always acted, upon just and reasonable principles, the differences and disputes with regard to the law itself, would never have been pushed so far. But in reading the history of prizes, and the result which the most reasonable remonstrances have often had, one is disposed to excuse the neutral governments, for rising against what are truly rights of war, but executed with injustice.

If the causes to be treated, before the tribunals destined to judge of the legality, or illegality of prizes, were less frequent, or less important, or less complicated, it would perhaps be sufficient, that they were treated in the manner practised in military tribunals, courts martial, and in police courts, where the proceedings are simple and summary. Indeed, in their origin, courts of admiralty were a kind of military court. But, if we consider the number and importance of processes, their complication in many cases, when circumstances obscure both the facts and the law, we shall find that there must here be tribunals of justice fully organized, and subjected to forms like those, which have to judge of civil causes. With regard to the details of the organization of these tribunals, or Conseils des Prises, it must be left to the determination of the governments, who have the right, and whose duty it is, to establish them. The number of judges, the mode of proceeding, the relations of the inferior to the superior tribunals, the judicial formalities, may be regulated in different ways; provided the object of them be always kept in view, and aimed at, namely, the administration of justice, the most exact, and the most prompt.

There are, nevertheless, essential points, with regard to these institutions, which ought to be particularly taken into consideration. The political or national relation of the persons who come to plead them, is of that number, independently of the importance of the causes, or of the value of the goods captured and reclaimed. Usually, in these processes, neutral foreigners are the pursuers, who reclaim their properties seized, and the defenders are the owners of the privateer, the fellow countrymen of the judges. It is necessary, then, not only to be just in these tribunals, but also to be so manifestly just, that neutral governments may be assured of it. The latter, so deeply interested, that there be no derogation from the neutral rights of commerce and navigation, can never be indifferent to the manner in which their subjects are treated in such affairs. They have, then, just reasons for being fully informed of the organization of the tribunals, whom the powers at war employ to make their rights be respected. There must also, then, be so much more circumspection on the part of belligerents, against the unjust sentences, which may emanate from these courts, that acts of injustice here are public and national disgraces. Indeed, the reputation of being just and honest, forms the primary basis of the true honour of a nation.

In Nos. 3 and 4, the author treats of the tribunals of prizes under the authority of the belligerent sovereigns. The governments at war establish the courts of prizes, nominate the judges, and give them authority. It cannot be disputed, that this furnishes the means of influencing the decisions, if the governments wish to abuse it. There are persons, who have found in this single point, a defect so great and important, that they have declared this kind of tribunal essentially vicious, and altogether incompetent to satisfy the end proposed. They are judges, it has been said, in their own cause, or what is nearly the same thing, in the cause of the people, who have acted by their orders. If it were so, there would be, doubtless, a moral nullity attached to this mode of proceeding; and force alone could support it.

But a little reflection only is necessary to see that this last objection is altogether unfounded. Even supposing that the government itself becomes immediately the judge in these cases, which, however, it could not do without abusing its authority with regard to the tribunals of justice, it would be so only, in the causes of its military agents against foreign subjects, and often even against its own subjects, who are interested therein. Indeed, in these tribunals, the question is seldom concerning the rights of nations, nor even those, which the belligerents might have arrogated to themselves, unjustly, against neutrals. The judgments here turn only upon, or merely regard, the acts of the military agents, and the conformity of their conduct, with the orders and instructions given with reference to illicit commerce and navigation. They are, therefore, the subjects of the government, who are called into court, and of whom the latter is the natural judge. For it cannot be disputed that a government is entitled to judge the actions of its own agents, and itself to decide whether they are in conformity with the laws and rules prescribed. It is likewise incontestable, that, in the ordinary course of justice, it belongs to him, who has suffered damage or is injured, to prosecute his adversary before the superiors of the latter, if there be not already another tribunal competent for that purpose. And as, at sea, there is no territorial jurisdiction, the cruizers have no other superior but their own government.

It might however, possibly, be argued, that the neutral governments should also have admission, and some concurrence in the prize courts, considering the multiplicity and importance of the suits, which are instituted there by their subjects. These tribunals would then be mixed courts, or chambers, composed of judges, partly authorized or appointed by the government at war, partly by the neutral government, whose subjects might there have business. Doubtless this would be a very generous mode of acting on the part of the belligerents. They could not demonstrate more clearly, their desire to be just towards neutrals But it is not a maxim of natural law, to exact from them such condescension; and on considering matters more nearly, we may perhaps see many inconveniences, and few advantages, likely to arise from neutrals having such an active part in these tribunals.

With regard to the point of right, never, certainly, is a government bound to yield, or concede to another, a portion of its sovereign power, such as that of judging its own subjects, who are within its own proper territory. Besides, the question here, is not concerning affairs which are to be treated and discussed by committees, in order to come to an agreement upon matters, which are contested, or in disputes between the governments, and which, from their nature, cannot be regulated by one alone. The only question here, is concerning judicial causes, in which every thing ought to be decided according to laws already in existence, and in which, the facts being established, leave no room for arbitration. With regard to the participation of neutrals in the courts of prize, if it offers them some slight advantages, it would also be accompanied with very considerable expense. It would be necessary to maintain, in the places where the tribunals are established, professional lawyers, particularly well versed in maritime laws. The consuls, or ordinary commercial commissioners, could not supply their place. The latter may well assist the claimants of their own nation, with their advice and their instructions; and this is their duty: but they are not fit, or, at least, they are not presumed to be fit, for discharging the functions of judges. They may, therefore, in reality be more useful to the litigants of their nation, by their extra-judicial intervention, than they would be by their voice in the tribunal. It must likewise be added, that the publicity of the proceedings in these kinds of law-suits, is a stronger protection against the partiality of the judges, than would be the admission of a foreign assessor among the voters. In fine, there must be presupposed in the governments at war, the will and desire to be just; it must be presumed, they do not wish either to corrupt, or to allow the courts of justice, to be corrupted. Without this pre-supposition, it would be vain to rely upon any judicial forms; without that, these forms would cease to be, what they ought to be, safeguards against precipitation, and fraudulent circumvention.

There are cases, in which the neutral government or magistrate becomes in its turn a competent judge, in a cause concerning the act of capture. This is, when a captor has entered with his prize, into a port of the neutral territory, of which, he who complains of the seizure of the vessel or goods, is the subject. If the claimant is a foreigner, this no longer holds: in that case, the magistrate of the place would have nothing to unravel or decide in the affair; he is bound to protect the parties equally, as long as they are in the territory, under his authority; leaving to each of them the care of prosecuting his own right; he ought not even to aid the captured vessel to escape, and withdraw itself from the captor. It is only when the claimant is a subject of the country, that he has the right to reclaim the goods illegally taken from him, and which are found in the territory of his sovereign. There is, then, what is called the Forum rei sitae. The government of the country when that happens, naturally becomes judge in the causes of its subjects, and of foreigners, who are found within the limits of its jurisdiction; unless there be express conventions to the contrary, with respect to some class of persons.

In No. 5, the author discusses the establishment of prize courts in neutral countries. As no government can, in point of right, exercise its judicial power in the country of another independent nation, it is very clear, that the powers at war cannot establish councils or tribunals of prizes in neutral countries, nor authorize the adjudication there, of the causes of their cruizers against the parties reclaiming them. This would be to pretend, in a manner, to form a state within a state, status in statu. At least, it would then be necessary to have the formal consent of the sovereign of the country, such as takes place among the nations of the Romish communion, where the church has, on certain points, a jurisdiction, which it exercises, under the authority of a chief, or head, who is not the sovereign of the territory. But such arrangements can only exist by particular conventions. And, if the neutral powers consented to allow tribunals of prizes to be established in their countries, they behoved to grant the same liberty to all the belligerent parties. Now, this act, in its consequences, might be attended with the same inconveniences, as allowing armed forces to enter their territory, there to act in a hostile manner. It would almost indubitably compromise both the independence and the neutrality of the country.

Farther, if a government at war, wishing to relieve its cruizers from bringing their prizes into its own proper ports, in order to prosecute there, their legal condemnation, should decree, that causes of this description might be brought before its commercial commissioners, established among foreign nations, and that the sentence of these commissioners should be sufficient to justify the legality of the prize, could the absolute right of a state to authorize this mode of proceeding be denied or disputed? Now, if such an act be considered, either as a favour to private cruizers, or as a relaxation of military discipline, with regard to these people, it could not be said, that it contained an arrangement absolutely unjust, or absolutely prejudicial to the rights of neutrals. The latter have no interest in it, provided the proceeding be confined to those cases solely, where the prizes are evidently hostile property, and where there is no contradiction or claim on the part of a neutral. This mode, however, of having the prizes adjudicated, is not calculated, in all cases, to make the sentences be respected as legal, except with the subjects of the government, who may have authorized it. In order that the legality of such a mode of procedure be generally recognized, it is necessary that it be also avowed and approved of by the other belligerents, either by an express declaration, or by the adoption of a similar mode of proceeding. If it is only on one side, that it is pretended to establish new rules, hitherto not authorized by the general law of nations, there are no reasons which can impose on others, the obligation of submitting to them. It follows, then, that the opposite belligerent power is not obliged to recognize the captor, as possessor of a right to the prize adjudged to him. Therefore, also, if this prize should pass, by sale, into the hands of a neutral, this new possessor would neither be recognized nor respected as a lawful possessor; and he would, on the contrary, be exposed to the right of recapture, on the part of those, from whom the goods had been taken. This is another reason for neutral governments never permitting the cruizers of nations at war, to have access to their harbours, except in cases of necessity. Even when traffic in the goods, captured and brought in by cruizers, is profitable to the country, it may bring about inconveniences greater than these advantages; particularly for the individuals who may have acquired those effects, whether vessels or merchandise, subject to be recaptured by the belligerent to whom they belonged.

In Nos. 6 and 7, the author treats of the appeal from the inferior to the superior prize tribunals, and of recourse to the government itself. Finally, with regard to prize courts, it is very evident, that their object ought to be not merely to render justice to foreigners, but also to render it in the most prompt and most easy manner possible. There are many causes of such a description, that it is almost an equal misfortune for a neutral merchant, to see his process long delayed, as to lose it. It is on that account, that a term has often been fixed by conventions, within which prize causes behoved to be determined. At the same time, there are a great number of cases, in which that would be impossible, without derogating from a still higher law,—that of never precipitating justice. Fraud, which knows how to render the investigation of facts so difficult, and the distance of the places, from which the proof and information must be drawn, embarrass and retard matters. But the organization of the tribunal ought to be such, that it can never be reproached with being the cause of these delays.

Neutrals complain, also, of the excessive expenses of actions or suits, brought before the tribunals of prizes. If there are sufficient reasons for maintaining that justice ought always to be administered gratuitously to individuals, it may be said that it is here especially this principle ought to be applied. The question, in fact, is with foreigners, forcibly arrested by the states at war, and to whom the latter ought to render justice, without charging them expenses. One reason more, in these cases, for giving them gratuitous justice, and which cannot be alleged in favour of the proper subjects of the state, is, that the latter are bound to contribute to the public expenses, for which foreigners owe nothing. At least, justice ought not to be too burdensome for foreigners. For although it may be said, that it is necessary to check chicanery and frivolous disputes, against which the expenses of process operate as restraints; and although it may also be added, that these expenses are always of little importance, when compared with the value of the prizes in dispute, it is no less evident, that in this matter, the governments at war owe to neutrals all the equity, all the moderation, and even all the generosity, which the love of justice can suggest and permit. There is ground here for talking of generosity. Neutrals are even entitled to expect favour with the tribunals of prizes, in all the cases, which are not rare in practice, where what is precisely just cannot be attained. Doubtless, too often merchants, and the owners and masters of vessels, are knowingly guilty of fraud. But there are many instances where it is not so, and where, in good faith, from want of circumspection or from error, they have allowed themselves to be drawn into transactions, illicit according to the rigour of the law, although excusable in themselves. However just, during war, may be the preference of the rights of belligerents over those of neutrals, as has been expounded elsewhere, it ought not, however, to be forgotten, that it is war alone which causes this collision of rights, and which renders illicit for neutrals, what they might do and exercise, freely and lawfully during peace. It is the neutrals, then, who, in this respect, suffer from the quarrels of the belligerents; and it is quite conformable to the laws of general justice, to be indulgent towards those who suffer for us, in consequence of our hostile disputes, which, though otherwise inevitable, are foreign to them.

It is an essential point in the formation of courts of prize, that there should be an appeal from a first to a higher tribunal, and also recourse to the government itself. Such causes cannot be allowed to be decided, in the last instance, by one chamber solely, as in the ordinary matters of police. With regard to recourse to government, it ought, in general, to be left free to the claimants. Indeed, the justice or injustice of the sentence of these tribunals may depend on the meaning of treaties and conventions; as, for instance, on what ought to be reputed contraband. Recourse, then, must be had to an authoritative interpretation, which is the province of government. It is sometimes also expedient that there be room for the ministerial intervention of neutral governments, when their subjects have valid grounds for reclaiming against the judicial conduct of the judges.

In an appendix, the author has placed an article which might well have formed an additional section, on the property of prizes captured from the enemy, and on the right of recapture. In section sixth, he says it was remarked, that the condemnation of prizes by Conseils des Prises, established in neutral countries, could not be respected as legal and valid, so that the effects thus adjudged to the captors, should be held by them in full property, safe from all claim of restitution, on the part of the former possessors, from whence they were taken.

In analysing the reason of this invalidity, we come back to the principle of the right of recapture, or recovery; which matter merits a farther development than it has hitherto received.

In No. 1, he shows, that the possession of goods taken from the enemy in war, is not full and entire property by the law of nature. If we suppose it to be a principle of natural law, which, however, it is not, that goods taken from the enemy in war, belong to the acquirers in full property, provided always, they have been acquired in a legal manner, then the points for discussion, in cases of capture, are reduced to these; was the prize really hostile property? Has the prize been made in conformity with the rules of war? If all is regular in these respects, the effects captured ought to be adjudged to the individual captor, or to the state, under whose authority the prize was made.

In conformity with this, every government being the natural judge of the conduct of its agents, and of the rights of the state, in relation to individuals, is entitled itself to prescribe the formalities necessary for ascertaining the points in question, under the condition, however, that they be conformable to the laws of war, and in no respect infringe the rights of nations. It depends, then, upon it, to determine, by what persons, and in what places, it pleases to make the necessary investigations, with regard to the prizes, and to judge of the right of the captor. In wars on land, the soldier who has seized some booty, mentions it, or carries it to the commanding officer; and the latter, in virtue of a general rule, or of a special decision, adjudges the property of it to the seizer. Then, after twenty-four hours possession, and without much other formality, the new owner may sell these goods, assign them, transfer them lawfully to others, without being exposed to the claims of the first possessor, from whom they have been taken. On sea, the rules require, that the captor have brought his prize into a port of his country, or to a squadron, or fleet of his nation, or to another place of safety; infra praesidia. After having had it for twenty-four hours in his possession, and after having also established the legality of his conduct before a court of admiralty, he is declared possessor in legal right, and in full property. All these formalities to arrive at the right of possession, make part of the positive or conventional (consuetudinary) law, which might well enough be changed, without touching the natural law.

It is, therefore, very evident, that the supposed principle, with regard to prizes, does not form part of the natural law. If we followed the latter, without regard to the positive law, we could regard the effects taken during war, by the one party from the other, only as articles, of which the party stripped or deprived, is dispossessed by force, and which the former possesses only by the sole act of seizure, viâ facti. Each party judges his own cause to be just; and sees in the occupancy and the captures of the enemy from him, only wrongs and acts of violence, for which he has a right to seek or enforce reparation, as long as the war lasts; for peace fixes the property of new. Each party may therefore regard, as still his own, or as belonging to him in property, what the other has taken from him. He may believe himself entitled to take it from the enemy, not merely as every other hostile property, but as being that which he may retake or resume as his own. It is from this right of retaking or resumption, that there is derived the right of still claiming restitution of the article, even from the hands of a third party, who may have become the possessor of it. This is what is called the Jus Postliminii.

In No. 2, the author shows, that the right of retaking

by the law of nature, holds with regard to immoveables. It is from this principle of natural law, that we must set out in these enquiries. It is preserved entire in the positive law, with regard to immoveables and the rights of territory.

The belligerent who takes possession of a territory, of a city, or of any other immoveable subject, possesses it merely in a military capacity or mode. He disposes of it by force as far as the law of war permits. He may sell it, hypothecate or mortgage it, transfer it in any manner whatever to another; but the right of the first proprietor subsists all along with the right of resumption, and of claiming restitution against every possessor who enjoys merely a title, transmitted by a party who has acquired only by forcible means.

In No. 3, the author explains the modifications which have been agreed upon in practice, with regard to moveable effects. With regard to moveable things, on the contrary, it has been almost generally agreed, that the capture of them from the enemy, made, nevertheless, in a manner conformable to the laws of war, should, in some manner, be for the captor a sufficient title of full property. In this respect, however, there is a great deal of diversity in the positive law, (or rather administration of international law by particular states). Sometimes the greatest extent has been given to the class of things moveable, which should thus remain with the acquirers, without even making any distinction between those taken from individuals, and those which belonged to the state, as vessels, cannons, and arms. There are countries in which, whatever has been taken by the enemy, is considered as having become a property, of which he may dispose lawfully as owner; having the right of gifting these captured articles, of selling them, or of abandoning them, so that, in this last case, they would belong to the first occupant who might get possession of them. Doubtless, if the property in full and absolute right of effects, taken by the enemy, be granted without restriction, there is thereby renounced the right of retaking, or the right of claiming in restitution, with reference to these articles. Most governments, however, have maintained and exercised the right of retaking or resumption, at least with regard to articles of public property. With regard to the effects of individuals, there are countries where prizes at sea are restored to the proprietor, when the ships of war of the state have made the recapture, exacting, then, a duty for rescue, and what is very natural, indemnification for the expenses attending the recovery; as, on the contrary, this restitution does not take place when private cruizers have recaptured the goods. There are still, in this respect, other modifications. Sometimes the restitution is confined to the benefit of the subjects of the state only; in other cases it is extended also in favour of allies. But universally, it is granted to proprietors, not hostile, or neutral, in the cases of the goods recaptured having been captured in an illegal manner, and by unauthorized people, except, however, the duty for rescue or recovery, which must be paid to the recaptors. These diversities in the particular positive law of recapture show, that nations have fallen back upon, or reverted to, or rested upon the general principle of natural law, that acquisition by force cannot annihilate the right of property in the former owner, although for particular reasons, exceptions are made in favour of some acquirers, or with regard to certain articles.

In No. 4, the author treats of the conventional, obviously meaning or including consuetudinary, formalities, for the excepted cases of recapture. It is clear, that property in full and entire right, with regard to goods taken from the enemy, not being a rule of the natural law, has no other basis in the positive law, than that of tacit or express convention, (rather express convention, or tacit, but virtual acquiescence, or consuetude). In the cases in which they are claimed, it is necessary that the acquisition and de facto possession, be conformable to the rules of the positive law, and that the forms, followed in practice, and recognised as valid, to render the acquisition legal, be carefully observed. It follows from this, that belligerent powers, in order to secure to their cruizers the peaceable possession of the prizes which they make, are obliged to conform to the usages recognized by the conventional (and consuetudinary) law of nations. If these were arbitrarily departed from on the one side, this would give the other party a right to depart from them in the same way, and to recur to his natural right of recapture.

A government may easily support its captors against the claims for restitution of its own proper subjects; but if the prize were to pass into the hands of neutrals, the latter would, by no means, be in safety against the right of resumption, in case the forms should not have been observed. These forms are not, by any means, indifferent ceremonies. Cruizers, for instance, could not obtain a regulation, that the judgment and condemnation of the prizes, which they make, might take place in neutral ports, as in those of their own country, without often occasioning thereby great disadvantage to the opposite party: and if, in particular cases, that is, of no importance, it ought, however, always to be borne in mind, that the one of the two nations at war cannot arbitrarily depart from established usages, without the other, by the law of reprisals, becoming entitled and empowered to do so, as much.

TENTH PERIOD.

Of Maritime International Law during the period from the General Peace of 1815 *to the present time.*

Since the peace of 1815, happily no maritime war has occurred, in which the principles of Maritime international law were required to be applied, or received farther illustration or development, or were subjected to any material change in practice. And this was one of the reasons for giving so detailed an abridgement, if the expression may be used, of the work of M. Tetens, as exhibiting in its most important branches the principles on which the present Maritime international law of Europe, as actually administered, is founded, as developed by, and resting upon, not only the British authorities of Lord Stowell in the court of admiralty, and of the court of appeal in prize causes, for a long time guided by that most acute and sound lawyer, Sir Wm. Grant, which authorities, as being British, may be considered liable to national bias and consequent partiality, but also upon the authorities of such recent able and learned foreigners, as Lampredi and Tetens, who were at least free from any British bias, and the interest or supposed interest of whose native countries, if they had allowed themselves to be influenced by such a motive, would have led them to expound different doctrines from those which, in the sound exercise of acute and impartial intellect, they actually did.

In giving the abridgement of the truly valuable work of M. Tetens, the most philosophical, perhaps, on international law, since the days of Grotius, we have to apologise for the inelegance of the language, arising in a great measure, from anxiety to represent exactly the original in his own dress, without attempting a more liberal translation, or to adapt the expressions more to the English idiom.

The only at all important discussion, since 1815, of any of the rules of Maritime international law, has been the recent one respecting the right of visitation, and its extent, under the conventional treaties, between Great Britain on the one side, and France and the United States of America on the other, for the more effectual suppression of the African slave trade. But this discussion regarded the right of visitation and search during peace, not during war; and as resting on special convention, not on general legal principle, or consuetude. It therefore does not immediately fall under our inquiries into the right of search during war. And the positive consuetudinary law of past ages, does not afford any direct illustration of this point comparatively new. But it can scarcely be disputed that all nations, who have any claim to be deemed or called civilized, are morally, if not legally, bound to concur in the requisite measures, for the suppression of this odious traffic in human kind, to the degradation of the species. And if this obligation has been recognized by conventional treaties, there do not appear to be any sound or valid reasons, why the right of visitation and search should not be recognized by convention, and resorted to, as the chief, if not the only farther measure, which can be adopted, for the suppression of that abominable traffic—a measure, which has for centuries been recognized in Europe, as indispensable for the ascertainment of hostile from neutral vessels, and for the discovery of hostile and contraband goods at sea, during war. All depends upon the nature of the offence, or injurious act, to be prevented, or punished and suppressed. If the prevention, or punishment and suppression of the act be just and generally expedient, the chief, if not the only practicable means of effecting that end, it should seem, must be conceded as a necessary consequence.

From the more recently disputed important questions of the common consuetudinary maritime law of nations during war, not having become the subject of actual contest, or conventional arrangement, since the general peace in 1815, we have few treaties to mention, later than those already noticed. In the course of this period, no doubt, a considerable number of treaties of commerce and navigation have been concluded among the different maritime powers, if not between every one of these powers, and other states; such as Britain, France, the United States of America, the Low Countries, Denmark, Sweden, Russia, Prussia, Austria, Sardinia. But almost all, if not all of these treaties, agreeably to the uniform practice in such cases, were for short definite periods, such as ten or twelve years, and consequently, many of these have expired during the intervening period, when not renewed. And it is therefore to be wished, that Baron Charles de Martens, would undertake the task of continuing the work of his uncle, G. F. de Martens, published in 1801, in three volumes, 8vo., entitled, Cours Diplomatique, and divided into the Guide Diplomatique and Tableau Diplomatique, downward from the end of the eighteenth century to the present time; exhibiting distinctly such treaties as are now actually in force. From the limited nature, however, of our present researches, we do not feel the want of such a view of the actual and real conventional law of civilized nations. For the treaties of commerce and navigation since 1815, are almost entirely occupied with stipulations and provisions for the regulation of maritime commerce during peace. And such of them, as contain any stipulations relative to a contingent state of war, appear to be confined, to the allowance for a definite period for foreigners to depart, with their goods, upon a rupture, a recognition of the common law of blockade, as maintained by an adequate naval force, and a special enumeration of the articles to be held by the parties, as contraband of war. We have not observed that any of these treaties, which, of course, are detailed in the continuation of the Récueil des Traités, by G. F. de Martens, attempt even between the contracting parties, any revival of the theories of Hübner, Totze, and Rayneval, or to resuscitate the other doctrines of the armed neutrality of 1780 and 1800. And we are not aware that any of the treaties here alluded to, either renew, as between the contracting parties, any of these doctrines, or make any attempt, or express any desire to do so, except the treaty between Prussia and the United States of America of March 1829, by which,[1] in Article XII., these two governments renewed part of their treaty of 1799, and declared their continued desire, to provide by treaty, either between themselves, or in conjunction with other maritime states, for ulterior stipulations, which might serve to secure a just protection and liberty to the commerce and navigation of neutrals, and to aid the cause of civilization and humanity. Of the continued desire of these two wise governments, to aid the cause of civilization and humanity, we cannot entertain any doubt. But it is equally im-

[1] Martens' Nouveau Recueil, VII. 615.

possible, not to perceive, that the aid which the Prussian government here desired to give, was at the expense of other states, and tended directly to promote its own national interest. What would Frederic II. have said, or done, if any neutral government had presumed to interfere,—to protect from occupation, and forced contributions, the towns and villages, the moveable effects and funds of the hostile state, whose armies he had vanquished in the field of battle,—and thereby to counteract and defeat the effects of his victories?

Farther, from the happy continuance of peace generally, during the period we are now to contemplate, we have no records to notice of prize law questions, settled by the determinations of prize tribunals. And what chiefly remains, is, to give some account of the principal treatises, which have appeared, during this period, on international law, so far as they relate to the maritime department.

But if our task, during the period we are now to survey, becomes, in a great measure, limited to a review of the principal works on Maritime international law, which have appeared since the termination of the French imperial war, we may hope, such a review will not be without its use For, as formerly observed, in the course of this review, under the disadvantage, perhaps, of occasional and too frequent repetition, we shall have an opportunity of supplying such deficiencies, in the narrative of events, in the first volume, as may have arisen, from its being too brief, under any of the former periods, we contemplated. And we shall in this way, also, have an opportunity of pointing out what we conceive to be the demerits of these works, and of guarding the reader against those plausible, but unfounded assumptions, and those ingenious, but inconclusive arguments, to which recourse is frequently had, from undue national bias, or for the promotion of national interests, at the expense, and to the injury of other states.

CHAPTER VII.

Notice of the Histoire des Traités de Paix par M. F. Schoell.

To this proposed analytical and critical review of the more eminent systematic writers on Maritime International law, from the general peace of 1815 to the present time, we humbly conceive we shall proceed with advantage, by departing, in a small degree, from the strictly chronological order, and commencing with the notice of an excellent historical work, of which a part only, treats of our subject. We allude to the Histoire des Traités de Paix par M. F. Schoell, published in 1817–18, in 15 tom. 8vo. M. Schoell appears to us to have been an able, independent, and, in general, impartial historian. But, like many other writers, he seems to us to err, in ascribing much too great effect to treaties and conventions.

The history of Maritime International law, M. Schoell has divided into five or six different epochs, or periods of change, but we apprehend, without sufficient foundation in fact, for the rather numerous distinctions he makes. The doctrines of the Consolato del Mare, namely, neutral goods on board hostile vessels are free, and the neutral vessel does not neutralize or protect the hostile cargo, of course form the basis of what he calls the first epoch of modern maritime law. And these maxims, he says, the law of nations does not disapprove. He might farther have said, and we humbly conceive should have said, they are the maxims, if not the only maxims, which the law of nations or natural justice, applied to independent states, does or can approve. For what can be more unfair or unjust, than to confiscate the goods of a friend, because they happen to be carried in the vessel or waggon of his neighbour, with whom we have a dispute? Or what can be more unneighbourly, or more inconsistent with real neutrality, than to attempt to conceal or cover the property of one neighbour, which another neighbour has a just title to seize, in self-defence, or in prosecution of his violated rights, and thereby counteract and so far defeat the operations of the latter for obtaining justice, or extract a profit from the exigencies of the former, which have been occasioned by the contest, to the direct loss and damage of the latter?

But M. Schoell, for whose fairness and impartiality we have great respect, as well as for his talents, goes on to observe. "In the middle ages, these maxims of justice were of more easy application than they are now. The commerce of these times differed essentially from that of the present day. What is called commerce by commission, or the commission-trade, was not then known; the merchant proprietor usually made the voyage himself, along with his goods, going from port to port, in search of a market, where he might dispose of them to the greatest advantage. It was then easy to decide, in each particular case, whether the cargo belonged to the enemy, or to a friend. In the present times, however, when goods are no longer sent upon chance, or by way of adventure, but are ordered or commissioned before hand, or are sent on consignment, against the advance of a part of the value, it often becomes difficult to decide upon their quality or character; and it is no longer possible to execute strictly the principles of the Consolato del Mare, without sometimes infringing upon (sans froisser quelquefois) the interests of neutrals."

The correctness, in point of fact, of this observation, we so far admit. There can be no doubt, that the change here alluded to, in the mode of conducting mercantile business, has rendered it more complicated, and increased the difficulty of distinguishing the property of friends from that of the enemy. And this actual change in the mode of conducting business, affords a much stronger argument for a change in the rules to be applied, than all the idle declamation about neutral flags, and floating territories. But it by no means, in our opinion, affords any adequate ground, for altering the rules of law and justice, for making war upon a friend, and for allowing a friend to act as an enemy. There can be no trafficking with the rules of justice. The increased difficulty of ascertaining the matter of fact, by no means amounts to impossibility, and affords no valid ground or reason for altering the rule of law. What should we think of the judges of a court of common law or equity, administering the internal criminal and civil jurisprudence of a country, if, from the greater difficulty in ascertaining the fact in a certain class of cases, they should decline applying the law to that class, or in order to save themselves the trouble of minute investigation, and to save the litigants on one side, the risk of occasional error of judgment, should adopt a rule, which would allow crimes and frauds to pass with impunity, to the manifest injury of all those who would have been litigants on the other side. But, in reality, the increase in the difficulty of distinguishing the property of the bonâ fide neutral, from that of the enemy, arises, in comparatively only a small degree, from the change in the mode, now prevalent, of conducting foreign trade, by commission or order, and by consignment, on a partial advance of value. The chief difficulty arises, and has all along arisen, from the preconcerted and fraudulent schemes of the traders in neutral countries, in collusion with the subjects of belligerent states. And how such fraudulent and collusive schemes should merit such an inversion of the rules of law and justice, as neutrals contend for, it is not easy to see.

The second epoch of the modern maritime law of nations, M. Schoell seems to make the fifteenth and the sixteenth centuries, when he says, the principles of the Consolato del Mare were altered; the second proposition was maintained as favourable to the belligerents, who had the superiority at sea, and the first was renounced. But that this second epoch is imaginary, we have already seen, and is manifest from the very slender basis, on which M. Schoell himself founds this distinction, or alleged alteration of the law of nations. This basis is no broader, than the treaty formerly noticed of 1417, between Henry V. King of England, and John, the fearless, Duke of Burgundy, which declared neutral goods on board a hostile vessel to be lawful prize; and the ordonnance, also formerly noticed, of Francis I. in 1543, which enacted, that hostile merchandise found on board a neutral vessel, should involve the confiscation of all the rest of the cargo, and even of the vessel itself. But it is plain, that a single treaty between two powers, could not alter the international law of Europe, especially when, as we have seen, the practice, even of the parties to that treaty, as well as of other nations, was different, with regard to these other nations. It is equally plain, that the single severe ordonnance of Francis I., although it might warrant other nations in adopting a similar severe regulation with reference to France, could not alter the general law of nations, as practised for centuries preceding.

The third epoch of maritime law, M. Schoell commences with the observation, that it was reserved for a power, which has remained a stranger to the progress of the sciences, but which, in its barbarous policy, respected the law of nations, to give the first example of a more humane legislation; alluding to the arrangement between the Sultan Achmet I., and the King of France, by which it was agreed, that goods belonging to the enemies of the Porte, on board French vessels, should not render these goods liable to confiscation. Under this third epoch, M. Schoell proceeds to notice the different treaties between the several European nations, during the seventeenth century, down to the peace of Utrecht in 1713; as if these treaties constituted the whole law of nations, or altered the general law by their special stipulations. In this inference, we can by no means acquiesce, especially, as we have seen, that excepting under these treaties, the practical administration of Maritime international law by these very nations was very different. But we shall follow his statement of these treaties, in order to ascertain still more distinctly, the point to which we formerly alluded, whether the report of Napoleon's minister, as to the rights of neutrals having been finally settled by the treaty of Utrecht, be well founded or not.

In 1646, France granted to the United Provinces, a privilege similar to what in 1604 it had obtained from Turkey, but only for four years; and this favour was alternately bestowed, or refused, by subsequent conventions and declarations, down to the treaty of commerce of Utrecht, concluded in 1713, for twenty-five years, by which France, while it maintained the ordonnance of 1543, that neutral goods on board hostile vessels should be confiscated, recognized the rule, that the neutral flag should cover the hostile cargo.

The Republic of the United Provinces, M. Schoell goes on to observe, had in 1612, also obtained from the Ottoman Porte, the observance of the first rule of the Consolato del Mare, that the goods of their subjects, found on board hostile vessels, should be respected. But this was not enough for the Dutch. The commission trade, which formed the principal branch of their industry, could not well exist, or must suffer greatly in time of war, unless the rule which declares the merchandise of the enemy to be covered by the neutral flag, were generally admitted.

Accordingly, by its zealous and persevering efforts to establish this legislation, this Republic, continues M. Schoell, became in fact the creator of what has been called the new maritime law of Europe. The maritime treaty, which in 1650, Philip IV. concluded with the ancient subjects of his crown, laid the foundation of it. And there was thus established in all its rigour, the rule, that the merchandise follows the flag in all cases; so that neutral merchandise found on board a hostile vessel was liable to seizure, while hostile merchandise was held sacred, when found under a neutral flag. This new maritime law was, in every respect, the opposite of that, which the Consolato del Mare had established. In all its arrangements, it was for the advantage of the commerce of the Dutch. The flag of the Republic neutralized the merchandise, which the nations involved in the war, might be disposed to entrust to it; while the Dutchman, who should have so little patriotism as to load his merchandise in foreign vessels, would thereby renounce the protection which the Dutch flag insured to a stranger.

England, too, so far admitted the rule of the liberty of the neutral flag, by its treaties with Portugal in 1642 and

1654, by its treaties with France in 1655 and 1677, by its treaties with Spain in 1667 and 1670, and by its treaties with the United Provinces in 1667 and 1674.

This new legislation, however, continues M. Schoell, was not generally admitted. Denmark and Sweden, who had nothing to export, but the products of their soil, remained faithful to the ancient principles. These form the basis of all the treaties, which in the course of the seventeenth century were concluded between Great Britain and the Northern Kingdoms. Indeed, these powers did not, M. Schoell observes, do homage to this new maritime law, till the occasion of the armed neutrality, of which we have in the first volume, given some account.

Before leaving what M. Schoell has thus described, as the third epoch of the Maritime international law of Europe, we must again remark, that he founds his statement entirely on treaties, leaving entirely out of view not merely the statements and opinions of their international jurists, but also the practical administration of the law during the seventeenth century, by the different European powers, when not controlled by these special conventions, as appearing from their respective ordinances, statutes, and judicial determinations. As he writes the history of treaties, he seems to have been led to hold, that all international law is contained in, and founded on them. But this is a limited and erroneous view, as we have endeavoured in the first volume to establish, at considerable length. And we may only here add, that beyond their special stipulations, for the period of their duration, these treaties afford evidence of the law of nations, only so far as acted upon, and thus prove actual practice or usage, but not if by mutual tacit consent, they are departed from, or left in abeyance by the contracting parties.

What M. Schoell designates as the fourth epoch of maritime law, he appears to date from about the middle of the reign of Louis XIV. For he proceeds then, under this head. The pride of Louis XIV. rendered vain all the efforts made by the Dutch to give prevalence to the new rules. It was at the time when he saw his marine increased to 100 ships of the line, and to nearly 700 other ships of war, armed with 14,000 cannons and 100,000 sailors, that regarding himself as the master of the seas, this monarch promulgated his celebrated ordonnance of 1681, by which, despising treaties (but only, it must be here observed, following out the previous ordonnances from the reign of Francis I.) he declared that all vessels loaded with goods belonging to the enemy, and all goods found in a hostile vessel, should equally be good prize; in other words, that the neutral flag should not cover the merchandise, while the hostile flag should render hostile the neutral merchandise. Nor did the government of France stop there. In the war for the succession of Spain, it endeavoured to establish a new maxim, by which the quality or character of the merchandise no longer depended on that of the proprietor, but every production of the soil, or of the industry of the enemy, whoever might be the proprietor, was subjected to confiscation. Frequently even the seizure was extended to neutral vessels, which after having taken on board their cargoes, in hostile ports, sailed towards a port, other than those of their own country.

What M. Schoell here states is quite true. But it does not follow that it constitutes a fourth epoch in the maritime law of Europe. The proceedings of the French government under Louis XIV. were merely the aggressions of one nation, and were checked in time by the combination of other nations, whom they injured, or excited. They could not, and did not, alter the common general law of nations, farther than authorizing other nations, upon the principle of reciprocity, to treat France in the same way, in which France treated them.

What he designates as the fifth epoch of maritime law, M. Schoell commences by stating that Great Britain considered it a duty to give a salutary check to the excesses of the French government just alluded to, by the treaty of commerce of Utrecht in 1713. And we now come to investigate and ascertain precisely, what arrangement was really concluded by that treaty, so much relied on by the minister of Napoleon.

The chief stipulations in this treaty relative to navigation and maritime commerce, in the event of the contracting parties being in future the one at war and the other neutral, are contained in the articles xvii. to xxvii. inclusive.[1] And the substance of these provisions appears from art. xvii. "It shall be lawful for all and singular the subjects of the Queen of Great Britain, and of the most Christian King, to sail with their ships with all manner of liberty and security, no distinction being made, who are the proprietors of the merchandise laden therein, from any port, to the places of those who are now, or shall be hereafter at enmity with the Queen of Great Britain, or the most Christian King. It shall likewise be lawful for the subjects and inhabitants aforesaid, to sail with the ships and merchandise aforementioned, and to trade with the same liberty and security from the places, ports, and havens of those who are enemies of both or of either party, without any opposition or disturbance whatsoever, not only directly from the places of the enemy aforementioned to neutral places, but also from one place belonging to an enemy, to another place belonging to an enemy, whether they be under the jurisdiction of the

[1] Chalmers Coll. Vol. I. p. 402 to 407.

same prince, or under several. And it is now stipulated concerning ships and goods, that free ships shall also give a freedom to goods, and that every thing shall be deemed to be free and exempt, which shall be found on board belonging to the subjects of either of the confederates, although the whole lading, or any part thereof, should appertain to the enemies of either of their majesties; contraband goods being always excepted; on the discovery whereof, matters shall be arranged according to the sense of the subsequent articles," by which contraband goods are specified and limited to warlike instruments, and all other merchandise and things specified or not, are declared free goods, "so that they may be transported and carried in the freest manner, by the subjects of both confederates, even to places belonging to an enemy; such towns or places being only excepted, as are at the time besieged, blocked up round about, or invested."

The treaty of navigation and commerce, signed the same day, 11th April 1713, between France and the States' general, contains similar provisions. But it is only in the two treaties which France thus concluded at Utrecht, with Great Britain and the States' general, that such provisions are contained. They are not repeated in any of the other treaties, which, taken together, are commonly comprehended under the appellation of the treaty of Utrecht. In particular, the treaty of peace and commerce concluded between Spain and Great Britain, and also in the year 1713, does not contain the same special stipulation, but merely renews the old treaty of 1667.

In fact, the British government appears to have been induced to admit this rule into this treaty with France, partly to provide, for a time at least, against the severity of the ordonnance of Francis I.; renewed by the ordonnance of Louis XIV. in 1681, by which the carriage of hostile goods was held to confiscate the neutral vessel, and likewise the remainder of the cargo; partly to favour the Dutch, whose influence at that time with the British government was very great. It is well known the treaty of Utrecht was forced upon Louis XIV.; and France, against whom this rule had been first brought forward, appears to have deemed it due to her dignity to oppose its taking root, or being generally established. Indeed, so averse was France to such restraints as those imposed by this treaty, that in the treaty of commerce, concluded with the Hanse towns only three years afterwards, in 1716, it was stipulated, that goods belonging to the enemy found on board Hanseatic vessels, should be confiscated; but derogating so far from the ordonnance of 1681, should not infer the confiscation of the remainder of the cargo, if neutral, or of the vessel.

What M. Schoell designates as the sixth epoch of maritime law, appears to extend from the peace of Utrecht to the armed neutrality of 1780. And in the interval, there appears to be only one treaty, by which France conceded the entire liberty of neutral commerce; namely, the treaty of commerce and navigation, which, at the expiration of that of 1713, was concluded in December 1739, with the States' general. As this treaty was a renewal of that of Utrecht, it contained the same stipulations, and the rule by which the neutral flag covers the hostile cargo, is there more distinctly expressed. But this treaty expired in 1764, and was not renewed.

The ordonnance of Louis XV. of 1744, declared good prize, not only hostile goods found in a neutral vessel, but also in general, all the productions of the soil, or of the industry of the enemy, with the exception of those which should be found under the Dutch or Danish flag. Even the règlement, which Louis XVI. promulgated in

1778, does not announce the rule, that the neutral flag covers the cargo. It does not, indeed, any more, after the example of the preceding laws, enunciate the opposite rule; but, as the 15th Article maintains the ordonnance of 1681, in all points in which it is not derogated from, by the reglement, the necessary conclusion is, that in 1778, France did not concede to the neutral flag, the prerogative of covering hostile cargoes. As a still farther proof, reference may be made to the treaty of commerce, which Louis XVI. in 1779, concluded with the Duke of Mecklenburg Schwerin, and which stipulated, "Les marchandises de contrabande, &c. ainsi que tous les éffets, denrées et marchandises, généralement, quelconques, appartenant aux ennemis du roi, qui se trouve, sur les navires du dit Duché. seront confisqués." Such was the legislation of France in 1779; it was not till 1780, that that government suddenly changed its tone and language, but only, as we formerly saw, conditionally, and for a short time.[1]

"The simple exposition of these facts," says M. Schoell, "is sufficient to demonstrate the futility, it may be added, the falsity, of the report, which, according to the Moniteur, the minister for foreign affairs made to Napoleon, in March 1812, that the rights of maritime neutrality had been solemnly regulated by the treaty of Utrecht, so as to have become the common law of nations, and that that law had been literally renewed in all the subsequent treaties."[2]

Again, when noticing the report of M. Maret in 1812, M. Schoell observes: "Such were the preparations in the course of being made, for the grand struggle, which was to decide upon the independence of Europe. Bonaparte, however, covered his immense preparations, under the pretext of the war, which he was carrying on against

[1] Schoell Hist. des Traités, Tom. IV. p. 10. [2] Tom. IV. p. 20.

Great Britain, whose preponderance was going to be menaced with a decisive blow. It was, at this epoch, that, to replace by some new invention, the superannuated terrors of federal system, and of continental system, which no longer made any impression upon the nation, his minister for foreign affairs, invented that doctrine, by which the stipulations of a particular treaty, between France and Great Britain, were raised and exalted into a kind of common law of nations, regulating for ever the maritime rights of neutrals;—a doctrine, which this simple exposition of facts is sufficient to refute."[1]

[1] Tom. X. p. 125.

CHAPTER VIII.

Review of part of the Précis du Droit des Gens Moderne de l'Europe, by M. G. F. de Martens.

In chapter X. of volume I. of this work, we noticed at considerable length, the excellent treatise by M. G. F. de Martens, Sur les armateurs et sur les Prises. And we did not, in surveying the period from 1793 to 1801, deem it necessary then to notice the early editions of his general work on the law of nations, as it did not appear to contain much in addition to his maritime treatise on the subject of our present enquiries.

At the commencement of this volume, too, we again postponed any detailed account of this work, until the appearance of the last improved edition. But on reflection, as the second edition of this work, in 1801, preceded by so many years, the treaties of Schmalz and Schmelzing, which we are soon to notice, and as the third edition, although enlarged and improved, does not materially alter the doctrines contained in the second, we think it due to the author to place our review of his work nearly at the commencement of this last period; especially, since there can be no doubt his successors, during that period, have been greatly indebted to his labours.

The first edition in German had appeared in 1796; the second edition in French in 1801. The changes which had taken place in Europe during the interval, required revisal and enlargement. A new edition was demanded. And placed between the necessity of consenting to a mere re-impression, or of undertaking to retouch the whole, the author informs us he had no hesitation in preferring the latter course; "Nonobstant, que des occupations d' un autre genre, dont je suis chargé, et mon éloignement de cette riche Bibliothèque de Göttingen, à laquelle il m' etait longtems permis de puiser à loisir, m' aient fait éprouver des difficultés auxquelles j' etais peu fait autrefois." This third edition of the Précis du Droit des Gens Moderne de l' Europe, was considerably enlarged and improved by the author; and was published at Göttingen in 1821, about the time of the author's death. But M. de Martens, although aware in 1820 of the subsequent works of Saalfeld, Schmalz, Schmelzing, and Klüber, adhered in this edition to his original arrangement, partly because he still considered it well calculated to facilitate the investigation of the individual questions, upon which it might be desired to have recourse to his work, and partly because he wished this edition to serve, like the second in French, as an introduction to his Cours Diplomatique, which appeared at Berlin in 1801.

Only a portion, of course, of this general treatise on the Droit des gens de l' Europe moderne, relates to Maritime international law. And before adverting to that portion, we have merely to repeat here, the objections we have elsewhere stated, to the doctrine propounded by this most useful writer in his introduction, § 7, with regard to the idea we ought to form of the Droit des gens général et positif de l' Europe, or of the common positive law of nations.

The following is the section to which we allude; and that our readers may judge of the correctness of the construction we put upon it, we subjoin both the original and a literal translation.

"Idée qu' on doit se former du droit des gens général et positif de l' Europe. Rien n' empêche d' imaginer qu' un plus grand nombre d' états, que même p. e. tous les états de l' Europe s' accordent à mieux fixer leurs droits reciproques, par des conventions générales et même à se fédéraliser pour se les garantir. Alors, il y aurait un code de Droit des gens positif de l' Europe, fixe et obligatoire pour tous. Mais jamais ni les conciles, ni les congrès de paix nombreux, tel que ceux de Westphalie, d' Utrecht, de Vienne, ou d' Aix-la-Chapelle, ni les projéts infructueux de republique universelle n' ait produit, une telle convention générale conclue par la plupart seulement des Etats de l' Europe. Ce n' est donc pas dans ce sens qu' existe un droit des gens positif de l' Europe, ou que probablement il existera jamais."

"D' un autre côté, ce qui ne tient qu' aux traités, ou aux usages particuliers établis dans les rapports individuels entre quelques états, n' est, comme tel, obligatoire que pour ceux-ci, et non pour le reste des peuples, indépendament des forces et du nombre, des uns ou des autres; il n' existe aussi aucun point si uniformement règlé par chaque état dans ses relations particulières avec chacun des autres, que l' ensemble de ces arrangemens particuliers pourrait équivaloir à une convention générale."

"Cependant on peut fort bien former par abstraction une théorie de ce qui se pratique le plus généralement entre les puissances et états de l' Europe, en considerant 1. que dans bien des points les nombreux traités particuliers des Puissances se ressemblent tellement dans l' essentiel, qu' on peut abstraire de là des principes comme reçus entre tous ceux qui ont formé des traités sur ces objects; 2. qu' il en est de même à l' égard des usages particuliers établis entre des états qui ont liê commerce ensemble; 3. que des usages une fois établis entre la plupart, surtout des grandes puissances de l' Europe, s' adoptent, et même s' imitent aisément par les autres, surtout par les moyens et petits états, en tant qu' il y a lieu pour ceux-ci; 4. les Puissances de l' Europe, en provoquant si souvent au droit des gens coutumier des nations civilisées, semblent lui accorder une force, qui ne suppose pas toujours la preuve particulière du fait de l' introduction de tel usage dans le rapport individuel, auquel il s' agit de l' appliquer; 5. Même, les traités, quoique obligatoires pour les seuls contractans, servent souvent de modele aux traités de ce genre à conclure avec d' autres puissances, d' où resulte une manière usitée de contracter. Quelquefois même, ce qui est règlé par traités avec telles puissances, s' observe avec d' autres par un simple usage, de sorte, qu' un même point, peut être de droit conventionnel pour les uns, et de droit coutumier pour les autres."

TRANSLATION.

"Idea, which ought to be formed, of the general and positive law of nations of Europe.

Nothing prevents us from imagining, that a majority of states, nay, even for instance, that all the states of Europe agree with each other, to fix better their reciprocal rights by general conventions, and even to enter into a confederacy in order to secure them. There would then be a code of the positive law of nations of Europe, fixed and obligatory upon all. But never have either the councils, or the numerous congresses of peace, such as those of Westphalia, of Utrecht, of Vienna, or of Aix la Chapelle, or the fruitless projects of an universal republic, produced such a general concluded convention, by the majority merely of the states of Europe. It is not, then, in this sense, that there exists a positive law of nations of Europe, or that, probably, it will ever exist."

"On the other hand, what belongs only to the particular treaties, or usages established in the individual relations between some states, is, as such, only obligatory upon the latter; and not upon the rest of nations, independently of the strength and number of either; there also does not exist any point, so uniformly regulated by each state, in its particular relations with each of the others, that the whole of these particular arrangements could be equivalent to a general convention."

"There may very well be formed, however, by abstraction, a theory of what is most generally practised between or among the powers and states of Europe; on considering, (1.) that in many points, the numerous particular treaties between powers, resemble each other so much, in what is essential, that there may be abstracted from them, principles, as received between or among all those, who have made treaties upon these objects; (2.) that it is the same, with regard to particular usages established between states, who are connected with each other in commerce; (3.) that usages once established among the majority, especially of the great powers of Europe, are easily adopted, and even imitated by the others, especially by the middle and smaller states, in so far as there is any room for the latter; (4.) the powers of Europe, in appealing so often to the consuetudinary law of civilized nations, seem to grant to it a force, which does not always suppose the particular proof, of the fact of the introduction of such a usage in the individual relation, to which it is required, (the business is) to apply it. (5.) Even treaties, although obligatory on the contracting parties only, serve often as a model for treaties of that kind to be concluded with other powers; whence results an usual mode of contracting. Sometimes, even what is regulated by treaties with such powers, is observed with others by a simple usage; so that one and the same point may be a matter of conventional law for some, and of consuetudinary law for others."

Now we do not at all object to our author's attempt to form by abstraction, out of treaties, a scientifically arranged system of the contents of these treaties, binding on the contracting parties, to the extent of their respective stipulations, and for the period of their endurance. This would be an unexceptionable, and an useful labour, as giving a scientific view of the actual conventional law of the European nations, properly so called. But we do seriously object and protest against his farther attempt, however ingenious, to rear up by abstraction, out of these treaties, which he admits, in § 58, are annulled by each successive war, unless renewed by the subsequent treaty of peace, a sort of law, which exists, after its parent has ceased to have any validity; which binds a nation, not merely towards the nations, with whom it has contracted, but in consequence of its having entered into such a treaty with one, two, or three other states, binds itself likewise towards other nations, with whom it has never so contracted; in short, a sort of general law, which, some how or other, rather mysteriously, arises out of treaties or conventions, and continues binding generally, although these treaties may never have been entered into, by the parties alleged to be bound, or may have ceased to have any validity. Such a doctrine is manifestly untenable.

All the possible effect of treaties is, to bind the contracting parties to the extent of their terms, and while they last; and to afford evidence of such and such agreements having been entered into at such and such times—of the views entertained by the parties on such occasions—of their conviction of the necessity or advantage of such treaties, for the attainment of objects conceived to be desirable, which could not be otherwise attained,—and of the habits or customs of nations to contract in certain modes generally, it is to be hoped, with the intention, but experience sometimes shows, without the intention, of executing the engagements undertaken by them, when the occasion arrives. A habit of contracting does not afford any ground for presuming a consent or liability, beyond the terms and the duration of the contract; else, why the necessity for the renewal of treaties? A habit or custom of contracting does not, like a habit of action, afford ground for presuming a general consent, or for holding the party bound generally, to enter into a similar contract with the same, or other states; as a habit of action does, for holding an individual or a state bound to receive from others, the treatment which it gives. In short, treaties contribute towards the formation of the common consuetudinary positive law of nations, only so far as they may afford evidence of the usual conduct of nations, independently of special paction.

But it is unnecessary here to push this argument any farther, at least against M. de Martens, since in the section just quoted, and in a note thereto subjoined, he admits "that there does not exist any point so uniformly regulated by each state, in its particular relations with each of the others, that the assemblage of these particular arrangements could be equivalent to a general convention; and that although the system of the armed neutrality, adopted in its time by so many powers, ap proaches nearer to this idea, it could not be held as received, even among the maritime powers only, for the relations of each with each among them; not speaking of England."

We proceed to notice the parts of this work, which relate to Maritime international law. In book I. chap. i. M. de Martens gives a short but distinct account of the law of nations, with regard to the straits of the sea, bays, gulfs, and adjacent seas, as being subject to jurisdiction, or territorial, and with regard to the open sea or oceans. In book IV. chap. iv., he gives a more full account of the rights of nations to the sea. In book VIII. chap. iv., he treats of the reciprocal rights of belligerent powers, respecting the mode of making war.

§ 280. "In continental wars, the enemy, in making himself master of a hostile province, becomes entitled to take possession of the domains and revenues of the state, of the fortresses, of the ships of war, and of every thing subservient to war. He may even in strictness appropriate the private effects, whether of the hostile sovereign, or of his subjects, so far as necessary for his satisfaction. And he may destroy the effects of the enemy, so far as subservient for the purposes of war, or so far as, if abandoned, they would strengthen the enemy, or when to spare them, would be injurious to military operations, or where the devastation of a country is necessary to deprive the enemy of subsistence on his march, or in reprisals. With these exceptions nearly, civilized nations have substituted for pillage and devastation, the practice of exacting war contributions, either in money, or in kind, under the penalty of military execution."

§ 281. "In maritime wars, in which private individuals cannot be reached by war contributions, as in wars on land, there has been preserved the rigorous right of seizing and carrying off the merchant vessels and their cargoes, belonging to peaceful subjects of the enemy, of condemning them as good prize, and of adjudging them to the ships of war or privateers, that have captured them, so that by the laws of most states, the captors are not allowed to release them, by means of ransom."

§ 282. "In continental wars, it has been pretty generally established, that if the effects have been twenty-four hours in the hands of the enemy, a third party may acquire them, by a valid title, and that all claim of restitution ceases. In maritime wars, the ancient principle of the Roman law, and of the Consolato del Mare, that the enemy becomes full proprietor, when his lawful prize has been conducted to a place of safety, (into a harbour, or the middle of a fleet) is still retained by several powers; but most of the European states have now adopted the principle, that the right of property passes from the ancient possessor to the captor, when the latter has remained twenty-four hours in the possession of his prize. § 289. The abuses almost inseparable from the arming of privateers, have sometimes caused their abolition to be talked of: but no attempt of this kind has hitherto succeeded."

In Book VIII., Chap. vii., M. de Martens treats of neutrality. § 305. Of the right to remain neutral. § 305. Of the obligation of the belligerent power. § 306, § 307. Neutrality, perfect and limited; conventional. § 308. Objects of neutrality. § 309. Assistance to belligerents. § 310, § 311, § 312. Principles of the universal, and of the positive law of nations, with regard to the neutral territory. § 313. Of neutral goods in the territory of the belligerent powers. § 314. Of neutral commerce, according to the universal law of nations. With regard to the important point of commerce in time of war, a belligerent power, 1, may prohibit its own subjects, and the inhabitants of the hostile provinces, of which it has taken possession, from all commerce whatever with the enemy; 2, may prohibit all commerce with or towards a hostile place, fortress, port, or camp, which it keeps so besieged or blockaded, that it is in a state to prevent the entry into them; and in all these cases, it may proceed to the confiscation of goods, ships, and even to severe penalties and death, against those who should attempt to carry on commerce with the enemy, in violation of these prohibitions. But the natural law does not authorize belligerent powers to prohibit, in general, neutrals from having commerce with the enemy, and to pronounce the confiscation of goods or vessels destined towards the enemy, as far as this commerce does not involve a violation of the duties of neutrality, or as far as there do not exist cases of urgency, so extraordinary, that the care of self-preservation becomes the first of all laws.

In the three following sections, Martens treats of the other leading points in Maritime international law, according to what he calls the natural law, or the universal law of nations; and we shall first quote the passages, and subjoin the remarks which they appear to require.

§ 315. "Of commerce in warlike stores. In time of peace the subjects of each nation have the natural liberty of carrying every kind of merchandise, to such nations as are disposed to trade with them. A neutral power does not lose this right by a rupture occurring between two nations; so that, continuing the bonds of friendship with each of them, it may continue also to permit that commerce, without distinction, even between the kind of merchandise with which it is carried on. And farther, if the war opens new speculations for its commerce and its navigation, it is not always a departure from the sentiments of neutrality, to profit by them, while it is the allurement of gain alone, that guides the merchant to the places where he finds purchasers."

"The neutral nation only violates the natural duties of neutrality, of which the essential character is impartiality, 1, if it permits its subjects to carry warlike stores to one of the belligerent powers, prohibiting them from doing so to the other; 2, if it violates the engagement undertaken to one of the belligerent powers, not to permit the conveyance of warlike stores to the ports of the enemy of the latter; 3, if not confining itself to the permission of this commerce to its subjects, it sends itself, warlike stores to one of the belligerent powers, tending to reinforce it; and thus shows a partiality, of which it often attempts in vain to conceal the exterior, by offering the same supplies to the other belligerent power."

"In these cases of the violation of neutrality, the belligerent power that suffers from them, may not only confiscate such goods and such vessels of neutral powers, but may even gradually go to the length of declaring war against such an ally, open or concealed, of his enemies."

Nevertheless, while, excepting these cases, the belligerent power is not authorized according to the natural law, to confiscate the ships and their cargoes, destined for the open ports of his enemy, and with, or in which commerce ought to remain free for all nations, without judging of the motives which guide the subjects of a neutral power, in their commerce with the enemy, it cannot see with indifference, that the latter is reinforced —strengthened by goods which serve directly and indubitably the purposes of war; and it does not infringe the law of nations, if it prevents these goods from reaching the enemy, by detaining them—either paying the value thereof to the proprietor, or restoring them, when the danger is past. Cases may even be imagined, in which extraordinary circumstances might justify such a detention of goods, which are not so exclusively subservient to the purposes of war, and over which it cannot regularly or usually, arrogate any power of disposal."

In this section, Martens endeavours to exemplify the distinction he made at the outset of his work, between the natural law, or the universal law of nations, and the positive law of nations. Now of the latter, it is easy to form a pretty correct notion of what is meant, as being what is actually observed and enforced among independent states in their intercourse with each other. But by the former it is not so easy to understand precisely, what is meant. It is evidently a law, not arising from the acts of men, but from nature, that is, the act of the Creator in forming the constitution of the human race, as individuals united in civil societies or states, and as states, having relations to, and intercourse with, each other, occupying different portions of this earth as territories, and thus placed so far in similar, so far in different circumstances, with certain limited powers bestowed on them. But what is meant by the universal law of nations, is not so clear. The universality, of course, is limited to the nations of this earth. But to embrace even all these, the rules must be very general, and not extended into ramifications; since they must embrace and be applicable to all the nations and tribes of men at present in existence, however much they may vary, from their being in different successive stages in the career of civilization. But the collection or aggregate of the general and simple rules, which may thus be applicable indiscriminately to all nations, rude as well as refined, obviously do not constitute the universal law here meant by Martens; for he considers it as applicable to the various cases which occur in modern maritime warfare, among the most civilized nations that have yet existed.

At the outset of his work, § 5, Martens informs us "the law of nations is called natural, universal, and necessary, inasmuch as its precepts are derived from (puisés dans) reason alone, as they are obligatory on all nations; and as it depends not on the will of these nations to depart from them. Yet, in § 6, he goes on to say: "If two nations have intercourse with each other, and wish to establish a regular commerce, the simple natural law would no more be sufficient for them. Different motives may induce them sometimes to mitigate the rigour of the natural law, sometimes to determine doubtful points, or to regulate the points, which it (the natural law) passes over in silence, sometimes even to depart from that reciprocity of rights, which the universal law establishes equally for all nations. It is the total or aggregate of these determinations, which forms the external public law, or law of nations, positive, peculiar, (proper) particular, and voluntary, of these two nations; and, according as it rests either upon conventions, whether express or tacit, or upon simple usage, it may be divided into conventional and consuetudinary.

Now there is here manifestly a good deal of ambiguity, inconsistency, and confusion For, if the simple natural law, the universal law of nations, be not sufficient to regulate the commercial intercourse of two nations, how can it be sufficient, as applied by Martens in the section under consideration, to determine the nice questions involved in the commercial intercourse of neutrals with belligerents in time of war? And the only way of elucidating the obscurity which thus prevails in the writings, not only of Martens, but of many other international jurists, seems to be, by holding that they recognize two significations of the terms, the natural or universal law of nations.

In the first place, they recognize a simple natural and universal law of nations, whether rude or civilized, and therefore very general, and yet limited. And the rules of this law they derive from the relations which naturally exist among independent tribes or nations, about the time they become agricultural, and settle in particular territories. And this simple law of nations arising in, and formed as applicable to, comparatively rude times, of course, requires extension, mitigation, and improvement, by conventions and usages, when nations become commercial and manufacturing, and what is called more civilized. But such a simple and comparatively rude law of nations can never, it is plain, be held as a standard for determining the difficult particular questions between neutrals and belligerents in modern times.

In the second place, however, Martens and many other international jurists, appear likewise to recognize under the terms, natural and universal law of nations, another notion, the aggregate of the various juridical relations, rules, rights and obligations, which gradually arise among nations, as independent states, in the course of their advancement through the different stages of progressive civilization. Such relations, rules, rights and obligations, arise naturally, and exist independently of the acts, or voluntary arrangements of men. And the chief object of the positive law of nations, is to enforce and give effect to these rules, rights and obligations, in the intercourse of states and their subjects. As the relative successive circumstances, in which nations are placed, vary, the application of the rule, and the resulting right or obligation, may also vary.

These relations, rules, rights and obligations, are discovered by observation, and ascertained by experience. And in investigating and deducing the principles, any attempt to be extremely minute, would probably be of little avail, since, in order to be universally, or (to speak less hyperbolically) generally applicable to the number and variety of individual cases or questions, the rule itself must be general. Indeed, it rather appears it would be vain to attempt any more particular enumeration of principles or maxims, than those mentioned in the first chapter of this work, or what is comprehended under the terms compulsory justice, reciprocity, and general expediency, with equity in maintaining proportional distribution, and in alleviating the application of general rules to individual cases. And, according to such an interpretation as this, of what is understood by the natural and universal law of nations, we have no objection to its being assumed as a standard or criterion, for judging of what ought to be observed and enforced as the positive law of nations, in such cases as those here considered by Martens. With this explanation, we acquiesce in the doctrine delivered by Martens in the section last quoted; but with the exception, and under the protest, that a government allowing its subjects to carry arms or other warlike stores to one of two belligerents, although solely for the purpose of mercantile profit, is, by the natural and universal law of nations, inconsistent with that impartiality which is the essence of neutrality. The selling such articles in the neutral country, to the belligerent state or its subjects, who may send for, or come to purchase them there, is the extreme verge of neutral right. To take a lowly and familiar example;—if two men were fighting with their natural corporeal weapons,—boxing with their fists,—what human being would say a third person acted with impartiality, who, though for an adequate price, handed to the one of the combatants a bludgeon or a sword? yet the cases are quite parallel.

In § 316, Martens thus inquires whether the vessel

covers or confiscates the cargo. "There can be no doubt that the enemy may confiscate hostile vessels and their hostile cargoes. But since war does not authorize the exercise of hostilities in a *neutral place*, it *seems* that even the natural law prohibits the seizure of hostile goods, innocent in their quality, which are *met with* on *board* a *neutral* vessel, and for a stronger reason, the confiscation of the vessel; and that as the war does not authorize us to appropriate the goods of the subjects of a state, with which we are at peace, although found in a hostile place, it is equally prohibited to confiscate the neutral cargo of a hostile vessel; so that the natural law would be sufficient to establish the principle, that the vessel covers the cargo, (frey Schiff, frey gut) but that it does not confiscate the cargo: verfallenes Schiff macht nicht verfallenes gut. It must, however, be admitted, that the opinion opposite to the first of these principles; namely, that according to the natural law, regard must be had to the property of the cargo, rather than to that of the vessel, is not in want of specious arguments to support it; and that a simple theory will never be sufficient to reconcile nations upon a point, with regard to which their interests are not the same."

Now, that the conveyance of neutral goods in a hostile vessel, affords no valid ground in law, for the seizure and confiscation of these goods, we quite agree with M. de Martens. And such, we have seen, has been the general practice of nations from the ages preceding the Consolato del Mare, and of England for centuries past. But we cannot admit that he expounds correctly the natural law of nations, when he maintains, that the fact of being carried in a neutral vessel in the open seas, is valid in law, to protect hostile goods from seizure and confiscation by the opposed belligerents. Indeed, like Surland, Martens states this doctrine chiefly in a negative way, and with great diffidence; "il semble, que la Loi naturelle defend," &c. And as his argument proceeds solely on the theory of the hostile goods being in a *neutral place*, when on board a neutral merchant vessel, it obviously rests on a mere fiction or fallacy; namely, that of a merchant vessel in the wide ocean, being an extension, or piece of the territory of the neutral state, to the subjects of which the vessel belongs in property. This fiction and fallacy we have already frequently exposed. It has been refuted by Rutherforth, Lampredi, and Tetens, and laughed at by Schmalz and even Schmelzing. To have any valid foundation in natural law, rights must rest on truth and fact, not on fiction or imaginary analogies and conceits. A merchant vessel in the open sea, or its flag, has manifestly none of the qualities or attributes, which characterize the stable and immoveable territory of a state. Accordingly, Martens is forced to admit, that the opposite opinion to what he has laid down with such hesitation, may be supported by specious, he might have said valid and well founded arguments; such as that in determining the property of the cargo, the cargo itself ought to be regarded, not the vessel; and that, if, as he argues, the vessel or vehicle cannot alter the nature of the cargo, or convert neutral goods into hostile, as little can it convert hostile goods into neutral.

A simple theory, he justly observes, will not reconcile nations that have opposite interests. But while the opinion he supports is the hypothetical theory, the opposite opinion is the true theory, being founded in fact. Farther repetition, however, on this head, is superfluous. And it would, perhaps, be tasking human nature, and expecting too much, that M. de Martens, a native of Hamburgh, should admit the fallacy of the doctrine, which, we have seen, the Hanse towns in former ages laboured so long to establish.

In § 317, Martens thus treats of the visitation of vessels met with at sea. "The simple neutral flag hoisted by a merchant vessel met with at sea, affording no sufficient proof that she is not hostile, the natural law cannot refuse to the belligerent powers the right of visiting the merchant vessels, which their ships of war or privateers meet with, in a place where it would be permitted to seize the hostile vessel; and consequently, to bring into port such vessels, if the proof adduced, that they are not subject to confiscation, be insufficient. But, according to the universal law of nations, the decision of the litigation arising between the subjects of the two nations upon the legality of the prize, should belong to neither of them exclusively; and if an amicable adjustment does not take place, there should be established a mixed tribunal to adjudge the question.

In this section, Martens resumes his good sense, by admitting, that as the neutral flag affords no evidence of the neutrality of the vessel, visitation is necessary to ascertain whether the vessel be hostile. But he urges the necessity of establishing a mixed tribunal of judges. The inefficacy, if not incompetency, of such a tribunal, and its practical disadvantages even for neutrals, our quotations from Lampredi and Tetens have already shown, as the convictions of able jurists living in countries usually neutral. And in point of authority, Martens merely refers to Hübner, the professed advocate of neutral traders, adding, that the impartial Lampredi is opposed to him.

In the sections from § 318 to § 323 inclusive, Martens treats of the principles of the positive law, anterior to the first system of the armed neutrality. And these sections we shall transcribe, as they state concisely, and upon the whole correctly the progress of the law, with some material exceptions, which, of course, we shall remark.

§ 318. "The positive law of nations has modified some of the principles before expounded, leaving others to exist entire. It is thus, that without generally prohibiting neutrals from selling at home every kind of goods, and even warlike stores, to the individual purchaser who presents himself, it is considered, by the avowal of all the nations of Europe, as contrary to neutrality to permit their subjects to convey to the ports of one of the two, or of both belligerents, certain commodities designated by the name of contraband of war. With regard to the question, what are goods of this kind? the treaties to which we must pay attention in the first place, do not answer it with uniformity; but the greatest part of them confine contraband to objects which are directly subservient to war, and of which the use is not doubtful; such as arms, bullets, bombs, &c., gunpowder, soldiers, horses, and their articles of equipment, and ships of war; often also saltpetre and sulphur, declaring free the other goods, and sometimes particularly provisions, wood for building vessels, cables, pitch and tar, hemp, sails and other materials for marine purposes, and coined money."

"In the absence of treaties, the powers, when they were neutral, maintained, long before 1780, that the goods of the first kind alone could be considered and treated as contraband by the belligerents. But in comparing attentively the principles, which several of these powers, who were the first to accede to the system of the armed neutrality, then put forward, with those, which they maintained during periods, when they were powerful by sea, and at war, it cannot be dissembled, that principles have often been modified according to interests."

"When belligerent powers began, by the end of the sixteenth century, to issue ordinances or proclamations, in order to extend uni-laterally, the catalogue of goods, of which they allowed themselves the confiscation or detention, this gave rise to reiterated complaints, as well on the part of the powers, who had treaties to allege in their favour, as on the part even of other neutral powers. And if the middle-sized and smaller states, sometimes conformed to these ordinances, by prohibiting their subjects from carrying to the enemy, the goods comprised in these lists, this does not prove they believed themselves obliged to do so."

In § 319, Martens goes on to state the penalty inflicted on commerce in goods contraband of war. "With regard to the goods, which, according to the rule, are to be considered as contraband, the belligerent power that seizes them, believes itself authorized to confiscate them. In former times, they often confiscated even the vessel which was loaded with them in whole, or in part. Now a days, almost all the treaties of commerce bear, that, regularly, there shall be confiscated only the contraband goods, permitting the vessel to continue her voyage, with the remainder of the cargo; and that the neutral vessel shall either never be confiscated, or only in some particular cases. Towards the nations, however, with whom this point has not been regulated by treaty, the conduct of the belligerent powers has not been always uniform, especially if the greater part of the cargo, or the whole cargo consisted of contraband. With regard to the goods which the belligerent power admits, are not properly or indubitably contraband, it sometimes confines itself to detaining them, offering to pay the neutral proprietor the value and the freight."

On the account given by Martens, in these sections, of contraband goods, we cannot help remarking, it is far from satisfactory: partly because it is rested chiefly on treaties, which may be, and frequently are, of very short duration, besides being binding only on the contracting parties, and not sufficient to establish any general rule; partly because it does not show, what, independently of treaties, is the positive law of nations, with regard to contraband of war. For that, independently of such treaties, there exists a positive international law on this subject, a law actually observed in practice, founded on reason, and on the natural law of nations, we have already seen, in reviewing the works of Lampredi and Tetens, and the judgments of Lord Stowell, to which we beg to refer.

In § 320, Martens next treats of commerce with blockaded places. The positive as well as the natural law of nations, authorize the belligerent power to prohibit all commerce with a place, which it holds blockaded, and to punish by the confiscation of the vessel and the cargo, and even by corporal pains, those who shall deliberately contravene this prohibition. But even before 1780, there were disputes about the notion of a blockaded place; often arbitrarily extended by the belligerent power." What is the correct idea of a blockade, and what the undue extension thereof, sometimes attempted, we have repeatedly had occasion to consider.

In § 321, Martens thus treats of visitation at sea. "In order to watch over the maintenance of the right of belligerent powers, to prevent the illicit commerce of neutrals, or that of the enemy, which is carried on under their flag, it has been hitherto universally recognized and sanctioned in almost all treaties of commerce, that when a ship of war or privateer meets a merchant vessel, the latter, after having been required by a summons to come to, must, under the penalty of being confiscated, undergo the visitation; that is to say, that he must show his ship's papers to the person or persons who are sent for that purpose; that if these ship's papers prove that the vessel and the cargo are exempt from confis cation, or if the vessel offers to give up the confiscable part of the cargo, she must be allowed to continue her voyage; but that if this proof be insufficient, or if the vessel refuses to give up the suspected part, or if the vessel which arrests cannot take it on board, the latter is entitled to take the former into a port, to have the legality of the prize adjudicated. But in more recent times, the question has been raised, whether this visitation can take place with regard to a vessel, which hoists the military flag of a friendly nation, or with regard to merchant vessels sailing under the convoy of a friendly power; or whether in those cases, the ship of war or privateer, is bound to look to the flag alone, or to be satisfied with the declaration solely of the ship of war which acts as convoy, that these vessels are neutral, and are not loaded with contraband."

On this section we may remark, that the mode of proceeding here narrated, is not founded on commercial treaties only of doubtful duration, but on reason in the actual circumstances, on the natural law of nations, in the more extensive sense before explained—on general usage, independently of special treaty; in other words, upon the common consuetudinary law of nations. With regard to the question, how far, independently of treaty, the protection of a convoy should limit the examination into the legality of the commerce, carried on by neutral merchants, we may refer to the impartial opinion of Tetens, formerly recited, as well as to Schlegel and Croke.

In § 322, Martens thus treats of the adjudication of prizes. "Although it is recognized in Europe, that the captor has no right whatever to dispose of his prize, until she has been adjudged to him, usage and treaties ascribe the jurisdiction in the disputes, which arise in this respect, between the captor and the claimants, to the sovereign of the captor alone, even when the latter has been forced to take his prize into the port of a third power. And although the courts of admiralty acknowledge, that it is according to treaties; and, in their absence, according to the general or universal law of nations, and not according to the particular or municipal law of their country, that they ought to judge, the unilateral interpretation of treaties, and the diversity of the principles, which, in their absence, are adopted as the law of nations, offer a vast field for the complaints of neutral powers, against the procedure and the decisions of these tribunals, whether upon the merits of the cause, or touching the admission of farther proofs, or touching the subjection in expenses of process, often enormous," &c. On this section we have only to remark, that while we regret these complaints of neutrals are too often well founded; they are also very often to be attributed to the fraudulent devices of neutral speculators and adventurers, and are frequently groundless, or made, not by honest bonâ fide neutrals, but by enemies under the semblance of neutrality. And it is singular, that Martens should here refer chiefly to controversial writers, such as Tötze, Steck, and to his own treatise on privateers, and that, although he was so many years Professor in the University of Göttingen, he should take no notice whatever of the judgments of Lord Stowell.

In § 323, Martens enquires, whether by the positive law of nations, the vessel covers the cargo. "But the question, whether the vessel covers, and whether it confiscates the cargo, has not always been determined in Europe in the same way. Down to the seventeenth century, the regulation of the Consolato del Mare, chap. 273, which has regard only to the property of the merchandise, and not to that of the vessel, was almost universally adopted in Europe, as well in the concluded treaties, as in general, in the tribunals which adjudicated prizes; so that the vessel did not cover the cargo. But the progress of commerce having shown, how hurtful and burdensome this principle is to neutral powers, there began in the seventeenth century, to be introduced by treaty, the opposite rule, agreeing that the vessel covers the cargo; but agreeing also, that the confiscation of the hostile vessel, carries and involves the confiscation of the cargo, though neutral; and these treaties have been multiplied in such a manner, that there remains only a small number of treaties, in which the ancient rule is expressly preserved: and some others, in which still different modifications have been adopted. The question, however, whether this new rule ought also to be followed in relation to the powers, with which there has been no treaty, or with whom the treaties do not decide the principle, is differently viewed, and has long divided England, and many of the other powers." Martens adds, § 344, note. "The question whether Great Britain ought to adopt, as a general rule, the principle frequently introduced in Europe since the seventeenth century, that the vessel covers the cargo, rests upon another doubtful and disputed question; namely, which of the two principles is conformable to the natural law."

Now, while we entirely acquit M. de Martens, of any intention in this section to deceive or mislead, we cannot avoid observing, that the statement it contains is to a great extent incorrect and fallacious. It is not true that the principle of the Consolato del Mare, admitted by Martens to have been universally adopted in Europe, and observed for centuries, had regard only to the property of the goods, and not to that of the vessel. On perusal, it will be found that the principle recognized or recorded in the earliest collection of maritime usages now extant, which bears the title of Consolato del Mare, or Costumbres Maritimas, actually had regard to the property of the vessel, as well as to that of the merchandise. It enquired and ascertained what was the property of the vessel, that is, to whom it belonged in property; condemned it if hostile, and exempted it, if friendly or neutral. It next enquired and ascertained what was the property of the cargo, that is, to whom the goods belonged in property; subjected them to confiscation, if they belonged to the enemy, and released or restored them, if they belonged to friends or neutrals. It was neither so unjust nor so absurd as to judge of the property of the cargo, *not* from the cargo itself, but from that of the vessel, or of the property of the vessel —not from the vessel itself, but from that of the cargo. The rule of the Consolato was, and is, the only mode of distributing justice. But this distribution of justice, it appears, was found hurtful and burdensome to neutrals; and the opposite rule was therefore introduced, to screen the property of the enemy, and to confiscate the property of friends.

But in what manner, and to what extent was this alleged change of the law brought about? Martens himself admits, it was introduced solely by treaty and convention. And we have seen in the first volume of this work, how strenuously, first the Hanse towns, and afterwards the Dutch and other nations, chiefly interested in the carrying trade, the commerce de fret, struggled for the adoption of a rule, which they found, or believed to be, more advantageous for themselves, and how the Dutch succeeded in persuading various powers to agree to the insertion of that rule in treaties. And so far as the rule was inserted in these treaties, it was binding while they continued in force. But its insertion in these treaties could not bind any others than the contracting parties, or beyond the terms of these treaties, or after they expired, or were annulled by supervening hostilities; it could not constitute a rule advantageous only for one party, and detrimental to another, a part of the natural or common consuetudinary law of nations. If it had been a portion of the common natural law of nations, it would *not* have required temporary treaties and special pactions to introduce it. It would have found its way into general usage, without any treaties, as the rule which preceded it confessedly did.

Farther, while he admits the new law was introduced by treaty, Martens can here find no other foundation for it, than the multiplication of treaties containing the provision, so as to form the great majority of treaties bearing reference to the subject. He does not show, that the new law is founded in justice, reciprocity, or general expediency. On the contrary, he dismisses, as untenable in justice, the half of the alleged new law, which confiscates the property of a friend, because he has put it on board of the vessel of his friend, who happens to be our enemy. And, if it be unjust to judge of the property of a friend by the quality of the vessel, or other vehicle, in which it is carried, it is equally unjust to deprive another friend of his right to take the property in question, by holding it to belong, not to the person to whom it really belongs, but to another, against whom that other friend has no claim. Neither does Martens show, in point of fact, that the exemption thus claimed for the goods of the enemy, rests upon any prior occupancy by a state, having this jurisdiction, and a right to interfere. A neutral state has no power over the effects of either belligerent, no right to interpose between them. The only argument is founded on the fiction, that a neutral vessel in the open sea, is a part of, or equivalent to, the land territory of a neutral state, which is manifestly contrary to the fact.

As little has Martens shown that the new law has been followed by any nation, except under the treaties by which they had bound themselves. On the contrary, we have seen, that, independently of the treaties concluded in the latter part of the seventeenth, and in the earlier part of the eighteenth century, all nations continued to follow the former rule, with regard to all other nations than those with whom they had so contracted, and frequently even with regard to them. The ancient common consuetudinary law of nations, therefore, was not substantially changed. It remained the same and entire, except when departed from, or modified by special paction. And Martens was not warranted in saying the new law was substituted for the old, except to the extent of these treaties; just as the internal common law, or jurisprudence of a people, is affected by the contracts which individuals make with each other. In short, this new rule rests solely on the multiplication of treaties. But even this limited and unstable foundation, this mere scaffolding, has fallen from under the new theory. For, as formerly shown, the treaties founded on, so far as Great Britain is concerned, have expired, or have been annulled by infringements committed by the opposite contracting parties, or have been terminated by intervening hostilities, and not renewed.

In the sections from § 324 to § 326 inclusive, Martens treats of the origin and the principles of the armed neutrality in 1780, of the adoption of that system by various powers, of the new association for its renewal in 1800, of its abandonment by Russia by the convention of 1801, and of its final cessation, or de facto dissolution. But, on this subject, we have already discoursed perhaps at too great length, as the system has ceased to form any part, even of the conventional international law of Europe. And although we conceive we can detect an error or two in the narrative, they are not so material, as to require animadversion.

In § 326, Martens gives the following brief, but more correct account, than that of Klüber, of neutral commerce, from the year 1803, of the continental system of the French Emperor, and of the British retaliatory Orders in council. "If, notwithstanding the efforts of so many of the European powers to arrive at a universal maritime code, which might serve as a rule for ages to come, the maritime powers remained divided in opinion upon several individual points touching the extent of the liberty of neutral commerce, they were at least all at one upon the principle founded on the natural law, that no belligerent power is entitled to prohibit other nations, neutral or armed, from having any commerce whatever with its enemy, or even from having any traffic in the productions of the latter. And, although before the end of the eighteenth century, we find some instances of attempts made to prevent all commerce by neutrals with the enemy, they at least remained without effect, or had been promptly abandoned. It was reserved for the commencement of the nineteenth century, to make astonished Europe feel, by experience, to what length the contempt of the law of nations could lead a fortunate conqueror in his rage against the enemy, who alone still seemed to oppose his ambitious projects, to give law to the world."

"The vain attempts at descents by the French upon England, the fruitless projects of attacking the English in India, through Egypt, projects baffled before, but pursued after the peace of Amiens, down to the new rupture which took place in 1803, and still more the victory of Trafalgar, 21st October 1805, made the Ruler of France alter his plans for the ruin of English commerce. Aided by the astonishing successes gained by him in 1805 and 1806, over Austria, Italy, Germany and Prussia, the French Emperor promulgated the Berlin decree of the 21st November 1806, of which the principles, faintly concealed under the veil of reprisals, bore, that the British Isles are declared in a state of blockade, all commerce and all correspondence with them interdicted, every individual Englishman in the countries occupied by France or her allies, declared prisoner of war, all English property declared good prize, all commerce in English merchandise prohibited, every vessel having touched England, excluded from the continental ports."

"This decree, promulgated in all the states occupied by France, and communicated to the allies, provoked the Order of the English government of the 7th January 1807, bearing a prohibition of commerce from one to another of the ports belonging to France, or to her allies, or which might be occupied by them, or under their influence; and this order having been made stronger by that of the 11th November 1807, the French Emperor, rising above the measures of the Berlin decree, promulgated that of Milan of 17th December 1807, bearing, 1, that every vessel which shall have suffered the visitation of an English vessel, or shall have submitted to a voyage to England, or shall have paid any impost whatever to government, is by that alone declared de-nationalised, to have become English property, and to be good prize; 2, that the British Isles are declared in a state of blockade, by sea as by land, and every vessel fitted out in ports subject to the English, or going thither, is good prize."

"These violent measures, however," continues our author, "by which the Emperor put himself in opposition to all the principles of civilization, did not produce the desired effect, although the Emperor, in all his treaties of peace, concluded at this period with other powers, had imposed on them the condition of shutting their ports against the English, and although he had promoted the object by farther decrees, and on the other hand, endeavoured to reap advantage from it by means of licenses. After the loss of almost all the French colonies, he still believed he could give a mortal blow to the colonial commerce of Great Britain, by charging (by the decree and tariff of Trianon of 5th August 1810,) with an enormous contribution, the entry of colonial produce; and to complete the measure of unheard of acts of violence, he ordered, by the decree of Fontainbleau of 19th October 1810, that all English merchandise should be burned in France, in Italy, and in all the states subdued or occupied by France. And after having succeeded in causing the whole of these measures, known under the name of the continental system, to be adopted by the states in alliance with France, and by the most part of the friendly states, he must have expected to be approaching near to the accomplishment of his object, if measures so unnatural could lead to it. But providence put a stop to these excesses; and in blessing, in 1813, the arms of the powers who united to release Europe from the yoke, which oppressed it, made the cause of liberty and that of the law of nations to triumph. The continental system adopted every where with regret, and already abandoned in 1812, by Prussia and Sweden, in their treaties with Great Britain, was then every where promptly proscribed."

We have thus been led to extend our critical remarks on the maritime department of the general work of Martens, much farther than we originally intended, or could have wished. But the reasons are obvious. For this treatise is not a mere controversial writing of the day, but a systematic work, bearing ex facie and ostensibly to be a scientific impartial exposition of the Droit des Gens de l' Europe Moderne; and, although it can never supersede Grotius, Bynkershoek, and Vattel, is likely, from its being more recent, and from its brevity and facility of acquisition, to be more generally perused, and to have a more extended influence. Although professedly impartial, however, this systematic work appeared to us to contain several incorrect representations in point of fact, and several erroneous conclusions in point of law. And against these, it seemed necessary, to put the student of law, and also the general historical reader, on his guard.

CHAPTER IX.

Review of part of the work of F. J. Jacobsen, entitled, Seerecht des Friedens und des Krieges im bezug auf die Kauffahrteischiffahrt, 1815.

Of the treatises which appeared about the commencement of this period, one of the most practical and useful is that of Jacobsen the Danish lawyer. In 1804–1805, he had published at Hamburgh, Handbuch über das Practische Seerecht der Engländer und Franzosen in Hinsicht auf das von ihnen in Kriegzeiten angehaltene neutral Eigenthum; a manual on the practical maritime law of the English and French, with reference to what was held by them to be neutral property in time of war. And towards the end of 1814, he published at Altona, the more valuable work before alluded to, entitled, Seerecht des Friedens und des Krieges in bezug auf Kauffahrteischiffahrt, laws of the sea, with reference to maritime commerce during peace and war; which was translated by Mr. Wm. Frick, American counsellor at law, and in 1815, published at Baltimore. Of this work, by far the greatest part, namely, books first, second, and third, are almost entirely devoted to the private law of maritime commerce, of which we have treated historically elsewhere. But chapter iii. of book IV., which treats of the legal relations and papers in capture, and chapter iv. of book IV., section ii., which treats of military salvage and ransom, contain a great deal of sound doctrine in Maritime international law. And we consider the author well entitled to the following eulogy bestowed on him by Dr. Hoffman, in his "Course of legal study." "This work is particularly valuable on three accounts: first, it is eminently practical; its learned author having collected his facts during a long professional experience, and from a correspondence maintained with the most distinguished maritime jurists of Europe: secondly, M. Jacobsen was a civilian of great learning, equally well acquainted with the legal literature of ancient and modern times, and of all nations: and lastly, his work is based on no overweening attachment to any theory of international law, but derives its facts and principles from the maritime regulations and conduct of all nations, and educes from the whole a system of maritime jurisprudence, remarkable for candour, justice, and reciprocal concession."[1]

While with a view to practice, and particularly with a view to the safety of neutrals, he gives an account of the administration of the Maritime international law adopted or observed by the different European governments, Jacobsen, at the same time, marks the deviations from the correct principles of that law, which have taken place in that administration, either generally or on particular occasions, on the part of these governments. In noticing these deviations, like Tetens, he does so with the intelligence, independence, and impartiality of a mind of a higher order. And it is gratifying to an inhabitant of this country to find the judgments of Sir Wm. Scott, so often quoted by this truly respectable foreigner, not merely as showing the practice of the British maritime prize courts, but as consistent with,

[1] Vol. II. p. 471.

and illustrative of, the genuine principles of international justice. With reference to some of the more important of these principles, it may be proper to recite at some length, the doctrines laid down by the author.

In book IV. chapter iii., after quoting the remark of Sir Leoline Jenkins, that privateers are like the astrologers of ancient Rome, every one condemns them, but whenever occasion offers, every one makes use of them, the author proceeds thus: "The passions which generally precede a declaration of war, so far from enabling us to look to the practical event and issue of it, and inducing us to establish rules and principles of war, not more rigorous than we should sanction in a state of peace, rather encourage the practice of privateering; and independent of these, there are other grounds in favour of them."

1. "If, at the commencement of a war, a government has but few national vessels, privateering, as formerly among the Netherlanders, is among the best means of acquiring larger vessels of war; and, like skirmishing on land, is a school of practice in warfare. Many naval heroes of Dutch and French history, are the pupils of this school. A government should look upon this as the more exalted aim of private maritime warfare; and in the prosecution of a war, sanction no petty privateers."

2. "As it has been a principle of every age and nation, to permit a trade with the enemy, only under special license of the government, private cruizers are the best adapted to restrain it. Their interest to scrutinize every case, is the best security, that a government has no need to inflict a more rigorous penalty upon a prohibited trade, than confiscation; because care is taken that the threatened confiscation of the law does not become a nugatory provision."

3. "Privateering makes the war, to some extent, a

war of the people; and assists a portion of the people to bear the burdens of the war."

4. "Privateering assists the government to bear the burdens of the war."

5. "As long as the one power, against whom a government wars, encourages privateering, the right of retaliation justifies and forces it on the part of the other."

"All those arguments, with the exception of the last, inasmuch as their objects can only be imperfectly attained, are incompetent to supersede the following objections, which go to restrain, and ultimately to destroy the beneficial effects of privateering."

1. "The guarantees against the abuse of private commissions, can rarely be more effectual, than they have hitherto been, by existing laws; and will always remain inadequate to the real injuries, which a private cruizer may inflict upon the captured."

2. "Most owners of privateers, instead of applying their profits to larger and more extensive equipments for the war, dissipate them upon subjects of luxury, setting an example of prodigality and licentiousness, which is doubly deleterious in a state of war."

3. "As the subject of decision in maritime controversies is most frequently valuable, it opens a door to bribery on the part of him, whose hopes are most desperate, whether captor or captured. If the captured return with their property restored, a bribe is one of the articles of the account rendered; and while the bribery is unknown in the country, where it either has been, or is pretended to have taken place, it is accredited by foreigners. This case is rare in captures made by national or state vessels."

4. "The commanders of national ships, bred in the school of honour, seldom violate the maritime laws, as private cruizers do; whose real or pretended injuries

frequently involve their government in disputes with other nations."

5. "If disputes arise out of captures by national vessels, a government has always more power to repair the injuries, resulting from the conduct of her captors, if so disposed, than to bring private captors to account for their conduct, which is for the most part ineffectual."

6. "Private cruizing too easily degenerates into privateering pro formâ; that is, merchants avail themselves of it, to give their commerce with the enemy an armed protection. If they, and the officers of the ports which they frequent, understand each other, the evil is difficult of prevention."

"From these and other principles," continues Jacobsen, "the period will probably arrive, when our posterity shall be blessed with the renunciation of this species of private warfare; and with the adoption of other and more liberal and humane principles, affecting the neutrality of hospitals during war, and the like."

In the hope of this event, although we are apprehensive not likely to take place soon, we sincerely concur with the author, as more equal and just, than any of the nostrums which neutral traders, and their interested supporters, have suggested, such as the fiction of holding the national character of the cargo, to be determined by the national character of the vessel.

In book IV. chap. iii. Jacobsen proceeds. "In a period of maritime war, nothing can be more important to a state, as involving national honour, its relations with other powers, and the prospects of indemnity and safety for the future, than the judicious selection of those, who are to preside over prize courts. * * * After the choice of judges, the next care of belligerent nations should be, to give the greatest possible publicity to the decisions of their prize courts; and that the grounds of decision in every case, but more particularly between a foreigner and a native, should be fully set forth in the report of the decision. * * * Nothing is more unfair in monarchies, as well as in republics, than to scrutinize too closely, what counsel, in their zeal for truth and justice, may have too forcibly or too incautiously expressed, in defending the interest of a client; and ex officio to investigate its merit or demerit, without any regard to this connection; conceiving, as we do, that the first quality which entitles a lawyer to our respect, is his independence of mind. * * * It is not to be denied, that theoretical views and scientific acquirements, connected with this branch of legislation, are highly useful and desirable; but experience teaches, that the more simple the laws and regulations of commerce and navigation are, the more beneficial are the consequences. It were, therefore, desirable, that the same class of merchants, who have retired from business with reputation and experience, and who, in independent states, are called to take a share in the regulation and direction of maritime commerce, should also in monarchies, be called to participate in a service for which they are best qualified."

In book IV. chapter iii., the author proceeds thus: "As we are now about to advert to the principles of maritime warfare, which regulate, and will remain the practice of national vessels, whatever may be the fate of privateering, we feel authorized (even though the declaration be found dissonant with our former opinions,) to declare, after a length of experience, as a practising advocate, that we hold the principle of 'free ship, free goods,' less conducive to essential justice, than the principle of the Consolato, that an enemy's property on board a neutral ship is confiscable; and that much more injustice may arise, where every thing depends upon the regularity or irregularity of the papers, than from the practice of England, which investigates the real essence of the transaction."

"It appears to us, that the doctrine of England relative to the question, neutral or not neutral, depends generally upon the harmony between the examination of the crew, and the ship's papers; and how imperfect soever the proofs adduced to establish the property, yet the party is entitled to farther proof; that is, to the exposure of the whole transaction, by the production of the correspondence, extracts from the books, and examination of the clerks, &c., provided the party has acted bonâ fide; but if the party has been grossly in malâ fide, the question, neutral or not neutral, depends exclusively upon the papers and the examination of the crew, however unsatisfactory the result."

"We would recommend the universal adoption and application of the following principles, which we subjoin from different prize decisions." (The principles here selected by Jacobsen, are taken from the Decisions du Conseil des Prises, under the direction of the eminent French lawyer, Portalis, as well as from Robinson's Reports.)

"Prize laws severe in their operation, should be interpreted restrictively."

"Prize courts may revoke their decisions, founded on error, as soon as such error is brought to light."

Where the laws are ambiguous, where their observance varies according to the different interpretations of them in different courts of one and the same country, it is to be wished, that whenever foreign property comes in question, the principles in the case of the Juffrow Maria Schroeder,[1] may prevail. "It is in vain for governments to impose blockades, if those employed upon

[1] Rob. III. 157.

that service will not enforce them. The inconvenience is very great, and spreads far beyond the individual case; reports are eagerly circulated, that the blockade is raised; foreigners take advantage of the information; the property of innocent persons is ensnared, and the honour of our own country is involved in the mistake."

"In cases of disaster, as when, to avoid shipwreck, a vessel runs upon the strand, or puts into the port of a hostile country, the principle of decision should be invariable, release and restitution." Diana, Conseil des Prises. 13 Ventose an IX.

"In interpreting the principle of the French prize law, that the ship's papers, which are produced after the capture, are entitled to no credit, Portalis held, in the case of the Danish East Indiaman, Antoinette—The expression of the law, 'rapporter,' presumes, that a paper at the moment of capture was not on board, and that it has since been procured. To satisfy the object of the law, it is sufficient that we cannot reasonably doubt that a paper discovered or produced after the capture, must have been on board at the time, and not subsequently brought forward, and secretly interpolated among the others. Principles, which one nation at war applies to another, in the condition of a neutral or ally, are, in the reversed relation, applicable to such, according to the laws of retributive justice."

"The captor may not be bound to state his reasons. He takes the vessel at his own risk, and responsibility for all cost and damages, in the case of the illegal exercise of his right."

"In this doctrine of indemnification from the captors, it becomes often an important question, how far the possession of the original captors, in the event of a vessel being lost upon recapture, was, in its inception, a legal bonâ fide possession; and whether such original possession, bonâ fide acquired, might not, by the subsequent misconduct of the captors, have become illegal and untenable? although such bonâ fide possessor, in the first instance, is not answerable for any accident, yet by subsequent misconduct, he may so affect his claim to the legal seizure and possession of a ship, as to make himself a wrong doer ab initio."

"Of sea territory, we conceive three kinds. 1. The stretch of sea bordering upon the shore, within the reach of cannon shot from the shore. 2. The gulf, or stretch of sea, between adjacent islands. 3. The sea territory at the embouchure, or the mouth of rivers, where the river disembogues itself. As soon as there is no navigation without the river bed, or such river bed lies between beacons and buoys, the river may be held to commence, as respects the sea territory."

"Within the neutral sea territory, neutrals alone exercise their jurisdiction; and the courts of belligerents, upon the claims of neutrals, are bound to refer cases, occurring within such territory, to the neutral tribunals. The rule, observed M. Portalis, reserving two leagues (lieues) extent of sea territory, implies less a disposition on the part of the sovereign to enlarge his territory, than to protect misfortune, and afford her a place of refuge; and is, therefore, to be considered and received as an act of general benefit."

"During the period of the unfortunate so called continental system, it was conceived a meritorious thing, to trade with the enemy. General opinion effected an opposition to the measures of the belligerents, mightier in its operation than the secret tribunals of the middle ages. A thousand abuses crept into society; and its very existence became endangered. The proper point of view on this subject should never be lost sight of. In the maritime jurisprudence of England, there exists a general rule, by which all trading with the public enemy, unless with the permission of the sovereign, is interdicted. Ex naturâ belli, commercia inter hostes cessare, non est dubitandum. It is a general principle of law in most, if not all, of the countries of Europe."[1]

"Contracts for the transference of property in transitu, in contemplation of war, are illegal, if it be proved that the contract has been concluded immediately and fundamentally in contemplation of war, on the part of the seller, and that it would not otherwise have fallen into the hands of the purchaser. A contract on the part of the neutral, with a privileged company of the enemy, under the avowed motive of securing the produce of the colony from the enemy, is illegal. But if the apprehension or prospect of war, is not in the contemplation of the contracting parties, then property transferred before hostilities, and captured as enemy's, in itinere, is not subject to condemnation. When a person born in a belligerent, has acquired a right of citizenship in a neutral country, and is temporarily in an enemy's country for the purposes of trade, his shipments are thus rendered very hazardous. With regard to the trade of merchants of interior countries, that have no sea ports, the privilege of carrying on trade through the ports of the enemy has been allowed to them, in consideration of the hardship they would sustain, were they altogether restricted from becoming merchants for the supply of their own wants, or for the export of their native produce and manufactures."

"An intercourse from one port of the enemy to another port of the same country, with a cargo, has the consequence of precluding a neutral from freight, charges, and the production of further proof."

"The continuity of voyage, which becomes so often

[1] Rob. I. 198. Bynkershoek, Lib. I. cap. 3.

prejudical in colonial trade, and in cases of blockade, extends the same prejudice to the coasting trade."

"It is to be feared, that England in future, is likely to set up a more rigid than lenient principle, with regard to the prosecution of an enemy's coasting trade, as she is extending the principle, to allow to neutrals no trade which they had not in time of peace; when they should be entitled to an equivalent for the limitation of their trade, in regard to contraband. The intercourse from the ports of a belligerent to the ports of her allies, however, is not prohibited. In the introduction to this principle, we come to the particular trade, which was unfortunately the origin of a war between that country and the United States; the trade to the colonies of the enemy, which, from the above principles, the English have declared illegal; assenting to a voyage from the mother country of the neutral ship, to a colony of the enemy, or vice versa; but not from the colony to any belligerent country, nor to a colony of the enemy. Importations into the neutral country must be conducted bonâ fide. The produce of the hostile mother country, may be transhipped from the neutral country to a colony of the enemy; but that produce must have been bonâ fide imported."

Although quite excusable in him, it is amusing to find the generally independent, just, and impartial Jacobsen, on some occasions, as in some of the preceding passages, under the influence of national mercantile bias. He seems to think neutrals entitled to an equivalent for the limitation of their trade, in respect of contraband of war; apparently forgetful, that abstinence from the carriage of arms and military stores to either belligerent, is essential to the maintenance of the neutral character; and that this small restraint on neutral trade, arises necessarily from the constitution of mankind, as distributed into civil societies or nations, inhabiting portions of this earth, or territories contiguous or adjacent to each other, or having communication and intercourse by sea; and from these nations having no other means than war, of self-defence, or of enforcing their just rights. He seems, also, so indulgent to their cause, as to believe that those neutrals were really misled, who thought they could destroy the continuity of a voyage, by mere fictitious transhipment, in which they ostensibly paid the duties leviable in the neutral country on importation; but on re-shipment, without any attempt at sale in that country, recovered the duties in the shape of draw-back.

To proceed with extracts from Jacobsen. "No subject of maritime law is more enveloped in doubt, than the doctrine of contraband. In general, it may be laid down, that every article, which, in the strictest sense, is used in the prosecution of war, or the equipment of vessels, is reckoned contraband by Great Britain. In Great Britain, however, the contraband articles alone, and not the vessel in which they are shipped, unless they belonged to one and the same person, or if he was informed of their being on board, are liable to condemnation. Almost all necessaries destined to a port of naval equipment, are liable to condemnation. Ports both of mercantile and military equipment, are not so dangerous as are ports of mere naval and military equipment. The French have always been desirous to exclude masts and ship timber from contraband."

With regard to the right of pre-emption, of necessaries of war, and provisions, Sir William Scott remarked,[1] "The right of taking possession of neutral cargoes, consisting of commodities or provisions going to the enemy's ports, is no peculiar claim of this country. It

[1] Rob. II 182.

belongs generally to belligerent nations;—the ancient practice of Europe, or at least of several maritime states of Europe, was to confiscate them entirely; a century has not elapsed since this claim was asserted by some of them. A more mitigated practice has prevailed in later times, of holding such cargoes subject only to the right of pre-emption, that is, to a right of purchase, upon a reasonable compensation to the individual, whose property is thus diverted. I have never understood that on the side of the belligerent, this claim goes beyond the case of cargoes avowedly bound to the enemy's ports, or suspected upon just grounds, to have a concealed destination of that kind; or that on the side of the neutral, the same exact compensation is to be expected, which he might have demanded from the enemy in his own port."

"Hitherto treaties have been so little a subject of general notice, that owners and masters are for the most part ignorant of those of their own country."

"To the credit of humanity, a new species of contraband has arisen of late years, namely, slaves."

"In the overwhelming superiority of Great Britain at sea, the right of blockade, as it has extended and perfected itself in the English legal decisions, will long be maintained, particularly with regard to the blockade of enemy's ports. It is, however, incident to the nature of the subject itself, that every nation, which may hereafter obtain the preponderance, will probably adopt the same principles. Upon no other subject in the books, and in practice, have we perceived more error, than upon this right of blockade."

"The English adopt two kinds of blockade; the one blockade in fact, and the other by notification to the ministers of foreign governments in England. The first is properly confined to ports; the other extended to whole coasts, and even to neutral rivers, as was the case in 1805, when the French had possessed themselves of Hanover."

With regard to this last paragraph, however, it is but right to remark, that it does not correctly represent the British administration of the law of blockade, prior to the orders in council of 1807, or subsequent to the revocation. For these orders, even while they were in force, did not establish a blockade in the proper sense of that term; but were temporary and conditional, and, as explained by Lord Stowell, a retaliatory measure, prohibitory of intercourse with France, deemed necessary, or at least adopted pro tempore, in order to counteract the continental system of Napoleon, by which the British were excluded from all communication with the neutral nations of Europe. And as from the date of the revocation of these orders, they ceased to form a part of Maritime international law, as administered by Great Britain, we confidently trust they will never be again resorted to by the government of this country. Accordingly we hold, that, although there may be a blockade of a definite portion of the territory of the enemy bordering on the sea, as well as of a single port or harbour, the English prize courts would require, that, to be legally effectual, such a blockade must be real and actual,—a military operation of such magnitude and force, as to deter the enemy from approaching.

In book IV., chap. iv., part 2, Jacobsen treats of ransom and of military salvage; but it may be sufficient to quote a few passages relative to the transfer of property by conquest, recapture, and salvage.

"Property retaken out of the power of an enemy, before, according to recognized law, it has become theirs, is a recapture, and entitles the recaptors to salvage. With regard to the transfer of property by conquest, some nations, particularly with reference to their own vessels, allow, that after twenty-four hours hostile possession, the right of property is acquired by the enemy."

"In general, it has been agreed by publicists, that by capture, a ship does not become the property of the captor, until it be carried into a port, or into a fleet of the enemy's country, or infra præsidia."

"The English have latterly adopted the principle, that the right of property of the original owner to a captured vessel, with respect to English vessels, can only be effected by an act of condemnation in the country of the captor. With regard to foreign nations, they waive the discussion of the point." Jacobsen ought rather to have said: in restoring to foreign nations, upon payment of salvage to the recaptors, or not, they proceed upon the principle of reciprocity.

"Upon this subject, Von Martens," says Jacobsen, "lays down a theory totally different from the practice. He asserts that, by the law of nature, no complete property, without distinguishing between conquest, plunder, or prize, however lawful the capture, however safe the subsequent possession, can vest in the captor before a peace; and that during the continuance of the war, it may be demanded by the proper owner, from any third possessor; that, therefore, every recaptured vessel, the recapture occurring in whatever stage of the war it may, the prize being lawful or unlawful, having been made by a national vessel or a privateer, is to be returned to the original owner, whoever he may be, upon payment of the reasonable costs and damages of the recaptor, provided the recapture was not in itself unlawful; in which no salvage is due.[1] The opinions on this subject have been exceedingly various at different times.[2] It has been held, 1, that the property vests in the captor by

[1] Martens Essai, § 45, § 46. [2] Note by translator.

capture alone; 2, only after twenty-four hours quiet possession; 3, only after it is conveyed infra præsidia; 4, only after condemnation; 5, only after peace."

1. "Those who support the opinion, that capture vests a title in the captor, and that there is no spes recuperandi, or jus postliminii, are certainly not fortified in that opinion by principle or reason: since war is a state of contention, whose object is to procure satisfaction for some injury sustained; if the capture per se vested a title, it might be when no injury had been sustained, or after full indemnity had been made. 2. The second rule is equally groundless; for the spes recuperandi may be as great after twenty-four hours as before. No certain period can be fixed; for fixing a period is predicated upon the idea of such a quiet possession, as deprives the proprietor of all hope of recovery. 3. The rule of infra præsidia appears to be most generally received. 4. Condemnation is the English rule. But still, 5, Peace, it is said by others, can alone vest a full title in the captor. Mart. 125, 126. If the treaty is silent, it has the same effect; it vests the title in the captor. According to this opinion, all recaptures must be restored upon salvage; the jus postliminii is never gone; and until peace, that is, during the entire course of the war, the first proprietor may claim it from any third person, whether bonâ fide acquired or not; whether by sale, after twenty-four hours possession, or infra præsidia, or condemnation. This doctrine, however, is not admitted by Great Britain. The courts there hold condemnation to be necessary; and any sale after condemnation, vests the title absolutely in the purchaser. The French writers, on the contrary, hold that all titles acquired during war, are, during war, defeasible, and that no recapture can vest an absolute title in the recaptor. They do not admit the doctrine

of jus postliminii, which they say, arises merely from the distinction introduced in England, between a right of property in the recapture, and a mere right to salvage. Martens, 123, 177. The French doctrine involves this absurdity, that neither vessels nor goods, if liable to seizure, could ever be sold at any time during war. The French say, that the goods or vessels captured, may, at any time, and any where, during the war, be seized, though bonâ fide purchased; for that the title of such purchaser is invalid. The English rule is one which quiets possession, and is entirely reasonable; as the idea of settling accounts, and adjusting reciprocal losses by peace, is a mere fiction, and is never practised."

"There are few subjects of prize law so complicated as that of recapture. The recapturing vessels may belong either to the sovereign or his subjects. The recapture may be made by each singly, or by them jointly, or by the crew of the captured vessel, or by persons from the shore. The vessel recaptured may belong to the sovereign himself, or to his subjects, or to allies, or to a neutral, or auxiliary power. The vessel recaptured may have fallen into the power of the belligerent legally, or against the laws of war. All these cases are far from being duly considered in legislation, much less in the compacts between nations." The author proceeds to detail the practice of the different European nations, and of the United States of America, in the different cases just noticed, so far as settled by their respective statutes or ordinances, and judicial determinations. But into that detail we cannot here enter farther.

CHAPTER X.

Review of Dr. Wheaton's Digest of the Law of Maritime Captures.

The next work on Maritime international law, in point of time, is the Digest of the law of maritime captures and prizes, published at New York in 1815, by Dr. Wheaton, the distinguished American jurist. And although it cannot be strictly called a valuable accession to the legal literature of *Britain*, it gives us much pleasure to record our opinion, that, in point of learning and methodical arrangement, it is very superior to any treatise on this department of the law, which had previously appeared in the English language.

On a former occasion, we deemed it necessary to object to the great, and too extensive effect, which Dr. Wheaton appears to us, to ascribe to treaties or conventions among nations, as establishing a description of international law, binding on all nations, and beyond the terms or the duration of these treaties. And to such a doctrine we must still object, if such was the author's meaning. But what we chiefly regret is, to observe throughout the work we are now to review, besides the national bias, arising from attachment to our native land, to which we are all so liable, on the one hand, a disposition adverse to Great Britain,—a disposition to exhibit in strong colours, if not to exaggerate, all her errors and alleged deviations from the strict rules of international law; on the other hand, a partiality for France,—a disposition to palliate, extenuate, and excuse her excesses in maritime war, and to overlook or omit all notice of her still greater excesses in continental warfare. Such sentiments, as we formerly observed, were more excusable during the last generation, from the aid afforded by France to the United States, when they threw off their connection with their mother country. But that generation has passed away, and another succeeded. And these jealousies and animosities, instead of being indulged, recorded, and thereby transmitted to succeeding generations, ought to be buried in oblivion, and sunk in the cultivation of a friendly intercourse between two nations still so intimately connected. Indeed, among the educated classes of Great Britain, any such feeling of hostility towards the United States, or even towards France, the ancient rival of England, appears to have, in a great measure, if not entirely, ceased. And while we can smile at the intemperance and extravagance of the populace of Paris, or New York, and of the journalists, who profit by pandering to their prejudices, we are sorry indeed, to remark any such tendency among the educated classes of the United States, especially in a lawyer of such eminence, as Dr. Wheaton.

After such long extracts from the works of Tetens, Martens, and Jacobsen, our historical sketch would become too long, were we to adopt the same plan with regard to the work now under consideration. And it is not necessary we should do so at such length; because the work is easily accessible to the English reader, although apparently not yet much known in this country; and because we shall have occasion to revert to some of the same points, in reviewing Dr. Wheaton's more recent work on the history of the law of nations. While, therefore, we make extracts, sufficient to show the author's views, and the great value of this work, we shall chiefly notice those passages, in which he accuses Great Britain of having departed from the law of nations, and exercised her might, beyond her right.

In chapter I. Dr. Wheaton treats of the commencement of war, and of captures made before the declaration of war; and the following paragraphs contain the substance of the chapter. "By the modern customary law of nations, a formal declaration of war to the enemy is not considered necessary, nor generally practised; letters of marque and reprisal are issued, as the first step which is generally taken at the commencement of a war, and which is considered as equivalent to a declaration of it. Reprisals are either general or special. They are general, when a sovereign or state, who have, or think they have, received an injury from another, issue orders to their military and naval officers, and deliver commissions to their subjects or citizens, to take the persons and property of the subjects of the other nation, wherever they may be found. * * * The modern rule would seem to be, that tangible property belonging to an enemy, and found in the country at the commencement of war, ought not to be immediately confiscated; and in almost every commercial treaty, an article is inserted, stipulating for the right to withdraw such property. This rule seems to be totally incompatible with the idea, that war does of itself vest the property in the belligerent government. It may be considered as the opinion of all, who have written on the Jura Belli, that war gives the right to confiscate, but does not itself confiscate the property of the enemy."

In chapter II. the author treats of the authority to

make captures, and of things exempt from capture. "The sovereign power of the state, too, alone has authority to make war. Whatever belongs to the enemy, state or sovereign, or to their citizens or subjects, may be termed things belonging to the enemy, res hostiles. A state taking up arms in a just cause, has a double right against the enemy. 1st, A right of putting itself in possession of what belongs to it, and which the enemy withholds, and to this must be added, the expenses incurred to this end, the charges of the war, and the reparation of damages. 2nd, A right to weaken the enemy, for the purpose of disabling him from supporting an unjust violence; the right to take from him all means of resistance."

"All moveable things taken from the enemy, belong to the sovereign or state making war. They may reserve the property to themselves, or grant it to the captors. * * * Captures made by private armed vessels, are in virtue of commissions, or letters of marque granted to them by the sovereign or state. Subjects are not obliged to weigh scrupulously the justice of the war; but in case of doubt, are to rely upon the judgment of the supreme power of the state. A question here arises, whether the owner and officers of a private armed vessel, are liable for illegal acts committed during the cruize, beyond the amount of the security exacted and given; and if so, whether they are thus liable to a greater extent than the value of the vessel, her tackle, apparel, and arms. * * * It is evident, that any limitation of the liability of the parties, must depend upon the positive provisions of municipal law; and that, unless it be thereby expressly confined to the value of the vessel and her appurtenances, it must be indefinite in its extent. The conduct of public vessels of war, or of private armed vessels, commissioned as letters of marque, is regulated by instructions from the sovereign, or supreme executive power of the state. It has been the great object of every maritime nation, to restrain and regulate the conduct of its privateers; they are watched with great anxiety and vigilance, because they may often involve the nation, by irregularities of conduct; in serious controversies, not only with public enemies, but also with neutrals and allies. Hence the instructions issued by governments to privateers. But though such instructions may bind the judges of the prize courts of the nation, under whose authority they are issued, where these instructions relax the law of nations in favour of neutrals, yet if they attempt to extend that law to the prejudice of neutrals, they are not conclusive upon the judges, whose decision must, in that case, be regulated by the paramount authority of the law of nations."

"A maritime capture is the seizure of a vessel or goods on board the same, or both, belonging to a real or supposed enemy, or from some other cause justifiable by the laws of nations, under authority from the belligerent state; with the intent to divest the actual owner of the property, and to carry it into port for adjudication, before some competent court."

"The rights of war can only be exercised in the territories of the belligerents, upon the high seas, or in a territory belonging to no one. Hence hostilities cannot be exercised within the territorial jurisdiction of a neutral power, who is the common friend of the belligerents. This jurisdiction extends to the ports, harbours, bays and chambers, formed by headlands of the neutral power. The usual addition allowed for this, is a distance of three English miles, or a marine league, or so far as a cannon shot will carry from the coast or shore."

"A vessel, with the cargo laden on board, sailing

under a pass-port, safe-conduct, or license from the belligerent state, whether the property belong to the citizens, or subjects of the belligerent state, or to the enemy, is exempt from capture by the armed vessels of the belligerent state."

"Of the same nature, are licenses granted by the belligerent state to trade with its enemy. All commercial intercourse being suspended by war, such trade can only be legalized by license, granted by the sovereign power of the state; which is alone competent to decide on all the considerations of commercial and political expediency, by which such an exception from the ordinary consequences of war must be controlled."

In chapter III. the author treats of enemy's property, as an object of capture; and inter alia, lays down the following doctrine. "By the general usage of maritime nations, transfers of ships and other vessels are made in writing. If, therefore, the vessel captured has been transferred from the original proprietor, it seems reasonable to require the production of the bill of sale, in order to determine the validity of the capture. Where it appears, that the transfer was made from an enemy to a neutral, during the war, various rules have been adopted by the particular ordinances of belligerent nations, as to the effect of such transfers, when valid or otherwise. By the French regulations of the 23d July 1704, 10th October 1744, and 26th July 1778, no such transfer to a neutral was held valid, unless made before the declaration of war. And the British orders in council of the 11th November 1807 provided, that the sale to a neutral of any vessel belonging to His Majesty's enemies, shall not be deemed to be legal." But as these ordinances, Dr. Wheaton correctly observes, make no part of the law of nations, so neither are they founded on the principles of justice. In this we quite agree.

But the author might have added, that the orders in council of January and November 1807, were provoked by the previous greatly more unwarrantable measures of the Emperor Napoleon; were so far justified by the fraudulent collusion of neutrals with the enemy, in protecting vessels really the property of the latter, were merely conditional and temporary, and were actually revoked in the course of the war.

The author goes on to observe, "The rules which have been laid down by the ordinances of belligerent nations, requiring the production of certain prescribed proofs, to ascertain the bonâ fide nature of such transfers, and inferring the existence of hostile interests from the absence of proofs, are more just and conformable to the law of nations. So also, it has been held, that such transfers, made by an enemy to a neutral in time of war, must be an absolute and unconditional sale. Besides these, the following proofs of property in the vessel or cargo are usually required: The passport or sea letter, the muster roll or rôle d'équipage, the charter party, the bills of lading, the invoices, the log book or ship's journal. But, as the whole of these papers may be fabricated, their presence does not necessarily imply a fair case, neither does the absence of any of them furnish a conclusive ground of condemnation."

"It is evident, that goods, the property of the enemy, laden in enemy's vessels, are subject to capture. But that the goods of a neutral, laden on board the vessels of an enemy, should be subject to capture and condemnation, is manifestly contrary to reason and justice. But unreasonable and unjust as this rule may be, it has been incorporated into the prize law of certain nations; as in the case of France and Spain."

"A question arises, whether the captor of an enemy's ship is entitled to freight upon the goods of a neutral thus captured and restored, according to the foregoing principle. And the Consolato del Mare, c. 273, has determined, that the freight is to be paid to the captor by the neutral, in the same manner as if the voyage had been terminated. But this determination is justly contested by Bynkershoek, upon the ground, that the freight was not due to the ship, unless the goods had been carried to the destined port, or the captor is ready to carry them thither. This doctrine is adhered to in practice."

Now, that freight is only due to the captor of a hostile vessel, by the owners of neutral goods, when the contract is fulfilled, by carriage of the goods to the port of destination, is certainly quite consistent with legal principle; it being kept it view, however, that by his own act, the neutral voluntarily exposes his goods to the risk of not being carried to the port of destination, by loading in a manifestly belligerent vessel. But we do not quite agree with Bynkershoek, and Dr. Wheaton, that the Consolato actually and absolutely decides the question otherwise. In the case of the vessel being neutral and the cargo hostile, the Consolato declares the captor liable in the freight, which the owners of the hostile goods would otherwise have paid the neutral owners of the vessel. When the vessel is hostile and the goods neutral, the Consolato recommended a reasonable bargain, if practicable—a composition between the merchants, owners of the goods, and the captor. And it was only when the former rejected such a reasonable arrangement, that the latter was held entitled to carry the cargo to his own port, and the former held obliged to pay freight, as if the goods had been carried to the port of original destination. But if the captor rejected such a reasonable arrangement, the merchants were declared not bound to pay freight, in whole or in part, and were declared entitled to reparation for damage."

"The regulations and practice of certain nations at different periods, have not only considered enemy's goods laden in neutral vessels, as subject to capture, but have also confiscated the neutral vessels, on board of which they were laden." The author here instances the practice of France and Spain, before mentioned by us. But England and Holland never appear to have adopted the severe practice here alluded to; namely, that of confiscating neutral vessels, on account of their carrying hostile goods. That England, however, may not appear to have adopted, in any respect, a milder system than France or Spain, the author here introduces the treaty between England and Holland, in August 1689, and the British order in council, of November 1807, although neither the treaty, nor the order, authorized or directed the confiscation of neutral vessels, on account of their carrying hostile goods; but were both notifications of blockade, without being supported by adequate naval force, and therefore certainly unwarranted, and were accordingly passed from; the former, by England admitting the error, and making reparation; and the latter by Great Britain, having in 1809 greatly modified, and subsequently, as soon as it had any authentic notice of the revocation of the Berlin and Milan decrees, recalled these orders in council, which were at first merely a retaliatory and conditional measure, and could be pronounced illegal, merely with regard to such neutrals, as had not sided with, or sacrificed their national independence to Napoleon.

§ 12. "Another," continues our author, "and a more difficult question presents itself, regarding enemy's goods laden in neutral vessels; whether the goods themselves are lawfully subject to capture and condemnation. The conventional law of maritime nations on this question, has fluctuated; but has most commonly decided, that free ships should make free goods. The customary law and practice of those nations has varied less, and has generally determined, that enemy's property, on board the ships of a friend, should be liable to capture and condemnation. Without going back, beyond the middle of the seventeenth century, the times preceding which, partake too little of the spirit of civilization and humanity, to furnish precedents of conventional law for the present age, we may enumerate the treaties mentioned in the margin, which sanction the principle, that free ship makes free goods."

In this, almost wholesale denial of all spirit of civilization and humanity to the European nations, during the ages of Grotius and Pufendorff, we certainly can by no means agree; it seems to us rather presumptuous. But to proceed with our author. Dr. Wheaton here gives a long enumeration of the treaties referred to in the former parts of these enquiries, chiefly during the seventeenth, but partly also during the eighteenth century, as establishing the rule of "free ship, free goods." And it is amusing to observe the zeal with which he searches out, not merely every conventional stipulation, however much mutually neglected, or tacitly passed from, by the contracting parties, but even almost every admission or opinion, expressed by any British diplomatic agent or statesman, which has a tendency to bind the British nation, as approving of, or acquiescing in this rule, as a principle or maxim of the maritime law of nations. Thus, after pointing out the treaties of navigation and commerce of Utrecht in 1713, and the treaties of Aix la Chapelle in 1748, of Paris in 1763, and of Versailles in 1783, as confirming the treaties of Utrecht, and thereby sanctioning the rule in favour of "free ships making free goods," he proceeds. "In the negotiations at Lisle in 1797, between Great Britain and France, it was proposed by the British plenipotentiary, to renew these treaties confirmatory of those of Utrecht; which proposition was objected to by the French plenipotentiaries, for several reasons foreign to the present subject, to which the British plenipotentiary, Lord Malmesbury, replied, that these treaties were become the law of nations, and that infinite confusion would result from their not being renewed. They were not, however, renewed by the treaty of Amiens of 1802, nor by that of Paris of 1814."

But it does not require much acquaintance with modern history to perceive, that in urging in 1797 the renewal of the treaty of Utrecht, the British plenipotentiary had in view, not the 17th article of that treaty, quoted in our first volume, p. 271, bearing, "it is *now stipulated* concerning ships and goods, that free ships shall also give a freedom to goods," &c., but to the far more important provisions of the treaties included under that appellation, which set bounds to the excessive ambition of Louis XIV., and by the establishment of the barrier fortresses, secured for a time at least, the independence of Holland.

Again, after noticing the declaration of the Russian Empress in 1780, endeavouring to establish her favourite system of the armed neutrality, he proceeds. "Among the belligerent powers, France, Spain, and the United States acknowledged its principles; and Holland having become subsequently involved in the war, the British government offered to make peace with her, on the basis of the treaty of 1674, between Great Britain and the Republic; by which the principles of the armed neutrality are established in their widest extent." But he is obliged to add, "These principles were again recognized by the convention of 1800, between the United States and France, and were renewed by the second armed neutrality of 1800; which was dissolved by the naval power of Great Britain, and the particular principle in question relinquished by Russia; enemy's property on board neutral vessels, being liable to capture and confiscation by the convention of June 1801, between Great Britain and Russia." And the result of all this anxious specification of treaties is, that Great Britain, on these occasions, and for particular considerations, consented to give to certain neutrals the privilege of protecting the goods of her enemies. But that this was a privilege, and not a recognized general rule of the law of nations, is manifest from such a number of special pactions, and from the renewal of them from time to time having been deemed and found necessary, on all these occasions, to obtain and secure this privilege. If it had been clearly a maxim of the natural law of nations, there would have been no necessity for such anxious stipulations from time to time, on the part of the maritime powers interested in the adoption of the new rule. Indeed, the rule is obviously founded on a fiction, that the hostile cargo is the property of neutrals, contrary to the real state of the fact; and is manifestly the creation of interested parties, desirous of profiting by the disputes, in which their neighbours are unhappily involved, or attempting by this pacific measure, to defeat the effects of the military operations of their adversary. Nay farther, the rule itself, we have seen, is not, from its nature, capable of being made the subject of a merely mutual bi-lateral contract; because it involves the interest and conduct of a third party, not included in the treaty; and to be equal or just, is dependent upon a contingency, the eventual conduct of that third party; because, as the Spanish government truly and justly replied to the Russian Empress Catherine, unless that third party, the opposed belligerent, referred to in the treaty, adopt a similar line of conduct, the one contracting party cannot, in equality or justice, be held bound to the other contracting party, on the subject of this stipulation in the treaty. And such seem to be the reasons why this stipulation, inserted in the treaty of Utrecht, and renewed certainly in several subsequent treaties, at least by a general reference, does not appear to have been fulfilled, but, as by mutual tacit assent, was allowed to become a dead letter, and to fall into abeyance, even before it was actually annulled.

By this specification of treaties, however, Dr. Wheaton appears to consider himself warranted in stating, that this rule of "free ship, free goods," forms a part of the conventional law of maritime nations. And if he means merely, that these treaties, entered into in the course of the seventeenth and eighteenth centuries, first introduced this stipulation, afterwards referred to it generally, and were binding on the contracting parties to the extent of their provisions, and, as long as they remained in force, or were renewed, his statement is clearly well founded. But if, like Martens, by the conventional law of maritime nations, he means something more, than the mere accumulation of these treaties, scientifically digested—a law arising from the habit or custom of having so treated, without fulfilment of the treaty—binding upon nations, who have never so contracted, or generally upon those, who have occasionally so contracted, with particular states, after the treaties have ceased to be in force, and in relation to all other nations; we must again deny the existence of any such inferential law, as distinct from the natural and the common consuetudinary law of nations, founded on their customs or practice, and habits of reciprocal action. A habit of stipulating or agreeing to act, in a particular manner, is very different from a habit of acting for ages in a particular manner.

And in point of fact, when wars broke out after such treaties, these contingent stipulations were seldom observed in practice on either side, when the parties became belligerents.

Farther, as it appears we have been accused of here misunderstanding our author's meaning, and ascribing to him a doctrine which he does not maintain, it may be right, in justice to our author, to quote one of the passages, from a perusal of which, we were led to form the opinion we did, that the reader may judge for himself, whether or how far that opinion is erroneous.

After the specification of treaties just alluded to, Dr. Wheaton observes, p. 78: "A celebrated controversial writer has criticised the above expressions, conventional law of nations, as used by these modern champions of neutral rights, Hübner and Schlegel; but it is evident that this criticism can only apply with force to its use in an unlimited extent. For, as between the nations stipulating, a treaty must be the law, 1st, as long as it subsists; 2nd, so long as its provisions are to subsist by its terms. Such treaty must also be the law, as between the contracting parties and all others to whom its provisions, relaxing the primitive rigour of the customary law of nations, are to be extended; and it must be the law, as between themselves, and to be observed by them towards all the rest of the world, if the provisions of the treaty be declaratory of the original and pre-existing law of nations. This last characteristic applies to the convention of 1801, between Great Britain and Russia, which Lord Grenville, in his speech delivered in the British House of Lords on the 10th November 1801, states, and conclusively proves to be a recognition of universal and pre-existing rights, which, as such, could not be justly refused by the contracting powers to any other independent state."

But really, it is impossible to admit the soundness, or consistency with correct legal principle, of such mysterious doctrine. That a treaty must be the law between the nations reciprocally stipulating, while it lasts, there can be no doubt. But it is not easy to perceive the distinction here made between the cases, so long as it subsists, and so long as its provisions are to subsist, by its terms. A treaty is binding on the contracting parties, to the extent of its terms, so long as it subsists, without distinction, whether its endurance be specially limited by its terms to a particular period, or be left to be determined by subsequent events, such as to require renewal.

Nor can we admit, so far as we understand it, the justice or legality of the assumption, that a treaty must be the law, not only as between the contracting parties themselves, but to be observed by them towards all the rest of the world, if the provisions of the treaty be declaratory of the original and pre-existing law of nations; and that this characteristic applies to the convention of 1801, between Great Britain and Russia, which Lord Grenville, in his speech in the House of Lords on the 13th November 1801, conclusively proved to be a recognition of universal and pre-existing rights, which, as such, could not justly be refused by the contracting powers to any other independent state. So far as the provisions stipulated in the treaty are merely declaratory of the original fundamental and pre-existing law of nations, universally binding on all states, there can be no doubt, the insertion of such provisions in a treaty, cannot render them less binding, but is a positive recognition by the parties of these provisions or rules, as long as the treaty lasts. But the observance of such provisions or rules, in the practice of a nation for ages, would be a much stronger recognition of them, than any temporary treaty liable to be terminated by so many occurrences; such as the decree of the national convention of France in 1793, by which it annulled all treaties with the powers with which it was at war. And, while we doubt very much whether the convention of 1801, between Great Britain and Russia, was in all its provisions, merely or really a recognition of universal and pre-existing rights, we cannot admit the conclusion, that this convention was binding on Great Britain towards all other independent states, whatever might be their reciprocal conduct. We have a great respect for the opinion of Lord Grenville as a statesman. But, while we do not think Lord Grenville's speech here alluded to, contains the conclusive proof imagined by Dr. Wheaton, we do not consider Lord Grenville to have been such an able international jurist, as Sir Wm. Scott, Lord Stowell, or Sir Wm. Grant, or the late Lord Chancellor Eldon, who in that debate maintained the convention alluded to, was, like every other treaty, merely binding on the contracting parties.

And, although the contracting parties may clearly relax the rigour of the primitive law, by special compact in favour of each other, it by no means follows, they are bound to extend the same relaxation to all other nations, however different their conduct may be, and least of all, to abandon such an important right at common law, as the grant of such a privilege to others implies,—a privilege which is not only founded in fiction, and dependent on the will of third parties for such equality of operation, as to render it reasonably practicable, but is contrary to the doctrines of the Dutch, German, and Swedish jurists, Grotius, Cocceii, Loccenius, Heineccius and Bynkershoek, and is shown by the Italian jurist Lampredi, and particularly by the Danish and Hamburgh jurists, Tetens and Jacobsen, to be partial and unjust to one or other of the belligerent nations, and not perhaps ultimately beneficial even to neutrals themselves.

Dr. Wheaton's third argument, or rather assumption, is, that a treaty must be the law, not only as between parties themselves, but also between those parties and all others, to whom its provisions, relaxing the primitive rigour of the customary law of nations, are to be extended. If the contracting parties be so generous as to attend not only to their own reciprocal interests, but also to the interests of other nations, relaxing the rigour of the primitive law, the parties themselves may, no doubt, insist upon the fulfilment of such provisions in favour of these third parties. But it does not appear at all consistent with general legal principle, to hold that other nations, not parties to the treaty, can compel the observance of these provisions in their favour, which the contracting parties have so generously made, against these very contracting parties, or either of them. Such generous provisions in relation to third parties, are res inter alios acta, of which the third parties may take the advantage, with the consent of the contracting parties, but cannot by force compel the observance.

Dr. Wheaton next proceeds to the customary law. "Considering the question in regard to the customary law and practice of maritime nations, we shall find that enemy's goods in neutral vessels were declared to be liable to capture by the Consolato del Mare. And in conformity with this rule are the authorities cited," as we have already seen at length, in volume first.

"Bynkershoek is of opinion, that freight is not payable to the neutral carrier of enemy's property by the captor, because freight is not due, unless the goods have been carried to their port of destination. But a different rule is laid down in the Consolato del Mare, which is more reasonable in itself, and is supported by the whole current of authorities. A capture is considered as delivery; and enemy's goods are condemned ex re only; the carrier of them not being guilty of any offence against the law of nations."

"This rule," continues Dr. Wheaton, "is adopted by the English prize courts; but with so many exceptions and limitations, that its practical effect is almost destroyed. 1st, It is refused to a neutral ship, taken while engaged in the coasting trade of the enemy. 2nd, To a neutral ship engaged in the colonial trade of the enemy. 3rd, Where there has been a spoliation of papers by the master. 4th, Upon the carriage of contraband. As the two first of these exceptions are grounded upon a doctrine peculiar to the British courts of prize, which subjects to capture a neutral trade not open in time of peace, and as this doctrine makes no part in the law of nations, and is not recognized in the practice of any other nation, it is evident that these exceptions have no legal foundation."

These round and unqualified assertions or assumptions, call for some animadversion. With regard to the allegation of the doctrine here alluded to, being peculiar to the British courts of prize, if true, the circumstance appears to have arisen from Great Britain, and the other maritime countries of Europe, except France, never having opened their colonial trade to foreigners during war, otherwise rival belligerent nations would have objected to an aid so important, being given by a neutral to their enemy during war, so inconsistent with real neutral spirit or conduct. And as to this doctrine making no part of the law of nations, however convenient for the United States to say so, it is a manifest and necessary deduction from the primary fundamental principles of that law. To entitle a nation to the benefit of neutrality, it must act impartially between the contending parties. And, if the successes of the one belligerent have, during the war, reduced the other belligerent to such a state, as to be no longer able to carry on their coasting and colonial trade, and have thereby obtained a near prospect of peace, what act can be more partial and unfair, on the part of pretended neutrals, than officiously to interpose their services, and when applied to by the one belligerent, to carry on for them their coasting and colonial trade, to the same extent nearly as during peace, under the burden merely of the freight, payable to the neutrals. Such is a direct interference with, and counteraction of, the military operations of the other belligerent.

Farther, in our analysis, or rather extracts, (for frequently it is too concise to admit farther analysis,) from the truly impartial and profound work of M. Tetens, we had occasion to mark the measure or boundary of the rights of neutrals. They are entitled during war, not to be put in a worse situation than they were during peace, and to carry on their accustomed trade. Nay, they are entitled to increase their mercantile shipping, to carry on their direct trade with either of the belligerent nations, whose mercantile navy may have suffered, or been diminished by the events of the war, to the effect of supplying that deficiency, and thereby increasing their profits from that part of the carrying trade, which was formerly carried on by the vessels of the belligerent. But this is very different from ultroneously, or upon the invitation of the belligerent, carrying on for that power its coasting and colonial trade, from which neutrals were during peace excluded, and thereby relieving that power from the pressure and effects of the military operations of its enemy, and enabling it to maintain its position, and to continue the war, to the direct injury of its adversary. In short, neutrals are entitled to avail themselves of those events of the war, which may enable them to increase their trade, without occasioning damage or loss to either belligerent. Thus, that they may not be deprived of the supply of colonial produce, which they were accustomed to receive during peace, directly from, or through the medium of the European mother country, they may be entitled to import that produce directly from the colony of that country. But they are not entitled to interject themselves, and to carry on for the behoof of the reduced belligerent, his colonial trade, to the direct injury and damage of the other opposed belligerent. They are not entitled to reap profits from the disputes of their neighbours to the direct damage and loss of one of these neighbours. They are not entitled to enrich themselves at the expense, and to the detriment, of their neighbours; non debent locupletari, alienâ jucturâ.

The author proceeds thus, in the exposition of the subject of this chapter.

"If the property in the ship, or her cargo, appear by the papers found on board, to be in the enemy, no liens in a neutral claimant, or in a subject or citizen of the belligerent state, upon the same, by way of pledge for the payment of the purchase money, or hypothecation, are sufficient to found a claim in a prize court, and to defeat the rights of the captors."

"The property in ships and their cargoes, which was enemy's property, at the commencement of the voyage, cannot be transferred to a neutral, in transitu, so as to protect it from capture and condemnation. In a state of war, existing or imminent, it is held that the property shall be deemed to continue as it was at the time of shipment, until the actual delivery; this arises out of a state of war, which gives a belligerent a right to stop the goods of his enemy. A transfer in transitu, in time of war, is prohibited, as a vicious contract, being a fraud on belligerent rights, not only in the particular transactions, but in the great facility which it would necessarily introduce of evading these rights, beyond the possibility of detection."

"Contracts of purchase, effected on the part of the belligerent, but left executory as to payment, and contingent on a delivery at an ulterior port, at the risk of the neutral merchant, are not allowed in time of war; the goods sailing under such a contract, and taken in transitu, are held to be the absolute property of the enemy."

"By the prize codes of several nations, the want of papers found on board the captured vessel, and the suppression, concealment, or spoliation of papers, is considered as furnishing presumptive evidence of the existence of hostile interests; and unless rebutted by contrary proof of a satisfactory nature, as affording a ground of condemnation."

"The right of visitation and search is a right of belligerent powers, consequent, not merely upon the right of capturing enemy's goods in neutral vessels, but upon that of capturing enemy's vessels, and enemy's goods laden on board the same, contraband of war, and vessels committing a breach of blockade, or of detaining vessels, transporting military persons or dispatches in the service of any enemy. Even if the rule, that free ships make free goods, be adopted, the exercise of this rule is essential, in order to determine, whether the ships themselves are neutral, and documented as such, according to treaties and the law of nations. Indeed, it seems, that the practice of maritime captures could not exist without it. Accordingly, the unanimous authority of the writers on public law, establishes this right in the armed and commissioned vessels of the belligerent states."

"Various treaties and ordinances of belligerent states, prescribe the mode, in which the right of visitation and search is to be exercised, so as to prevent disorder and illegal violence."

"The penalty affixed to a violent resistance to the exercise of this right, by the universal law and usage of nations, is confiscation."

"In the supreme prize courts of the United States, a majority of the judges held, that a neutral had a right to ship goods, his property, on board a belligerent armed merchant ship, without forfeiting his neutral character, unless he actually concurred and participated in the vessel's resistance to capture."

In chapter IV. the author treats of the property of persons resident or having possessions in the enemy's territory, considered as an object of capture. And he justly remarks, "that time is the grand ingredient in constituting a domicile, and that the natural domicile easily reverts."

In chapter V. the author treats of the liability to capture of property sailing under the flag and pass, or license of the enemy; and justly observes, "that the acceptance from the enemy of a license to trade, is a cause of confiscation."

In chapter VI. the author treats of neutral property, considered as a legal object of capture. And beginning with articles contraband of war, he labours, along with Bynkershoek, to limit, as much as possible, this description of articles, so as not to interfere with neutral commerce. It is the duty of neutrals to observe an exact impartiality between the belligerent parties, and to afford no assistance to either, to the prejudice of the other. Their commerce with the belligerent powers, is generally free and unrestrained by the war. But to this general freedom, there are several exceptions.

Among these is included the trade with the enemy, in certain articles denominated contraband of war. The almost unanimous authority of elementary writers, of the ordinances of belligerent powers, and of treaties, agrees to enumerate among these all warlike instruments or materials, by their own nature fit to be used in war. But beyond this enumeration, there is some difficulty in reconciling the different authorities, which are extremely discordant, and at variance with reason and justice. * * Indeed, when we once go beyond the line of warlike instruments or materials, by themselves fit to be used in war, we know not where to stop, until we come to the entire proscription of neutral trade."

After thus representing the difficulty of discrimination, in ascertaining what are contraband articles, as much greater than it appears to be, and urging the necessity of confining the description to instruments or materials, by themselves fit to be used in war, the author proceeds to charge the British prize courts with a disposition to extend; nay, with the actual "extension of the law of contraband, so as to embrace bread-corn, and naval stores."

Thus, § 3, "As little foundation is there for the distinction raised by the British courts of prize, by which articles of promiscuous use are considered as contraband, when destined to a port of naval equipment; since the trade to such ports must be as free as any other, unless they are actually besieged or blockaded. Nor is the nature of the port material, as Sir Wm. Scott has himself observed, since naval stores, if they are to be considered as contraband, are so, without reference to the nature of the port; and equally, whether bound to a mercantile port only, or to a port of military equipment." * * "Another distinction," continues the author, "which has been adopted by these courts, considers certain articles as contraband, only so far as to give the belligerent power the right of taking them to his own use, paying the neutral a suitable indemnification; and it is said, the practice of pre-emption has been substituted in certain cases, in the place of confiscation by the modern law of nations. But this practice appears to have been derived from the principle laid down by Grotius, which restrains the right of intercepting things of promiscuous use, to the case of necessity, and under the obligation of restitution or indemnification. And unless it can be shown, that by the ancient law of nations, these articles were deemed contraband, this practice, so far from being regarded as a mitigation of the rights of war, can be considered in no other light, than an unlawful innovation."

On this occasion, as formerly, Dr. Wheaton seems also to resort to treaties, as constituting a conventional law, superior to the treaties themselves. But this fallacy we have frequently detected. And the practice of the English courts, here attacked, will, upon investigation, be found perfectly consistent with the first principles of international law, as well as with the consuetudinary law, and the opinions of judicious foreign jurists, unconnected with Great Britain.

It is manifest, as has been pointed out by several disinterested foreign jurists, particularly Lampredi and Tetens; and the acute Dr. Wheaton would have seen it also, if his vision had not, in this particular, been obscured, like that of Bynkershoek, by patriotic bias in favour of the supposed interests of his country; that immediate or direct fitness in themselves, for the purposes of war, whether natural, or by artificial adaptation, is not the sole characteristic or criterion of contraband of war. Contraband or prohibited goods, that is, unlawful supplies to the enemy, may be constituted by the time and place of destination, independently of any siege or blockade. To render arms and ammunition, or the other direct implements of war, available for success, the land or marine forces must be properly provided with naval conveyance, subsisted, and maintained. The sending naval stores to the naval arsenal of a belligerent state, whose government is known to be occupied in there fitting out ships of war for the invasion of the territory of the other belligerent, or the sending bread-corn, or other provisions, to a port or roadstead, where a belligerent has assembled a large fleet of ships of war for such a purpose, is giving as real and effectual aid to the military operations of that belligerent, and is as great a deviation from the impartiality incumbent on neutrals, as sending to him cannons, balls, and gunpowder. That such articles as those first alluded to, though not contraband generally, from their nature or adaptation, may become so from particular circumstances, or from the purposes to which they are applied, from their being supplied at a time when, and in a place where, they are required for rendering the instruments of war of use, is abundantly obvious. And in such circumstances, though not otherwise, such articles become legally liable to confiscation.

As little can the British enforcement of such a rule, be correctly represented, as a new recent practice. For, as admitted by Dr. Wheaton, it had the sanction of Grotius, more than two hundred years ago; and it was precisely upon this principle, that Queen Elizabeth seized the cargoes of the merchant vessels, which the Hanse towns had sent for the requisite supply with provisions, of the grand Spanish fleet then fitting out, and destined for the invasion, and contemplated conquest of England. And instead of finding fault with, Dr. Wheaton ought rather, according to his own laudable zeal for softening the asperities, and mitigating the fierceness of warfare, especially when neutrals are concerned, to have approved of the practice of the English prize courts, in requiring the belligerent captor to pay the neutral the price of his goods; and in thus substituting in more doubtful cases of contraband, than those before alluded to, the right of mere pre-emption, instead of the more severe measure of confiscation.

Dr. Wheaton proceeds to observe, § 5, "There is reason to believe that the ancient law of prize did not subject contraband articles to confiscation, but only gave the captor a right of appropriating them to his own use, paying the owner a reasonable compensation for the same. For the French ordinance of 1584, art. 69, permits the capture of neutral vessels laden with munitions of war destined for the enemy, and the retention of the cargoes, according to a reasonable estimation to be made thereof by the admiral or his lieutenant." But we have already seen it proved by Sir Christopher Robinson,[1] that the inference drawn from the terms of this old ordonnance, improbable in itself, is altogether unfounded: for these terms relate solely to, and imply merely, a reservation to the crown, to take the warlike stores captured by privateers, at a reasonable price to be fixed by the admiral—a right of pre-emption on the part of the government for purposes of state. Indeed, as Sir Chr. Robinson remarks, what encouragement could it be to the private captor, to have the liberty of purchasing such a catalogue of useless articles, as are comprised in the old enumerations of contraband? But we have already shown the erroneous, as well as improbable nature of the supposition here made.[2]

The author proceeds. "To this right of pre-emption, if it formerly existed, has succeeded the penalty of con-

[1] Coll. Marit. p. 124—5. [2] Vol. I. p. 281.

fiscation, which is applied to contraband goods captured on their destination to the enemy. And as they are thus condemned ex delicto, the carrier-master is not entitled to his freight upon them, as he is upon innocent articles, which are condemned as enemy's property. Where the ship and the cargo belong to one and the same person, the carriage of contraband, under the fraudulent circumstances of false papers or false destination, will work a condemnation of the ship as well as the cargo. The same effect is produced by the carriage of contraband articles in a ship, the owner of which is bound by the express obligation of the treaties subsisting between his own country and the belligerent state, to refrain from carrying such articles to the enemy. Except in these instances, the remainder of the cargo and the ship, unless they belong to the owner of the contraband articles, are not involved in the confiscation of the latter. But where the ship and the innocent articles of the cargo belong to the owner of the contraband, they are all involved in the same penalty."

"This penalty," the author proceeds, § 7, "has lately been attempted to be extended to the return voyage, by the British courts of prize, in cases where contraband had been carried outward with false papers. But it is evident that this innovation is not founded upon principle; for in order to sustain the penalty, there must be a delictum at the moment of seizure. To subject the property to confiscation, whilst the offence no longer continues, would be to extend it indefinitely, not only to the return voyage, but to all future voyages of the same vessel, which could never be purified from the contagion communicated by the contraband articles. From the moment of quitting port, indeed, the offence is complete; and it is not necessary to wait till the goods are actually endeavouring to enter the enemy's port."

As usual, the author here seizes the opportunity of censuring the practice of the British courts of prize. But here he does not show the impartiality, which might have been expected; and the charge of an attempt to extend indefinitely, the rule of confiscation on account of contraband, is not well founded. The practice of the British courts generally, with regard to the effect of contraband, is thus stated by Sir Wm. Scott, in the case of the Imina, 1st August 1800.[1] "The rule respecting contraband, as I have always understood it, is, that the articles must be taken in delicto, in the actual prosecution of the voyaye to an enemy's port. Under the present understanding of the law of nations, you cannot generally take the proceeds on the return voyage. From the moment of quitting port, on a hostile destination, indeed, the offence is complete; and it is not necessary to wait till the goods are actually endeavouring to enter the enemy's port; but beyond that, if the goods are not taken in delicto, and in the actual prosecution of such a voyage, the penalty is not now generally held to attach."

In making the charge of the indefinite extension of this rule, Dr. Wheaton does not refer to any particular case. But he is supposed to allude to that of the Aramintha, 17th Dec. 1804, in the vice-admiralty prize court, at Halifax in Nova Scotia; in which, apparently, under the authority of the judgment of Sir Wm. Scott, in the Rosalie and Betsy, 5 Feby. 1800,[2] Dr. Croke decided, that contraband upon the outward voyage, under false papers, was a ground of condemnation upon the return voyage.[3] On examining this case, however, it will be found there was no attempt at any such indefinite extension. The outward and the return voyages were one unbroken transaction, in which the owners of the vessel and of the whole cargo, were equally impli-

[1] Rob. III. 168. [2] Rob. II. p. 343. [3] Stewart's Rep. p. 47.

cated by the charter party. By their joint agent, the outward contraband cargo, under false papers, was sold; and the home cargo was purchased by him out of the proceeds, and credit given by him for the freight, as per charter-party.

Dr. Wheaton thus proceeds, § 8: "Of the same nature with the carrying of contraband, is the transportation of military persons or dispatches in the service of the enemy. § 9, A neutral vessel which is used as a transport for the enemy's forces, is subject to confiscation. § 10, The fraudulent carrying the dispatches of the enemy, will also subject the neutral vessel, in which they are transported, to capture and confiscation."

In § 11, the author states, that another exception to the general freedom of neutral commerce in time of war, is to be found in the trade to blockaded ports; and proceeds, in § 12, to remark, that the right of blockade has been, in various periods of history, abused by belligerent powers, to the total prohibition of neutral commerce with the enemy, or for the purpose of obtaining a commercial monopoly for the private advantage of the state imposing the blockade. And here the author indulges in an enumeration of the cases, in which he conceives the law of blockade has been abused; bringing forward all the instances he can against Great Britain.

With regard to the true principle of the law, blockade is a military operation; and it has been decided by the highest prize tribunal in Great Britain, that the blockade to be legal, so as to support the consequences attached to the breach of it, must be actual, de facto, and maintained by such a force, as to deter, or keep the enemy at a distance. Whatever may have been done in extreme cases, in former times, it is clear, an effectual blockade cannot be created by the mere declaration or notification of it made by a belligerent government.

And from this rule, the instances here enumerated by the author were certainly deviations, in so far as they tended to give to an unreal, the effects of an actual blockade.

But in enumerating these deviations from the correct principles of the law of blockade, it is rather singular that Dr. Wheaton, especially in the case of Britain, omits to mention the particular circumstances, in which they took place, and which, while they do not legally justify, at least morally extenuate the culpability of these deviations in relation to neutrals. Into the convention of 1689, by which all the ports of France were declared to be in a state of blockade, England was induced to enter with Holland, in order to protect that industrious free people against the aggressive policy of that ambitious monarch, Louis XIV., and to maintain generally the liberties and independence of the European nations. And upon the remonstrance of Sweden and Denmark, this declaration, so far as liable to objection on the part of neutrals, was abandoned.

By the treaties which Great Britain concluded in the year 1793, with Russia, Spain, Prussia and Austria, the contracting parties, no doubt, agreed to unite their efforts to prevent other powers not implicated in the war, from giving, on this occasion of common concern to every civilized state, any protection whatever, directly or indirectly, in consequence of their neutrality, to the commerce or property of the French, on the seas, or in the ports of France. But, although not warranted by the law of blockade, this measure was manifestly resorted to, from the strong pressure of necessity, in order to counteract the unjustifiable attempts of the French Republic to excite internal revolution and anarchy among the different European states, by seducing and corrupting the less informed portions of their population, and teaching them their wild and dangerous doctrines, impracticable to any beneficial effect.

Dr. Wheaton here next brings forward, in comparatively full detail, and in grand array against Great Britain, the orders in council of 1807, without noticing the conditional nature, the subsequent modification, and the ultimate recall of these orders during the war; while he only shortly alludes to the Berlin decree of the French Emperor, of the 21st Nov. 1806, which, we have seen, was in fact the great cause of the consequent severe British retaliatory orders in council, of the 7th Jan. 1807, and 11th Nov. 1807; and was followed up by the Milan decree of the 17th Dec. 1807; and makes not the slightest allusion to the gross infringements of the law of nations, which the French Emperor was then in the course of perpetrating on the continent, to the sad humiliation, spoliation, and almost total subjugation of Holland, Prussia, and Austria. That the British non-intercourse orders in council, however justifiable, as measures of retaliation against the inordinate ambition, extravagant animosity, and unprecedented hostility of the French Emperor, were warranted by the ordinary rules of the maritime law of blockade, in so far as they infringed upon the rights of independent and really impartial neutrals, we by no means maintain. Nor do we think that these orders in council, with the licensing system, consequent thereon, were for the advantage of Great Britain, or well calculated to attain the object which the British government had in view—the restraint and defeat of the schemes of conquest and aggrandisement, on which Napoleon was bent. But, if we view their nature correctly, these orders, so far as they were not accompanied de facto, by the military operation of a real and actual blockade of the ports or coasts, against which they were directed, do not belong to the law of blockade, and ought not, properly to be introduced in that department of maritime international law. They rest on a different principle, as explained by Sir Wm. Scott, in his judgment in the case of the Fox, 30th May 1811, before quoted, p. 27—28. In his judgment in the case of the Success, 28th Jan. 1812, Sir Wm. Scott also observed: "The relative situation of British subjects to Sweden, must depend upon the order in council, by which not only the countries, with which we are actually at war, but those also from which the British flag is excluded, are placed in a state of blockade. The blockade which has thus been imposed, is certainly of a new and extended kind; but has arisen necessarily out of the extraordinary decrees issued by the Ruler of France, against the commerce of this country, and subsists, therefore, in the apprehension of this court at least, in perfect justice."

And with regard to these measures of retaliation, so far as they were directed against France and its dependencies, there can be no doubt whatever of their justice and consistency with the recognized rights of war. The only difficulty with the impartial spectator of nations, or unbiassed international jurist, is, whether one belligerent nation can, by its illegal act against its antagonist, entitle that antagonist to perform that illegal act with reference to any other nation than itself. The perpetration of an injurious act by one nation against another, may not authorize, as a measure of just retaliation, the reciprocal perpetration of the same identical act by the latter against the former, if this retaliatory act affects the rights and interests of other nations. Accordingly, with regard to another article of the orders in council, prohibiting the sale to a neutral of any vessel belonging to the enemy, Dr. Wheaton quotes against Sir Wm. Scott,

[1] Dodson's Adm. Rep. I p. 133.

the opinion delivered by him in the case of the Flud Oyen, as to the condemnation of British vessels by French consuls in a neutral country. "The true mode of correcting the irregular practice of a nation, is by protesting against it, and by inducing that country to reform it. It is monstrous to suppose, that because one country has been guilty of an irregularity, every other country is let loose from the law of nations, and is at liberty to assume as much as it thinks fit." But, however well founded and applicable to that case, this general observation of the most able and learned judge may have been, it is obviously inapplicable to the case now under consideration. Even Dr. Wheaton will not pretend that Great Britain was entitled to resist the Berlin and Milan decrees, merely by a simple protest and admonition to reform. In the passage just referred to, p. 63, he admits that retaliation is just, if it strikes only the offending power. And the justice of the orders in council as against France, and its dependencies and allies, being thus acknowledged, it only remains to enquire, what was then the condition and conduct of those other nations, whose commerce was affected by these orders. Now, the United States appear to have been then the only civilized nation in a condition, from the intervention of the Atlantic, to resist the victorious arms of Napoleon. At the date of the Berlin and Milan decrees, all the more northern and eastern states of Europe, if not actually subjugated, were originally so weak, or had been so reduced by military operations, or had become so alarmed for territorial invasion, as to be unable to resist the wishes of Napoleon, and some of them even rendered themselves actively subservient to his views. But if a belligerent state adopts a mode of conduct towards a neutral, which amounts to an act of hostility, or at least to an act of sovereign power over it, and if that neutral acquiesces and submits, the other belligerent thereby acquires a right to retaliate against the enemy, although his doing so should affect the interests of the neutral state who has thus ceased to be independent and really neutral, or to be entitled to exercise the rights attached, or to exact the obligations due to that character.

If a neutral submits to an interdict by a belligerent power, against his trading with another belligerent, from favour to the former, he thereby makes himself a party in the war, and lays aside the neutral character; and retaliation becomes strictly applicable, just and legal. If the neutral submits to such an interdict, from weakness, or from any other motive or cause, not hostile or fraudulent, the opposed belligerent acquires a right to insist, that the neutral shall suffer from him what he suffers from the interdicting belligerent; otherwise the neutral would relieve the latter from the pressure of the war, and would become an instrument in the hands of the latter, for the infliction of that illegal pressure upon the former or opposed belligerent. The retaliation becomes just, not only against the enemy, but also in so far as the neutral is concerned, because the injury by the interdict cannot be inflicted without the participation of the neutral. And on this point, as Dr. Wheaton seems inclined to refer to the speeches of British statesmen as authorities, reference may here be made to Lord Holland's speech on the orders in council, 26th February 1808, and to Lord Erskine's speech, 8th March 1808, and also to the pamphlet of Mr. Baring, now Lord Ashburton, on the orders in council, p. 110, 111.

In the remainder of this chapter, the author gives a definition of blockade, and treats of the requisite notification, of the acts of violation, and of the penalty for the breach of blockade. "The appropriate penalty for a breach of blockade, is the confiscation of the vessel and cargo. But when the owners of the cargo, are not, at the same time, owners of the vessel, the confiscation cannot be extended to the cargo, unless its owners were, or might have been, conusant of the blockade, before they shipped their goods."

In chapter VII. the author treats of the property of the subjects of the belligerent state, or its allies, engaged in trade with the enemy, considered as an object of capture. § 1. "In a state of war, between two nations, declared by the authority in whom the municipal constitution vests the power of making war, the two nations, and all their citizens or subjects, are enemies of each other. The consequence of this state of hostility is, that all intercourse and communication between them is unlawful. This principle of public law forms a part of the municipal jurisprudence of every country."

§ 5. "The same course of decisions which has established that the property of a citizen or subject, taken trading with the enemy, is forfeited, has decided also that it is forfeited, as prize. The ground of the forfeiture is, that it is taken adhering to the enemy; and therefore the proprietor is pro hac vice to be considered as an enemy, and his property must be condemned to the captors."

§ 9. All the apparent exceptions which have been supposed to exist, to the rule of law we are considering, far from weakening its force, do but confirm and strengthen it.

In chapter VIII. the author treats of ransom, recapture, and claims for salvage. § 1. "Where a ship and cargo, the property of the enemy, is taken on the high seas, it is the duty of the captors to seize the papers found on board, and to send the vessel into some port for adjudication. But where circumstances will not permit this to be done, or render it inconvenient, they may permit the captured to ransom their property, for such sum as may be agreed upon between the parties."

§ 2, "This contract is unquestionably legal, on the part of the captors of every country, although the municipal law of Great Britain prohibits it to be entered into, in relation to the property of her subjects, captured by her enemies."

Under recapture, the author gives an account of the municipal, or peculiar national laws of the different maritime states, when the vessel or cargo recaptured, belonged to subjects of that state, and of the law of reciprocity, as applicable when the vessel or cargo belonged to other states than the belligerent. He concludes with rescue and derelict.

In chapter IX. Dr. Wheaton treats of the jurisdiction and practice of courts of prize. § 1. "The validity of maritime captures, is, with certain exceptions, determined in courts of prize established in the country of the captor, and judging by the law of nations. § 2. Among these exceptions is included, the case of a neutral power, the prize courts of which have the exclusive authority of determining the validity of captures made by the cruizers of the belligerents, within its territorial jurisdiction. 3. And a neutral state will restore the property of powers in amity with it, or of their citizens or subjects, taken by armed vessels fitted out within the dominions of the neutral state, in violation of its neutrality, when brought into its port. 4. So also when captured property is brought into a neutral port, the neutral state will restore the property of its own subjects, if it has been illegally taken from them. 5. But subject to these exceptions, the right of property acquired by capture, continues in the captors, who have brought their prize into a neutral port, or within the territorial jurisdiction of a neutral power. For, though the civil right of property in the prize, may not be vested in the captor, until a sentence of condemnation, yet the military right of property, which is evidenced by possession, is completely vested in him by the capture. By what right, then, shall the neutral sovereign, who is the friend of the captor, take from him these things which belong to him, jure belli, and give them up to another, though he be equally his friend?"

6. "It is the opinion of many writers, that belligerents have a right in neutral ports to sell their prizes, and to recover and appropriate to themselves the proceeds. But unless it is permitted by the municipal law of the neutral country, impartially to all the belligerents, or exclusively allowed to one or more by special treaty, there seems to be nothing in the principles of public law, which can prevent the neutral from withholding it entirely."

7. "Another exception to the general rule, is, in the case of prizes carried into a port of an ally in the war, or of a co-belligerent, and adjudicated upon by a consular tribunal of the captor's nation, established in the country of the ally or co-belligerent. The exercise of such a jurisdiction on the part of the consul of a foreign, though friendly power, is unquestionably unlawful, unless it be expressly permitted by treaty. But if the ally or co-belligerent choose to waive his strict rights of sovereignty for this purpose, other parties cannot complain of it, since he thereby violates no duty, as a neutral would do in a like case. 8. Subject to these exceptions, the validity of maritime captures is always determined in courts of prize, established in the country of the captor; and that whether the property be carried into his own port, or a port of an ally or co-belligerent, or whether it be carried into a neutral port. § 10. Where the property is carried into a neutral port, it may appear

more doubtful, whether the validity of the capture can be determined even by a court of prize, established in the captor's country. There is not only a want of original jurisdiction in the belligerent country, from the want of possession, but there is likewise a substantial defect of that authority, which is required for the attainment of justice, and which is essentially necessary to give effect to the ceremony of condemnation. But the conclusiveness of these reasonings has been contested; and the practice of nations sanctions the condemnation of property brought into neutral ports, by courts of prize established in the country of the captor."

§ 11. "These courts of prize are established in every country, acccording to the municipal constitution of each; and there is in all a superior court of review, consisting of the most considerable persons, to which the parties who think themselves aggrieved, may appeal; and all these courts, whether supreme or inferior, judge by the same rule, which is the law of nations." The author proceeds to give a short account of the prize courts, subordinate and supreme, of France, of Great Britain, and of the United States of America.

§ 15. "The judgments or sentences of the courts of prize, thus having authority to determine the validity of maritime captures, are conclusive as to the title of property in the thing, which is the subject matter of adjudication in such courts. A legal condemnation is, therefore, an essential muniment of the title of a neutral purchaser of captured property, without which he is liable to be evicted. A sentence of a court of admiralty is said not only to bind the subject matter, on which it is pronounced, but to prove conclusively the facts which it asserts."

"This principle has been maintained in the courts of municipal law in England, particularly as applying to cases of insurance; and has been adopted by the supreme court of the United States. Croudson and others, *v.* Leonard, Cranch's Rep. The decisions of a court of exclusive jurisdiction, are necessarily conclusive on all other courts, because the subject matter is not examinable in them. With respect to itself, no reason is perceived for yielding to them a farther conclusiveness, than is allowed in the judgments and decrees of the municipal courts of common law and equity. They bind the subject matter as between parties and privies. The whole world, it is said, are parties in a prize cause; and therefore, the whole world is bound by the decision. § 17. The jurisdiction of these courts extends, as well to goods taken on land by a naval force, or in consequence of the operations of a naval force, as to property captured on the water."

In § 18 and § 19, the author gives an account of the mode of procedure in the prize courts of the United States; and in § 20, § 21, and § 22, of the American distribution of prize money. In § 23, § 24, § 25, he gives an account of the British distribution of prize money.

In chapter X and last, the author treats of the effects of a treaty of peace, on questions of prize.

"A treaty of peace binds the contracting parties from the date of its conclusion, and to carry it into immediate execution, unless there be a stipulation to the contrary. But it binds the citizens or subjects of each party, only from the time it is notified to them. Those, however, who, by their fault, are ignorant of the conclusion of a peace or armistice, although they may not be liable to punishment, are responsible for the damages, occasioned by their own want of diligence. In order to avoid such questions, it is a frequent practice to stipulate, in the preliminary articles of peace, for a cessation of hostilities at certain times, in different places, and for the restitution of property taken afterwards; and this, as well within, as beyond the period assigned for the ratification of the preliminary articles themselves. § 5. It has been determined, that such a stipulation extends to recaptures, as well as to original captures. § 6. A treaty of peace has the effect of quieting all titles of possession, arising from the war. Therefore, where a question arises as to the title of a neutral purchaser under consular, and other condemnations, it was held, that the intervention of peace had the effect of curing whatever defects might otherwise exist in such titles."

CHAPTER XI.

Review of part of the work of M. Schmalz.

THE next work we have to notice, in point of time, after that of Dr. Wheaton, is the Europäische Völkerrecht of Privy Councillor Schmalz, which appeared at Berlin in 1817: and was translated into French in 1823, by the Count Leopold de Bohm. In his preface, the author thus briefly announces his opinion, with regard to the basis or foundation of the law of nations; which, it will be observed, is to a considerable extent, different from those of his German contemporary or predecessor, Martens, and his German successor, Klüber. "That I found the law of nations, solely, upon customs and usages, will appear from the book itself. Treaties cannot be the foundation of it; but they show well enough what the Powers (the different European states) have thereby set forth, or expounded, as consuetudinary law, and have, in this way, recognized as such."

Only a small part of this excellent work relates to maritime law. In book V. chap. iii., M. Schmalz treats of the commerce of nations, of the excessive value put upon foreign commerce, and of the consequent commercial jealousy of nations; but with regard to Maritime international law, he here merely notices the establishment of commercial consuls in foreign ports. In book VI.

chap. iii., the author treats of the law of nations during war. And passing over his account of the military operations by land, which are sanctioned by law, we shall extract the following brief account of the law of maritime war, as exhibiting the views of an able statesman and lawyer, a member of a state possessed of comparatively little marine territory, and which therefore should be more impartial in this department, and free from national bias. "Acquisition by means of arms, is most frequent in maritime war. Except the rare cases, when a fleet has to disembark land forces, or to supply a fort with provisions, war at sea, is especially directed against the commerce of the enemy; for erroneously regarding foreign commerce as the principal source of the wealth of nations, each state believes, it deals the most fatal blow against its adversary, by annihilating this support of his power. The principal object, then, of maritime war, besides that of pursuing and destroying the armed fleets and vessels of the enemy, is to seize his merchant vessels. Although the damage falls principally upon individuals, yet as, by this means, they believe they render themselves masters of the commerce of their adversary, the maritime powers will, with difficulty, renounce this custom. Nor can this, in reality, be regarded as more oppressive, than the treatment which the peaceful inhabitants often experience in war by land. The property of the latter ought more to be respected, seeing they have ransomed themselves by war contributions; which is not the case with those who fit out or charter vessels. It must be added, that by seizing the vessels of the enemy, his adversary deprives him at the same time of the mariners, whom he might employ in manning his fleets."

"Nor is it the state only, that arms vessels for capture; individuals also equip such vessels at their own expense. We should renounce with pain, the hope of one day seeing this immoral mode of making war abolished. Prussia and North America are the only powers, between whom there exists a treaty, by which they reciprocally agree not to grant such licenses in the event of a rupture. Other states had already set such an example, but without putting it actually in execution."

"The commander of the privateer must be always furnished with the express permission of his government; and always carry with him the papers, by which this is ascertained. This document, known under the name of letters of marque, is thus denominated, because it authorizes the exercise of hostilities out of the limits (marquen) of the country; in opposition to letters of reprisal, which the sovereign, in former times, granted to the authorities, to be used in the interior of his dominions. The captains of this description of vessels, are always under the orders of the admiral of their nation; and consequently, must not capture vessels, which have obtained a safe-conduct from him."

"The privateer that has captured a hostile vessel, is obliged to conduct her into one of the ports of his sovereign. The prize is examined and judged of, before the competent authorities. He cannot arbitrarily dispose of any part of the ship or cargo; he appears in the character of complainer against the owners, or charterers and merchants, who appear in the cause as defendants. The captor who makes the demand, that the vessel and the cargo be declared good prize, must prove, in order to have them adjudged to him, that both are really the property of the enemy."

"The privateer pursues the enemy into all seas; but must nevertheless respect the maritime limits of neutral powers. It is regarded even as unlawful, to chase a vessel into a river of the hostile territory; and if the privateer is there captured, he may be refused the privileges enjoyed by prisoners of war belonging to the state, and commanded by naval officers."

"When the captured vessel has been declared good prize, it becomes the property the owners, or charterers of the privateer that has captured it; who divide the proceeds among themselves, according to agreement; allowing, however, a share to the captain and crew. Usually the crown allots to itself a part, according to the laws existing in this respect, in different countries."

In book VIII., chapter ii., M. Schmalz treats of neutrality. And for the reasons before assigned, it may be proper to give an extract, containing his views of international law, in this department.

"No principle can be more clear (p. 278,) than that a state, which does not wish to take any share in the disputes and contentions which arise among other powers, and is not bound to do so by anterior treaties, enjoys, in virtue of its independence, the right of remaining neutral. Beside the evident injustice of wishing to force a pacific government, which has given no offence, into a war, common prudence forbids a state to increase the number of its enemies by resorting to such force."

"Neutral states (p. 281,) have a right to exact from belligerent powers, that they abstain from every act of violence towards them, as in times of general peace. Their territory is inviolable; no armed man belonging to the contending parties, can there set foot. * * * If, on the one side, (p. 282,) all neutral states enjoy the rights just mentioned, on the other, this same neutrality also imposes on them corresponding duties. It is thus they must scrupulously abstain from all participation in the war, and from favouring, in any respect, the one power, to the prejudice of the other; or from refusing to the latter, what is granted to the former. Even ancient treaties, with one of the belligerent parties, would not justify such partiality, unless the other consented. For a stronger reason, an auxiliary power cannot make any pretension to neutrality, if the adversary of his ally withholds his assent. But it is entirely in the choice of the neutral state, to grant, or to refuse a favour to both parties, provided it observes an exact equality or parity. It would be, for example, a deceitful impartiality, in a war between a maritime and a continental power, to open, to the ships of war of the former, all the ports from which it might menace and endanger the latter, by offering to this latter the enjoyment of the same privilege. In a war between two maritime powers, a neutral state may shut its ports against the cruizers of both, or permit them both to bring in, and there sell their respective prizes. Yet, unless with special authority, no foreign government can retain prisoners of war by main force, in a neutral country. When merchant vessels meet hostile cruizers in a neutral port, the latter are not allowed to depart till twenty-four hours after the departure of the former."

"Every thing which lightens or facilitates the war for either of the belligerent parties, being regarded as a favour, the permission to purchase warlike stores in the neutral country, must be granted or refused to both equally. It would, however, be contrary to the rules of justice, to view a liberty, which the enemy had taken by force in a neutral country, as an infringement of the neutrality on the part of the latter; and to exact, in consequence thereof, a similar concession. But as it is permitted to go in quest of our enemy, into all places from which he threatens us, if he takes refuge, when armed, on the neutral territory, we cannot be prevented from pursuing him there."

"These principles of justice, simple though they be,

are, nevertheless, involved in numerous difficulties, in their application to the multifarious relations and cases that occur."

"Hence in all times reciprocal complaints, sometimes of the violation of the rights of neutrality, sometimes of the non-observance of the obligations of neutrality; and in all times, the pretexts of state policy, for actually permitting both. The difficulty of unravelling the truth, in a series of individual facts, often itself makes it impracticable for the most impartial and enlightened judge to pronounce a correct judgment; for here there is no legislator to establish those presumptions of law, which must be assumed as true, until the opposite be proved. And still greater difficulties attend the determination of the rights of neutral powers in maritime war. For not merely the application of the principles to the facts, but the principles themselves are so uncertain, through the diversity in the relations of the different maritime states to each other, that nothing is more unlikely, than an agreement upon a Positive code of the maritime law of nations in war."

"It is, indeed, clear in itself, that the ships of neutral countries in general, should be secured against hostilities; and that their cargoes should not be seized by the cruizers of the nations engaged in war. But as this is an incontestable, and actually uncontested principle, so, on the other side, it is equally incontestable, that the ships and subjects of neutral powers should not favour the one of the belligerents to the prejudice of the other, and should facilitate neither offensive nor defensive operations. Now it is the conflict of these two principles which it is so difficult to reconcile, in individual cases, that complicates and embarrasses the decision. It has been attempted to establish a third equalizing conciliatory principle, namely, That every vessel is a part of the soil, or territory of the country to which it belongs, in whatever place it may be; and that nothing can be done, or take place on board a neutral vessel, from which belligerents must abstain in the neutral territory itself."

"But this principle bears so decidedly the impress of an hypothesis, that it is manifestly unfit for the discovery of a juridical truth. A ship lying in a foreign harbour, or sailing in a foreign territorial sea, is there subject to the jurisdiction of the country, and is no part of the territory of its native land. Not the keel or hull of the vessel, but the place where she is found, determines, according to the law of nations, whether she is within this or that territory; this determines also, that in the free open sea the vessel is in no territory; that it is not the law of any territory whatever, but the general law of nations alone, which determines the privileges and obligations of the vessel. On the other hand, from the principle that a neutral vessel can, to no belligerent, facilitate either attack or defence, it follows immediately, that the neutral vessel, which ventures to do so, oversteps the boundaries of neutrality, and takes a hostile part in the war.

"Now it is easy to comprehend, how difficult it is to determine, what facilitates and favours the attack or the defence of the enemy, and how the views of neutral and belligerent powers, on that subject, must always be different. Of old, it has been always chiefly the most powerful maritime states, that have been accused of having, from the feeling of their superiority, cared little about annoying or giving offence to the weaker neutral states. We find, accordingly, that formerly the Spaniards, then the Dutch, restricted the navigation of neutrals more severely, than is now charged against Great Britain; and justice requires the admission, that France herself, in the late war, by which she pretended she was to conquer the liberty of the seas, acted much more harshly, with much greater rigour, against neutral vessels, than the British. In fact, we come to this conclusion, that the contest of the belligerent with the neutral maritime states, must be contemplated from impartial points of view, in order that we may ever approach the possibility of having general principles, fixing the boundaries of the legal rights of both parties distinctly recognized. Equity requires, that even the prejudices, with which, as yet, all the nations of Europe are beset, should be allowed to prevail. Truly, it would be different, if people had once formed a just notion of the relation of maritime trade, to the internal wealth of countries."

These views and sentiments of M. Schmalz, certainly indicate great impartiality, and zeal for the peace and prosperity of all nations. But we humbly conceive, he has magnified too much, the international legal difficulties, and has represented, as still to be solved, problems, which have already received a satisfactory solution. Nor do we see, that any exercise of impartiality, or farther investigation of the rules of justice, reciprocity, and general expediency, and still less, the attainment of more correct notions than were entertained by Adam Smith, with regard to the comparative value of the domestic and fóreign commerce of countries, will lead to a more equitable adjustment of the relative rights of belligerents and neutrals, than the exposition of the just and the unjust among nations, given by all the international jurists, with apparently one exception, from the fifteenth to the middle of the eighteenth century; from Albericus Gentilis to Vattel, and subsequently elucidated in the works of Lampredi and Tetens, distinguished alike by the acute examination and ascertainment of matters of fact, to the exclusion of all hypotheses or fictions, so inadmissible confessedly in this department, and by sound logical reasoning in point of law.

CHAPTER XII.

Review of part of the Droit des Gens de l'Europe by Von Klüber.

The next work we have to notice, so far as it relates to maritime international rights, is the concise, yet comprehensive treatise of Von Klüber, entitled, Droit des Gens Moderne de l'Europe, published at Stuttgart in 1819. As already observed elsewhere, Klüber, like Martens, appears to ascribe a great deal too much to the efficacy of treaties, as creating a sort of general positive international law, binding on states generally, beyond the really contracting parties, and beyond the duration of these treaties. But the groundlessness of this assumption, a mere fictio juris, we have already on various occasions, pointed out. And we shall now proceed to select the leading passages in Klüber's work, in this department of international law.

§ 250. "Of the number of legitimate means of annoying the unjust enemy, is also the right of appropriating, as far as the object of the war requires it, the effects and rights of the enemy. § 260. A lawful mode of annoying the enemy, is that of authorizing by letters patent, or of marque, private individuals to fit out and arm, on their own account, vessels, called privateers, in order to make war upon hostile vessels. Privateers are distinguished both from state or government ships of war, and from pirates or sea robbers. § 261. Privateers are under the orders of their sovereign and his admirals. They must conform to the laws of war, and to the rules and instructions, which they have received for their cruizing. They are legitimate enemies, such as the soldier in war by land, who may appropriate what he takes from the enemy. They must respect the maritime territory of neutral nations, and must not there commit any hostilities. Their booty, or prize, is not regarded as their property, until they have brought it into a port of their own country, or of an ally, or of a neutral power; and until it is besides declared a good prize by the sentence of a court of admiralty, or tribunal of maritime prizes. Express regulations, in each maritime state, determine whether the privateers shall, in such and such circumstances, receive a reward, and what shall be its amount, whether the state shall divide the value of the prize, and what shall be its share, the proportion which shall be reserved for the captain of the vessel, the security which shall be found by the owners of the privateers, in order to prevent abuses. Privateers are almost generally prohibited from releasing, without special authority, the captures they have made, even for a ransom. A prize may be recaptured by the government ships of war, or by the privateers of the enemy. It is in vain that several powers have proposed to abolish privateers, and to secure for the objects of commerce, belonging to individuals, the same liberty and safety, which they almost generally enjoy by land."

As Klüber's work is so recent, and seems to be considered, on the continent, an authority, in the present or existing law of nations, a remark or two appear necessary, in correction of his preceding statement of maritime law between belligerents. In the first place, his statement is so vague and equivocal, that it is doubtful whether he does not mean to say generally, and without limitation, that maritime prizes may be carried into a neutral port, and there legally condemned. Now, it is plain, that it would be equally inconsistent with neutrality, and with legal principle, for any court in a neutral country, to adjudicate upon a capture made by a belligerent, unless the capture was alleged to have been illegally made from the subjects of that neutral power, and unless the ship and cargo were captured or actually brought within its maritime jurisdiction. And it has not only been decided by the prize courts of Great Britain, and of the United States of America, but admitted by some of the most eminent continental jurists, that a condemnation by a commercial consul of one of the belligerents states, resident in a foreign neutral country, elevated by that belligerent, during the war, from obvious considerations of partial conveniency, to the rank of an admiralty or prize judge, is quite illegal.

Again, the expression of Klüber seems to imply, that the abolition of privateers, would merely give to merchandise the liberty and security by sea, which they enjoy by land. Now, although we agree with him, that the abolition of privateers is highly desirable, though not easily attainable, we conceive, that such a measure would give merchandise conveyed by sea much greater liberty and security, than what is enjoyed by it on land, in a state either of depositation or conveyance. For although, in continental warfare, the goods of merchants, in particular, may not, in general, be directly seized by the troops, the military exactions being usually, in the first instance, indirect in the shape of requisition, upon the governors of provinces, or upon the magistrates of local municipal communities, and of forced loans and contributions, it is equally true, that merchants and bankers have to bear a large proportion of these forced loans and contributions. And when the accumulated merchandise consists of grain, flour and other provisions, the invading army usually procures its subsistence by the immediate seizure of these articles. Such, at least, appears to have been the mode of continental warfare practised during the nineteenth century.

Klüber afterwards thus expounds the relative rights and obligations of belligerent and neutral nations. § 279. "That state is called neuter (medius in bello,) which, in a war, gives assistance to none of the belligerent powers. Neutrality is the resulting condition of that state, with reference to these powers. In virtue of its natural liberty, each state may, in any war between other states, maintain its right of neutrality, even when one of the powers at war may have given it offence. There is only one exception to this liberty of remaining neuter, namely, when a state may have engaged itself by convention, to take a part in the war, as a member of a confederacy, or of a composite state, or in virtue of a treaty of alliance." After distinguishing neutrality, in § 280, § 281, and § 282, into natural and conventional, voluntary and obligatory, entire and limited, general and partial, armed, continental and maritime, Klüber thus proceeds to state the obligations of belligerent towards neutral powers, and of neutral towards belligerent powers. § 283. "Belligerent powers are bound, in no respect, to disturb the tranquility of neutral states. They must, consequently, abstain, in the territory of the latter, (in territorio pacato, i. e., gentis mediae) from all kinds of hostilities, not only against these neutral states, but also between or among themselves." § 284. "A neutral government in the war, is neither judge nor party. It must not only not permit, on the part either of itself or its subjects, the slightest action which may favour or aid the one of the belligerent parties, in its warlike operations, but also not suffer, on the part of one of these belligerents, the least violation of its own rights of neutrality. The laws of neutrality consequently prohibit it from giving warlike assistance to one of the two enemies, or permitting its subjects to do so, especially in the capacity of privateers; as also from voluntarily suffering the one of the belligerent parties, to commit, upon its neutral territory, continental or maritime, acts of hostility. A violation of these laws would immediately authorize the belligerent party, thereby prejudiced, to use force against the neutral state, and also to pursue his enemy in the territory, where he had found assistance and protection."

In § 285, § 286, and § 287, Klüber proceeds to discuss the rights of neutral states against belligerent powers; 1, with regard to the neutral territory; 2, with regard to the country of the enemy; 3, with regard to the relations of commerce. And these last, to which our enquiry is chiefly directed, he considers, first, according to the natural law of nations, and then according to what he calls the European law of nations. § 287. "An object of the greatest importance is the commerce of neutral states during war, particularly with the states who take part in it. A power which makes war, may prohibit both its subjects, and the inhabitants of the hostile country occupied by its troops, from trading either with the hostile state, or even with the neutral countries. But it has not, in the ordinary case, the right of requiring a neutral state to abstain from commerce with its enemy; the state of enmity which has arisen between two powers, not being sufficient of itself alone, to prejudice the rights of third parties."

"The natural law of nations does not forbid trade, even in the immediate necessaries for war, provided it is not carried on, with the design of favouring the one of the belligerent parties."

This section also calls for a remark. The statement of what is here called the natural law of nations, is rather dogmatical. How is the design of favouring one of the belligerent parties to be discovered, except from the nature of the act? The distinction pointed out by M. Tetens, between the commerce of the neutral, and the commerce of the enemy, is entirely overlooked or omitted. § 288. "Indeed," continues the author, "the usage of nations now-a-days recognized in Europe, permits the commerce of neutral states with those at war. It merely imposes on it certain restrictions, with regard to the immediate necessaries for war, and blockaded places. It prohibits not the sale of the immediate necessaries for war to a belligerent power, or to its subjects, when the latter purchase the articles in the neutral country, and export them themselves. If, on the contrary, the neutral government, or its subjects, carry these necessaries to one of the two enemies, this is a violation of the neutrality, and the goods are then called contraband of war. Under this denomination are comprehended, in general, all sorts of arms, the harness of horses, and warlike stores, with the exception of those destined for marine purposes, (pour la marine.) If there be any uncertainty as to the quality of contraband, attaching to an article, the terms of the treaties concluded on this subject, must be strictly adhered to. In the absence of such treaties, the natural law of nations, establishing the entire liberty of commerce, becomes again in force; (rentre en vigueur) and the goods must be presumed free."

Now this statement also requires animadversion.

Why, articles necessary for maritime war, should be exempted from confiscation, any more than articles necessary for war by land, no reason is assigned. We have already seen, that naval stores, such as timber for building vessels, cordage, canvass and other such articles, although not from their nature immediately sub-servient to war, may become contraband, by their direct destination to a port of naval equipment, where fleets are usually fitted out. Independent states reduced to the necessity of going to war, it is plain, continue to have rights as well as neutral states. And the rights of the former impose restrictions upon the commerce of the latter, as well by the natural and common law of nations, as by European usage or conventional treaties.

§ 289 § 290. "The following principles," continues Klüber, "determine the rights of belligerents, with reference to the commerce of neutrals, and to contraband of war. 1. It must at the outset, be presumed, that neutrals do not carry on any trade in contraband; therefore, and seeing neutral states are, besides, independent, the belligerents cannot, in the absence of particular convention, arrogate to themselves, the right of visiting their convoys of merchandize, either by land or by sea; it is sufficient, it be proved that the merchandise belong to them."

Now for this presumption in favour of neutrals, here made a postulate by the author, there does not appear to be any foundation in reason or law; except the ordinary negative presumption of innocence; and in the case of neutrals, the experience of ages unfortunately warrants a directly opposite conclusion. It is quite sufficient to protect neutral innocent merchandize, that it be proved to belong to neutrals. But how is this fact to be ascertained, except by a visit, and examination of the documents, which afford evidence of property.

And such a visit has notoriously been the practice among the European nations for ages. The only authority referred to, by the author, for the principle, as he calls it, is a treaty in 1785, between Prussia and the United States of America. But how can a single treaty between two nations, towards the end of the eighteenth century, be said to alter the common consuetudinary law of nations, which has been observed in Europe for ages?

2. "All goods, which are not contraband of war, may be freely carried by neutrals, if not to places besieged, blockaded, or invested. The enemy cannot take possession of them, except when he has urgent need of them for his own subsistence, and then always on paying their full value." This is correct, if it includes contraband by direct hostile destination; but the distinction between the commerce of the neutral and the commerce of the enemy, is altogether lost sight of.

3. "If, nevertheless, a neutral state or its subjects," continues the author, "shall carry contraband goods, and they fall, on their passage, into the hands of the enemy, still the latter can appropriate them, only upon paying for them, or he may send them away, upon security that they shall not be brought back, and that all such commerce shall cease thenceforth. The confiscation of contraband of war, and still less of other merchandise, found in the same convoy, or means of conveyance, as ships, waggons, horses, &c., cannot then be justified upon principle."

Now, the author's reasoning here, is not satisfactory; nor his meaning distinct. The second sentence is stated as a deduction from the first; but they seem to be both nearly identical unsupported assumptions. If a neutral government or its subjects, actively supply the enemy with the instruments of war, the seizure and confiscation of such articles, if met in transitu, is, upon the principles of natural justice, a very moderate retribution for such a breach of neutrality, approaching to a positive act of hostility; and so, the nations of Europe have thought, before there were any treaties on the subject.

4. "The greatest part, however," continues our author, "of the treaties now in force, permit the confiscation of contraband of war; but not the rest of the cargo, nor ships, waggons, or horses. In a few treaties only, is the confiscation of these last articles admitted in certain cases."

5. "Finally, in the absence of treaties, the principles of law have not yet been sanctioned by an uniform and general usage. Policy or power often decide. Usually, articles contraband of war are confiscated, and the remainder of the goods taken at their value." Now here again, our author's statement requires correction. For, upon investigation, it will be found, that apart from, and independently of treaties, the usage in Europe of confiscating goods confessedly contraband of war, has been both uniform and general. The disputes which have occurred on this head, have merely been, whether such and such articles were comprehended, under the denomination of contraband or not. It will likewise be found, that the captor of a cargo, partly contraband, has not, in practice, been held bound to take and pay for the innocent part of the cargo, but to have discharged his duty, by restoring it to the neutral owners.

In § 291, and § 292, the author observes: "The maritime commerce of neutral with belligerent nations, presents, in these days, peculiarities according to the treaties, usages, and pretensions of the European states, which have often enough formed the subject of diplomatic and literary discussions. The maritime powers themselves, have not always followed the same principles.

* * * The uncertainty which prevails in this respect, and the distressing consequences which it entails, have excited a strong desire for a general maritime code for Europe, composed with unanimous consent of all the powers interested."

That such a conventional code would be highly desirable, we entirely agree with the author. But past experience affords little prospect of its accomplishment. In the composition of such a code, it can never be reasonably expected, that maritime states should agree to restraints in their mode of warfare, to which continental nations have never submitted in their wars by land, and in all probability never will submit, or should abandon the means afforded them by nature, of maintaining their self-defence and independence, and of prosecuting their just rights, against the violators thereof, or should allow any of the surrounding nations, who, ostensibly and nominally remain at peace, to practice war in disguise, more injurious than their open and avowed hostility, and for their own mercantile profit, to counteract and destroy the effect of these military operations, by which the former were in the course of successfully enforcing their rights, and bringing about peace on fair and equitable terms.

In § 293 and § 294, Klüber thus treats of the visitation of neutral merchant vessels: "When a neutral merchant vessel meets a ship of war, or privateer of a belligerent power, in the maritime territory of the latter, or in that of one of its allies, or in the full open sea, she must, according to the usage of the European nations, upon a signal given, (semonce, ou coup d' assurance,) approach it, and submit to a verification or ascertainment, that the vessel, as well as the master and crew belong in reality to a neutral state, and that they do not carry goods contraband of war, to another belligerent power. If the vessel sails under convoy, that is to say, under the escort of one or more neutral ships of war, the verification consists in the declaration of the officer commanding the convoy, giving his word of honour, that the vessel, as well as the master and crew belong to his state, and that the former carries no merchandize subject to confiscation." § 294, "If the merchant vessel sails without convoy, the verification is made by the production and examination of the ship's papers on board, or log book. The property and destination of the cargo, are ascertained by the charter-party of affreightment, the bill of lading, and the certificate of a magistrate, to the declaration, which has been made before him upon oath; the neutral property of the ship is proved besides, by the deed of conveyance, the bill of sale or vendition, or by other deeds duly executed, expressing the title of property; the neutrality of the master, or person entrusted with the management of the vessel, as well as that of the crew, is proved by the pass-port, or patent of navigation, by the muster-roll of the crew, or by letters of naturalization. If the ship's papers are suspicious, the visit or search of the vessel may take place, but in the forms that are stipulated, or sanctioned by usage."

On these two sections, it may be enough to remark, that what is said of the visitation of merchant vessels when under convoy, was agreed to in the convention between the Russian Emperor Alexander, and Great Britain, in 1801, to which Sweden and Denmark afterwards acceded; but is not, as Tetens shews, sanctioned by the natural law of nations, and is not established as a part of the common consuetudinary law of nations, by long continued and uniform usage.

In § 295 and § 296, our author treats of the procedure with regard to prizes, and of the competent tribunal in prize causes. "If the captain of the ship of war or privateer, after the result of the verification, or of the visit, has reason to believe that the merchant vessel may be entirely subject to condemnation, he is entitled to capture and to carry her into port, without, however, appropriating her by his mere act, (viâ facti) or maltreating the crew. He must conduct the captured vessel, if practicable, into a port of his sovereign, or cause her to be conducted thither by an officer or prize master, and there abide the judgment of the admiralty prize court, until she be declared a good prize, or not. This often gives rise to a formal lawsuit in the courts of first instance, and of appeal. When, on the contrary, the cruizer claims only a part of the cargo, and the vessel offers to give up that part, she ought forthwith to be released; a principle of law, which, however, is but too often neglected; and gives rise to numerous complaints. If the vessel refuses to abandon what is contraband, or what the officer commanding the cruizer alleges to be such, the vessel remains under arrest; and it then belongs to the competent tribunals to decide. The burden of the proof, in such a case, lies on the master of the merchant vessel. The judgment is pronounced according to the arrangement of the public treaties, and in the absence of treaties, according to the principles of the natural law of nations; the laws of the country do not at all enter into the question, with the exception of what regards the expenses of the procedure."

§ 296, "The ocean," continues our author, "being perfectly free, the belligerent powers cannot there exercise any dominion over the merchant vessels of neutrals. These vessels are no more bound to submit, in anything whatever, to the vessels of these powers, than their governments recognize, in virtue of their political independence, nor any superiority of the governments at war, nor any common judge. The consequence is, that agreeably to the natural law of nations, no tribunal is competent in prize causes, if the vessel has been arrested in the open sea. In former times, treaties often enough attributed competency to the admiralty courts of the neutral state. The modern usage, on the contrary, recognizes, most generally, the jurisdiction of the belligerent state; whether because it is in some measure founded by the seizure or capture, (forum arresti) or upon the principle, that the owner of the prize, in the character of pursuer, must follow the defendant before his own proper courts."

"Finally, neither the one nor the other of these reasons can be applied, when the prize has been carried into a port of a third power, as sometimes happens in cases of distress; then the jurisdiction of the belligerent state is more frequently contested even by the third power."

In a note to this section, Klüber admits that the doctrine here laid down by him as the law of nations, is disputed. And it is surprising so learned a man, not writing a polemical pamphlet, in support of a particular nation or interest, but expounding the modern European law of nations, should have stated such erroneous doctrine as that law. The chief authority he refers to for this doctrine, is Hübner, (of whom we have already said enough,) passing over all the other international jurists, from Albericus Gentilis, and Grotius, to Wolfius, and Vattel. The ocean is perfectly free to all nations, for the purposes of navigation, and the conveyance of their own innocent commodities. But the liberty of the ocean is not licentiousness; it does not authorize delinquency, or the violation of right on the ocean. The liberty of the open sea does not authorize a nation to be the friend of another nation, and at the same time, to convey the implements of war to the adversary of that nation, to his manifest damage. Nations forced into war in self-defence, or in prosecution of their just rights against their adversary, do not lose the rights formerly belonging to them as nations. The nation at war has a right to seize the property of his enemy. Another nation, pretending to be a friend, has no right to obstruct the exercise of that right on the ocean, with a view to his own emolument. No nation, it is quite true, has dominion or jurisdiction over another independent nation. But each independent nation having no superior on earth, is the judge of its own rights, and of the violation of these rights. The belligerent state has clearly jurisdiction over the captor, as one of its own subjects, and over the prize itself, when brought within its territory. And if the neutral owner claims the prize as illegally captured, he thereby avails himself of, and consequently subjects himself to, the jurisdiction of the belligerent. The case here stated by Klüber, of the captor being forced by stress of weather, to carry the prize into the port of a third nation, seldom occurs, and does not affect the question, as it does not give this third state any right to interfere, or adjudicate upon the legality of the prize, unless one or more of its own subjects claim the vessel or cargo as their property, or allege piratical conduct on the part of the captor. If he had consulted Rutherforth, who wrote about the same time as Hübner, instead of the latter, Klüber would have found sounder doctrine; or if he did not choose to quote British authority, he might have founded, as we have seen, on the Italian authority of Lampredi, the Danish authority of Tetens, or the Prussian authority of Schmalz, who all smiled at the absurd, as well as untrue hypothesis of a merchant vessel being a part of the territory of the state, such as to have the effect of creating or constituting a territorial jurisdiction.

In § 297 and § 298, Klüber treats of commerce with blockaded places. "A place is said to be a blockaded place, whether a port, a fortress, a city, or a camp, where by the arrangements of the power, which attacks it, with troops or vessels, stationed sufficiently near, there is evident danger in entering without consent of that power. Such a place, in so far as it is considered to be blockaded to this effect, for example, a port on the coast of the sea, ought to be regarded by neutrals, as being in the power of the belligerent state, which holds it blockaded. This power is, therefore, entitled to exclude at will, neutral states and their subjects from all communication, whether navigation or commerce properly so called, with this same place. The time of the commencement of the blockade, must in general, be fixed, according to the determination thereupon; it cannot, however, in any case, occasion prejudice to vessels and individual traders, before they have been sufficiently informed of it. What is certain is, that a mere verbal declaration by one of the belligerent powers, Blocus sur papier, cannot establish a blockade, in the sense, and with the legal consequences of the law of nations, § 297. "The power which maintains the blockade, may use force and vindicate its right against the neutrals, who, against its express declaration, have knowingly carried on, or endeavoured to carry on, commerce with the blockaded place. Usually belligerents are contented with the confiscation of the vessel and cargo; but sometimes those who have infringed the rights of blockade, are also punished in their persons. The cargo is often restored if the neutral owner, or his agent, prove that he had given the order to convey the goods by sea, before the blockade was known, and that it was not in his power to recal that order before the time fixed for the departure of the vessel.

In § 299, § 300, § 301, and § 302, Klüber discusses the questions respecting hostile goods in neutral, and neutral goods in hostile vessels. And here it is singular, that a writer, not of a polemical pamphlet, but of a system of the modern European law of nations, should take a side, like an advocate for a party, should invert the order of natural law, which, while it permits the use of force and the seizure of the property of the enemy, as the means of self-defence, or of obtaining justice, enjoins respect for the property of one's friend and neighbour, and should assume, as a legal proverb, the fiction which determines the quality and character of goods not from their own nature, but from the quality or character of the vehicle, in which they are transmitted from one place to another. Yet such is the account of the natural or common law of nations, which Klüber gives in this important department, very different, indeed, from what we found in the first volume of this work, to have been the true common law of nations, through a long series of ages, as appearing not from treaties or special compacts between nations, but from the records of the actual conduct of nations towards each other, as contained in their own statutes, ordinances and edicts, or proclamations, in their judicial determinations, and in the writings of their international jurists. Thus, § 299, "Upon the ocean, every vessel is held to be ex-territorial, with reference to all foreign nations. A merchant vessel ought to be considered as a floating colony of her state. Consequently, no belligerent power ought to allow itself, upon the ocean, to visit a neutral vessel, nor to confiscate the hostile goods with which it may be loaded, and still less to appropriate the vessel on account of the cargo belonging to an enemy. This is expressed by the legal proverb: the neutral flag covers the cargo, or, 'free ship, free goods,' that is to say, the neutral vessel renders the cargo neutral. It is the same with the goods of neutrals loaded in hostile vessels, which the belligerent power is no more entitled to confiscate, than if they were found on the continental territory of his enemy."

This theory of the maritime law of nations, Klüber obviously founds entirely on the fiction of a merchant vessel being a part of the neutral nation, and equivalent in law to the part of the globe occupied by that nation, as its fixed and stable territory. But that absurdity appears to have been first introduced by Hübner, and rests very much on his authority, such as it is, and that of some other controversial writers. Even Professor Totze seems ashamed of it, and rests his theory upon a more plausible basis. And for a refutation of it, it is sufficient to refer to the passages already quoted from Rutherforth, Lampredi, Tetens, and Schmalz.

Accordingly, Klüber is obliged immediately to admit, that the principles actually observed by the European nations, are different from what he has stated to be the principles of the natural law of nations. Thus,

§300, "These principles, however, of the natural law of nations, have not been always followed in Europe. The Consolato del Mare, which was composed or compiled towards the middle of the thirteenth century, established as a principle, the absolute liberty of the property of neutrals; that is to say, that the property of the enemy on board a neutral vessel, should be liable to confiscation; but that neutral property in a hostile vessel, should not be so. Free ship, unfree goods; unfree ship, free goods. This principle was recognized in almost all the maritime treaties, and by all the maritime tribunals, till the middle of the seventeenth century."

"But since that period," continues Klüber, § 301, (all the origin of the system of the armed neutrality, adopted in 1780,) many treaties have sanctioned two contrary principles; namely, that the flag or the vessel covers the cargo or merchandize, or the friendly flag saves the hostile merchandize, or 'free ship, free goods,' and that the vessel confiscates the cargo, or verfallenes Schiff, verfallenes Gut; in other words, that a neutral vessel has a right to convey free hostile goods, with the exception of contraband of war. And that the goods of friends, loaded in a hostile vessel, may be confiscated with the vessel." In the notes to this section, Klüber refers to the controversial writers, Hübner, Totze, Galiani, Büsch, and Schlegel, and particularly to the different treaties, which we formerly noticed when surveying that period, as having been concluded between various European nations, including England, from about the middle of the seventeenth century, downwards; stating, that from 1642 to 1780, there were thirty-six treaties, in which was adopted the rule, that the flag or the vessel covers the cargo; and fifteen only, which followed the contrary rule. But into the arithmetical accuracy of this enumeration of treaties by Klüber, or these other authors, we do not consider it material to enquire. That these treaties formed the conventional law between the contracting parties, to the extent of their stipulations, and for the periods of their duration, we have never disputed. Any two nations may, of course, by mutual consent, concede to each other, privileges or advantages which they could neither exact from each other, nor be compelled to give at common law. But such bi-partite pactions, containing mutual concessions or grants, for reciprocal considerations, do not alter the natural and necessary, or general and common consuetudinary law of nations, especially where those very nations continue to observe that common conseutudinary law, with regard to all other nations, except those with whom they have made such special compacts. Bi-lateral contracts between A and B, C and D, E and F, although of the same or similar import, can never bind A or B to C or D, or to E or F; or vice versa. Contracts can become binding on nations, as on individuals, only by their becoming principal or original parties, or by their accession to such original or principal contracts. The fact of having entered into a convention with one nation, can never impose an obligation to enter into a similar treaty with another different nation. Treaties afford evidence merely of reciprocal stipulations; not of actual conduct, or of custom or usage of action. And when the two contracting parties, have each tacitly allowed certain stipulations and engagements to remain unfulfilled, no third party has any right to complain. A government which treats the subjects of another government in a particular way, may, upon the principle of reciprocity, give the latter a right to insist, that its subjects shall be treated in a similar way. But a government that makes a particular contract with another government, does not thereby, give a third government a right to insist, that the former shall enter with it into a similar arrangement. A majority of nations cannot, by entering contemporaneously into similar separate conventions between each two, or into one grand or principal convention among two or three, acceded to by a number of others, impose upon the minority of nations, any legal obligation to enter into, or observe a similar convention. And as little can any series of similar conventions, entered into in succession, by the majority of nations, either one between each two, or one principal convention between two, acceded to by the others, bind the minority of nations to give up the treaties which they have found, or may find it expedient to conclude with each other, or to observe the conventions which the majority have entered into, but to which they have not consented at all, or only by particular treaties, or special pactions with certain members of the majority.

And that such, besides being agreeable to legal principle, was the feeling and understanding of nations generally, is manifest, not only from the parties to these conventions observing them, only with regard to the opposite contracting parties, and acting otherwise according to the previous recognized common law of nations, with reference to all other nations; but also from treaties of a different or contrary import, being entered into by the minority with each other, or even with many of the majority who had concluded the treaties, which are represented as having changed the face of the whole law of nations in this department. For in § 302, Klüber is forced to make the following admissions. "There are, however, many treaties in which the ancient principles have been preserved, with this modification solely, that it is forbidden to furnish to the enemy contraband of war, and to trade with blockaded ports. A small number of treaties permit also a belligerent power to confiscate on board neutral vessels, not only the property of the enemy, but also goods contraband of war destined for the enemy. Finally, a good many treaties contain no arrangements sufficiently clear and general upon this subject. There are even many states, between which there exists in this respect no conventional arrangement. France had established by a law of 1681, that hostile merchandise on board a neutral vessel, behoved to subject to confiscation the vessel and the remainder of the cargo. But now-a-days that power has publicly recognized the principle, that the flag covers the merchandise; while Great Britain has declared the opposite."

In this passage, although it seems to imply as much, Klüber surely could not mean, that Maritime international law rests solely upon treaties or conventions; or that the French government, even by its celebrated Ordonnance of 1681, which we have seen only repeated in the respect alluded to, the ordonnances of the preceding century, or that the British government, by its proclamations or orders, could constitute the law of nations, unless these ordonnances or proclamations enforced principles or rules founded on justice, reciprocity and general expediency, or sanctioned by long and generally established usage. But we cannot so easily excuse his holding out in his note as an authority, or as containing a true statement of facts, the mendacious report, which, in 1812, Napoleon caused his minister for foreign affairs to make, with regard to the rights claimed by neutrals having been finally settled by the treaty of Utrecht, and having been from that time observed by France; a report, which, as we formerly noticed, although notoriously unfounded and fallacious, M. Schoell informs us, not only the French, but the subjects of the other continental governments, were required to believe, under the penalty of being held an enemy of the Great Empire.

In § 303, to § 309, inclusive, Klüber gives an account of the scheme of the armed neutrality. And although perhaps we have enlarged enough on that subject in Chapters IX. and X. of volume first, when surveying the periods from 1776 to 1793, and from 1793 to 1801, yet as Klüber's work being very short, is easily procured, and is likely to be generally read, and as the account he gives of these events, appears to be partial and not quite correct or fair, a few observations on it seem to be requisite.

In § 303, Klüber informs us, that even the conventional rights of the neutral flag were not duly respected by the belligerent powers, especially after France and Spain had, in 1778 and 1779, taken part in the war between Great Britain and her American Colonies; that the definitions of contraband of war, and of a blockaded port were often extended, and applied at pleasure; that these arbitrary measures, led Russia to establish in 1780, a system of principles in favour of the navigation and commerce of neutrals; and that according to this system, the belligerent powers, who should refuse to recognize it, should be constrained to do so, by the naval force of the neutral nations. "En suite de ce systême, les puissances belligerentes, qui se seraient refusées à le reconnoitre, devaient y être contraints, par une force navale des nations neutres."

Now, we are not aware that at the period here alluded to, any of the European nations, then neutral, except the Dutch against the French, had any conventional right to protect the goods of the enemy from capture by belligerents. The conduct of Holland in that war, in contravention of former treaties, released Great Britain from any obligation to continue to concede to that republic, the indulgence which she had stipulated at the peace of Utrecht. If France, Spain, and Britain, chose each tacitly to pass from any reciprocal stipulations in favour of each other, by which their goods, though hostile, might have been protected by the neutral flag, no third party had any right to complain By the then existing treaty between Prussia and Britain, these governments had agreed, that their maritime commerce during war, should be regulated à l' usage, by the established practice of the European states, which certainly did not give the neutral the privilege of protecting hostile property in the open seas.

The system of the armed neutrality, therefore, was not warranted by any violation of the conventional rights of neutrals, strictly and properly so called. And with regard to the alleged extension and arbitrary application of the definition of contraband and blockade, the fact appears to have been, that, in the course of the war between Great Britain and her American colonies, in which they had taken part, France and Spain, on the one hand, stood very much in need of materials, raw and manufactured, for the construction and equipment of ships of war, while Russia, Sweden, and Denmark, possessed an ample supply of such materials. In these circumstances, the latter nations were naturally anxious to sell and convey, and the former nations to purchase and receive, or import such naval stores, without the risk of capture by British cruizers, and of confiscation, on the ground of the conveyance of such materials to the enemy, being inconsistent with that pretended neutrality, inasmuch as, if not strictly arms, guns or ammunition, they were at least naval stores, directly destined for the naval arsenals of the enemy, and obviously intended to be used for warlike or military purposes. Such seem, at least, to have been the political motives, towards the adoption of the armed neutrality. But even although the scheme had been less the dictate of national interested policy, and had had a meaner origin, neither Russia nor any other state, could, in the language of Klüber, of its own authority, "establish a system of principles," except for its own subjects. And, although Klüber appears to have considered the use of force, in support of this system, as quite justifiable, if not praiseworthy, there seems to be more reason for holding it was, not a little presumptuous in these neutral states, not merely to frame a set of rules, obviously for their own respective advantage, and quite different from the practice, which, except in cases of special paction, had existed in Europe for centuries preceding; and to threaten to compel other nations to submit to such a deviation from established usage, by force of arms, to the effect of de-

2 A

priving these other nations, of an important portion of the means afforded them by nature, for maintaining their independence, and vindicating their just rights.

In § 304, § 305, and § 306, Klüber details the principles and consequences of the armed neutrality of 1780; and states, that having been destined to be the basis of an universal maritime code, it was soon fully inserted in many conventional treaties; thus, leaving it to be inferred, that it was universally adopted; whereas, it was not permanently recognized and acted upon, either by France or Spain, any more than by Great Britain. So far from being recognized as an universal maritime code, we have seen, it was expressly departed from in 1793, by the Empress Catherine herself. And it is amusing to observe, how Klüber slurs over this fact. "Si dans la suite, pendant la guerre de la revolution, (1793) la Russie, et la Prusse s' en éloignèrent quelquefois, cette inconstance ne fut que transitoire; et elle donna lieu à la Suède, et au Danemarck de s'y attacher de nouveau." But the fact is, that by the conventions with Great Britain in 1793, both Russia and Prussia reverted in such matters, à l' usage, to the former practice, or common consuetudinary maritime law of the European nations.[1]

In § 307, Klüber proceeds to observe, "that the long duration of the war between Great Britain and France and her allies, of new, made the powers of the north feel the necessity of securing, by defensive alliances, what he calls, les droits du pavillon neutre;" and as the result, gives an account of the suddenly adopted scheme of the Emperor Paul, in 1800, called "the Second Armed Neutrality." But of this scheme we have already said enough, in the proper place. And, in § 308, Klüber himself states, "this new armed neutrality was not adopted

[1] Martens Recueil, V. 117, 169.

by so many powers, and was of short duration; as six months after its conclusion, Great Britain, in June 1801, effected an alliance with Russia, by means of a maritime convention, to which Denmark and Sweden found it necessary to accede." Yet such, we regret to observe, is the anti-British bias or prejudice of M. Klüber, that even the import or effect of this convention, whether intentionally or not, is not correctly stated by him. Thus, "Il est vrai, que dans cette nouvelle convention le commerce des neutres avec les ports et les côtes des puissances en guerre, fut également déclaré libre, a l'exception seulement de celui de la contrebande de guerre, et de la propriété ennemie; mais du reste, il fut permis aux vaisseaux de guerre, (non pas aux armateurs) de visiter les navires neutres, et même ceux naviguans sous convoi, dès qu'il y aurait quelque soupçon contre eux." Now, it is plain, that the freedom of neutral commerce and navigation, with the ports of the enemy, except in contraband of war, or the case of blockade, or in carrying the goods of the enemy, did not, in 1801, require any new conventional declaration to support it, because it had been recognized in practice, and had formed the common consuetudinary maritime law of Europe for at least four centuries. And while the latter part of the passage just quoted, obviously implies, that, by this convention, it was permitted only to ships of war, not to privateers, to visit neutral vessels, the truth is, that this convention permitted, agreeably to the common consuetudinary law, not only ships of war, but also privateers, to visit neutral vessels, if not under convoy, and merely precluded privateers from visiting neutral vessels, when under convoy, confining that right to state, or government, ships of war.

Farther, in § 309, Klüber seems so pleased with the system of the armed neutrality, that he alleges it was subsequently adopted of new, and a second time abandoned by Russia and Sweden. And, to make out this, he avails himself of the temporary misunderstanding, which, in 1806-7, occurred between the Emperor Alexander and the British government, partly from the refusal of the latter to accede to a new loan, partly from the unfortunate seizure by Britain of the Danish fleet, and partly also from the influence which the then recent success of Napoleon against Prussia, in the decisive battle of Friedland, could not fail to have, prudentially, on the Russian Emperor. But, by this time, in fact, none of the continental governments could be said to be altogether independent of French domination. Although, in November 1807, the Russian government may have declared, it regarded the convention of 1801 annulled, no such actual hostilities appear to have followed between Russia and Britain, as to require a formal renewal of that convention. And, by the treaty of July 1812, between these governments, if the maritime convention of 1801 was not renewed, as little, Klüber admits, was the system of the armed neutrality, in any respect, recognized; matters being left to be regulated upon the basis of usage, that is, agreeably to the common consuetudinary maritime law of nations.

In § 310, Klüber gives an account of certain new restrictions alleged to have been imposed on maritime navigation and commerce, by the conduct of Great Britain towards neutrals. And as he here concentrates the alleged transgressions by Great Britain, of the law of nations, prior to the Berlin and Milan decrees of Napoleon, it may be proper here again to ascertain, what foundation there may be in fact or law, for such serious charges. Klüber thus commences:—"Dans la lutte, aussi longue, qu' opiniâtre, entre la Grande-Bretagne et la France, qui se renouvella quatorze mois après la paix d' Amiens, le commerce maritime des neutres, et même toute communication par mer, et par cela, aussi le commerce continental dans toute l' Europe, furent reduits à un tel point, qu' on ne l' avait jamais vu. La nécessité d' une code maritime universel, n' en fut, que plus vivement sentie." Now, in the first place, it is rather strange, that while he thus talks of the long and obstinate struggle between Great Britain and France, renewed under Napoleon, as having been so injurious to neutrals, and as making them feel more sensibly the necessity for an universal maritime code, Klüber should omit all notice, at this place, of the contemporaneous struggles between France and the other European states, of the series of stratagems and victories, by which Napoleon annexed Belgium and Italy to France, reduced Holland to the condition of a province, for a time subjugated Spain and Portugal, humbled the sovereigns of Austria and Prussia in their respective capitals, oppressed and ultimately destroyed the Russian capital—which certainly inflicted infinitely greater miseries on mankind, than any maritime operations during the same period did, or could do on neutrals, and still more urgently required the establishment of an universal code of the law of nations, to prevent the recurrence of such gross aggressions upon neutral and peaceful nations.

Klüber thus proceeds to charge Great Britain: "La Grande Bretagne, surtout depuis 1806, employa sa prépondérance maritime pour faire valoir contre les neutres le même principe, qu'elle avoit déjà établi précédemment dans plusieurs traités, notamment dans ceux avec les Etats-Unis d'Amérique, et avec les villes Anseatiques, portant que le pavillon ne couvre point la cargaison ou la marchandise. Elle y joignit la prétension, que même les navires marchands naviguans sous convoi devaient se soumettre à la visite de ses vaisseaux de guerre, et de ses armateurs."

Now, here it is not easy to abstain from charging this learned expounder of the Droit des Gens Moderne de l'Europe, either with ignorance, or with such gross bias and prejudice, as to be inconsistent with bona fides. With what regard to truth could this writer allege, that Britain sought, by treaties merely, as if it were a new claim, to establish her right to capture the property of her enemies, when found in the open seas, although on board neutral vessels, when it is notorious, that England had for centuries, invariably, and independently of any treaty, exercised that right, under the common consuetudinary maritime law of nations, and, as we have seen, agreeably to the practice of every state in Europe, except when the right was departed from by special paction or treaty? It is, indeed, equally a perversion of legal principle, and a violation of historic truth, to represent the proposition, "the flag covers the cargo," as having been recognized to be the general rule of law. The obvious rule of law is, that the moveable property of the enemy may be seized, whether in his own territory, or in the oceans and open seas, which admit not of any territorial dominion; but that the property of friends and neutrals ought to be respected. And the claim of neutrals to protect the property of the enemy from capture, when exposed in the open seas, to the manifest injury of one of the belligerents, is an exception from the general rule of law, and a pretension, which Klüber himself, in § 300, tell us, was not put forth till the middle of the seventeenth century, and then attempted to be realized only by special paction or treaty. Farther, to represent the right of visit and search, which is, in law, the necessary consequence of the admitted right to capture the property of the enemy, and contraband goods, as a separate and novel pretension in 1806, is equally untrue, as absurd. And the fact is, that the plan of protecting neutral merchant vessels from search by means of convoy, is only a recent pretension; which we saw, was attempted to be enforced in 1651, by Christina, Queen of Sweden, but was then abandoned, as untenable or hopeless.

The following is the remaining charge here brought forward by Klüber, against Great Britain. "Elle soutint, que des côtes, et des provinces entières, dans le sens le plus étendu, pouvaient être mises en état de blocus par une simple déclaration, (blocus fictif ou sur papier); qu'à cet éffet, il devait suffire, qu' elle donnât une notification publique quelconque (blocus per notificationem) ou envoyât croiser sur les côtes en question, des navires armés en guerre, (blocus de facto); qu' enfin tout bâtiment neutre naviguant vers les côtes ou ports désignés, devait être réputé avoir rompu le blocus, dès qu' il y aurait de la probabilité, que la déclaration de la mise en état de blocus etait parvenue à sa connaissance, avant, ou durant sa course." But in his note, Klüber is obliged to add, "Cependant, il faut avouer, que cette extension de la notion du blocus, n' appartient pas exclusivement à la Grande-Bretagne." And, as we formerly saw, this blockade by notification, was frequently resorted to in early times, in modern Europe.

There can be no doubt, however, that such a blockade is inconsistent with legal principle; because, it is not a fact, on which a right can be founded, but a fiction. A true or real blockade, is a military operation by one enemy against another; and, if not carried into execution by an adequate force, is no such military occupation, as neutrals are bound to respect, but a mere fiction; like the social compact of Rousseau, like the fiction by which a merchant vessel, sailing in the wide ocean, is represented as a part of the stable territory of the sovereign, whose subjects navigate the vessel; or, like the decree of the French convention, that the property of the vessel should be determined by the property, not of the vessel, but of the cargo. Such fictions are altogether inadmissible in the law of nature and nations. And accordingly, if he had consulted the proper authorities, somewhat more to be relied on, than the French memoir of 1812, concocted by the foreign minister of Napoleon, to which he refers, he would have found, that neither the British orders in council, from 1803 to 1806, nor the judgments of Sir Wm. Scott, during that period, authorized or sanctioned, or gave effect to any blockade, which was not actual, or maintained by a sufficient force. Indeed, nothing could be more equitable, than the judgments of Sir Wm. Scott in this department, prior to the Berlin and Milan decrees.

In the sections, from § 311 to § 316 inclusive, Klüber proceeds to give first, a very brief, and then a little more detailed account of the new restrictions imposed on neutral navigation and commerce, by the French continental system, and by what he calls the British system of blockade. And this account, certainly, resembles more the ex-parte contemporaneous political brochure of an advocate, desirous to justify the French conventional system, as necessary to counteract and repress the previous aggressions of Great Britain, than that of an impartial historian of events, writing sometime after their occurrence, and the native of a country different from that of either of these contending powers. It, therefore, becomes necessary here again, accurately to examine the nature, and the dates, of the respective proceedings of these two governments, in order to ascertain, with which the alleged new restrictions on neutral commerce, and the alleged breach of the maritime law of nations, originated.

Section 311 commences thus: "A ces prétensions de

la Grande-Bretagne, Napoléon opposa dans les années 1806 et 1807, par des décréts datés de Berlin et de Milan, son systême continental, qui défendit non-seulement tout commerce, mais aussi toute autre communication avec l'Angleterre, et nommément le trafic de marchandise d'origine Anglaise, et des denrées coloniales Anglaises, tant pour la France, que pour les états des souverains du continent alliés avec elle." But the British pretensions here alluded to, are those specified by the author in the preceding section. And these, we have seen, were neither many nor new. The first was the right to visit neutral vessels, and to capture the property of the enemy, and contraband goods, when found in the open sea, though on board such vessels; a right which, unless departed from by special treaty, we have seen, had existed at common law, and in the general practice of all the European nations, from the ages preceding the compilation of the Consolato del Mare. The other claim was the right of blockade, which, when actual, and supported by adequate force, has been deemed a lawful military operation from time immemorial, and which, although attempted to be exercised by notification merely, by different nations on different former occasions, had not been attempted to be so exercised by the British government, or so sanctioned by the British courts of prize, either during the French revolutionary war, or during the war renewed in 1803, prior to the French Berlin decree of November 1806. It was not till after the French had, in spring 1806, effectually excluded all English commerce from the ports in the south of Germany, that the British government, by the order in council of May 1806, declared all the coasts, rivers, and ports, from the Elbe to the port of Brest, inclusive, in a state of blockade, with this modification, that it should be free for neutral vessels, which should have on board neither hostile property, nor contraband of war, to approach these coasts, and to enter or sail from the said rivers and ports, except the coasts, rivers, and ports from Ostend to the Seine; provided the said vessels, which should thus approach and enter, had not taken on board their cargo in any port belonging to the enemies of Great Britain, or in their possession; and that the said vessels which should sail from the said rivers and ports, should not be destined for any port belonging to the enemies of Great Britain or in their possession, and should not have previously infringed the right of blockade. But, although a general notification was thus given of the coasts, rivers, and ports, against which the blockade was to be directed, which is proper, if not necessary, in the case of an actual, as well as of a paper or fictitious blockade, the blockade here notified was not a paper or fictitious blockade, such as to subject to confiscation, vessels which had entered or departed from any of these rivers or ports, when there was not an adequate force stationed near them. In general, such an adequate force was so stationed. But when there was no such force so stationed, namely, a force such as to render it dangerous for the enemy to approach, the neutral vessels were not condemned for breach of blockade.[1] There was here no departure from the common recognized mode of warfare; and even when there was an actual blockade, maintained by an adequate force, the express exception in this order of council in favour of neutrals, left their own proper commerce, as distinct from that of the opposite belligerent, almost entire.

Such were all the military operations of Great Britain, in the shape of maritime blockade, prior to the Berlin decree of November 1806. But Napoleon having before

[1] Rob. Rep. III. pp. 147, 148; V. pp. 256-262; and VI. pp. 64-67, pp. 112-122.

that time, by the victory of Friedland, laid Prussia prostrate, and having concluded the peace of Tilsit, with that power, and with Russia, foresaw and proclaimed, that the system of continental blockade would no longer be an empty name; and from the capital of Prussia, in November 1806, issued the decree, by which the British isles were formally declared in a state of blockade. By this French Berlin decree, according to Klüber, "all commerce and correspondence with these isles were interdicted. In consequence, letters and packets, addressed either in England, or to an Englishman, or written in the English language, were not to pass by post, and should be seized. Every individual subject of England, who might be met with in a country occupied by French troops, or by those of the allies of France, was to be made prisoner of war. All stores, merchandise, or other property belonging to the English, were to be declared good prize. Trade in English merchandise was prohibited. And all merchandise, the produce of English factories or colonies, was declared confiscated. No vessel coming directly from England, or the English colonies, or having been there since the publication of this decree, was to be received in any port. The vessels which, by means of a false declaration, contravened this regulation, were to be seized and confiscated with their cargoes, as if they were English property."

In self-defence against, and in order to counteract the operation of this French Berlin decree of November 1806, which was certainly at least an unprecedented mode of warfare, the British government resorted, in January 1807, to a similar measure, which was not properly a legal military operation, like a blockade, but a general retaliatory interdiction of commerce, to cease as soon as the French Emperor should revoke the decree of Berlin. This British order in council of January 1807, according to Klüber, declared, "That no vessel should trade from one port to another, of those ports, which belonged to, or were in the possession of France or her allies, or were under such subjection to her, as to have no commerce with England; and that every neutral vessel, informed of this order, who should be found on a voyage for such a port, should be captured, brought into port, and declared, as well as her cargo, a good and lawful prize." And, as several of the continental nations, such as Prussia, Denmark, and Russia, had, in the course of the year 1807, under the influence of Napoleon, acceded to his continental system of blockade, the British government, by another order in council in Nov. 1807, directed, according to Klüber, "That all the ports and places of France and her allies, those of every other country at war with Great Britain, those of the European countries, from which the English flag was excluded, although these countries were not at war with Great Britain; finally, that all the ports and places of the colonies belonging to the enemies of this power, should henceforth be subjected to the same restrictions relative to commerce and navigation, as if they were really blockaded in the most rigorous manner; that all commerce in articles, the produce of the soil, or manufactures of the before-mentioned countries, should thenceforth be deemed illegal; that every vessel whatever, departing from these countries, or on a voyage to them, should be lawfully captured, and the prize, with her cargo, adjudged to the captor; that every vessel which should carry a certificate of origin, according to which the goods on board were not the produce either of English possessions or of English manufactures, should be declared, if the owner had knowledge of the order in question, a good prize, and adjudged to the captor, with all the goods belonging to the persons, by whom, or for whom, the certificate had been taken."

On the other hand, in order apparently to counteract the British orders in council, of January and November 1807, Napoleon pushed still farther his system of continental blockade, by the decree of Milan in December 1807, bearing in substance, according to Klüber, "that every vessel belonging to whatever nation, which should have allowed itself to be visited by an English cruizer, or carried into an English port, or should have paid any tax whatever to the English government, should by that alone be de-nationalized; that this vessel must be regarded as English property, and declared a good and valid prize, as soon as she should be captured; that every vessel, to whatsoever nation she might belong, and whatever might be her cargo, fitted out from the ports of England, or of the colonies, whether English, or occupied by English troops, or going to England, or to the English colonies, should be declared good prize, and when captured by ships of war or privateers, should be adjudged to the captor."

Such was really the order, in point of time, in which these extreme measures of hostility were adopted by the French Emperor, and by the British government; although, from the mode in which these events are recorded in the narrative by Klüber, it would appear, the British government first resorted to the measure of a general interdiction of commerce with France and its allies; whereas, under the orders in council of 1803, and of May 1806, the British government merely exercised the ancient warlike right of capturing the property of the enemy, when found in the open seas, although on board neutral vessels; and of confiscating neutral vessels that had committed a breach of an actual blockade, maintained by an adequate force; while the Berlin decree of Nov. 1806, was not an actual blockade, but a general interdiction of commerce. With regard to the French continental system, Klüber states, it was acceded to by Prussia, Denmark, and Russia, in 1807, by Austria in 1809, by Sweden in 1809—1810, by Holland in 1810; that it was abandoned by Russia and Sweden in 1812, by Prussia in 1813; and that the fall of Napoleon put an end to it even in France. It may, therefore, be here remarked, that whatever opinion may be entertained, with regard to the legality of the British orders in council, as affecting nations who retained their independence, and remained absolutely and completely neutral, there can be no doubt, that against those European states, who thus acceded to the continental system of Napoleon, these retaliatory measures were perfectly justifiable; because, through the influence or dread of Napoleon, these nations had not only sacrificed the character of independent states, but had also completely laid aside the character, and forfeited the rights of neutrality, and subjected themselves, as allies of the enemy, to such operations as were necessary to counteract the new hostile measures, in which they thus concurred and participated.

With regard to the British orders in council, Klüber states correctly, that the order of November 1807, was revoked by that of April 1809, with reference to all ports, other than those of Holland, to the Ems inclusive, of France, of the colonies and dependencies of those two powers, and of the northern part of Italy. But in the same partial spirit, he takes care to remark, that this revocation was confined to the north of Europe, and south of Italy. And he omits to mention, that the British orders were conditional, and to cease, as soon as the Berlin and Milan decrees of Napoleon were recalled. On the other hand, in § 316, Klüber assumes gratuitously, the existence of the pretended decree of the 23rd April 1811, recalling the Berlin and Milan decrees, with regard to the United States of America, although no evidence has yet been adduced, that any such decree was actually passed till the following year; and adds, that in June 1812, the British government likewise recalled the former orders of council of Jan. 1807, and April 1809, without observing that this was done, as soon as the revocation by Napoleon was authentically communicated to that government.

CHAPTER XIII.

Review of part of the work of Dr. Schmelzing.

As contemporaneous with Klüber, we may place Dr. Julius Schmelzing, whose work, entitled, Systematisches Grundriss des Practischen Europäischen Völkerrechtes, consists of three parts, which were published successively at Rudolfstadt, in the years 1818, 1819, and 1820. As we have observed elsewhere, we do not think, Dr. Schmelzing has been fortunate in adopting the defective general arrangement of the Roman law, as his model for arranging the doctrines of the modern law of nations. But his more minute arrangements are more distinct and complete; he abounds in learning; and his views are, upon the whole, less partial, than many of the German controversial writers, from 1780 downwards. Of course, only a small part of his systematic outlines, in three volumes, of the general law of nations, relates immediately to maritime law; and we shall here merely notice shortly that part.

In Chapter III. of the second division of his work, on the real rights of the European nations, he treats of the right of dominion over the sea; of the customary sea ceremonial, in the parts of the sea subject to the dominion of maritime states, in the parts of the sea not subject to such states or territorial, and in the wide open seas, or oceans. In chapter iv. of this second division of his work, the author treats of the customary modes of making use of the sea; of the exclusive right of navigation; of the title to levy certain duties or tolls; of the exclusive use of the produce of the sea, generally, and of what is thrown on shore by the sea.

In part III. of his work, the author treats of the "obligation-rights," as he calls them, of the European nations; in the first chapter of that part, of the rights and obligations of the European nations, arising out of their friendly relations; and in the third section of that chapter, of traffic in merchandise among nations, of the natural freedom of trade, of the trade of the European powers, in Europe, and with other parts of the globe, of particular arrangements by particular treaties, of the maintenance of commercial relations through consuls.

In part III., chapter ii., the author treats of the rights and obligations of the European nations, from their hostile relations. In section I. of this chapter, of the origin of hostile relations among nations; of the violations of the laws of nations. In section II., of the different modes of prosecuting and enforcing rights among nations. In title first of this section, of the means for the amicable settlement of disputes among nations. In title second, of the settlement of existing disputes by war. In this title, after some preliminary explanations, with regard to the right of making war, and the mode of carrying it on, the author treats, 1, of the rules and usages of international law, which relate to the person of the enemy; 2, of those international legal rules and usages, which relate to the public property of the hostile state, and to the private property, and the goods of the individual subjects of that state, including capture as prize in maritime war, transference of the property of vessels captured as maritime prize, and postliminium in immoveable property, and in moveable effects; 3, of the rules and usages of international law, which relate to single warlike operations or enterprises; 4, of conventions with the enemy during war; 5, of the rights and obligations of allied, auxiliary, and subsidizing nations; 6, of the rights of neutrality.

Under this last head of neutrality, the author treats, 1, of the territory of the neutral state, and of the hostile persons, and goods, that may be found therein; 2, of the commercial relations of neutral states; 3, of ex-parte assistance by a neutral state; 4, of the rights of neutrality at sea. Here the author considers the chief points in dispute, hitherto agitated between belligerent and neutral maritime powers. And although his observations on the subject are not very acute or profound, they are distinct and sensible; and he discusses the several points, in the shape of questions, with much greater modesty and fairness, than Klüber, and some other Germans. Thus, 1. What articles are to be considered contraband of war? Immediate necessaries for war; mediate necessaries for war; and goods, which cannot, at all, be considered even as mediate necessaries for war. Mode of proceeding with contraband goods, and with vessels carrying them. 2. How far the right of search by belligerent powers extends against neutral vessels, with, or without convoy? 3. Whether "the free ship makes free goods, and the unfree ship, unfree goods?" 4. Whether, or not, it is lawful for neutrals to carry on in time of war, a trade, which they are prohibited from doing during peace? 5. What extent ought to be given to the idea of a blockade? 6. To whom belongs the decision of disputed cases, respecting prizes captured from neutrals? 7. How far does the right of postliminium take place in the case of the recapture of prizes, taken from neutrals?

Of the preceding sub-divisions of the title on the rights of neutrality, we shall merely translate a part of the sixth, on the question whether the vessel covers the cargo; as a specimen of the author's historical correctness and fairness of view; which, on this point, seems to coincide with that of M. Schmalz.

§ 540, vol. III., p. 300—301. "In the middle ages, the sea laws of the Consòlato del Mare decided, that hostile goods, even when on board neutral vessels at sea, should be confiscated; but that neutral goods, although loaded in hostile ships, must be freely delivered to the owner. This decision was repeated almost without exception, in all the treaties during the fifteenth, sixteenth, and in the beginning of the seventeenth century; and the same maxim was followed in the prize and admiralty courts. After the discovery of America, and the settlements in the East Indies, this principle became of greater importance; and was, on that account, even frequently contested. The enemy, by means of his cruizers, interrupted the trade with the colonies, and captured their costly produce. People also loaded, more frequently, their goods on board neutral ships; and these might not only withdraw the booty from the enemy, but also spare the mariners of the unemployed merchantmen, for the fleet of the enemy."

"The neutral powers saw the great advantage to their ship-owners, which would accrue from, and accordingly set up, the principle, that the flag should always cover the cargo; that from neutral ships hostile goods must not be taken, contraband excepted. The same principle is found mentioned in the treaties of the European powers with the Turks and the Barbary States; from which, since the middle of the seventeenth century, down to the origin of the armed neutrality, it was likewise adopted into most of the treaties between the European powers, although, in a great measure, with small effect. On the other hand, contrary also to the Consolato del Mare, people chose to allow belligerent powers to declare as good prize, neutral merchandise found on board hostile ships. And there was introduced a proverbial rule, 'free ship, free goods, unfree ship, unfree goods; forfeit or confiscate ship, forfeit or confiscate cargo.'"

"It is not to be perceived, how this contest may come to an end, so long as people believe, that to destroy the maritime trade of the enemy is the annihilation of the most important source of his acquired wealth; so long, as a belligerent power certainly cannot be expected to tolerate, that a neutral ship-owner should, so decidedly, defend or support and protect his enemy; so long, as that belligerent cannot be expected to remain satisfied with the compensation, which is proffered to him,—namely, to capture neutral goods on board hostile vessels, along with the vessel itself; for what neutral merchant would willingly run the risk of shipping his goods on board a hostile vessel? Then, only, is an equitable adjustment to be hoped for, when it is discovered and perceived, that all these captures merely ruin the fortunes of individuals, but never deprive the enemy of the most important source of his wealth."

"Belligerents, too, according to the ancient international law of the Consolato del Mare, have done the greatest injustice, in condemning also the neutral ship, as lawful prize, on board of which hostile goods have been found. To such a ship-owner, it is a sufficient punishment that he loses his freight, and that, in consequence of his being carried into the hostile port, he misses the opportunity of another voyage, and of earning a new freight." In this observation we quite agree; but happily, as we have seen, this charge of injustice, can only be brought against the governments of France and Spain, not against those of England or Holland.

The author concludes the part of his work, which falls under our present inquiries, with an account of the system of the armed neutrality, and of the continental system of Napoleon, with the retaliatory measures of the British government. But these subjects we have already discussed, at more than sufficient length. And while we make due allowance for national partiality in an author, whose nation is engaged in the contest, and who writes in support of the cause of his party, we certainly conceived ourselves entitled to expect, that Dr. Schmelzing, an author, who, several years after the events narrated by him took place, and in a period of peace, writes systematical outlines of European international law, for academical lectures, or private study, would have transmitted to the future generations of Germany, a more correct, fair, and impartial account of the conduct of Great Britain in those memorable transactions.

CHAPTER XIV.

Review of part of the work of M. Emile Vincens.

About the period at which we have now arrived, there appeared at Paris in 1821, in three vols. 8vo, the able work of M. Emile Vincens, Chéf du Bureau du Commerce au Ministère de l' Interieur, entitled, Exposition raisonnée de la Législation Commerciale. In this work, M. Vincens treats very fully, distinctly, and methodically, of the commercial, including the maritime, laws of France. Although apparently, not a professional lawyer, he exhibits the experience and sagacity of the merchant; and occasionally discusses, not only what the French commercial laws are, but what they ought to be. Almost the whole of the work, however, is devoted to private commercial and maritime jurisprudence, which from its common, similar, and almost uniform nature, has frequently, though rather incorrectly, been denominated the law of nations. Only a small part of the work relates to what is properly international doctrine, namely, chapters 17 and 18 of book XII, on maritime commerce. To these chapters, therefore, on the "Etat de guerre," and "Des neutres," we shall confine our attention, as alone falling within the scope of our present inquiries; and making allowance for the absurdly strong national bias and antipathy, to which, like most of his countrymen, he is liable, we deem it but justice to observe, that in international questions, he is comparatively fair, and, although occasionally not correctly informed, does not misrepresent, by exaggerated statement or false colouring.

The 17th chapter of book XII., Vincens commences with an exposition of the inconveniences of the "armemens en course," or privateering system. And, although he describes the modern recognized mode of proceeding in continental war, as milder or less severe than that adopted in maritime war, in a greater degree, or to a greater extent, than what the experience of the eighteenth and nineteenth centuries appear to warrant; and as a merchant, evidently labours under the mercantile bias, which would sacrifice all the other rights of nations, to that of carrying on, at all times, an entirely free, and perfectly unlimited commerce, we shall willingly quote part of his argument against the use of privateers; because it is our conviction, that the abolition of this system, is the chief farther improvement, which is likely to take place in maritime warfare, or which perhaps can take place, consistently with justice to all parties concerned. For, although we may find it necessary in some points, to correct and moderate his statement of facts, and must continue to resist any attempt to alleviate the severities of war, at the expense of doing manifest injustice to one or more of the parties, we cordially concur with Vincens, and the other rational philanthropists of the age, in recommending and endeavouring to promote any measures, by which, while the right of war, that is, the power of maintaining by force of arms, the independence, territorial integrity, and other just rights of each nation, against hostile aggression, is preserved entire, this primary object may be attained and secured, with the least possible hardship or suffering to individuals, in their commerce or otherwise.

Among civilized nations, observes Vincens, it is said to be admitted as a principle, "To do each other in peace all the good they can; and in war the least possible evil." How the first part of this adage is observed in practice, may be seen from all the existing laws of customs and duties, monuments of reciprocal and constant jealousy. But the protection due to the national industry, the preference for itself which each nation has the right of exercising within its own territory, colour these defensive and offensive measures. It is, besides said, they are just as reprisals; and this reason, (motif) which each repeats, is a confession that a spirit of hostility continues to find refuge in these regulations, even during the intervals which war permits."

"In war, it must be admitted, on the contrary, that on land at least, a tacit convention among Europeans, a holy alliance, unwritten, but which has for its guarantee the incontestable progress of civilization, and of the spirit of humanity, now willingly spares, as far as practicable, all useless cruelties and ravages. It is true, that nothing is abstained from, which promotes the success of military enterprises; the armies are made to live at the expense of the countries which they traverse, and their food and provision are taken, wherever they can be found. There are exacted from the provinces, cities, and towns, occupied by the military forces, contributions, and labour or services; but these requisitions are made upon the magistrates, and not upon the private individual. These sacrifices, commanded under the pretext of necessity, and in order to subsist, or defray the expense, of the conqueror, are considered as drawn from the public treasuries; the citizens are not called to furnish them, except by way of contribution; private property is not gratuitously attacked; at least, if that happens only too often, those who permit it, are considered to act contrary to the laws of war; and from the act of the strongest, there is not fabricated a right against the weaker. There is no confiscation, except in cases of contravention; those, in which the exercise of pillage is permitted, are foreseen; it is never avowed or authorized against the unarmed individual, who has made no resistance."

"But at sea," Vincens goes on to observe, "it is otherwise. Every thing is seized which is found to belong to the enemy, unarmed, and who surrenders without defending himself; and this regular pillage has so little the pretext of the self-defence of him who exercises it, or of necessity, that people go in quest of the property of the enemy, even on board the vessels of neutrals, to whom it is impossible to impute any hostile attempt or design. Not only the vessels of the state, pursuing their military enterprises, seize or destroy the properties which they meet by chance—a proceeding which might strictly be compared to some of those, which armed troops commit in their marches; but each power authorizes individuals, under the name of privateers, to traverse the seas, in order to capture there, whatever they shall find belonging to the enemy. Here the evil is gratuitous; these privateers are not auxiliaries, who serve for the operations of naval armies or fleets; they are no more in a state to co-operate in war, than the ships which they pursue, and which, solely occupied in commerce, are not in a state to do harm."

"The legal origin," continues Vincens, "de la course—of privateering, is to be found in the ancient formula of the declaration of war, in which a power ordered its subjects de courre sus à l'ennemi.* * * It was also the ancient right of war, to put to ransom the persons of prisoners, for the profit of him who had taken them.* * * This odious custom has come to an end; but maritime prize, in some measure, holds of it; those, are there made prisoners, who, on land, would be allowed to go free; it seems to be, by an extension of the right of stopping them, that there is exercised the right of stripping them of all they have with them. If the captor release them, with their property, he is in a condition to exact ransom.* * * If these (customs) are still preserved, if the defence of them is sometimes undertaken, let us, in good faith confess, it is because each people believes it loses by what its neighbours gain. This sentiment, which, in peace, dictates more than one regulation, but is there under constraint and disguised, in war, takes a free course. He, who, even with arms in his hand, would abhor pillaging a house, believes he promotes a just policy, by sending to sea to capture vessels and merchandise, in the hope of disturbing the commerce of others. Avarice answers to the appeals thus made to it, and comes to take part in the enterprise, as a lucrative speculation; but the principal sentiment which covers or justifies this ardour for plunder—this sentiment, so remote from the maxim of doing the least evil possible, is, that the interest of the national commerce requires, we should always seek, first, its prosperity, and next, the evil or loss of others."

"Although this miserable principle could be admitted, a person must be blind, he must never have observed the salutary complication of the affairs and interests of universal commerce, who believes he can promote or effect the prosperity of the industry of a country, by ruining some merchants in another country. How frequently does the confiscation by a government, fall upon itself or its subjects, upon the insurers or underwriters of that nation, upon creditors, from whom their pledges are pillaged? How many counter-blows may be felt by one's-self, from the evil which one believes he has done to others?"

"Whatever truth there may be in these observations," continues Vincens, "the inconveniences, and especially the abuses before alluded to, have often excited attention; on several repeated occasions, it has been mutually proposed to suppress privateers; unfortunately, the power which takes the initiative in this overture, immediately passes for having acknowledged his inferiority in this fatal game; and then the other party feels himself called upon, or that he has got a hint to avail himself of the advantage he possesses. This calculation is strange in each of those who make it; it consists in finding profit in a certain number of merchants, owners, and freighters of vessels in his country being infallibly ruined, provided there is more of loss in the country of the enemy, and, in estimating more highly what a small number of privateers will take from others, than what a crowd of merchants will lose of their property. But, although this compensation of real evils and fortuitous acquisitions should not be ideal, and there should result from it a gain, is this a commerce worthy of a great nation? Doubtless, it ought not to be in the power of any one, to compare the European powers in the nineteenth century, to those Barbary powers, who could not be reduced to renounce privateering, or plunder at sea, because it is their trade—by which they earn their bread. How worthy would it be of sovereigns, in their councils, in the midst of peace, to agree upon the abolition of 'this savage custom'!"

In the preceding passages, Vincens obviously exaggerates the superior civilization and refinement, which he ascribes to modern warfare by land, when compared with modern warfare by sea. We do not find much moderation, clemency, or tenderness, displayed in modern continental wars, from those of Louis XIV. to those of Catherine and Frederic, Napoleon and Nicholas. Vincens evidently forgets, that the sufferings inflicted in war by land are much more extended, affect the homes and families of individuals, and embrace all classes of the community. And although each individual is not directly pillaged, in an invaded province—the plunder exacted being in the shape of requisitions and contributions—he is forced directly to give up any articles he may have, which are requisite for the subsistence and supply of the invading army; and although the money contribution, or forced loan, may be exacted circuitously, in the shape of requisitions upon the magistrates or local authorities, it does not come solely from the public treasury; the wealthy individual also is obliged to pay; and, though circuitously, loses part of his wealth, as really as if it were taken from him directly. In maritime war, on the other hand, the great body of the nation are not directly affected; their homes and families are not assailed. The direct plunder is taken from part of the more wealthy classes of the community—the mercantile, manufacturing, and naval capitalists, who expose their property to capture, by embarking it in foreign trade. Nay, even in the case of neutrals, the inconveniences or hardships, to which they are incidentally, but unavoidably subjected, in consequence of disputes arising among other nations, who are neighbours, or with whom they have intercourse, it is these more wealthy classes of the community chiefly, who are affected in their foreign commerce.

With these animadversions, we quite agree with Vincens, in his humane recommendation and argument, in support of the abolition of the system of privateering, by general or universal consent, expressed in a treaty or treaties, or perhaps more effectively established, by general or universal usage, reciprocally observed. Of course, all the maritime states behoved to concur in this measure; and it does not appear, that any nation can reasonably object. To employ privateers, is a particular mode of making war; and it may be given up, in the same way, as the practice of killing or enslaving prisoners, or of using poisoned weapons. It does not, like the maxim, "free ship, free goods," give one class or description of nations, a right of superiority over other nations. It does not counteract or defeat the military operations of one or more nations, for the behoof and protection of other nations, who may have injured the former. It reduces or narrows the power of inflicting damage or loss; but it affects all nations equally, and does not give one an advantage over another. And while the abandonment of this mode of warfare, operates equally and justly, as between nations, who may unfortunately find it necessary to become belligerents, it puts an end to the great majority of occasions, in which abuses are likely to be committed by belligerent, in relation to neutral nations. It places maritime warfare on nearly the same footing as continental warfare, and gives the former all the civilization and advantages, which have been ascribed to the latter. As the right of legitimate warfare, between state and state, must flow from the sovereign or government of each state, it is generally expedient, that the military operations should not merely be authorized by the government, in letters of marque, or commissions to private individuals, but should be conducted under the control and direction of the government, and by means of the regular forces of the government,—the portion of the population of each state set aside, and trained for such operations.

By such an arrangement, indeed, neutrals will not

obtain the power of benefiting by the unfortunate disputes of other nations, or of extending their commerce, and reaping profit at the expense of these nations, beyond what naturally, and incidentally, unavoidably arises from these other nations going to war with each other, solely by means of their regular navies. But by such an arrangement, neutrals acting bonâ fide, will be relieved from the great proportion of the abuses of which they complain, and as far as seems to be practicable in justice—in consistency with the rights of other nations, who may be forced into war for self-protection, and in consistency with the inconveniences to which they are, from the nature of their situation, liable, in consequence of their proximity to, or commercial intercourse with, these other belligerent nations. To avoid, or escape altogether, from the inconveniences and constraints, arising naturally and necessarily from their being members of the great society of civilized independent nations, neutrals would have to learn the lesson taught by the Prussian Professor, Schmalz, to consider their foreign trade as of comparatively little, or almost no value, contrasted with their internal or domestic trade.

In the meantime, we must return to the consideration of Maritime international law during war, as it exists at present. The section of which we have quoted a great part, Vincens concludes with the just remark, "that, in authorizing privateers, there is no government which is not aware, to how many abuses their enterprises may give rise, and which has not evinced a wish to subject them to severe regulations." And he goes on, in the following sections, to indicate those regulations which exist in France, in their latest state. In the sections, from the 2nd to the 12th inclusive, he treats of the general rules for privateers; of letters of marque; of the caution or security to be given by the owners or fitters out of privateers, for their correct conduct; of co-partnership in fitting out privateers; of the encouragement given to them; of their crews; of their share in the prizes taken by them; of the sale and liquidation of the prizes; of the competent tribunal and procedure; of the instructions given to their commanders; of the exercise of the right of capture by privateers, and of the limitations thereof, arising from neutral territory, and from the liberty of fishing.

In section 13th, Vincens thus enumerates the cases in which the captured vessel is a good prize, without distinction of the flag. "La facilité, qu' auraient les vaisseaux ennemis de se déguiser sous un pavillon neutre, les conditions auxquelles les neutres eux-mêmes doivent impartialement se soumettre entre les puissances belligerantes, et diverses circonstances, dont nous parlerons incessamment, autorisent aussi à sommer ceux, qui sont rencontrés en mer, à entrer en explication dans des formes déterminées. Or le neutre vrai, ou prétendu, l' allié, celui même, qui porte le même pavillon que le corsaire, qui, au coup de canon de semonce, refuse d' amener ses voiles, peut y être contraint par la force; et, s' il fait résistance, il est de bonne prise, quelle que soit sa nation. Le navire, qui n' a pas son passeport (ou congé,) celui qui en aurait un sous un nom différent du nom indiqué par les autres pièces de bord, celui, qui en aurait de plusieurs puissances, celui dont les papiers auraient été jettés à la mer, peuvent être arretés et déclarés de bonne prise."

In sections 14, 15, 16, Vincens treats of the conduct of the captor with regard to the prize, of composition, ransom and prisoners; of recapture; and of goods captured from Frenchmen, and brought back into France. In section 14, he observes, "All the precautions, we have just indicated, have evidently for their object, to put authority and justice in a state to decide upon the lawfulness of prizes; to protect the true proprietors, according to laws or treaties, from the avidity of captors; to prevent that avidity, which is exercised by the display (appareil) of force, in the open sea, far from all control, from degenerating into pillage, to the prejudice of the fitters out of the privateers themselves." And he thus concludes his 17th chapter. "We have shown, that on certain occasions, neutral vessels may be stopped by privateers; and we are going to resume the subject. But their prize may always be contested; it can be adjudged only for some contravention of the laws of nations; no presumption can supply the place of the sentence of a competent tribunal. Till then, the captor has not been invested with the property; and consequently the recapture, even after the lapse of the twenty-four hours, can transfer no right to the new captor."

In book XII. chapter xviii., Vincens proceeds to the consideration of the rights of belligerent, in relation to neutral nations. And as he is one of the latest systematic (also official) French writers, on the subject; and his talents, information, and usual fairness, and impartiality, entitle him to our respect, we shall continue to quote such leading passages, as exhibit his views of the existing maritime international law during war, and subjoin our animadversions, where we find his statements are not well founded, or his argument inconclusive.

"What right," Vincens here commences, "have powers, who make war upon each other, to disturb the commerce of neutral states? There is no such right, having a solid foundation in reason. All that belligerent parties can claim, is, that those, who take no part in the quarrel, remain impartial, and do not give to the one, to the prejudice of the other, any effective supplies, which aid hostilities. These principles are not denied; their general consequences are also generally enough recognized. The neutral cannot furnish troops, arms, or warlike stores to the one of the parties; his vessels must refrain from entering the ports, against which a hostile force is really acting. It is in the application of these rules, that enormous deviations (écarts)—differences are found. And as the powers at war traverse the sea in force, while neutral merchant vessels are unarmed, and their governments are usually the weakest, or afraid of compromising themselves, and in their state of peace, are not in a condition, or inclined, to repel, or avenge, by force, each violent act of injustice, it is seen at a glance, by whom, and in what sense, doubtful cases are interpreted, or usages established, which become the law of nations."

"The enemy may be concealed under a false neutral flag—the neutral himself may be loaded with arms and ammunition, in contravention of the rules of his proper neutrality; hence, a right claimed by the belligerent powers, to stop and to visit neutral vessels, or those calling themselves such; and the effects of this right are singularly extended. It has even been pretended, that the neutral not being able to give an asylum to deserters, there existed a right to make the visit, in order to discover and retake them; and in this case, the stronger party, not embarrassing himself with much scruple, in deciding the questions of identity, the English law of impressment has been exercised on board American vessels."

"Finally, there has been found a marvellous invention, derived from the impartiality which neutrals ought to observe. It has been declared to them on all sides, that whatever injustice one of the belligerent parties may do them, the other acquires a right to do them as much injustice. When treaties are made between nations, it is usual to promise, in good will, to grant all the advantages which may come to be conceded to any other nation. Here the contrary takes place. To reserve to do to a neutral, all the mischief which he may have received from others, is the treaty of the strong against the weak; and the last is more exactly fulfilled than all the others."

Now, at the commencement of the passages just quoted, Vincens, evidently in his great zeal for neutral commerce, loses sight of, or wilfully keeps out of view, the higher and still more important right, competent to all nations, to use force for the maintenance of their independence, territorial integrity, and security against foreign aggression, and the limitations, which, in the collision of these two opposite rights, the right of commerce, as being not only inferior and subordinate, but susceptible of compensation, or reparation for the damage arising from its non-observance, must of necessity, undergo. But this, we have seen, has been so distinctly expounded by these impartial authorities, Lampredi, Tetens, and Jacobsen, who are unquestionably free from British bias, that it is strange, Vincens, when alluding to solid foundation in reason, should not have noticed the grounds in reason and justice, on which these preceding jurists founded their doctrines; unless his silence has arisen from his own national bias.

That maritime nations, who have to go to war with each other, being armed, are more prepared for forcible contention, than neutral nations, who are unarmed, is a truism. And experience proves, that nations and governments, like individuals, when in possession of superior power, are apt to exceed the bounds of moderation, and to dictate to their weaker and more peaceful neighbours. It is likewise true, that in Europe, there are a good many small states. But, it is equally true, that there are in Europe, a good many large maritime states, able to contend with each other, singly or in union, and able and willing to protect the smaller states, against any aggressions attempted by any of the larger. And from our researches in the preceding volume, we have seen, it is not historically true, as here insinuated by Vincens, that by the greater maritime powers, such as Spain, France, Britain, Holland, Russia, doubtful cases have been uniformly, or generally, interpreted in such a way, as to lead to the establishment of international usages, inconsistent with justice.

While he next again, admits, but to appearance reluctantly, the right of belligerents to stop, and visit neutral vessels, Vincens complains of the extension of this right, so as to comprehend the search of neutral vessels, for the purpose of discovering deserters; and alleges, that the British exercised their internal or municipal law of impressment, on board American vessels. But Vincens does not here venture to maintain, that neutrals are entitled to entice seamen to desert from their native vessels, or that neutral vessels can afford a legal asylum to such deserters; and, in reclaiming these deserters, the British did not, it is manifest, proceed upon their own municipal law of impressment, but merely exercised the right, competent to every nation and government, to demand restitution of its subjects, who have deserted its service, so as to prevent their acting against their native country. This obviously unfounded insinuation was unworthy of Vincens. The right to reclaim such deserters is indisputable; and when the nations are distinguished by speaking different languages, there can be very little risk of mistake, or consequent injustice. But when the two different nations speak the same language, the risk of mistake, and the difficulty of ascertaining the identity, are great.

And, if any of the British naval commanders used force, and caused seamen to be seized and detained, without having previously ascertained their national character, they committed a wrong, and an act of injustice, for which all practicable reparation ought to have been made, and measures adopted for preventing any repetition of it.

With regard to the remaining tirade in this section before quoted, we shall willingly indulge Vincens in this ebullition of national bias, as directed against Britain; because it bears as much against, and equally affects, the Berlin and Milan decrees, the continental system of Napoleon, as the British orders in council of 1807, which it occasioned; and which can only be justified, as conditional and retaliatory, and directed against the enemy, not against neutrals; unless the latter had forfeited the character of neutral independent states, and become, in a great measure hostile, by entering into treaties with the enemy, submitting to his insults, complying with his unjust demands, promoting his schemes, and excluding all British vessels from their ports.

In section 2d of this chapter, Vincens treats of the goods of neutrals met with at sea on board the vessels of the enemy; and he says, they are now reckoned good prize, the cargo following the fate of the vessel, whose flag decides. He adds, indeed, the publicists are in general agreed, that this is a great infringement of the natural law; and it appears even to be a singular extension of a quite different regulation. But, he concludes, "this jurisprudence has prevailed; it has become an express article in the treaties; and, in fine, it is every where received, without discussion."

Now we must protest, against this most erroneous doctrine, as forming any part of the natural, or common and general consuetudinary law of nations. With regard tò France, it is, no doubt, true, as we have already seen, that for the encouragement of French cruizers, the ordonnances of 1543, and 1584, as afterwards that of 1681, declared the goods of a friend, in the ship of an enemy, to be subject to confiscation, contrary to the old practice of the Mediterranean states, as recorded in the Consolato del Mare. The government of Spain, we have also seen, adopted a similar regulation. And the undue severity of these regulations, probably rendered the Dutch and other carrying nations, more anxious and urgent, first to obtain a relaxation of these unjust restrictions, and afterwards to push their own pretensions to an unjust length on the other side. But it does not appear, that the maritime states of the Mediterranean, or England, or Holland, or the smaller maritime states of the North Sea and Baltic, ever confiscated neutral goods on account of their being in the vessels of an enemy, unless they were contraband of war, or destined to a blockaded port. Indeed, that we should confiscate the goods of a friend, when they happen to be conveyed in the vessel, or waggon, of his friend, because the latter happens to be our enemy, is evidently contrary to the ordinary feelings of natural justice, as well as confessedly contrary to the opinions of all the international jurists, and to that, we have seen, of the great French lawyer Pothier, himself, although he admitted it to have been, and still to be the law of his own country. And this unjust rule has obviously been admitted, or acceded to, by the neutral carrying nations, who, after they had succeeded in getting introduced into a number of treaties, a clause, that their neutral vessels should cover the goods of the enemy, in other words, that the character of the vessel should determine the character of the cargo, instead of its own real and proper character, according to the dictates of common sense, felt they could not, with any consistency, or decency, object to the application of this fictitious, and absurdly unnatural rule, to neutral goods, when in the vessels of the enemy.

But Vincens, like some of the later German writers, seems to think it sufficient to render this severe and unjust rule, adopted in the sixteenth and seventeenth centuries, by France and Spain, a part of the general law of nations, that it was inserted in a number of treaties, such as those during the American war, and at the peace which terminated that war, and the treaty between France and the United States, 8 Vend. An. IX. That this stipulation was binding on the parties to these treaties, while they lasted, and thus formed a part of the particular and temporary conventional law of Europe, is not disputed. But the very insertion of the stipulation in these treaties, contrary to the natural feelings of justice, and contrary to the immemorial usage of the great majority of the European states, shows it was not then understood to be a part of the natural and common law of nations, independently of such paction. And with regard to these treaties themselves, so far as Great Britain is concerned, besides the French republic having expressly annulled them, and the Dutch having forfeited all benefit from this stipulation in previous treaties, by their having failed to fulfil the counter obligations undertaken by them, the treaties referred to were de facto and de jure abolished and extinguished, by the two subsequent successive wars, without having been renewed at the conclusion of either of these wars; so that the rule stated by Vincens, to be every where recognized, does not now form a part, even of the particular conventional maritime international law of Europe.

In the third and following sections of this chapter, Vincens considers hostile goods under a neutral flag;

and here also we have to correct several inaccuracies in view and narrative. He commences with the remark: "To admit that neutral property, found on board a hostile vessel, was good prize, was adhering to a maxim often invoked—'the flag covers the merchandise'—for it is by professing that all merchandise, even that of the enemy, is protected by the flag of the neutral who transports it, that it would be natural to maintain, that the hostile flag compromises the neutral cargo." And it must be acknowledged, this mode of arguing the case is ingenious, though very fallacious. Vincens begins by attempting to establish by treaties, the manifestly unjust rule, which subjects to confiscation, the innocent goods of neutrals, on account of their being put on board the vessel of an enemy, though their friend; in order that he may thus give the appearance of its being natural, and a plausible foundation for the rule, which protects the goods of the enemy in a neutral vessel. But in reality, both these rules are unjust, though not perhaps in equal degree. And the absurd fiction of holding, that the property or national character of the cargo is to be discovered from, and determined by, the national character of the vessel; and not from, and by that of the cargo itself, can never become a good foundation, and valid in law for any just rule.

Vincens goes on to observe, that the Consolato del Mare decided, that an armed vessel or cruizer has a right to cause to be delivered to him, the goods of the enemy, which he finds in a friendly vessel, on paying the freight, and allowing the neutral vessel and the rest of the cargo to go free. But the Consolato was not a statute or supreme ordonnance of any particular nation or government; it did not enact or decide; it merely recorded the rules of practice, which, in the course of their experience for ages, the trading maritime states of the

Mediterranean had found it just and reasonable to observe, towards each other. He next observes, that the French ordonnances of the sixteenth century, adopted this rule. And if they had merely done so, they would have been in conformity with the Consolato, and with the practice of the other European maritime states, of England and Holland, of Sweden and Denmark. But they went much farther; and Vincens admits, that the ordonnances of the sixteenth century, involved the neutral vessel also in the confiscation, and that subsequently, the celebrated ordonnance of Louis XIV. in 1681, and the réglement of 1704, confirmed that severe and unjust addition to the simple forfeiture of the property of the enemy.

In section 5th, Vincens vaguely states, that the treaty of Utrecht solemnly stipulated, that the flag should regulate the fate of the cargo; every thing was confiscated on board the hostile vessel; and was free, without distinction of property, on board the neutral vessel; apparently bonâ fide, but groundlessly believing, or affecting the belief, that the general international law of Europe, or at least the law of his own country, was thereby changed. But he is mistaken in both these points. For, besides the idea of a treaty between two or three states altering the general law, being quite absurd, the stipulation alluded to, was introduced merely into the treaties between Great Britain and France, and Holland; apparently through the great influence then possessed by the Dutch with the British government, or from the intestine broils, and negligence of the British ministry at that time. No such new stipulation was introduced into the treaty of Utrecht between Great Britain and Spain, or any other nation, but merely a confirmation of the old treaty with Spain in 1667. Neither does it appear, that either France or Britain, ever observed this stipulation in relation to each other; both appearing to have tacitly departed from it, as unequal and unjust, unless the neutral could procure the observance of it by both belligerents—the ground, upon which the Spanish government afterwards declined to adopt the stipulation in 1780. As little did the treaty of Utrecht alter the French maritime law, except with regard to the contracting parties. With regard to all other nations, with whom there was no treaty, the French government, we found from Valin, continued after the treaty of Utrecht, to enforce the ordonnance of 1681, and the réglement of 1704. And Vincens errs greatly, in blaming, in section 7th, the government of Louis XV. for renewing the confiscation of the goods of the enemy in neutral vessels. Such continued all along to be the law of France, as well as the general law of Europe, independently of treaty. And so far was the government of Louis XV. from being to blame, for reviving more severe measures, that, by the réglement of 1744, while it retained the old common law rule of capturing and confiscating the property of the enemy, when found in the open seas, this government abandoned the peculiarly severe ordonnances of 1543, 1584, and 1681, which confiscated the neutral vessel on the ground of carrying hostile goods, and returned to the milder general law, which, from the ages preceding the Consolato, in such cases, always released the neutral vessel. Surely Vincens had not read the very learned and accurate work of his able and honest countryman, Valin.

Vincens goes on to state, that in the course of the following war, 1756–1763, the interests of the maritime states of the north, and the preponderance which Russia assumed in Europe, began to introduce more liberal principles; and that Russia and Sweden united to shut the Baltic against the cruizers of the belligerent powers. In truth and reality, however, what is here called the prevalence of more liberal principles, was just an attempt to extend the rights of neutrals, and to restrict the rights of belligerents, as these respective rights had been recognized, for centuries, as part of the common consuetudinary law of nations, in order that the naval stores, which the governments, or subjects, of France, or Spain, or Holland, might purchase, in these northern countries, might, though belonging to the enemy, be protected against the cruizers of the opposite belligerent. And the right of Russia and Sweden to shut up the Baltic, is a very questionable doctrine, which it is unnecessary here to discuss.

Vincens next states, that soon after the peace of 1763, Russia concluded with England a treaty, by which the liberty of commerce is recognized; that in time of war, neutrals should merely be prohibited from transporting to the enemy warlike stores, and from going to places actually blockaded; and, with regard to merchant vessels, that ships of war and privateers should conduct themselves, as favourably, as the usages of war, (la raison de guerre,) then existing, would permit, observing, as far as possible, the principles, and the rules of the law of nations, generally recognized. Vincens adds, "I know not, whether it was worth while, to make a treaty, in order to insert in it guarantees so vague; or rather, I am ignorant, whether the true translation of this embarrassing phrase, be not a sort of submission and recognition of the rights abandoned to the strongest." But we conceive, there was no occasion for these doubts and conjectures. The treaty referred to was a sufficiently plain recognition, so far as the treaty went, of the usage of war, which had been voluntarily adopted, as reasonable and just, not only by the maritime states of the Mediterranean, but also by all the larger states of Europe, kingdoms and republics, including France and Spain. And if the rule, thus universally recognized for ages, was unjust, as being merely the law of the strongest, why did these great states not merely enforce it against each other, however strong, but also submit to it from others, although weak? And, that this was understood by France, to be the rule of justice, and of the then existing law of nations, is plain from what Vincens adds, that a little after the treaty just alluded to, France, in full peace, granted to the city of Hamburgh, a convention, announced as a favour, by which, while the hostile flag was made to confiscate the friendly property, the hostile merchandise might be captured though under the Hamburgh flag, but the vessel behoved to be released, with such part of the cargo, as belonged to friends. And, if he had duly considered the pre-existing law of his own country, Vincens would not have been surprised, at this convention being announced as a favour on the part of France. For, while this convention recognized the established law of the European maritime nations, independently of treaty, in declaring, that the property of the enemy may be legally captured on the open sea, although in neutral vessels, it conceded to the citizens of Hamburgh, the abandonment of the severe ordonnances of 1543, 1584, and 1681, and the réglement of 1704, which added to the common consuetudinary law of nations, the confiscation of the neutral vessel, which happened to carry the goods of the enemy, and also of the remainder of the cargo, although neutral.

In section 7th, Vincens comes to what he designates the war of American independence; and after informing us, that France first concluded with her new allies, the United States, a convention, in which it was formally declared, that the "free ship shall secure the liberty of the goods," although the cargo, or part thereof, should belong to the enemy, exclaims, "behold, then, at last recognized the principle, that the 'flag covers the merchandise.'" From this exclamation, it might be inferred, that Vincens understood this rule was thus established as a part of the general maritime law of nations. But that it was merely a conventional arrangement between France and the United States, affecting only the two contracting parties, is manifest from the immediately following paragraph, in which Vincens states it as remarkable, that six months after the conclusion of this treaty, a réglement on navigation, in which were recited the different contraventions into which neutrals may fall, ordered neutral vessels with their cargoes, to be declared good prize, when the latter should belong to the enemy, to the extent of three-fourths; and reserved to annul all toleration of the liberty to transport the goods of the enemy, if the other belligerent powers did not agree to give that permission, within six months. But there is nothing at all remarkable here—nothing inconsistent between the French treaty with the United states, and the réglement. And it appeared so to Vincens, only, because he most erroneously supposed, that the treaty of France with the United States, altered the general law of nations; or established generally, and with reference to other nations, the rule for which he contends, or at least altered the ordinary administration of that law by France, in relation to other states; whereas, notwithstanding this special compact with their new allies, the law of France remained the same as it had been for centuries, with regard to other nations, and was not recalled or revived, but merely continued by the réglement of 1778, with an alleviating modification, requiring the hostile part of the cargo to be three-fourths of the whole, in order to authorize confiscation, and with a conditional concession of the pretension of the neutral flag, to be withdrawn at the end of six months, if not adopted by the other belligerents.

In section 8th, Vincens goes on to state, that the crowns of the north, allied for the purpose of causing their armed neutrality to be respected, insisted on the establishment of an uniform law of nations; and he narrates the maxims proposed by Russia, and the answers returned by the French and British governments. But of these we have already said enough; and we proceed with the subsequent observations of Vincens. These disputes were maintained with more or less eagerness, till the peace of 1783; but, it is here, he says, that we must carefully mark, what was the fate of the principles debated on the subject of neutrals. "The maxims for which neutrals had so strenuously contended, were received and solemnly consecrated; namely, the flag covers the merchandise; the liberty of neutrals has only two ordinary exceptions, contraband, and the violation of a blockade; the visit which may be required at sea, regulated in the form the most proper for preventing its being converted into an abuse, or act of violence, has no other object than to take cognizance of two documents, under the guarantee of which, the neutral is perfectly free, the passport for the vessel, and the certificate for the cargo. Homage could not be better rendered to the system of neutrality; it could not be more fully adhered to. All the treaties made at this period, and down to the following war, have general articles of the same import."

Now, this is, no doubt, a beautiful picture of the alleged triumph of the neutral system; but it is rather too highly coloured; and unfortunately the premises do not warrant the conclusion. That a clause to the effect of neutral vessels covering hostile goods, was inserted in most of the treaties entered into about this time, is quite true; such as between France and Britain in 1782—between France and Russia in 1787—and between Denmark and Russia in 1789.

In such clauses, the government of France had now for sometime felt, they might have contingently a material interest, inasmuch as these clauses not only enabled France to import all articles required for her internal consumption, and even naval stores during war, to export her superfluous commodities, and thus to procure the favourable disposition of neutrals, by securing to them the profits of the carrying trade for France, but also counteracted, and to a great extent weakened, the maritime power of her rival belligerent. Why the British government made any such concession, as these clauses import, to any of the European governments, who had each assisted, if not all combined, to effect the separation from Britain of her American colonies, it is not easy to see. But there can be no doubt, that these clauses, when inserted expressly, or renewed, were binding on the contracting parties, while the treaties lasted; and so far formed a part of the maritime conventional law of the European nations.

On the other hand, it is equally true, that, except to the extent of these treaties, while they lasted, the general and common consuetudinary maritime international law of Europe remained the same, with regard to all other states, between whom such treaties were not entered into. And this is manifest, even from what is stated in the next paragraph of the very work we are reviewing. "I must, however, observe," says Vincens, "that about this time, Russia, as soon as she became in her turn a belligerent power, and had to apply to neutrals, the rules, which she had claimed, did not precisely commit a breach of these rules; but, by a regulation in December 1787, declared, that the simulations or pretences, of the enemy, rendered it necessary to stop and visit neutral vessels, in order to ascertain their neutrality; and that, as the falsehoods, and double sets of ships' papers often served to disguise or conceal contraband articles found in these vessels, it was necessary to push the examination or search a little farther; and, therefore, gave permission to send to the vessel an intelligent pilot," &c.

In section 9th, arriving at the epoch of the war of the French revolution, Vincens states, that the legislative assembly of France offered to abolish the use of privateers; but that the Hanse towns only, responded to the invitation which perfectly suited them. Our author here refers to the law of the 29th March 1793. Like Martens, we have not been able to find this law; but, upon the statement of Vincens, we willingly give the legislative assembly due credit for this humane proposal.

Our author thus proceeds with his narrative. "France, thanks to the revolutionary administration, was soon in want of grain from foreign countries. The enemy endeavoured to intercept or carry away the neutral vessels, which brought subsistence to our ports. This occasion was seized, to establish a sort of reprisal. A decree of the convention of 9th May 1793, preceded by a recital of the proceedings of the English, declared good prize, the merchandise of the enemy found on board neutral vessels, and especially ordered, that there should be brought into the ports of France, all provisions, even those belonging to neutrals, which should be found at sea; that the vessels should be immediately released; that there should be paid to the captain, according to the bills of lading, the freight of the confiscated goods, with indemnity for the delay experienced; and with regard to eatables, that the price should be paid according to their value, at the place of destination. "This law, we see," continues Vincens, "established a right of pre-emption over grain; and this was its principal object. But, in the same law, there was a return to the maxim, so solemnly abandoned, of confiscating the property of the enemy, in general, under the friendly flag. It seems, that this principle of plunder continued to be considered as the true law of war, suspended only by treaties, which vanish with the peace. The Americans claimed the observance of their conventions, that their flag might continue to receive merchandise; and their particular right was sometimes observed, sometimes considered as abolished."

Vincens here reluctantly admits the true state of the law, at this time; and it is strange he should have had so much difficulty, in perceiving, or admitting it. The former common consuetudinary law had never been departed from, except between the contracting parties, to the extent, and during the subsistence of the particular treaties. And by the decree of May 1793, the convention did not return to, or revive, but merely continued the old maritime law and practice of France, as expounded by Valin, Pothier, Emérigon, and Bouchaud. Vincens, however, correctly observes, that this decree established the right of pre-emption, as claimed by France, in the same way, as this right was claimed and exercised by Britain.

In section 10th, Vincens states, "In 1794, the Americans submitted, in some measure, to receive the law from the English, in consenting, by treaty, that the goods of the enemy under their flag, should be good prize." Now, it is really lamentable, that a national bias or prejudice, when it has once taken possession of the mind, should so much obstruct and obscure the perception of fact and truth. In the treaty of 1794, the Americans, in no respect whatever, submitted to the dictation of Britain. They merely recognized, what had, independently of treaties, been the common law of Europe for centuries, and was at that time, and continued to be, the law of France and Spain. And Vincens himself here goes on to state, "that the government of France, founding on the convention of 1778, ordered by a decree of the Directory, 12 Ventose An. V; that all goods belonging to the enemy, or of which the neutral property should not be sufficiently ascertained, found on board an American vessel, should be seized and confiscated, and the vessel and the remainder of the cargo left free; and that timber for building, pitch and tar, hemp, copper in sheets or plates, and whatever was of use for the building of vessels, should be added to the list of articles of contraband of war."

In sections 11th and 12th, Vincens, who was originally a French merchant in Genoa, observes, "From this epoch, privateering totally changed its character, at least in the Mediterranean; it no longer had the enemy, but solely neutrals for its object. They were assailed without danger, since they had neither means nor authority to make any resistance." But we have no wish to dwell upon the abuses, committed under the revolutionary government, except in so far, as it was attempted to introduce a new principle of law. "Special laws," observes Vincens, "had been made against goods manufactured in England, whoever was proprietor, ordering the confiscation of every vessel which entered a French port, having the least particle of English produce. A new law, 10 Brumaire An. V, applied this rigour in the open seas, and even generalized it, by declaring, that the state of a vessel, in what concerns her quality of neutral or hostile, should be determined by her cargo, and that consequently, every vessel loaded in whole, or in part, with English merchandise, should be good prize, whoever might be the proprietor of the merchandise. Vincens adds, "One of the first acts of the consular government, was the suppression of this declaration, so violent and unjust. The réglement of 1778, was re-established, namely, that at sea, the quality of hostile or neutral, with regard to the vessel, should depend on the flag, (he must mean the deed of sale, or other evidence of the property of the vessel) and with regard to the merchandise, should depend upon their proprietors, and not on the place of their origin."

In section 13th, Vincens briefly narrates the disputes between Great Britain and Denmark, Sweden, and ultimately Russia, as to the right of neutrals by means of convoys, to prevent the visitation and search of their vessels by belligerents—the consequent battle of Copenhagen, and the attempt, in 1800, by the Russian Emperor Paul, to revive the system of the armed neutrality of 1780. And here, one cannot help being struck with the strong national bias, and antipathy to England, of which even a comparatively fair minded Frenchman seems to find it almost impossible to divest himself. In this short paragraph, our author tells us, "that the proceedings they thought fit to adopt against France, in 1793, in the hope of famishing that kingdom, had accustomed the English to restrict neutrals in their commerce of grain; that England protested she had always regarded the league of 1780 as hostile, and spoke of the ancient and just privileges of the British flag; and that, thereafter, her fleet forced the sound and attacked Copenhagen." The events of that period, we have already narrated at sufficient length. The imputation cast upon the British government, of having, in 1793, expected to reduce the French nation by famine, is absurd. Such an expectation and attempt would have been about as insane, as that of Napoleon, to starve the manufacturers and colonists of England, by ordering the destruction by fire, of all the British merchandise in France. The object of the British government in 1793, obviously was to intercept the supplies of provisions, from Denmark chiefly, destined for the French armies, then threatening to invade, or actually invading, the neighbouring peaceful nations on the north and east. If the conduct of Britain, on this occasion, was not in strict conformity with her existing treaties with Denmark, there was no departure whatever from her treaties with Sweden and Russia. And the attempt then made by Denmark, in conjunction with these two powers, to protect from visitation and search, their merchant vessels, by means of armed convoys, was a new scheme, which had been tried, or at least contemplated before, but without success; which was manifestly liable to great abuse, in affording a protection to goods contraband of war, and to the property of the enemy; and was so far inconsistent with the pretended neutrality. But although it may have been legally justifiable, we regret the attack on Copenhagen, and sincerely wish the government of the day had resorted to other measures, for the protection of British rights. For, although the language of Vincens and other French writers, implies a charge to the contrary, we are confident that the British government and nation, have no wish to enjoy any peculiar or exclusive privileges in war, over other maritime states, and claim no rights, in relation to neutrals, for the British flag, which they do not most willingly admit, to be equally competent to the flag of other nations.

In section 14th, Vincens narrates the fate of the second armed neutrality, as terminated by the convention between Great Britain, and the Russian Emperor Alexander, in 1801. These events, we have already narrated at sufficient length; and we have only to remark the anxiety here shown by Vincens, to make out, that the provisions of this treaty were universally adopted, as the general common international law of civilized states. After stating the substance of this convention, Vincens adds: "And these principles and measures are declared permanent, applicable to all nations, and proclaimed as the constant rule of commerce and navigation." Now that these rules were reciprocally binding on the two contracting parties, and on Sweden and Denmark, who afterwards acceded to the treaty, as long as the treaty remained in force, is undoubtedly true. But to say, that these rules and measures were, in consequence of this treaty, binding upon, or in favour of France, or Spain, or Austria, or Prussia, or Holland, or the Neapolitan kingdom, or the Hanse towns, is contrary to all legal principle; and would be scouted as absurd, were not the concessions made by Britain in this treaty to the northern states, very favourable, both to other usually neutral states, and to belligerents, who need the aid of neutrals. Accordingly, as Vincens states, in the next paragraph, "The treaty of Amiens, which followed soon after, preserves an absolute silence on these questions. Europe was escaping from a state of hostility. People abstained from exhausting each other, by debating, and stipulating for subsequent wars: they referred these matters to futurity."

In sections 15th and 16th, Vincens commences with stating, that the peace of Amiens was of short duration, and led to another order of discussions; and he thus describes the war which ensued. "Of the rival powers engaged in this fatal struggle, and resolved upon a war of extermination, the one, without difficulty, triumphed at sea, and there conducted herself as absolute mistress; the other delayed not to establish his domination over the continent, by his arms and his alliances. Each power scrupled not to avail itself of its peculiar advantages. England believed *she* could prevent all commerce undertaken without her. The Ruler of France believed he could destroy the enemy, by excluding her from all access to the ports of Europe."

Although by no means a correct account of the relative position of, and of the conflict between, the two nations, this may, perhaps, be considered as a tolerably fair representation by a French writer on such a subject. And Vincens proceeds to state the substance of the hostile measures adopted by the opposed belligerents; charging Great Britain with having devised, what he designates, blocus de cabinet; and charging France, under Napoleon, with the continental system. Of the injustice, and pernicious consequences of the continental system, he gives a pretty fair account; and remarks, that the war against hostile property, upon which the disputes with neutrals had formerly turned, was thereby directed against hostile production, without distinction of property. The charge, too, against Great Britain, of resorting to what he calls the blocus de cabinet, is true, in so far, as the British government issued the orders in council of January and November 1807, after being provoked to this retaliatory measure, by the Berlin decree of Napoleon in November 1806, interdicting all commerce, or correspondence, with the British isles.

But the author is incorrect in his statement, that Britain, in this war, resorted to the blocus de cabinet, or blockade by proclamation, without an actual force to give effect to it, prior to the Berlin decree, or until thus provoked to retaliate upon the enemy. Such general interdictions of commerce with the enemy, by belligerents, were not unknown in former ages. England, we have seen, was induced by Holland to concur in such an interdict against Louis XIV, in 1689; but upon the remonstrance of Denmark and Sweden, abandoned it, as not warranted by the law of nations. Bouchaud also mentions a blockade by notification. But the judgments of the British prize courts, in the course of the revolutionary war from 1793 to 1801, had, in repeated cases, distinctly defined, what is a legal and effective blockade; which may be either a blockade de facto merely, without notification, or a blockade by notification, and de facto likewise; both being actual, by means of armed vessels, stationed sufficiently near, and of sufficient strength and number, to put in danger any vessel attempting to enter, or depart from the port; it being understood, that the blockade, once regularly notified, and de facto commenced, does not cease by the ships of war being for a short time driven off the coast by stress of weather.[1]

Such being the only blockade sanctioned by the British administration of the law of nations, the orders in council prior to January 1807, were quite consistent with it. They, at the outset, directed the measures necessary for an actual and efficient blockade of the ports or places to be taken and notified to foreign neutral powers. And when an efficient blockade was not maintained, the British cruizers had no inducement to capture, because they knew, that, agreeably to the law of nations, as administered in Britain, the captured vessel and cargo would, in such a case, be restored to the owners, probably with expenses.

So far, therefore, the conduct of Britain was quite consistent with the maritime law of nations universally

[1] Rob. Adm. Rep. I 94, 149, 171; III. 147.

recognized. But, after the Berlin decree in November 1806, the British government, no doubt, issued the orders in council of January 1807, and November 1807, which have been called blockades, but erroneously. For a blockade is a military operation; and implies the actual use of a naval military force of adequate strength; and without such a force, does not exist. The British orders in council of 1807, therefore, were not blockades, but general retaliatory interdictions of commerce with the territories of the enemy, or the countries which afforded him supplies, or were under his dominion or influence. As directed against, and so far only affecting the enemy, such interdictions were clearly justifiable, as being strictly retaliatory measures, and only conditional and temporary. They appear also to have been clearly justifiable against those other nations, who, although they had not formally declared war against Britain, had entered into treaties with the enemy, by which they concurred in carrying into execution, his hostile schemes against Britain.

So far, again, as those interdictions affected what is the proper commerce of nations, really and bonâ fide neutral, we conceive, they were inconsistent with the genuine principles of international law, as admitted by England, so long ago as 1689. But, in point of fact, scarcely any European continental state could be said, in 1807, after the battle of Friedland, and the Berlin decree, to be altogether independent, and strictly neutral. The only plea that could be urged by these nations, was, that they were forced into a concurrence in the schemes of Napoleon, that they did not act voluntarily in their un-neutral conduct towards Britain. But although this circumstance may alleviate, or extenuate, it cannot justify such concurrence on the part of a pretended neutral, which is, in fact, a departure from the neutral character, and amounts to such a degree of hostility, as may warrant stronger measures, than the mere interdiction of commerce with the enemy. To entitle a nation to claim the rights of an independent state, it must be really independent; not the mere servant or tool of another government. An individual, who commits a personal assault upon another, cannot justify such conduct, by alleging, that he did so against his will, in consequence of his having been himself threatened with a similar assault, if he did not comply.

In the remainder of the 16th section, Vincens describes the grievous injuries inflicted on commerce by the continental system of Napoleon, and the British retaliatory orders in council down to 1812. But on these, we think it unnecessary to dwell farther, than to quote one of the remarks of Vincens on the continental system, that we may express a more pleasing hope and anticipation of the future state and practice of the law of nations, than he seems to have entertained. "Unfortunate pretensions," says our author, "which infringed the rights and liberties of all nations, which rendered alliances a burden, which contributed to nourish the desire of throwing off the yoke; fatal weapon, of which all the world abhorred the use, but which remains now-a-days kept in reserve; for, on the first occasion, Europe must expect it; people will see cited as a code of the law of nations, and invoked as principles, the examples, or practices, under which they have groaned."

Now, we do not entertain any such gloomy apprehensions; speramus meliora. We do not indeed expect, that in future, any more than in past times, the subjects of neutral governments will be held entitled at common law, that is, by the common law of nations, to earn a direct profit through the disputes of their neighbours, or from the attempts of these neighbours to obtain, what they believe to be justice from each other; or to nourish war, by supplying either belligerent, under the cover of neutral bottoms, with contraband articles; or to favour the one belligerent, and counteract the military operations of the other, by protecting under their cover the property of the former, and carrying on for them that commerce, which the operations of the opposed belligerent may have disabled them from carrying on for themselves. But we do hope, that the mode of waging maritime war by privateers, or by any but natural or government ships of war, may in time be relinquished. And, even although it should not, we are convinced, that governments, which are usually neutral, may, and we hope they will, by proper regulations, prevent many of the grievances, of which their subjects complain, by prohibiting their subjects, under suitable penalties, from carrying contraband articles to either belligerent, and from fraudulently covering the property of the enemy, either in ships or cargoes, by counterfeit documents, or otherwise. On the other hand, we are convinced, that governments which are frequently belligerent, may, and we hope they will, by proper regulations, under suitable penalties, prevent the commanders of their ships of war, or of privateers, if still continued, from any acts in relation to neutral vessels, beyond what are necessary for ascertaining the neutrality or non-hostility of the ship or cargo; still improving upon the well-arranged mode of doing so, now sanctioned by general practice. Of the continental system of Napoleon, or the British retaliatory conditional order in council being cited as authorities, in the law of nations, we have no apprehension whatever; and consider the dread of a recurrence to such measures, as a vain fear. To all appearance, there is no risk of any one of the continental nations obtaining such an ascendancy over the others, as to render the general re-adoption of the continental system at all practicable. And, if not excluded, by a general interdiction from the European continent, the government of Britain will never be so insane, as to attempt, by any such interdict, to exclude neutrals from their legitimate and accustomed commerce with the nations, with whom it may unfortunately happen to be at war.

Vincens concludes section 16th, with the observation, that, in the treaties of peace of 1814 and 1815, we find no stipulation regarding the rights of navigation in time war. The same precaution was not taken, as at the peace of Utrecht. The treaty between Britain and the United States, concluded at Ghent in 1815, observes the same silence.

In section 17th, Vincens inquires, what law of nations have all these events left to Europe? And we shall quote the greater part of this section, as containing the fairest account, by one of the most recent, and most respectable French authors we have met with, of the state of maritime international law, at present, or since the general peace; adding, however, after each paragraph, such remarks as may be necessary, to correct the errors which it may appear to involve.

1. "The principle," says Vincens, "of the treaty of Utrecht,—'the flag covers the merchandise,' is no longer the common law. Forgotten by France in 1744, resumed with some modifications of little consequence in 1778, mistaken or misunderstood under the legislation of the Convention and Directory, adopted under the Consulate, claimed, because the English trampled upon it;—at least the violent measures, which the imperial government substituted for it, were held out by it only as reprisals, which could not be objected to, as a disavowal of this conservative principle."

Now, there are here several errors. We have seen

from Valin, Pothier, Emerigon, and Bouchaud, that the rule of the "flag covering the merchandise," was never the general law of France; and therefore, could not be forgotten in 1744, or resumed in 1778. All along, the property of the enemy, on board neutral vessels, was held liable to confiscation, under the old monarchy for centuries, except for six months, at the time of the northern armed neutrality; and also under the Convention and Directory.

By the advice of Portalis, Bonaparte, when first consul, cultivated neutrals, because their aid was found necessary to protect French property, under their cover, against the cruizers of Britain. But finding this cover not sufficient, for the attainment of his more ambitious projects, when Emperor, he resorted to those, correctly styled, violent measures, which ultimately, almost entirely annihilated the rights of neutrals. In fact, the clause here alluded to, was forced upon Louis XIV., in the treaty of Utrecht, apparently through the influence, which the Dutch then had with the British government. And so far was this rule from forming a part of the general maritime law of France, that this merely conventional clause does not appear to have been observed either by France or Britain.

2. "The Americans," continues Vincens, "had defended this principle, as far as they were able. The nations of the north had supported it, as gloriously, as they are essentially interested in it. But the most preponderating power among them has made concessions, and consented to announce, as a permanent rule, the right of search, and of confiscating the property of the enemy under the neutral flag."

Now, it is true, that, like the Hanse towns, and the Dutch, in former ages, the Americans have endeavoured to support, and will, probably, for a time, continue to endeavour to support the rule, of which Vincens here regrets the non-establishment, from their having attained such a degree of advancement in their mercantile marine, as to possess more vessels, than are required for their own imports and exports; from their thus having it in their power to conduct the carrying trade, the commerce de fret, of other nations; and from their finding it for their interest, under the cover of this rule, so convenient for neutrals, to protect the property of such of the European nations, as have the misfortune of being obliged to go to war, and whose maritime commerce is reduced, or nearly annihilated, by the operations of the opposed belligerent. And so far, as the Americans can secure the observance of a rule, so convenient for them, by treaty, all is well. But no nation, in order to promote its own interest, as a neutral state, is entitled partially to interpose its services between two belligerent nations, so as to counteract or defeat the military operations of the one against the other. It may be added, that our author here omits to mention the accession of Sweden and Denmark to the convention between Russia and Britain, as specially provided for by that treaty.

3. "England," continues Vincens, "has passed over in silence the treaty of Utrecht; has dissolved by negociation, and by arms, the armed neutralities; and has spoken of the rights of the English flag. These rights are merely the right of force; and that right makes itself recognized, and lasts, only so long, as the party claiming it is the strongest."

This last injurious allegation, we shall, in good humour, excuse, in courtesy to the national prejudices of Frenchmen; and shall merely smile, at such a charge being urged on the part of a nation. which, in the course of the last two centuries, has so frequently exercised, what is here called the right of the strongest, (in reality no right at all,) to oppress the surrounding continental nations, and to aim at universal empire. But it is absurd to talk at this day of England passing over, in silence, the treaty of Utrecht, fallaciously referred to, in his report, by the minister of Napoleon in 1812; after that treaty had been expressly annulled by the French nation in 1793, after it had been dissolved by a long series of hostilities, without being renewed at the peace of Amiens, or at the peace of 1815; and when it does not appear, that the stipulation in that treaty, here referred to, was ever observed or complied with, either by France or Britain. The injustice—the unequal and partial operation of such a stipulation or clause, as a rule of maritime international law, we trust, we have already shown and established.

4. "The principle of the flag covering the merchandise," continues Vincens, "has been observed, without contention, only towards the Barbary states." The reasons for treaties containing such a stipulation being generally entered into with the Barbary states, are sufficiently obvious. And we have only here to remark this admission of the existing state of maritime international consuetudinary law, by an official commercial French author of talents, information, and respectability.

5. Vincens proceeds to notice other points, as now settled in the existing maritime law of nations. "The attempt," he says, "to add grain and eatables to the list of articles of contraband of war, has not had great results, because this kind of supply did not continue to be of material importance, for ports, which were not really blockaded." Now, we are not aware of any attempt, to hold neutral grain or eatables as contraband, or liable to seizure, unless directly destined for the supply of armies or

fleets, or to ports of naval and military equipment; and then only the right of pre-emption was exercised, both by Britain and France. The author adds, "the Americans have struggled, with all their might, against the pretension to rank among articles of contraband of war, their produce destined for ship building." But, here also, we are not aware of any attempt to hold such produce contraband of war, unless directly destined for ports of naval and military equipment.

6. "The blockade by proclamation," continues Vincens, "has been very much decried; but we must never be surprised to see the belligerent powers thus endeavour to impose on neutrals, and on the weak. The examples set in this respect, are those, which are most likely to be renewed. There is only one step beyond, to arrogate the right to confiscate, whatever goes to, or comes from, the country of the enemy, without distinction of the proprietor." But these appear to us to be vain apprehensions; and so far as applicable to Britain, are proved to be groundless, not only by the uniform practice of England for centuries, with the exceptions already pointed out—the proclamation of 1689, soon recalled, and the conditional retaliatory interdictions of commerce in 1807, entirely occasioned by the continental system of Napoleon—but also by the recent judicial determinations of her prize tribunals.

7. "The search," continues Vincens, "on board every vessel, and the capture as prize, not of what belongs to the enemy, but of whatever his manufactories have been able to produce, are among the most savage inventions —the most worthy to be sent back to the gothic ages." In this remark, we entirely concur. But we must add, that in the Consolato del Mare, the produce of these gothic ages, we find no such savage inventions, as those here alluded to, but conceive, we discover in it,

more good sense, justice and equity, than in the practice either of France or Britain, during the nineteenth century.

In section 18th, Vincens mentions several points, fixed by the réglement of 1778, which we notice, as being now the maritime law of nations, as administered by France. The passport of the neutral vessel is valid only for one voyage. The Americans had, by the treaty of 1800, obtained the concession, that their passport might serve for a year, in order to enable them to continue their coasting trade in Europe, without returning to their own ports each voyage. "The neutral property of vessels of hostile construction, is recognized only so far, as there is found among the papers on board, the contract in authentic form, which proves the sale or cession before the commencement of the war. A similar vessel, acquired after having been captured as prize, must carry on board, the deeds which prove the capture, the condemnation, and the sale."

"Neutrality can only be proved, by the pieces or documents on board; no credit is given to those, which are subsequently produced. It has, however, been frequently remarked, that although no simulation or concealment is permitted to neutrals, because they have no reason to conceal their quality, or their destination, allies have often reason to recur to it; and that it is necessary to admit them, when claiming restitution of their property, to prove the averment, of which they have not been able to put the documents on board their vessel, because, by doing so, they would have exposed themselves to the enemy."

"Among the circumstances," continues Vincens, "which the réglement reckons sufficient to warrant confiscation, is the presence on board, of an enemy, in the capacity of super-cargo, merchant, or agent, or staff officer, or a mixture of more than two thirds of hostile sailors in the crew of a neutral vessel; and the roll, which ascertains this number, by mentioning the place of birth of each individual embarked, has thus become an indispensable piece, or document on board, and of which the absence authorizes confiscation."

CHAPTER XV.

Causes Célèbres du Droit des Gens.

In 1827, there appeared at Leipsic, in two vols. 8vo, a work, entitled, Causes Célèbres du Droit des Gens, Redigées par le Baron Charles de Martens. This is rather an useful book, and makes no great pretensions, although dedicated to the Russian Emperor Nicholas. The Baron is a nephew of the celebrated M. G. F. de Martens; and mentions that this publication is extracted, (but of course popularized and improved,) from a large work published by his uncle in 1800–1802, entitled, Erzählungen Merkwürdiger Fälle des Neuern Europäischen Volkerrechts. Only a few of the disputed cases fall within the domain of maritime international law. But there are two of this description in the second volume; and we would particularly recommend the first case in that volume, as containing a full and distinct account, on both sides, of the difference, which arose in 1752 between Great Britain and Prussia, on the subject of captures, made by English cruizers, during the maritime war of 1744 to 1748, and of the arrest made by his Prussian Majesty, by way of reprisal, of certain sums lent by, and due to certain English merchants, secured upon the revenues of Silesia.

Although a little out of order, chronologically, we may here also mention, that in 1843, the Baron Charles de Martens, published other two vols. 8vo, at Leipsic and Paris, under the title of Nouvelles Causes Célèbres du Droit des Gens. In this publication, the Baron is again much indebted to the laborious collections of his uncle, and particularly to his Recueil des Traités, and other state papers; as likewise to that excellent work formerly noticed by us, at some length, the Histoire Abrégée des Traités de Paix, by M. de Koch, wholly recast, enlarged, and continued, in fifteen volumes, to the treaties of Paris in 1815, by M. F. Schoell, then counsellor of the Prussian embassy at the court of France. These two additional volumes contain some other important disputed cases in maritime international law; in the first volume, the differences, which arose in 1775—1780, between Great Britain and the republic of the united provinces of the Netherlands, on the subject of the commerce of the Dutch, with the revolted English-American colonies, and of the aid which the court of London demanded from that republic, in virtue of the alliance subsisting between the two countries; and the differences, which arose in 1778 between Great Britain and France, on the subject of the recognition of the independence of the Anglo-American colonies; in the second volume, the differences between Great Britain and the powers of the north, at the time of the new maritime association, for the maintenance of neutral navigation, from 1800 to the convention of June and October 1801.

It may also be here mentioned, that in 1832, Baron Charles de Martens published a work, entitled, Guide Diplomatique, of which a new and enlarged edition, in three vols. 8vo, appeared in 1837, with extracts from the works of Count d'Hautrive, &c. But this work treats chiefly of the privileges and duties of public ministers; and, while it contains a good deal of practical information, very useful to students of general diplomacy, and young Attachés, it does not enter into any discussion of the maritime rights of nations.

CHAPTER XVI.

Traité Complet de Diplomatie par un Ancien Ministre.

In the preceding remarks, we have considered, at great length, the small portion of the able work of M. Vincens, which relates to maritime international law, because we esteem him as an author of talent, of information, and, comparatively, of great fairness; though misled, occasionally, in the representation he gives of facts and events, by an overweening national partiality. On the next work we find, in the order of time, which appears also to be by a French author, we shall not dwell so long; partly, because, so far as it embraces maritime international law, we consider it not so much a work of science, as a polemical diplomatic brochure, calculated to mislead that portion of the French population who devote themselves to diplomacy; partly, because we have already either ourselves shown the groundlessness of his theory, or refuted it, by the more powerful arguments of Lampredi and Tetens, which are certainly free from British bias.

The work to which we allude, is the anonymous one, entitled, Traité Complet de Diplomatie, published at Paris in 1833. This treatise has been ascribed to different individuals; but, as the author has not chosen to give his name, we make no farther inquiry on the subject, and merely conclude, from the style, that he is a Frenchman, not a German or Dane, writing in the French language. For the student of general diplomacy, the work appears to contain a good deal of useful, but rather superficial information; and some of its best passages are apparently taken, without reference, from Count de Bohm's French translation of the German work of M. Schmalz, before mentioned. But the work itself, as a whole, is ill arranged; and with regard to that part of it, which relates to maritime international law, the author seems either not to have studied the practical administration of that law by the prize courts of his own country, and of the other countries of Europe, or perhaps, like a skilful diplomatist, to have concealed that knowledge. The opinions of foreign judicial tribunals, or of foreign jurists, he may have held in little estimation. But he does not even refer to the great jurists of his own country in this department, such as Valin, Pothier, Emérigon, Portalis. A party pamphleteer may be excused for omitting all notice of the doctrines of his predecessors, however talented or learned, if they happened to be adverse to the cause he wished to support. But somewhat different conduct was to have been expected from the author of a work, which he entitles, a complete treatise of diplomacy.

This anonymous author, indeed, seems to tolerate armemens en course, or the system of privateering, as being established in practice, and likely to be continued; while to us it appears, the universal abolition of the system would be more beneficial than any other improvement to be reasonably expected in the practice of maritime warfare. He recognizes also the lawfulness of those restrictions on neutral commerce with belligerent states, by which neutrals are prohibited from carrying supplies to ports under actual blockade, and from furnishing arms and ammunition as contraband of war. But, on the other hand, adopting the views of Hübner and Rayneval, and perceiving, as the latter did, the absurdity of holding a neutral merchant vessel, sailing in the ocean, to be a part of the territory of the neutral state, he resorts to the principle of national independence, and says, "It must be laid down as a fundamental principle, that the liberty of navigation is inherent in the independence of nations, as in that of the sea, which is res communis; and that all the modifications which are introduced into it, are so many exceptions, which are stricti juris, and not to be extended beyond their object."[1] And, agreeably to this assumed principle, he proceeds to argue, that contraband of war is founded solely on the commerce in the articles being dangerous, and embraces merely arms and ammunition, not naval stores, or other such articles; that the goods of the enemy, although in the open seas, are protected from capture by the neutral flag; that neutrals may carry on the coasting and colonial trade of one of the belligerents, who had been deprived of the power of carrying on that trade, by the military operations of the opposite belligerent, during the existing war; that there is a presumption in favour of goods, under a neutral flag, that they are really neutral property; that a deviation from the route or destination, indicated in the ship's papers, is lawful or innocent, and affords no ground for confiscation; that the pretended right of visitation and search is contrary to the elementary notions of the law of nations, and is even belied by the usages of war; that the faculty of violating treaties deserves no answer, (as if Britain, any more than France, had at any time maintained such a doctrine;) that resistance to the right of visitation and search is lawful;

[1] Tom. II. p. 348.

that the neutral military flag protects all neutral merchant vessels against all cruizers.

But this argument, (which our author borrows from Rayneval,) that the right of each nation to maintain its independence against any interference by other nations, implies or involves a right to protect the property of another nation, in its temporary custody, as a common carrier on the open sea, is neither grammatically, nor logically correct. The idea expressed by the term independence, is manifestly more of a negative or non-permissive, than of a positive or active nature—a right to exclude others cannot well be held to include, or comprehend a right to interfere between others. The negative right of a nation to maintain its own independence against, and by the exclusion of others, cannot imply or involve a positive right to protect the property of another nation against a third nation, having otherwise confessedly a right to seize it. It would be strange jurisprudence to hold, that the independence of a citizen entitles him to interfere between two other citizens, such as a debtor and his creditor, who has no other means of obtaining payment of the debt due, than by seizing the effects of his debtor; and to maintain that he has a right to protect the effects of the debtor, from any such attachment by the creditor.

Nor does the liberty of the open sea for navigation, any more than the independence of nations, imply or involve any right in one nation to protect the property of another nation against a third nation, having, confessedly, a right otherwise to seize it. The liberty of the sea is not licentiousness; it is for the legitimate purposes of navigation; it cannot legalize an act at sea, which is otherwise, and in itself, unlawful.

Towards the close of his seventh book, the author becomes less extravagant in his theory; admits the legal effect of blockade, if actual, which is all that is correctly contended for by belligerents; and that the prize courts of the country of the captor are the only competent tribunals for the adjudication of prizes, captured on the high seas; reserving to neutral governments, through their prize courts, to judge of prizes captured within their territorial seas, and of prizes captured from their subjects, and brought by the captors into their ports.

In imitation, apparently, of the great Montesquieu, this anonymous author expounds the theoretical doctrines, before alluded to, in a series of brief epigrammatic sections, and in a tone much more authoritative. But, how great the contrast, in extent of view and accuracy of reasoning! At the same time, this author never fails to gloss over his unwarranted assumptions and illogical reasoning, by constantly repeated appeals to humanity and philanthropy; forgetful that all such indulgences, which are deviations from, or are not based upon, impartial even-handed justice, are mischievous, not generally beneficial or expedient.

CHAPTER XVII.

Notice of Dr. Wheaton's Elements of International Law.

THE next author whom we have to mention, as appearing again, near the close of this last period of our historical inquiry, from the peace of 1815 to the present time, is the able and learned American lawyer, Dr. Wheaton, now American minister at the court of Berlin. We formerly noticed at length, and made long quotations from his Digest of the Law of maritime captures and prizes, published in 1815. We have now to notice his work, entitled, Elements of International Law, in two vols. 8vo, dated Berlin, and published at London in 1836.

This work, although not by a British author, was certainly, at the date of its publication, the most able and scientific treatise on international law, which had appeared in the English language. The arrangement is superior to that of Martens, Chitty, Schmalz, or Klüber. On the other hand, we have elsewhere, both formerly, and in the course of the present historical review, entered our protest against part of the author's doctrine, regarding the sources or foundation of international law—against the excessive efficacy, which appears to us to be ascribed by him, along with Martens, to treaties or conventions, as not merely constituting international law, pro tempore et inter paciscentes, and creating valid obligations on states, while the treaties remain in force, and to the extent of the stipulations contained in them; but as creating, also, a sort of conventional or consuetudinary law, separate and distinct from the treaties themselves—valid and binding, after the treatics themselves have, by the admission of these identical modern jurists, ceased to exist, through the intervention of subsequent hostilities, without being renewed;[1] and binding even in favour of other nations, with whom no similar treaty has ever been entered into. Such a deduction or conclusion, we humbly conceive, we have sufficiently shown, to be unwarranted by the premises. Indeed, it seems to be a mere fiction, got up to support a particular theory, convenient and advantageous for certain states, but unequal and unjust in itself, and injurious to other states.

Of this, Dr. Wheaton's principal work on international law generally, of course, only a part relates to the subject of our present inquiries—the maritime department of that law. And as in that part, we do not find any thing very material, in addition to what is contained in his Digest of the Law of captures and prizes, from which we have quoted largely, and which we have criticised at sufficient length, we shall reserve our farther observations for his more recent work in French—the History of the progress of the law of nations in Europe, from the peace of Westphalia to the congress of Vienna, published at Leipsic, in 1841.

[1] Martens Precis, § 64, Klüber, § 154.

CHAPTER XVIII.

Review of Mr. Oke Manning's work.

In the interval, there appeared in 1839, the work of Mr. W. Oke Manning, Junior, entitled, Commentaries on the Law of nations. And we congratulate the author in having produced the best recent work in the English language, on the law of nations, by a native of Great Britain. He does not, indeed, like the anonymous author before alluded to, who takes the designation of "un Ancien Ministre," call his work a "complete" treatise of diplomacy; he takes the more modest title of commentaries; but his treatise embraces international law generally as a system. Of course, only a part of this general treatise relates to maritime international law—the proper subject of our present inquiries. And our object, certainly, is not to repeat what has probably been better said before, and not so much to give any detailed account of recent British works, which speak for themselves, and are generally known, or easily accessible, as to make that portion of the British public who take an interest in such matters, better acquainted with the works of foreign authors on the subject; both of those, who, influenced by national bias, or less worthy motives, give statements, in point of fact, not altogether correct, or propound doctrines in point of law, which appear to be unfounded; and also of those, who, proving themselves to be above such influences, candidly and impartially state the truth, and propound the doctrines which they believe to be consistent with legal principle and justice. At the same time, in our historical sketch, we feel it a pleasant part of our task to notice, shortly, the literary labours of our countrymen. And, as there cannot be any rivalry between a work, embracing the whole range of the science of international law, and the result of our previous or simultaneous researches, having for their object to trace the history merely of the maritime department of that law, we shall feel no indelicacy in frankly stating our opinion, when, in our brief review, we happen to differ from our author.

With regard to the chapters of this work, which treat of the definition and sources of the law of nations, as natural and positive, as derived from the law of nature, from custom and convention, or as founded on the principle of general utility, we differ, in some important points, from our author. But we have already given our opinion on these subjects at sufficient length, in our Inquiries in the Science of Law, national and international; and this is not the place to revert to these discussions.

In his first book, containing a history of the science of the law of nations, our author gives a more full account of the successive writers on that law, and of the different collections of treaties, than had previously appeared in the English language. And, in general, his criticisms appear to be just. In particular, we agree with him in charging Klüber with statements of events not always correct, and, as we have seen, with a partiality or prejudice, for which it is not easy to account, but which it is not easy to excuse, on the score of patriotic zeal. But we do not entirely concur with our author in his almost indiscriminate censure of Klüber's whole work, or in his almost unqualified laudation of Martens, although a highly useful writer, and generally more correct and impartial than Klüber.

In his second book, our author treats of the sources of the law of nations; in his third book, of war; and in his fourth book, (marked Book III. apparently in error,) of neutrality. And we certainly do not consider this general arrangement as any improvement upon some of those which preceded it, or as affording an example of the application of the exhaustive analysis, recommended by Bentham. But this point, we have, elsewhere, sufficiently discussed. And our author's subordinate and more minute arrangement of matters, falling under the general heads, just mentioned, is greatly superior, being comprehensive and sufficiently special. This will appear from a recital merely of the titles of his chapters. In his third book of war, he treats of the rights and effects of war; of retorsion, embargo, reprisal, and privateers; of the declaration of war; of the state or condition of war; of the rights of a belligerent, with regard to the property of his enemy in a hostile country; of postliminium; of the right of war with regard to the person of the enemy; of prisoners of war. The chapters bearing these titles contain a great deal of valuable information on these subjects, derived from unexceptionable sources, and comprised in a condensed shape. But only a small part of this division relates to maritime international law. And it would be improper here to do more, than to refer to the work itself, so recent, and so easily accessible to the English reader.

In his fourth book, or, as it is entitled, Book III., of neutrality; the author enters into a more full discussion of the law of nations generally, and embraces almost all the leading questions on maritime international law. In chapter i., of the rights and duties of neutral nations with regard to hostilities; and in chapter ii., with regard to the right of passage through a neutral territory, our author treats almost entirely of the law of war as applicable to land. But the thirteen following chapters are almost entirely devoted to the doctrine of maritime international law during war. In chapters iii., iv., and v., the author treats generally of the rights of neutral and belligerent commerce in time of war; of the rights of neutrals to trade at all with belligerents; of the rule of 1756; and of the right of neutrals to carry on the coasting trade of a belligerent.

Now, while we concur in the result or conclusions, at which our author here arrives, we are not aware, that, by the natural or common consuetudinary law of nations, a belligerent was ever held entitled to prevent a neutral from having any trade at all with the opposed belligerent. Indeed, the early and universal recognition of articles of contraband of war, necessarily implied, that the commerce of neutrals with belligerents in articles not contraband, was generally free. The reciprocal proclamations of the Spanish and Dutch governments in the sixteenth century, prohibiting neutrals from having any commerce with their adversary, were held to be deviations from the law of nations, and were resisted by the Queen of England. The similar treaty between England and Holland against France in 1689, we have seen, was also remonstrated against by the northern powers, and was abandoned as unwarranted. Even the strong necessity of self-defence against the insane threat and attempt of the revolutionary rulers of France, to conquer and revolutionize the governments of all the surrounding nations, does not appear, although represented "as being a common concern to every civilized state," to have been held sufficient to warrant the provision respecting neutrals, in the treaties concluded in 1793, among the different European powers who then united against France. The Berlin and Milan decrees of the French Emperor Napoleon, prohibiting all neutrals from commerce with the British isles, are admitted, on all hands, to have been gross infringements of the law of nations. And the merely retaliatory, temporary, and conditional British orders in council of 1807, can only be justified against those other nations, who had ceased to be bonâ fide independent neutrals—who had forfeited the character and consequent rights of neutrality, by alliances with Napoleon, and concurrence in his schemes.

With regard to what has been rather absurdly called "the rule of the war of 1756," prohibiting neutrals from carrying on the colonial trade of belligerents, which is alleged, by some continental writers, to have been then first introduced by Britain, to have been discontinued during the American war, and to have been resumed during the French revolutionary war, we have already seen, that, while it is plain, a right cannot come into operation, or be exercised, until the occurrence of the events, and the existence of the circumstances producing or constituting the relations which give it birth; instances had occurred, prior to 1756, of the exercise of this right;[1] and that, even at the close of the seventeenth century, Baron de Cocceii had expounded the right of the neutral to be, the maintenance of his accustomed trade during peace; consequently excluding the colonial trade of the European nations, from which foreigners have been, and are uniformly excluded. Besides, the principle seems to be entirely the same, as that by which a neutral is held not entitled to step in and carry on his coasting trade for a belligerent, who has

[1] Rob. Adm IV. App p 1-25.

been disabled by his antagonist, from doing so himself as usual. For what is a colony, but a separate and more distant territory, dependent on the parent state. In these views of the common consuetudinary law of nations, relative to the coasting and colonial trade of belligerents, we quite concur with Mr. Manning; and merely doubt the propriety of the expression, that belligerents may prohibit neutrals from carrying on such trade, inasmuch, as the term, "prohibit," may be thought to imply the exercise of legislative or judicial power, which no nation has over another sovereign state. Perhaps the more correct phraseology would be, that belligerents are entitled to prevent neutrals from interfering to carry on the coasting or direct colonial trade of the enemy, not with, but for the behoof of that enemy, by the seizure and confiscation of the vessels, or at least, of the stipulated coasting freight.

With regard, again, to the conventional law of nations, relative to the coasting and colonial trade of belligerents, our author shows, that in this department there has been no consistent system in treaties among states; different nations, and even the same nation, stipulating and undertaking different obligations to different parties. Of course, there can be no legal result, but that each party is bound to fulfil the contract it has entered into while it exists.

In chapter iv., Mr Manning treats of the property of an enemy found at sea, by a belligerent, in the ship of a neutral, and of the property of a neutral found at sea, in the ship of an enemy. And this is the most elaborate and valuable part of our author's work. But this is not the place to give any detailed account of it, as we have done of some of those continental works in foreign languages, which seemed to be little known in this country; especially after we had passed over with such brief notices,

"War in disguise," and the other pamphlets consequent upon it, as being easily accessible to the English reader, and likewise even the excellent professional treatises of Mr. Plumer Ward, for the same reason, although certainly more liable to go out of print, from their having been published in the shape of pamphlets, instead of the ordinary shape of a standard scientific work, to which they were so justly entitled. Our author, and we, occasionally, appear to have been engaged in the same line of study. Our plan was to attempt to trace, historically, the condition of maritime international law generally, through successive ages; including, of course, the important questions here discussed. Our author's plan appears to have been, to distinguish the different rules of maritime international law, particularly the rules and questions discussed in this chapter, and to have traced them each separately and chronologically. And it is satisfactory to us, to find that we arrive, on the subject discussed in this chapter, at the same conclusions. Referring, therefore, to this chapter, as very worthy of perusal, and equally accessible, as these researches, we shall merely notice the order in which the author has conducted his inquiry. I. "What are the dictates of reason with regard to the right of the question; or in other words, what are the commands of the law of nature? II. What have been the decisions of the acknowledged authorities on the law of nations? III. How far the customary, or conventional law of Europe, has interfered to reverse or modify the law, as derived from the two preceding sources?"

Under the first of these heads, and the first section of this chapter, we wish our author, after quoting the brief and sound remark of Mr. Ward, that neutrals are at liberty to *trade with*, but *not for*, belligerents, had followed this up, by endeavouring to ascertain, what was really the commerce of the neutral, what really the commerce of the belligerent, prior to the war. Every inhabitant of a country, who sells or exchanges the produce of his land and labour for other commodities, as formerly observed, is not a merchant. A merchant is a person who purchases, or acquires commodities, with a view to sale In the same way, a nation that merely exchanges its surplus produce for other produce, which it requires for consumption, can scarcely be called a mercantile, or trading, nation. The commerce, or trade, of a nation, appears to consist in the employment of that part of its accumulated moveable capital, by which exchanges of commodities are effected between different nations, or the individuals of whom they are composed, by means of exportation and importation. And, in this way, an approximation, at least, may be made, to the ascertainment of what is really and truly the commerce of the neutral, as distinct from the commerce of the belligerent, so as to afford a measure of the right of the neutral. At all events, this is easily done in two descriptions of trade; the coasting trade, and the colonial trade, which nations uniformly reserve to themselves exclusively.

In section second of this chapter, Mr. Manning recites the decisions, or opinions, on this subject, of almost all the various successive authorities on the law of nations, from the Consolato del Mare, to Grotius, Pufendorff, Bynkershoek, and Vattel. He points out the inconsistency in the reasoning and doctrine of Hübner, and quotes also the authorities of Lampredi, Klüber, and Martens.

In our author's opinion, that the right of belligerents to capture the property of their enemies, in the open seas, although on board of neutral merchant vessels, not merely admitted of little doubt, but was also not now called in question, or disputed, we once concurred. But, after having perused not merely the works published during the late war, from 1803 to 1815, in France, and in the other continental countries, then under the dominion or influence of Napoleon, but even the systematic works on the subject, which have appeared since the general peace in 1815, we cannot say, with our author, that the right is not now called in question, and must admit, that it is still disputed, with great zeal and energy;—however completely, we may agree with him, in thinking, it is clearly well founded in reason and legal principle.

In our historical sketch, therefore, both in the earlier and later ages, we have, besides those mentioned by Mr. Manning, noticed some other eminent jurists, with whose works Mr. Manning, probably, was not acquainted, or which he might not deem it necessary to quote. We have already sufficiently commented on this portion of the systematic works of Klüber and Martens; and have deemed it right to bring, pretty fully, before that portion of the British public, who take an interest in such matters, the works of Lampredi and Tetens, as authorities, perfectly free from all British bias, and as approaching nearer to Grotius, in profound and extended views, and in acute discrimination, than, perhaps, any of the other more recent maritime jurists. We may also here, perhaps, be permitted to supply an omission, in our first volume,[1] by adding, that Dr. Zouch, whom we noticed, at length, in our general International Inquiries, and who was judge of the English Court of Admiralty in 1660, recognized, as also did Molloy, about thirty years afterwards, the authority in England of the Consolato del Mare, and thus laid down the doctrine we are here considering. After mentioning the

[1] P. 165.

French law, by which the hostile cargo was held to confiscate the neutral vessel, "Acquius, tamen, est, ut amicorum naves, ablatis tantum mercibus (nisi prohibitas deferant) dimittantur; et per Consulatum Maris quo Mediteranei jus continetur, qui in amicorum nave, hostium bona deprehendit, pro eo itineris, quod navis praestitit, naulum solvere tenetur."[1]

In section third of this chapter, our author treats of what he calls the customary and conventional law of nations on this question, till the armed neutrality of 1780: and in section fourth, of the armed neutrality and conventions since that period. In these sections, our author goes through, most laboriously and accurately, all the treaties, from about the middle of the seventeenth century, to the peace of Amiens in 1801, among the European powers, or between any of them and the United States of America, which contain any stipulation or provision, with regard to the protection from seizure at sea, of hostile goods on board neutral vessels. And the result of this laborious examination is, in our author's words, that he is not aware of any treaty, comprising this principle, existing at present between Great Britain and any other Christian Power. Indeed, we have already shown, that so far as regarded such a provision, all the treaties which were entered into during the successive periods, into which we divided our historical sketch, had all expired, or been expressly annulled, or been invalidated, in consequence of the infraction of the counter stipulations, or been dissolved by successive wars, and not renewed in the treaties of peace. And, as we may have occasion to revert to the armed neutrality, in our review of the still later work of Dr. Wheaton, we shall content ourselves with a reference to these sections, as worthy of perusal, and add a few remarks.

[1] Jur. et Jud. Fecial. P. II. § viii. p. 6.

In the terms of the title of section third, namely, of the "Customary and conventional law of nations," our author has not shown his ordinary precision of language. The conjunction of the terms, "customary and conventional," seem to confound these two descriptions of law, and to hold them either as identical, or at least, as parts of one and the same whole. But this we can scarcely suppose to have been our author's meaning. For these two descriptions of obligatory and compulsory law, appear to be quite distinct. Conventional law is formed by the special consent of the contracting parties, expressed in language, in treaties. The customary, or common consuetudinary law, is formed by long established, constant, and uniform usage, proceeding in its most important parts, upon the principles of natural justice and equity, and adopted, from necessity and mutual convenience; as recorded, not in special contracts or treaties, but in the concordant statutes, ordinances, proclamations, and judicial determinations of independant states, and in the concordant writings of the eminent international jurists of these different states, through a series of ages. Accordingly, although in the title he has added customary to conventional, our author, in these two sections, considers merely the treaties among nations, during the period he surveys. Indeed, it is plain, special treaties require no custom, or usage, to give them validity, however necessary or useful the latter may be, in ascertaining the right interpretation of such conventions.

But, in thus showing, that there is no existing treaty between Britain and any other nation, stipulating, that free ships shall make free goods, our author does not exactly, or altogether, meet the argument of his antagonists. They are aware, although they do not explicitly admit, that since the peace of Amiens, there has existed no treaty binding Great Britain to recognize such a rule. But they maintain, that, in consequence of Britain having entered into different treaties, with different nations, from about the middle of the seventeenth to about the middle of the eighteenth century, particularly the treaties of 1674 with Holland, of 1676 with France, and of Utrecht, in 1713, with France and Holland, containing stipulations and engagements in favour of their vessels, when neutral, protecting hostile goods at sea, Britain thereby became bound, in perpetuity, and by the law of nations, to recognize such a rule, independently of the existence of these treaties, and after they have been annulled by infringement, or otherwise. And so far as he makes any answer to this argument, we apprehend our author concedes more than he was called upon to do, in reason, or on correct legal principle. His answer seems to be,[1] "Such a collection of treaties, agreeing in the principle, that the cargo shall be free, or be confiscated, according as the ship is neutral, or enemy, seems to go far in establishing, not that this principle was enforced, (sanctioned?) by the law of nations, independent of treaty, but that it was the general wish of maritime powers that this practice should be adopted; and that it might probably become the conventional law of Europe among those states, and only those states which were entering into these engagements. But such an opinion was soon proved fallacious by the result. Not fifteen years from the date of the armed neutrality, the wars with France had involved almost every European state; and the principle, which appeared obtaining such general prevalence, was abandoned by nearly all the members of the northern confederacy; the great leader in that alliance, Russia, being the chief instigator of the unusual

[1] pp. 271, 272.

severities which were adopted towards neutrals. France was the first to alter the practice engaged in (undertaken by) the recent treaties."

Now, we not merely agree with our author, that the series of treaties he enumerates, shows it was the wish of a large number, if not the majority, of the maritime states, at different times, for certain considerations, that this practice should be adopted; and even also rendered it probable it might become the conventional law of Europe, among the contracting parties. We further admit, that these treaties, when concluded among the different nations, really constituted the conventional law of Europe, properly so called, pro tempore, among these nations; and that, if this series of treaties had legally constituted, or could have legally constituted a customary, as well as a conventional law of Europe, binding on all the maritime states, the subsequent conduct of certain governments in 1793, and afterwards, could not have justified a departure from such a common consuetudinary law, provided it had ever been actually established. But we deny, in point of fact, that either Spain or France, any more than Britain, then actually, absolutely, and unconditionally agreed to, and adopted generally, the doctrines of the armed neutrality. And, in point of law, we deny that any number of treaties, if simultaneous, or any succession of treaties, however long, can afford any adequate ground for inferring, or deducing legal obligations, beyond the terms and import, and the duration of the contract. The longer continued, and the more general the recurrence to the contract, the stronger proof is afforded, of the conviction, that the privilege wished to be obtained, does not exist in justice, or at common law, independently of special bargain.

We are rather surprised, too, that, while in this

section, he does so much justice to the merits of Hübner, our author does not notice the two anonymous works we formerly mentioned:[1]—La Liberté de la Navigation et du Commerce des nations neutres pendant la guerre, considerée selon le Droit des Gens universel, celui de l' Europe, et les Traités; and the Essai sur un Code Maritime general Européen pour la conservation de la liberté de la navigation et du commerce des nations neutres en tems de guerre. These works, published in 1780 and 1782, although, no doubt, posterior in date, appear to us equal, if not superior, to that of Hübner, and to have had as great an influence on public opinion on the continent. On the authority of Von Kamptz, we have ascribed them to Professor Cobald Totze. And whoever may have been the author, the origin of the works is, probably, connected with the antipathy to the government of Great Britain, which King Frederic II. of Prussia, confessedly felt and exhibited, about the period of their appearance. The recent publication, too, by Lord Malmesbury, of the diplomatic correspondence of his ancestor, Sir James Harris, throws additional light, to that afforded many years ago by Count de Görtz, upon the concoction of the scheme of the armed neutrality in 1780. The original incentive to this measure, in the mind of the Russian Empress Catherine, appears to have been a desire to be avenged for an affront, which she conceived the Spanish government had offered to her maritime flag. Of this opportunity, her astute minister, Count Panin, in his competition with Prince Potemkin, for the favour of their imperial Mistress, took advantage; and, apparently, under the influence of the King of Prussia, prepared, and got immediately promulgated, without delay, a set of rules for neutral navigation during war, which, while they

[1] Vol. I. pp. 326-342.

were represented to the Empress, as calculated to prevent the recurrence of such conduct on the part of Spain, more materially and injuriously affected the rights and interests of Britain. It does not appear, that, at first, the Empress understood the regulations proposed by her minister, were to affect Britain injuriously, or that she intended they should do so. For, when the matter was subsequently explained to her, by the British minister, at a personal interview, obtained through Prince Potemkin, she repeatedly protested she had no such intention. But, by that time, her declaration and invitation to the other powers, had reached the different courts of Europe, and it would have been awkward to retract her proposal. She was anxious, she admitted, for the advancement of her mercantile navy; being despotic in her own empire, she could not bear that Russian vessels should be subjected to any interruption, however just the purpose; she was delighted with the popularity of her measure among the maritime states, who were directly to reap benefit from it, at the expense of others; and her personal vanity was gratified, by the adulation of being represented as the glorious Vindicatrix of the liberty of the seas! Yet, a few years only elapsed, when this same Empress lived, to perceive and feel the folly of such vain pretensions.

Chapter VII. of Mr. Manning's work, is a concise essay on contraband of war; and we shall merely recommend it to perusal, with a very few remarks. We have already seen, that the general descriptions of goods, which have been held to be contraband, or illegal for neutrals to convey to belligerents, are, 1, articles which have been constructed, fabricated, or compounded into actual instruments of war; 2, articles, which, from their nature, qualities, and quantities, are applicable and useful for the purposes of war; 3, articles, which, although not subservient generally to the purposes of war, such as grain, flour, provisions, naval stores, become so, by their special and direct destination for such purposes, namely, by their destination for the supply of armies, garrisons, or fleets, naval arsenals, and ports of military equipment. But, as the detail of the first and second of these descriptions may admit of dispute, and even the first description may vary from changes in the art of war, we agree with our author, in the opinion, that it is highly desirable these articles should be ascertained by special enumeration in treaties, and that the consequences attached to the carriage of such articles, by confiscation, or otherwise, should also be thus defined.

But we do not see, that the effect of such enumerations in treaties can be extended beyond the contracting parties, or that, without an almost really universal convention, systematic writers on international law, such as Martens and Klüber, can, by collecting from treaties, such articles as are most generally included in these treaties, deduce a compulsory list, binding upon all nations generally, whether parties to a treaty containing the particular articles, or not. And, perhaps, our author has rather gone too much into the views of some of the late continental writers, in ascribing to a collection of simultaneous or successive treaties, or similar clauses, in such treaties, a mysterious power of creating legal obligations, beyond the stipulations and engagements, or duration of these treaties,—such an obligatory effect, as is the result only of long established, constant, and uniform custom and usage. Such a collection of treaties may, no doubt, prove the practice of treating in such a way; but it does not prove the actual conduct and practice of nations to have been in conformity with these treaties. The stipulations in the treaties of Utrecht in 1713, between Britain and France, and between Britain and Holland, were, no doubt, equivalent to "free ships, free goods." But for half a century succeeding, they had not been acted upon, in practice, not because either of the nations had violated, or failed to observe the contract, but because the circumstances in which, alone, the stipulations could be founded on, had not occurred. We agree, however, with our author, in his censure of the strange misrepresentation of the law by Klüber, that the confiscation of contraband of war has no foundation in principle. And such correction was the more necessary, because, the work of Klüber, being a recent systematic treatise, not a polemical pleading in favour of any interested party, is the more apt to mislead the young student.

In chapter VIII., our author treats of pre-emption. But the general right of pre-emption, which he notices, as having existed even in time of peace, in former ages, does not rest on any principle of the Common law of nations; having been exercised by sovereigns or governments, in virtue of their supreme power over their own subjects, or over foreigners importing commodities into their territories, or in virtue of special paction in treaties. And what has come to be termed the right of pre-emption in maritime international law, ought rather to be denominated the right of interception and appropriation, upon condition of the payment of the value, or current market price of commodities, which are not, from their nature or quality, or quantity, directly subservient to the purposes of war, but which may, from their direct destination, afford such supplies to the enemy, as to support or promote, or facilitate his military operations.

On chapter IX. and X., on blockade, generally, and on the continental system, and the retaliatory British

Orders in Council, we have little to remark. We have already seen, that blockade is a military operation; and, although notification thereof to neutrals, be highly proper, and is now generally practised, it is indispensably necessary, that, to be valid and effectual in law, so as to infer confiscation for a breach of it, the blockade must be actual, and maintained by an adequate naval force. Such was the law of blockade, as administered by the British prize tribunal, during the French revolutionary war. Under such an administration, the British cruizers could have no inducement to capture for breach of blockade, unless it was actual. And the British orders in council of January and November 1807, which proclaimed a quasi, and more extensive blockade, as a retaliatory temporary measure, directed against the continental blockade of Napoleon, were not issued, till after the promulgation of the French Berlin decree in November 1806.

In chapter XI., the author gives a concise view of the right of search of merchant vessels, without, or under convoy. And of chapters XII. and XIII., which treat of prize courts, of captures within neutral territory, and of prizes brought into neutral ports, we have only to regret the brevity.

CHAPTER XIX.

Review of Dr. Wheaton's History of the progress of the Law of Nations in Europe.

Section I.

In the course of our historical investigation, we come now to what, so far as we are aware, is the latest work that has appeared on our subject, Dr. Wheaton's Histoire des Progrés du Droit des Gens en Europe, dépuis la paix de Westphalie jusqu' au Congrés de Vienne. This work, we understand, gained the prize proposed by l'Academie des Sciences Morales et Politiques de l'Institut de France for the year 1839; and with additions, was published at Leipsic in 1841. His long residence at Berlin, as minister of the United States, has enabled Dr. Wheaton to draw his information from the best sources, the juridical and political literature of Germany. His learning is extensive and profound; and his views are enlarged, and generally impartial, except when his intellect appears to us to be clouded by his unfortunately strong national bias, and excessive zeal to promote the commercial interests of his country, by his rather too apparent antipathy to the land of his forefathers, and by his equally apparent strong predilection for France.

We are not aware, that Dr. Wheaton has published any edition of this work in the English language. But we shall use the French edition; making a literal English translation, and, of course, noticing only those parts of the work, which relate to Maritime international law.

To his history of the progress of the law of nations in Europe, from the peace of Westphalia to the congress of Vienna, our author prefixes an interesting historical sketch of that law, prior to that peace. His history he divides into four periods, of which the first is from the peace of Westphalia in 1648, to that of Utrecht in 1713. This first part, he very properly commences with a short account of the principal jurists of the latter half of the seventeenth century; and reverts to the equitable principles of the prize code of the Consolato del Mare. But these, in the course of our Historical view, we noticed at sufficient length; and we pass on, with our author, to the celebrated Ordonnance de la Marine of Louis XIV., and the Code des Prises François.

This ordonnance of 1681, like the previous ordonnances of 1543 and 1584, we formerly saw, departed from the common consuetudinary maritime law of nations, inasmuch as it subjected to confiscation neutral goods on board hostile vessels, and neutral vessels carrying hostile goods. Apparently, as an excuse, or palliation for these extraordinary and extreme severities, our author remarks, that Louis XIV. did not intend, by this ordonnance, to prescribe a law of nations to Europe, but merely established principles for the direction of his own Admiralty courts of prize, which, in their application, these courts might moderate, or relax, at their discretion, pro temporibus et causis; and in support of this observation, he refers to the authorities of Sir Wm. Grant, and of Portalis. We have, elsewhere, stated our admiration of Sir Wm. Grant, as the model of a judge; and we have given Portalis due credit for advising Buonaparte, when First Consul, to moderate the rigour and injustice of the French republican administration of maritime international law. And, along with Sir Wm. Grant, we have no doubt, that neither Louis XIV. nor his able ministers, ever imagined they were entitled, or could de facto, by their ordonnance of 1681, establish a general maritime law of nations for Europe. But, that the ordonnance of 1681, did not constitute the law of France, or was not practically observed in the administration of the law of nations by that government, it is difficult to believe. And, on such a point, we are more disposed to be guided by the testimonies of some of the greatest lawyers whom France has produced, such as Valin, Pothier, and Emerigon, than by the incidental remark—the obiter dictum even of Sir Wm. Grant, supposing the passage could be interpreted, so as to bear such a meaning; or by the oration of Portalis, when in the Conseil des Prises, 6 Thermidor An. 8, he advised indulgence to neutrals, of whose aid at sea, France, at that time, stood so much in need.

In this apparent endeavour to account for, or extenuate the undue severity of the French Code des Prises, it is rather amusing to find our author observing, that the French maxim, "Que la robe d'Ennemi confisque celle d'Ami," adopted by the ordonnance of Francis I. in 1543, and of Henry III. in 1584, was deduced by De Mornac, from the Roman fiscal law, and quoting Sir Leoline Jenkins, to prove, that these ordonnances, were not enforced. The passage here quoted from Sir Leoline Jenkins, is just the one we formerly quoted.[1] And, besides that passage being, it is obvious,

[1] Vol. I. p. 150–153.

merely the argument of Sir Leoline, in favour of an English vessel, against her condemnation in France, to all appearance under the severe rule here referred to, our author omits altogether the remark of Sir Chr. Robinson on that passage,[1] while the quotation by us from Valin,[2] places beyond doubt, that this was the law of France, even down to the middle of the eighteenth century. Our author farther observes, Grotius was of opinion, that under the French ordonnances of 1543 and 1584, the neutral vessel was confiscated only in the case of the vessel being loaded with hostile goods, with the consent of the proprietor. But Bynkershoek is of an opposite opinion. And Valin, who, in such a matter, is a much better authority than either, proves that the French law in all cases, confiscated the neutral vessel, along with the hostile goods.

In period first, § 13, under the title, Droit des Gens Maritime fondé sur des Traités, our author proceeds to give, what appears to us to be an account, not so much of the conventional maritime law of nations, properly to called, as consisting of, and constituted by the stipulations and engagements embodied in treaties still existing and in force, but rather of a maritime law of nations, founded upon treaties, yet somehow independent of such treaties, and binding not only upon the contracting parties in relation to each other, but on all parties, who may have ever entered into similar contracts, or even upon those who may never have entered into any such contracts. The fallacy of the doctrine, which seems to be here maintained, we humbly conceive we have already shown, on several occasions;[3] and to avoid repetition, we beg to refer to our former observations on the subject.

[1] Coll. Marit. p. 120–121. [2] Vol. I. p. 152.

[3] Vol. I. pp. 183-203, 270-274, 458-468, and Vol. II. pp. 253-257, 299-300

In period first, § 14, our author treats, at considerable length, of contraband of war, from 1648 to 1713; and it may be proper to follow him, referring, at the same time, to the account given in the first volume of these researches, of the state of maritime international law in this particular, during the seventeenth, and first half of the eighteenth century, as appearing from the statutes, ordinances, and judicial determinations of the different maritime states, from the works of their international lawyers, and from treaties or special conventions. Our author begins with the conventional law, and informs us, that, by all the treaties, from that of the Pyrenees in 1659, to that of Utrecht in 1713, goods, contraband of war, were excepted from the general liberty of neutral commerce, but were limited to those articles only which are of direct use as instruments of war; excluding from the list, provisions, timber, and other materials for the construction of ships, and all other goods, which are not yet converted into the form of instruments of war. We are not quite sure, that, in all the treaties here referred to, the description of contraband of war is so special and distinct, so limited, and so exclusive, as here represented. But, if so, we at once admit, that such special stipulations and descriptions were clearly binding on the contracting parties, while the treaties remained in force, and prove what articles were then usually agreed to be held contraband, by parties entering into such conventions.

Passing to the regulations of particular countries, our author states, that the French ordonnance of 1681, declared warlike stores only to be contraband; and that Valin and Pothier agree in holding, provisions were not regarded as contraband, unless destined for a blockaded place; Valin, however, adding, that during the war of 1700, pitch and tar were comprehended in the list of contraband, because the enemy regarded them as such, except when found on board Swedish vessels, in consequence of these articles being the produce of their country; that by the treaty of commerce concluded by France with Denmark in 1742, pitch and tar were also declared contraband, as well as rosin, cloth for sails, hemp, masts and timber for building vessels; and that, in this matter, the conduct of the English could not be blamed by the Dutch, unless there was a contravention of particular treaties between them; for, in law, (de droit,) says M. Valin, quoting the Chevalier d'Abreu, "those things are at present contraband, and have been so, since the commencement of the present century, which were not so before, as appears from the old treaties, particularly that of St. Germains, concluded with England in 1677."[1]

Not approving of this extension of the list of contraband articles, and in order to controvert the preceding statement and admission by Valin, our author resorts to an inquiry, what was the pre-existing law in this particular, as recognized by international jurists; and adduces as authorities, Grotius, Bynkershoek, Zouch, and Jenkins.

The division of things, by Grotius, into what are directly useful, for the purposes of war, and what are of promiscuous or doubtful use, we formerly noticed.[2] And our author admits, that Grotius prohibits, or permits the conveyance of the latter to the enemy, according to the circumstances or state of the war. The ground assigned by Grotius for the interception of such articles, is, as we formerly noticed, the necessity of self-defence; and it is permitted only under the burden of restitution of the articles, or their value; in other words, it is a right, not of confiscation, but of pre-emption.

[1] Traité des Prises Chap. V. Sect vi. No 1. [2] Vol. I. p. 114.

This, also, our Author seems to admit; but he labours to show, that the necessity here required by Grotius, to justify the interception, must be, that absolute or extreme necessity, which annihilates all general rules of right, with the exception of a place effectually besieged or blockaded. In this argument, however, we do not think he is successful. For, according to Grotius, the necessity which legalizes the interception, is made to depend on the state, that is, the events of the war, and is said to give a right under the obligation of restitution. The necessity, therefore, which Grotius here meant, must be a necessity consistent and compatible with the existence of right and obligation, not an extreme necessity, which annihilates all rules of right, and which very seldom occurs in human affairs. Grotius was too acute and consistent a reasoner, to found a right, involving an obligation, on circumstances, in which these juridical relations and rules could not exist or be applied. And with regard to the case of the carriage of goods to a blockaded port, being the only instance, in which such goods could be legally seized, it is manifest, the right of seizure and confiscation, in consequence of a breach of blockade, rests upon a different and distinct principle from that of seizure of contraband. It does not depend on the nature or quality of the goods. A blockade is an operation of war, an occupation of a place by military force. And the act of a neutral, in attempting any communication with that place, in opposition to such military force, infers not merely the interception and pre-emption of the cargo, but the confiscation of the vessel, as well as of the cargo, of whatever description the goods may be.

In his farther investigation, our Author finds, Bynkershoek states, that the general usage of nations, interdicted as contraband, only articles exclusively adapted for the purposes of war; and that the rude materials, out of which articles of contraband may be fabricated, are not contraband; but modifies this general position, by adding, "it may sometimes happen, that the conveyance of materials, for the construction of ships of war, may be prohibited."

Our Author also finds, that Bynkershoek, in commenting on the passage of Grotius, before quoted, understood it as permitting the seizure of articles of the latter class, or of doubtful or promiscuous use, in case of necessity, and then only under the burden of restitution; but it is not made out, that Bynkershoek understood the necessity, here mentioned, to be that absolute and extreme necessity, which annihilates all rules of right and obligation.

Our Author likewise finds, that Zouch, who wrote about the middle of the seventeenth century, merely transcribes the passage of Grotius, before quoted; and that Heineccius, the contemporary of Bynkershoek, declares, the usage of nations has comprehended in contraband of war, not only warlike stores, but provisions or eatables, and materials, which serve for the construction of vessels. But our author does not show, that Heineccius makes the right to seize these latter articles depend on the absolute and extreme, and very rare necessity, which our author contends was the meaning of Grotius.

Our Author next quotes the passage of the report of Sir Leoline Jenkins to King Charles II., in which that excellent lawyer says, "That, by the general law of nations, nothing can be adjudged contraband, but articles which may be used directly and immediately, for the purposes of war; and no other goods, except only in the case of besieged places, or of a general declaration to all the world, on the part of Spain, in which case, she will confiscate all the pitch and tar which she may be able to seize."[1] But this passage merely proves the correctness of the statement of Valin, that the addition of naval stores, especially for the construction of ships of war, to the ordinary list of contraband, did not take place till about the beginning of the eighteenth century; in consequence, it may be concluded, of maritime wars having then become more frequent, and of naval stores having then become more instrumental in these wars. Besides, in this passage, Sir Leoline is talking of contraband, as involving confiscation by the law of nations, not of mere interception and seizure, upon condition of restitution, or payment of the market value; which, as inflicting greatly less hardship on the neutral; it is plain, requires not an extreme, but a very inferior degree of necessity, to justify it as a right.

"The only conclusion," observes our Author, "which can be legitimately drawn from these authorities, is, that the change in the law of contraband, as it was understood by belligerents, (of which Valin speaks,) took place long before the period which he assigns to it; but the authority of the new rule, introduced in this manner, was still contested by the neutral states, whose interests were affected by the interdiction of their ordinary commerce in their native produce." But, while we are not prepared to admit, that our author has here convicted Valin of any error, we readily recognize the right of neutrals to indulgent considerations, when the goods conveyed by them are not intrinsically contraband, and are the produce, perhaps the chief produce, of their native country. And, with a view to such neutral interests, we would remark, that in reason and in law, the principle of contraband,—the principle upon which it is unlawful for neutrals to supply belligerents

[1] Wynne's Life of Sir Leoline Jenkins, Vol. II. p. 751.

with certain articles, is not so much, the natural qualities, or the adaptation by human art, of certain materials to immediate use in war, by construction or composition, as the direct and immediate tendency of the supplies, whatever may be the goods, to enable the enemy to maintain successfully, offensive or defensive warfare. Grain, and other provisions, are not contraband from their nature, and can only become so, from their immediate destination for the supply of invading armies or fleets. Timber is not contraband from its nature, and may not be so, though conveyed to the enemy for the construction, at ordinary sea-ports, of ordinary merchant vessels, in the coasting or foreign trade. But, it may become so, if of such dimensions or form, as to be applicable, only, or chiefly, for the construction of large ships of war, or if destined to a port, which is a national naval arsenal, a port of military equipment, at which fleets and ships of war are fitted out.

From this discussion of what is contraband, according to the Dutch and German international jurists of the seventeenth and eighteenth centuries, our author passes to the treaties in the seventeenth and eighteenth centuries, between England and Sweden and Denmark; partly, it should seem, for the purpose of assailing the judgment of the English prize court in 1799, in the case of the Swedish convoy. So far as the question turns upon the interpretation of these old particular treaties, it is of less general interest. And, did we think with our author, that the interpretation put upon these treaties, by Sir William Scott, was very bold or rash, (fort hazardée,) we should at once frankly make the admission; because we humbly conceive, the British Prize Court should not expose itself to any such charge, if at all well founded, for the sake of the interpretation of a treaty, entered into nearly two hundred years ago, and of questionable validity. But the judgment objected to, appears to us to be correct. For it proceeds, not so much upon the interpretation of these old treaties, as upon the change, which is admitted, by Valin, to have taken place about the beginning of the eighteenth century, in what was to be held contraband, in the then more frequent and more extended naval military operations of the maritime states of Europe. The import of the treaties of 1656, 1661, 1664, and 1665, taken together, is, that, in the event of one of the contracting parties being at war, the commerce and navigation of the subjects of the other party, who shall remain neutral, with the enemy, shall be free: and that, consequently, they shall be permitted to carry to the enemy, "all the goods, which are not expressly excepted by the eleventh article of the treaty of London in 1661, nor prohibited as contraband, or which are not hostile." Under the prohibition, as contraband, the alteration in the common consuetudinary law was legally admissible; and, if it was meant, that contraband should be here limited and restricted by the conventional enumeration of articles, what reason could there be, for introducing both terms?

Our Author next notices the treaty between England and Denmark in 1670, the treaties between France and Denmark in 1674, and 1742, and the treaty between Britain and Denmark in 1780, as distinctly fixing what are to be held contraband articles between these contracting parties.

Proceeding to the effect of the carriage of contraband goods, upon the vessel, our author remarks, the most ancient maritime law of France seems not to have confiscated such goods going to the enemy, as prize of war, but to have subjected them to the exercise of the more mitigated right of pre-emption. But as the ancient

French ordonnances of 1543 and 1584, as well as the ordonnance of 1681, confiscated neutral vessels for merely carrying hostile goods, and neutral goods, if found in hostile vessels, it was not very likely they would compel the captors to pay the price of the contraband goods they had taken. And here our author merely repeats the error, into which Vattel unaccountably fell, and which we formerly corrected, by a reference to these old ordonnances, as published in the Code des Prises of 1784.[1]

Our Author next quotes Bynkershoek and Heineccius on the point under consideration, according to whom, independently of special treaties, the confiscation of the neutral vessel, and innocent part of the cargo, was regulated by the knowledge and acquiescence of the proprietors in the loading of the illicit articles, or their ignorance of the fact. And here we beg to refer to our quotations from these authors.[2]

Like those of the other maritime nations, the English courts of prize all along confiscated goods contraband of war. And there were certainly as strong, if not stronger, reasons for confiscating neutral vessels, which carried to the enemy such illicit articles, as for confiscating, like the French ordonnances, the neutral vessels, which carried the goods of the enemy. But it does not appear, that the English prize courts ever confiscated, along with the contraband goods, the vessel, and whole cargo indiscriminately; the practice having been, to limit the confiscation of the vessel and innocent goods to the cases of their belonging to the proprietors of the contraband, or of there having been an attempt to conceal the conveyance of the contraband articles, under false papers, with a false destination.[3] And although the British

[1] See Vol. I. p 238. [2] Vol. I. p 210. III. p. 218 220.
[3] Rob. Adm. Rep. Vol III. p. 221, note A.

prize court of appeal in 1750, declared pitch and tar, the produce of Sweden, carried in a Swedish vessel, destined for a French or hostile port, liable to confiscation, as contraband of war, according to the more modern understanding and usage, goods of this nature, being the produce of Sweden, belonging to Swedish subjects, and carried in vessels of their nation, have, upon a principle of indulgence, for the produce and ordinary commerce of that country, been held by the British prize courts, as only subject to the right of seizure and pre-emption; in other words, to the right of preventing these goods from being conveyed to the enemy, and of appropriating them to British use, under the burden of paying a pecuniary indemnity to the neutral proprietor. According, also, to the more modern practice of the English prize courts, commodities, provisions, or articles of human food, are subjected only to the right of pre-emption.[1]

In Period first, § 15, our Author gives an account of the right of blockade, as recognized during the period from 1648 to 1713, and shows, by quotations, from Grotius and Bynkershoek, commenting on the edict of the States General in 1630, that, to be effectual in law, a blockade, as then recognized, behoved to be actual, and maintained by a sufficient force. In this we quite agree, and shall merely quote the concluding sentence of this section. "In the fourth chapter, he, (Bynkershoek,) blames the inconsistency of the States General, who boasted, in 1652, of having interdicted the English, from having any commerce with any part of the world; and, in 1663, had contested with the Spaniards the same right, which they had themselves exercised against the English."

[1] Rob Adm Rep Vol II p. 182

When such a general interdiction of commerce was thus attempted by the Dutch and the Spaniards, our author here contents himself with repeating the animadversions of Bynkershoek. But he devotes the whole of the next section (§ 16,) to the denouncement of the interdiction by England and Holland in 1689, of all neutral commerce with France; and suddenly passing from the seventeenth to the eighteenth century, avails himself of this opportunity for a tirade against the British exceptionable orders in council, during the late French Imperial war. The deviation by the English government in 1689, from the genuine law of nations, apparently occasioned by the great influence of Holland at that time, we have all along admitted. The English Government itself soon made this admission, and desisted from the attempt. The letter, here alluded to, by our author, of Pufendorff to Groningius, (not Gronovius,) we quoted at length, first volume, pp. 132–134, as containing a principal part of what Pufendorff had left of his view of international law, properly so called, and of neutrality. And, on perusal, it will be found, he, in this letter, gives his legal view of the question, as well as his moral or political reasons, to which we formerly alluded, not as justificatory of any undue extension of the right of blockade, but as an extenuation, or apology, for Britain and Holland, then struggling, the former for its independence and liberties, the latter for its very existence, against the unwarranted aggression of the ambitious Louis XIV.[1]

In Period first, § 17, Dr. Wheaton gives an account of the right of visit, not only as recognized from 1648 to 1713, in the ordinary practice of all the great maritime states of Europe, but also, as founded on legal

[1] Vattel, III. VII. § 112.

principle, as shown by the great Dutch international jurist, Bynkershoek. He notices, also, the fruitless attempts, made by the Dutch, with one exception; and also, the still more unsuccessful schemes of Sweden and Denmark, to resist this right by means of armed vessels. And he adds, "It appears also evident, from the testimony of history, that the right of visit was maintained in practice by the country of Bynkershoek, while it was a belligerent party, although the Dutch sought often to have their flag exempted from the application of the rule of visit, while they were neutral, in order to attract the carrying trade—the commerce de fret—under the protection of their favourite maxim, 'free ship, free goods.'"

In Period first, § 18, § 19, our Author treats, historically, of the Sovereignty of the seas, and notices the Mare Liberum of Grotius in 1609, the Advocatio Hispanica of Albericus Gentilis in 1613, the Mare Clausum of Selden in 1635, the opinion of Pufendorff in 1672, and the pretensions of England to the sovereignty of the British seas. But, into these matters, it is unnecessary to enter farther than we have already done. These points were settled, and at rest, even so far back as the middle of the seventeenth century, as we saw from Loccenius.[1] Before the close of that century, Sir Leoline Jenkins had defined the legitimate boundaries of the claims of England. And the lengthened revival of such discussions, as by Rayneval, in his treatise, De la Liberté des Mers, can have no other object, than to create a prejudice against Britain. It is to be regretted, that Albericus Gentilis, and particularly Selden, wasted their learning and their talents in support of such extrava-

[1] See Vol. I. p. 119.

gant claims. Such vain pretensions are always injurious to a nation. And Britain may rest quite satisfied with the maintenance of the rights, which she recognizes as belonging equally to every other independent state. The sovereignty claimed by Denmark over the Sound and the Belts, appears, according to our author, to rest very much on international conventions.

The Second of the periods, into which Dr. Wheaton divides this history of the International law of Europe, is from the peace of Utrecht in 1713, to the peace of Paris and Hubertsburg in 1763. And we shall here accompany him through his narrative; distinguishing, as formerly, the conventional law, as constituted by treaties, from the common consuetudinary law, as founded on the natural, legal, or juridical relations of independent states, and sanctioned and established as positive law, by long, general, constant, and uniform usage. We shall also state, as formerly, when, and why, we cannot agree with our author.

Period second, § 9. With regard to the treaties of Utrecht between Britain and France, and between Britain and Holland, about which so much was fallaciously written under the government of Napoleon, and continues still to be erroneously alleged, we formerly mentioned, that the stipulation of "free ship, free goods," which the Dutch got inserted in these treaties, through their then great influence with the English government, was never acted upon for above half a century. And this statement is confirmed, by the observation here made, by our Author, that the circumstances, in which the clause could come into operation, never occurred between 1713 and 1763. This boasted new International law, then, alleged to have been, it not first introduced, at least, firmly established, by the treaties of Utrecht, remained a dead letter, of no force or validity whatever. The different European nations, therefore, of course, continued to be guided by the old common consuetudinary law, which had existed since the ages preceding the compilation of the Consolato del Mare. "Each state," our Author observes, "continued to adhere to its own peculiar interpretation of the law of nations, as the rule, by which it was guided in its conduct towards neutrals." "The maritime powers," he says, "which adopted the maxims of the Consolato del Mare, relative to maritime prizes, continued to be directed by these maxims, with the exception of the modifications, introduced by particular conventions."

The phraseology here used, of the maritime powers having adopted the maxims of the Consolato del Mare, is not quite correct. For the Consolato was not an Imperial mandate of any Potentate, nor the theory of any international jurist, nor the lecture of any learned professor; but a record of the rules, which, in the course of their experience, practical men had found to be just and equitable, and generally expedient. And the Governments, their Admiralty courts, and their subjects, who acted agreeably to these usages and maxims of experience, did not adopt any new theory or system, but merely trode in the steps of their predecessors in such matters.

But, farther, we would ask, who were the maritime powers that adopted the new maxims? Spain did not do so expressly, even by the treaty of Utrecht; and, from D'Abreu, we have seen she did not do so, in her actual practice, except under special treaties with France and Holland. As little did France do so. By the ordonnance of 1744, France moderated the extreme rigour of her former ordonnances, by restricting the confiscation to the hostile cargo, and releasing the neutral vessel, that is, by adopting the milder rule of the Consolato, agreeably to the previous practice of all other nations, except Spain and herself. But while, by the ordonnance of 1744,[1] France thus adopted the milder practice of other states, she, in other respects, violated the common law of nations, by continuing, by that enactment, the ordonnance of 1704, by which all merchandise of the growth, fabric, or manufacture of the hostile country, were declared liable to confiscation, with the exception of the cargoes of neutral vessels, sailing directly from the hostile port to a port of their own country; and neutral vessels were prohibited from carrying a cargo, from one port of the enemy to another hostile port, whatever might be the origin, or to whatever person the property of the goods might belong. Thus, the French government, in the eighteenth century, not only extended the rule of the common law, by which neutrals are not entitled to interpose their services by carrying on the coasting trade of the enemy, so as to embrace goods, the produce and property, both of neutrals and of the enemy; but likewise directed the confiscation, by the right of war, not merely against the property of the enemy, agreeably to former practice, but likewise against goods, the growth or manufacture of the enemy, although the property thereof had been transferred to, and vested in, neutrals. And, in this respect, certainly, Napoleon and his ministers had not the merit of novelty in their Berlin and Milan decrees.

With regard to the treaties concluded by the French government with other maritime powers, during this period, when the treaties of Utrecht were a dead letter, or in abeyance, and the ordonnances of 1681, 1704, and 1744 were in strict observance, our author admits, that,

[1] Code des Prises, pp 249, 250.

by the treaty of France with the Hanse towns in 1816, neutral goods in hostile vessels were subjected to confiscation, as well as hostile goods on board neutral vessels, the vessel, in the latter case, only, being exempted; that the convention of France with Holland in 1739, merely renewed the commercial treaty of Utrecht in 1713, which had by that time expired; that, by a treaty of commerce in 1742, France extended the same exemption to Denmark; that a similar exemption was extended to Sweden; and that Spain enjoyed the same privilege, under the still subsisting treaty of the Pyrenees; but that the privilege conceded to Holland having been revoked by the ordonnance of 1744, the only states which had the privilege of "free ship, free goods," under the French administration of the maritime law of nations, at the time Valin wrote, were Spain, Denmark, and Sweden. "In other respects," continues our Author, "the ordonnance de la marine of 1681 of Louis XIV., remained in full vigour; and these two ordonnances of 1681 and 1744, continued to form the French prize code, during the maritime wars, which were terminated by the peace of Aix-la-Chapelle in 1748, and by the peace of Paris in 1763."

With regard to the practical effects of the boasted treaty of Utrecht in 1713, on the administration of maritime international law by England and Holland, we cannot do better than quote the following passages from our author, as supplying any deficiency, from the brevity of our historical sketch of the corresponding period in the first volume.

"We have already seen, in what circumstances were concluded the treaties between England and Holland; granting to this latter power, the rule of 'free ships, free goods,' as the favourite object for which her statesmen had struggled with so much zeal and perseverance, in their negotiations with the great maritime powers. This concession, on the part of England, was connected with treaties of alliance and mutual guarantee between the two states, which dragged Holland into the war between France and England, in 1747; while the treaty of 1739, by which this same concession was made in favour of Dutch navigation by France, was suspended by the ordonnance of this last power. In this manner the Republic lost, with its character of neutral, the advantages of this concession, with regard to the two belligerent powers, during the last years of the maritime war, which was terminated by the peace of Aix-la-Chapelle. As the alliance of 1756, between Austria and France, had delivered Holland from the danger which it had to dread, of the invasion of the barrier, which was secured to it in Belgium by the treaties of Utrecht, the Republic, when required by England, to fulfil the conditions of the guarantees, stipulated in its treaties with that power, refused, upon different pretexts, to comply with this demand, and at the same time, insisted on the execution of the treaties of commerce, by which the rule of 'free ship, free goods,' had been mutually stipulated. This interpretation of the conventions between the two countries, was rejected by the English government; and it continued to treat the Dutch navigation, upon the same footing as that of the other neutral nations, with whom there was no special convention in favour of the liberty of the flag. The treaty of commerce of 1739, between France and Holland, had been suspended from the year 1745; and in consequence of all these different circumstances, this last power derived no advantage as a neutral, during the seven year's war from its antecedent treaties with England and France, by which the rule of 'free ship, free goods,' was stipulated between the contracting parties."[1]

[1] Wheaton's Hist. p. 144–5.

"The treaty of Aix-la-Chapelle of 1748, between France, England, and Holland, (art. 3.) renewed in general terms, 'the treaties of Utrecht.' As the treaty of commerce signed at Utrecht, is not specified by name in the treaty of Aix-la-Chapelle, it might be considered as doubtful, whether it was the intention of the framers of that treaty, to renew the stipulations of Utrecht in favour of neutral commerce. This doubt is entirely dispelled by the treaty of Paris of 1763, (art. 2.) between France, England, and Spain, to which Portugal acceded, and which expressly renews, among other treaties, those of peace and commerce of Utrecht in 1713."

"Such," continues Dr. Wheaton, "was the maritime law of nations, established by the customs and the ordinances of the European states; and such was the maritime law of nations, recognized by the treaties between these states, during the period now in question. The two systems were in direct opposition to each other."[1]

Now, while we do not here dispute with our Author, the correctness of his historical narrative, we cannot altogether agree with him in the representation of the law, as deduced from the events narrated. We cannot admit that there were here two different, independent, and co-ordinate systems of law, in direct opposition to each other; the one established by the constant and uniform customs, and by the concurring ordinances and judicial determinations of the different European states; and the other recognized by the treaties between these states. The ordinances or statutes of any particular state, could not, and cannot, constitute a part of the general law of nations, in relation to other states, except against itself, upon the principle of reciprocity. The ordinances, statutes, proclamations, or judicial determi-

[1] Hist. p. 145.

nations of particular states, constitute the common and general consuetudinary law of nations, only so far as they agree, or are concordant or consentaneous in recognizing rules, which are just and equitable, according to the natural law of nations, or which have been found, by experience, to be generally convenient and expedient. According to the natural law of nations, the dictates of reason and justice, the operations of war, as the means of maintaining and enforcing the rights of nations, ought to be directed against the property of the enemy, not of friends or neutrals. And these principles were recognized, and adopted in practice, by the earliest trading maritime states of Europe; and generally acted upon from the twelfth and thirteenth to the middle of the seventeenth century.

In the progress of maritime commerce, certain difficulties, inconveniences, and hardships, came to be felt in the application of this rule of manifest justice. Certain nations rose to wealth and power, chiefly through maritime commerce, and were able so to increase their mercantile marine, as to become the carriers, not only of their own goods, but of the goods also of other nations. For such trading states, it was an obviously advantageous scheme, to cut short any difficulties, and to avoid any inconveniences experienced in the application of the plain rules of justice, by pretending they were entitled, not only to carry their own goods, but to carry and protect the goods of other nations from just seizure by injured third parties. The Hanse towns, as long as they had the power to do so, openly maintained this pretension, so far as other nations were concerned; but, when belligerents themselves, they refused to recognize it, and were, ultimately, obliged to abandon it.

As this new rule could not be maintained with common decency upon the footing contended for by the

Hanse towns, it was thought it might be rendered less exceptionable, by coupling it with a rule, apparently adverse to the interests of neutrals. And, as thus modified, the scheme became, "That neutral vessels should protect from just seizure, the goods of the enemy; and that the goods of neutrals should, unjustly, and without any valid reason, be confiscated, if shipped in the vessels of their friends, who happened to be our enemies." Such a strange combination could not well be supported, as a part of the natural or rational law of nations. And the Dutch, who succeeded the Hanse towns, as the great carrying nation, in the commerce de fret, struggled, for more than a century, to get the rule, advantageous for themselves, introduced into practice, by means of conventions or treaties. Clauses of this import, they certainly succeeded in getting inserted in various treaties. But, with what effect, we have just seen. And the true representation of the state of the maritime law of nations in 1763, is not two competing co-ordinate systems, but one original system, founded in justice and equity, confirmed by experience, and sanctioned by the usages of the European nations for a series of centuries; merely departed from and modified, pro tempore, in some particulars, in the course of the century preceding 1763, by special clauses in various treaties between particular nations, inserted at the instigation of interested parties. And such, our author cannot deny, is the account of the matter given by the contemporary Dutch and German international jurists, Bynkershoek and Heineccius, as appears from the passages quoted from these authors, in the first volume of this work.[1]

In this second period of his history, from 1713 to 1763, § 10, Dr. Wheaton gives an account of the ques-

[1] Pp. 209—224.

tion respecting the Silesian loan, and of the discussion between Britain and Prussia, relative to neutral navigation during war. This event, which occurred in 1751–1753, we formerly briefly noticed; and we inserted the substance of the state papers, on the part of Britain, against the threat of Frederic II., to retain the loan by British subjects, secured over the public revenue of Silesia, in reparation of damage alleged to have been done to Prussian vessels by British cruizers; partly, because the report, here referred to, was styled by Vattel an excellent Morçeau du Droit des Gens;[1] and by the great Montesquieu, une Réponse sans Replique.[2] Our Author here quotes the reply given by the Prussian government, from the Causes Célèbres, by Charles de Martens.[3] We would also have inserted it here, had we not already[4] given its argument at great length, contained in the works of Hübner, Totze, and Galiani, when we reviewed these works. And we shall only add the remark, subjoined by Charles de Martens, to his account of this discussion—"That it was Frederic II. who first supported the principles of maritime neutrality, and that M. de Hertzberg was the first defender of them." Hence arises a question, whether M. de Hertzberg, if not the author, did not contribute to the composition of the anonymous works, ascribed to Professor Totze, La Liberté de la Navigation, and Essai sur un Code Maritime Européen?

In this second period of his history, § 11, Dr. Wheaton proceeds to notice, what has been rather absurdly denominated the rule of the war of 1756, namely, the principle of the law of nations, which prohibits the commerce of neutrals between the parent state and its colonies, and upon the coasts of the enemy; representing that

[1] Tom. II. C. vii § 84. [2] Oeuvres, Tom. V. p. 437.
[3] Vol. II. pp 1-11, 12-41. [4] Vol. I. pp. 326–358.

rule, as first introduced by the English, in the war which commenced in 1756, and as a violation of the law of nations, of which neutrals, the Dutch and the Danes, had just reason to complain.

But here we differ from our Author, both in point of fact, and in point of law. In the first volume of this work,[1] we conceive, we have shown, that the war of 1756 was not the first occasion, on which this rule was enforced, and that neutrals are not entitled, actively, to interpose their services between a belligerent mother country and her separate dependent territories, and to carry on, for its behoof, the colonial trade of a belligerent state, after it has been disabled from doing so itself, by the military operations of the opposed belligerent. Indeed, in addition to our former statement, just referred to, our author is forced to admit, that this very rule had been practised by France, from the commencement of the eighteenth century, during the war of the Spanish succession, terminated by the peace of Utrecht, and during the war, terminated by the peace of Aix-la-Chapelle in 1748; as is placed, beyond doubt, by the ordonnances of 1704 and 1744, inasmuch as they prohibited neutral vessels from carrying goods from one port of the enemy to another, to whomsoever the property of the goods might belong. Of this part of those ordonnances, no complaint was made, as being a breach of the law of nations. Indeed, neutrals had not then become so very bold and presumptuous in their pretensions, as to allege they were entitled, so far to depart from their neutrality, as to interject their mercantile marine, and protect one belligerent against the warlike operations of the other, however just. Such an adoption of the trade of the enemy—such an identification of the traffic of the two nations—such a transference of their

[1] Pp. 305—311.

mercantile Marine to the enemy, the Dutch could not justify, under the concession which they had prevailed on the government of Charles II. to grant them by the treaty of 1674–5; besides their having forfeited the benefit of that concession, by their failure to fulfil the counter stipulations in the subsequent treaties which continued that concession.

At this time, also, the Danish government thought fit to complain and remonstrate against their subjects being prevented from carrying on for France, her whole colonial trade, which had formerly been confined to her own subjects exclusively. The minister employed, on this occasion, was M. Hübner, and the result, his clever treatise De la Saisie des Batimens Neutres. The Danish government had here no treaties to found upon. There was thus imposed on M. Hübner, the difficult task of upsetting and overturning what, independently of special paction, had been the common consuetudinary law of Europe for centuries, had been unfolded by experience, and found to be just and equitable; and had been sanctioned by general, almost universal, acquiescence and usage.

We have great respect for the patriotic wisdom of Count Bernstorff; and admit the justice of those smaller European states, whose population and territory do not enable them to take a leading part in the maintenance of national independence, and of the balance of power in Europe, being allowed to remain neutral, and to cultivate commerce with as little interruption as practicable, from the disputes of their more powerful neighbours, and to reap such benefit, as may incidentally and necessarily arise from the operations of one belligerent against another. But we cannot help thinking, that Count Bernstorff would have acted still more wisely, if he had remained satisfied with this incidental and necessary benefit, arising from warfare among the neighbouring nations, and had abstained from insisting on the subjects of his Sovereign being allowed to reap mercantile profit directly through the contests of their neighbours, by becoming, in a manner, the adopted and naturalized subjects of France, and being admitted to the privileges hitherto enjoyed, solely by them, to the effect of supplying France with the mercantile navy, of which Britain had, in the course of the war, deprived her. When of two individual combatants, the one succeeds in depriving the other of the use of his left arm, the by-stander, who by his intervention enables the latter to do, what he formerly did with his left arm, cannot be truly said to be a neutral, or impartial looker-on.

This second period of his history, § 12, Dr. Wheaton concludes, with an analysis of the work of Hübner. But having noticed this work, at such length, in the first volume of these Researches,[1] we shall only revert to it, to add to the refutation of Hübner's leading doctrine by Lampredi, as quoted by us formerly,[2] the following criticism by Dr. Wheaton:—"It is generally recognized," says Hübner, "that the goods of the enemy cannot be seized in a neutral place. Neutral vessels are, without dispute, neutral places. Consequently, a cargo belonging to the enemy cannot be seized on board a neutral vessel, any more than upon the neutral territory." "Hübner," says Dr. Wheaton, "appears here to have forgotten, that, in the preceding part of his work, he had conceded the right of the belligerent power, to capture the goods of his enemy in a place which belongs to no one, such as the sea, provided he does no mischief to his friend the neutral. Now, he

[1] Pp. 291—305. [2] Pp. 376—394.

assumes the principle, that a neutral vessel at sea, forms a portion of the neutral territory, although he does not give himself the trouble to establish, by proof, this proposition, which forms the basis of all his reasoning; and, although it seems difficult to reconcile it, with what he had already admitted, with regard to the exercise of the right of visit, in a place which belongs to no one, such as the sea. Bynkershoek, as we have already seen, deduces the belligerent right to seize the goods of the enemy, on board a neutral vessel, from the right to visit, in order to determine the character of the vessel. This argument would appear irresistible, if it were once admitted, as it is by Hübner, that the belligerent power may exercise this right, upon a neutral vessel at sea. According to him, the sole reason, why the belligerent power cannot exercise its right of seizing the goods of its enemy on board a neutral vessel at sea, is, that the vessel forms a part of the neutral territory. But the same reason must apply equally, to prevent the exercise of the right of visit, or any other belligerent right, on board a neutral vessel at sea."

On this passage, we have to remark, that we cannot agree with our author, in saying, that Bynkershoek deduces the belligerents' right to seize the goods of the enemy on board a neutral vessel, from the right to visit, in order to ascertain the character of the vessel. In our first volume,[1] the passage is quoted in the original language; and its obvious import appears to us to be, that the right of capture is founded on the fact of the goods being the property of the enemy, and being found on the high seas, not within the territory or jurisdiction of any nation. "Id emim capio, quod hostium est, quodque jure belli, victori cedit." And the objection to visiting or detaining the ship of a friend,

[1] P. 223.

Bynkershoek goes on to obviate, by answering, "you cannot reasonably object to such a visit, because it is necessary for your own safety, in the situation in which you have placed yourself." The visit is, manifestly, merely the means of ascertaining, whether the facts are such, as to give rise to, or support the right to capture. And to deduce the right to capture the cargo, from the right to visit the vessel, would have been but inconsequential reasoning. As neutrals admit, hostile vessels, in the open sea, are liable to capture, they must necessarily admit the means of ascertaining, whether the vessel, so met at sea, be hostile, or not. "Si constet," says Bynkershoek, "navem amicam esse, dimittam; si hostilem esse consteterit, accupabo. Quod, si liceat, ut omni jure licet, et perpetuo observatur, licebit quoque, instrumenta, quae ad merces pertinent, excutere, et inde discere, an quae hostium bona in navi lateant; et si lateant, quidni, ea jure belli, occupem."

The third of the periods into which Dr. Wheaton divides his history, is from the peace of Paris in 1763, to the French revolution in 1789. And the first article, relative to maritime law, is § 13, in which the French réglement of 1778 is announced, as establishing the rule of "free ship, free goods." But this réglement by one state could not alter the common consuetudinary law of nations. And, in fact, it merely altered the administration of that law by France, for the short period of six months. For, the adoption of this rule was merely conditional, and made dependent on its adoption within that period, by the other maritime powers. And, as this condition was not fulfilled, this article of the réglement was revoked in January 1779, and the ordonnance of 1681 was again in force.

Our Author proceeds, in the following sections, § 14 and § 15, to give an account of the armed neutrality of 1780; but, as we gave rather a full account of that extensive association in our first volume,[1] our review may here be brief. In our notice of this formidable combination of the majority of the maritime powers of Europe, we were content to allow it to be ascribed to partial views of national interest on the part of Russia, and the other northern states. But Dr. Wheaton adopts the narrative of the Count de Goertz, who traced its origin to the rivalry of the two ministers of the Empress Catherine, the Chancellor Panin, and Prince Potemkin. Into the details, however, of the manoeuvres of these Russian ministers, we shall not here again enter, and shall merely add, that, while we agree with our author, in his remark, "that the first armed neutrality of 1780 had not its origin in beneficent and liberal views of advancement in the maritime law of nations," we cannot admit, as fact, that the advancement here alluded to, as alleged by our author, had been, until that time, sanctioned by general practice. For, we have seen, the general practice, prior to that time, had been the reverse, except under special stipulations in treaties, and conventional concessions to neutrals, of the privilege of protecting the property of the enemy from seizure at sea.

Notwithstanding this most formidable confederacy, our Author admits, "England continued to act towards the powers that remained neutral, during the American war, according to the pre-existing law of nations, as she understood it, and practised it." "She, however," he adds, "advanced her maritime pretensions with moderation and caution; and allowed to fall into desuetude, the rule which she had established in the war of 1756, re-

[1] Pp. 321—342, and p. 357.

garding the colonial commerce of the enemy." But, we are not aware, that, on this occasion, England acted with any greater caution or moderation, than she was all along accustomed to do. And, most certainly, she did not abandon the right of preventing neutrals from interposing their services, in carrying on the colonial trade of the enemy. She did not, indeed, at that time, exercise that right; but solely because she had not an opportunity of doing so—because the circumstances did not occur, in which it could be exercised. Before the French government took a part in the American war, it seems to have been convinced of the inexpediency of the Dutch, or other neutral vessels, being permitted to carry on the colonial trade of France; apparently, upon the grounds, urged in the able Brochure, entitled, Considérations sur l'Admission des Navires Neutres aux Colonies Françaises, published in 1779.

The contest, maintained by the association, called the armed neutrality, was, of course, terminated by the treaty of peace of 1783. "That treaty between France, England, and Spain," our Author remarks, "renewed the treaties of peace and of commerce of Utrecht, and, consequently, confirmed the maritime stipulations contained in the latter treaty, in favour of the liberty of neutral navigation." But this is not quite correct. So far as regards France and England, the stipulations alluded to, in the treaty of Utrecht, between these countries, which, we saw, by our Author's account, had remained a dead letter, were resuscitated; but, again, destined to expire, or be of no avail, from the non-occurrence of the Casus Foederis. As the precise stipulations, here alluded to, did not exist in the treaty of Utrecht between Britain and Spain, these precise stipulations, at least, could not be resuscitated in 1783, by the mere renewal of the former treaty of 1667. And, our author admits, "that the treaty of 1784, between Britain and Holland, contained no equivalent stipulation."

Our Author adds, "That the same stipulations were again inserted in the treaty of commerce and navigation, between Britain and France in 1786." And, apparently, delighted to appeal to the speeches of *opposition* members in the British Parliament, he adds, that, "in the discussion which took place in that assembly, on the preliminaries of that convention, Lord Lansdowne objected to these clauses, as containing a complete recognition of the principles of the armed neutrality on the part of Britain; and that the only answer made to this objection, was, that the stipulations in question, were solely, destined to provide for the case, not likely to occur, of one of the contracting parties being, unhappily, involved in a maritime war, while the other may have it in their power to remain neuter; and do not furnish a general rule to be observed towards other nations." Our Author seems to consider this as a feeble and unsatisfactory, if not an evasive, answer. But, on the other hand, it may be argued, that it rather shows the sagacity of an intelligent ministry, who, while they made this concession to France, in consideration, no doubt, of some commercial advantage being conceded by the other contracting party, were aware, France had, comparatively, but little carrying trade, and was not likely to be neutral, when Britain was at war with Spain, or Holland, or any of the northern powers.

In this third period of his history, our Author devotes a section, (§ 16,) to the treaty of 1785, between the United States and Prussia; and articles 23 and 24 of that treaty, certainly contain several reciprocal regulations, highly laudable. But, it is easy for the Governments of two countries, situated in relation to each other, as Prussia and the United States are, to provide by treaty for events, which are not likely to occur, and thereby to earn the praise of making humane and liberal stipulations, when it can be done, without any sacrifice of national interests. And we certainly attach much more importance to the opinion of Dr. Franklin, given in the next section, (§ 17,) against the employment of privateers. In this opinion, we have repeatedly stated our entire concurrence, as one of the greatest meliorations to be expected in maritime warfare. The abandonment of this mode of warfare, may, no doubt, be a greater sacrifice on the part of those nations, who have a larger and more numerous mercantile marine. But, in other respects, the abandonment would fall equally upon all nations, and would, therefore, be just; whereas, to admit the pretension of cautious neutrals to protect, on the ocean, the property of one nation against legitimate seizure by another, is, to allow these nations to earn emolument, through the unavoidable exercise by their neighbour, of their respective rights of self-defence, territorial integrity, and national independence, and to tolerate an undue interference between belligerent nations, to the manifest advantage of the one, and to the manifest injury of the other.

In this third period of his history, § 18, our Author gives an account of the writings of Galiani and Lampredi, on what he calls the principles of the armed neutrality. But, in giving this appellation, he scarcely does justice to the works of these authors; for their works are not mere commentaries upon the scheme of the Empress Catherine, or of her ministers; they are treatises of the maritime law of nations generally. As the treatise of Galiani is very inferior to the other, our Author's account of it is brief; while he gives a pretty long and neat analysis of the treatise of Lampredi. But, after the notice we have taken of the work of Galiani,[1] and the full abridgement, we have given, of the treatise of Lampredi,[2] we deem it unnecessary to return to these works. And we may here merely remark, that Dr. Wheaton passes over, in silence, the doctrine of Galiani, with regard to the origin of the right of visitation and search, as founded on the physical difference of operations by land and by sea,—as existing in peace as well as in war,—as being no act of superiority or jurisdiction, but merely a reciprocal and equal right, any dominion on the free and open sea being impossible; and, while he gives a pretty full analysis of the views and arguments of Lampredi, he neither disputes their correctness, nor attempts to refute them; contenting himself with marking, decidedly, that he merely recites the views and arguments of that author, without expressing any approbation of these views and arguments, or noticing their coincidence with, and able elucidation of the doctrines of almost all the eminent jurists, from Albericus Gentilis, and Grotius, to Vattel.

Nor can we altogether agree with our author, in the remark, with which, in his third period, § 19, he introduces his account of Moser and Martens. "The age of classic publicists," he says, "terminated with Vattel. Since the publication of his work, the theory of the law of nations has made no real progress. The publicists, who have written since his time, down to the French revolution, are, in general, either compilers, more or less systematic, or polemical writers, occupied only with questions of a transient interest. The names of Moser and Martens, only merit our attention."

Now, without examining the merits of Burlamaqui, Pestel, Köhler and others, who wrote on the law of nations generally, about the time alluded to, we con-

[1] Vol. I. pp 349—357. [2] Vol. I. pp. 360—417

ceive, the two jurists, whom the author has just reviewed, contributed greatly by their works, to elucidate the principles, and promote the progress of the law of nations in the maritime department. Galiani, though not an accurate or sound reasoner, was a man of very considerable talents and ingenuity. And we are induced to think the Juris universalis Theoremata, of the Pisan Professor Lampredi, of which the third volume embraces the Jus Gentium, or International law generally, a more classical and elegant, if not a more philosophical and profound work, than that of Vattel. Moser, we are well aware, was merely a laborious collector of treaties, and but a very indifferent arranger of their contents. But Günther, who wrote in 1787, before the French Revolution, was, we conceive, a more acute and enlightened lawyer, than either Moser or Martens, or even than Vattel. And to Baron Von Ompteda, who also wrote before the French Revolution, we apprehend, the law of nations, as a science, is nearly as much indebted for its progress towards the end of the eighteenth century, as to Martens. His arrangements of the subjects are perspicuous and profound; and Martens had the good sense so far to profit by his views. Von Ompteda, indeed, had the merit of following out what appear to have been the views of Leibnitz, more scientifically, than either Wolfius or Moser; and of pointing out, how a complete exposition of the modern European law of nations was to be effected by a combination of its several parts or sources.

In our review of the maritime department of the Précis du Droit des Gens de l'Europe, by G. F. de Martens, as we were in possession of more than one copy of the work, particularly of the edition of 1821, revised by the author, a short time before his death, we did not think of procuring a posthumous edition, pub lished in 1831, by M. le Commandeur, S. Pinheiro—Ferreira, Ancien Ministre des Affaires Etrangères in Portugal. But we now find, that this posthumous edition of 1831, was accompanied with annotations by the editor, which Mr. Manning reprobates as indecorously abusive, but which are lauded by M. Hoffmans, who published, in 1837, a new edition of the Guide Diplomatique of Baron Charles de Martens, as rendering this last edition of the Précis du Droit des Gens, by M. G. F. Martens, published in France, much preferable to those formerly published in Germany.

In this third period of his history, § 19, after noticing the works of Moser and Martens, our Author gives an account from the Précis du Droit des Gens de l'Europe by the latter, of the plan upon which Martens constructed his general theory of positive international law. And, although we have, on various occasions, remarked, that this theory was, to a certain extent, but a baseless fabric, we shall again venture to state our objections to it, at the risk of being charged with superfluous repetition, and with misunderstanding the meaning of the author; because Dr. Wheaton does still appear to us to approve, in 1841, of what he urged in 1815; and because we shall be happy to be found in error, if it should lead to an explicit disclaimer of the doctrine.

To all appearance, holding treaties and usages to be identical, in legal effect, although they are really very different, our Author, if not in the identical terms employed by Martens, at least, in language of similar import, says, "Treaties and usages subsisting between particular nations, cannot be regarded as being obligatory upon the others, except in the case in which they are adopted as a general rule, for directing the conduct of others, who accede to them. Nevertheless, a general theory of the positive law of nations of Europe may be constructed, (en considerant) keeping in view the following considerations:[1]—1. "That special treaties between particular states, resemble each other so much in their essence, that we may deduce from them, the principles generally recognized by the nations who have been accustomed to make treaties upon similar matters." Now, this is rather vague and ambiguous. By comparing a number of treaties, either successive or simultaneous, doubtless, we may ascertain the general points on which they agree, and in which they differ. And, in this way, we may give a methodical or systematic arrangement of the points fixed by certain treaties, between or among, certain nations, as Martens himself has done, in an abridged form, in his Cours Diplomatique, down to 1801. But of what avail, in existing compulsory law, will this system of points agreed upon, be, if the treaties fixing them have expired, or been annulled, or otherwise ceased to exist? Will this systematic arrangement render the points or rules binding in law, beyond the duration of the treaties, or the contracting parties? When the treaties have ceased, will not this theory be merely a matter of history?

2. "In the same manner," continues our Author, "we may deduce from special usages, which have been established between two particular nations, the general principles, recognized by all, or at least, the greater part of nations." Now, here our Author appears to identify, or assimilate, and confound, the usage of acting, with the usage of treating, which are very different. The use of reciprocal action among nations is the principal mode, by which the rules of international justice, equity and conveniency come to be recognized and enforced among nations. The long established usage in

[1] Pp. 248 9.

time past, gives a reasonable ground for expectation of the continuance of that usage in time to come. And, in other important respects, it is necessary to distinguish the legal effects of treaties or compacts from the legal effects of the uni-lateral acts of nations to other nations. By treaties, two states may alter the common law of nations, so far as regards themselves. The one may surrender rights, which at common law it is entitled to exercise; the other may undertake obligations, which it is not otherwise bound to perform. And a particular conventional law may be thus formed between those two states, which may either relax, or render more rigid the common law, as between the contracting parties.

On the other hand, the uni-lateral act of any one state, although it may make concessions of its rights, cannot alter the general common law of nations in its own favour. Neither the celebrated Ordonnance de la Marine of Louis XIV. in 1681, nor the British Orders in council of 1807, could, of themselves, create any obligation on other nations, to obtemper the rules so prescribed. But the uni-lateral acts of a nation may, in other respects, have very material effects; when the statutes or ordinances, the edicts or proclamations, or public instructions, or judicial determinations of different states, in their administration of the law of nations, in their several international tribunals, are identical or similar, or consentaneous, the aggregate of the rules so observed in practice for ages, (if not inconsistent with the obvious principles of legal right or compulsory justice—a most improbable supposition,) constitute the positive common consuetudinary law of nations, as actually enforced. Thus, for example, with the exceptions introduced by particular treaties and special compact, between particular nations, the common law and practice of the different European States, was to respect the property of friends and neutrals in the open sea, even although in the vessels of the enemy; but to capture and confiscate the goods of enemies in the open seas, although in the ships of neutrals, upon condition, however, of indemnifying the neutral ship owner, and fulfilling to him the obligation undertaken by the hostile proprietor of the goods. So far as regarded the enemy, the practice of France and Spain was the same as that of England and Holland, and of the other northern and southern European kingdoms and states. But, so far as regarded neutrals, the practice of France and Spain was more severe; confiscating the goods of neutrals, if found on board hostile vessels, and the vessels of neutrals, if found carrying hostile goods. But this excessively severe practice never formed any part of the general common consuetudinary law of nations, and appears to have been departed from in later times. Farther, the uni-lateral acts of each state, its statutes or ordinances, its edicts or proclamations and instructions, its judicial determinations, and, in general, its administration of the maritime law of nations by its international tribunals, so far as they affect the interests of other states, or of their subjects, give those other states and their subjects a right to act in a similar manner towards the former, so far as the interests of third parties are not involved. But such are not the legal effects of treaties, or engagements for the future, to act eventually in a particular manner, for a particular time, or on particular conditions, and in particular circumstances. When the equality and fairness of the treaty depends on the will of a third party, the contract is imperfect, if not absurd. And the event upon which the stipulation comes into operation, may never occur, or may not occur for upwards of half a century, as in the case of the treaty of Utrecht.

Our author proceeds, 3, "The usages established in

this manner, among the majority of nations, especially the larger nations, are easily adopted and imitated by the others." So far as it applies to the second position, this observation seems to be a truism; and since it mentions usages only, it is not applicable to the first position about treaties.

Our author proceeds, 4, "The frequent appeals of the European powers to the consuetudinary law observed among civilized nations, gives it an obligatory force, which dispenses with the necessity of seeking for proofs of the introduction of the particular usage in question." Now, the appeals here alluded to, certainly show the conviction and belief of the European powers, in the existence of such a common consuetudinary law of nations, and their willingness to abide by it. But how these general appeals can give it any obligatory force, so as to dispense with any proof of the alleged particular usage, it is not easy to perceive. If a rule of the common consuetudinary law of nations be alleged, it must be proved by the statutes, edicts, or proclamations of sovereign powers, or by the judicial determinations of international tribunals, or by the works of international jurists, expounding the principles of natural justice applicable to nations, and recording the practice of nations in enforcing these principles, and sanctioning farther rules of conveniency, founded on experience, when views and feelings of the just and the unjust may not be applicable.

Our author returns to treaties, 5, "The treaties which bind only the contracting parties, serve often as models for other treaties to be concluded with other powers, and the habit of concluding treaties containing the same stipulations, insensibly establishes itself. It happens, also, that what is stipulated between certain powers is adopted as usage between others, which establishes in this manner, a conventional law for the former, and a consuetudinary law for the latter." Our author concludes. "By thus collecting or combining (rassemblant) the principles most generally followed, according to special conventions, express or tacit, identical or analogous, or according to usages of a like nature, we may establish a complete theory of the European law of nations, general, positive, modern, and practical."

Now, we own, we cannot form any clear or distinct, precise or accurate notion of this complete theory of European International law, from this combination and amalgamation of the shreds and patches of the different treaties of peace and commerce, which have been entered into since about the middle of the seventeenth century, without ascertaining, whether any, and, if so, which of these treaties are still binding and in force. We were amused with the account given by M. Lerminier, of the way in which the Code Napoleon de Commerce was compiled, by cutting down into parcels of sheets, or half or quarter sheets, the quarto and octavo volumes of Valin, Pothier, Emerigon, &c., and piecing them together again, in an improved order. And, in that case, the validity of the new code did not rest upon the excellence alone of the old materials thus dissected, and again combined. It rested upon the legislative sovereign power of France, and upon the power of the imperial despotic Napoleon. But, in the present case, among separate independent states, there is no such paramount despotic power presiding over them, so as to enforce observance of this collectanea of shreds and patches of expired, or annulled, or forfeited stipulations, now a dead letter. "Il existe, en Europe," (says Martens,[1]) "un bien plus grand nombre de traités tacitement prolongés, qu'on n'auroit lieu de le croire; vu l'importance de l'objet."

[1] Précis, § 342.

"There are, in Europe, a much greater number of treaties tacitly prolonged, than there would be room to believe, considering the importance of the subject."

The fourth period into which Dr. Wheaton divides his history, is from the French revolution in 1789, to the congress of Vienna in 1815; and here we again regret to observe the same pre-disposition against Britain, and in favour of France, as well as of the United States. For his national bias in favour of his own country, we make ample allowance in a citizen of the United States. But France is abundantly able to fight her own battles, in argument, as well as in arms, without American aid. And the effect of this too obvious predilection, is to make his history be considered by the impartial spectator, as more a polemical treatise, than a correct and fair record of events, doing justice to all, and showing favour to none.

In the department of the law of nations, which is the object of our inquiry, our author commences this period (§ 4 and § 5,) with the maritime law of nations, during the wars of the French revolution; and is, in the sequel, almost entirely occupied with the French revolutionary maritime war, strictly so called, from its commencement in 1793, to the peace of Amiens. Although not stating, in so many words, that the powers allied against France were the aggressors in this unfortunate war, our author indirectly represents them as such; and proceeds, in § 5, to assail the British Orders in council of the 8th June and 6th November 1793. So far as these orders merely directed the ordinary military operations of capture of the property of the enemy as such, and of the actual blockade of hostile sea-ports, there could be no ground for objection. But they were complained of, as authorizing the seizure in transitu, for the purpose of pre-emption, of cargoes of grain, destined for France for the supply of her invading armies, and the capture of neutral vessels carrying on the colonial trade of France, between the mother country and her colonies.

With regard to the first of these points, we beg to refer to our statement in volume first.[1] Sweden could not complain of the seizure, because, by her treaty with England in 1661, grain, and other provisions, are declared contraband of war. And Denmark complained of the seizure, not so much as an infringement of the general law of nations, as of particular treaties, by which it was stipulated, that such articles should not be deemed contraband. The answer of the British government was, that the right of pre-emption had been long recognized in the common consuetudinary maritime law of nations; and that there was no infringement of the treaties referred to; because these treaties merely provided against confiscation as contraband; whereas the orders in council did not authorize any such confiscation, but merely interception and seizure, under the burden of payment of the market price or value; in other words, a compulsory change of the market.

Our author proceeds to notice the proceedings which took place between Britain and the United States, relative to the order in council of June 1793, issued in the exercise of the right of pre-emption. This perhaps was not very necessary on the part of the United States, as the point was settled between the two countries by the treaty of commerce and navigation of 1794. By that treaty it was agreed, that military and naval stores, except unwrought iron and fir planks, should be comprehended under the denomination of contraband; and also, that when grain, provisions, and other articles, which are not generally contraband, become contraband,

[1] pp. 437-441.

according to the existing law of nations, they should not be confiscated, but the owner should receive a just and prompt indemnification. And the subsequent order in council of April 1795, to a similar effect, having been issued before the treaty was ratified, the captures made under it, were all agreed to be settled, and were actually settled upon the footing of the treaty. As our author, however, seems not contented with having this matter settled by treaty, and again brings forward the argument then urged, on the part of the United States, to show that no such right of pre-emption exists by the common consuetudinary maritime law of nations, we can have no objection to accompany him in his inquiry into the grounds, on which the right of pre-emption rests.

We have already seen, that we are not to look in the natural common law of nations for a complete catalogue of goods contraband of war, so as to infer confiscation; and that it is not so much the general principles, as the great diversities in the enumerations of these articles in the treaties entered into, by the different European states, that have occasioned the embarrassment and difficulties experienced in this matter. And these diversities appear to have arisen very much from the different interests, which these nations have, in consequence of the differences in their natural and industrial produce, in the description of their exports and imports, and in their relative advancement in navigation and commerce. In such circumstances, the proper mode of proceeding is, obviously, to apply the principles of natural justice to nations generally, and to leave any modifications of these principles, which may be required, from the peculiarities in the produce of particular countries, to be fixed by particular convention.

Now, in point of right, or legal justice, it is clear, that all nations who chuse to remain neutral, while others are obliged to go to war, are entitled to dispose, as they chuse, of the produce of their respective countries, natural or industrial, of whatever description it may be, within their own territories. The question of restriction or limitation only arises with regard to the transportation or conveyance of that produce to the countries of the nations at war; and the only limitation even upon this transportation or conveyance, to the countries of nations at war, by neutrals, of their commodities on the open seas, is the tendency of such transportation to assist the one belligerent against the other, by supplying the wants of the one, chiefly those occasioned by the events of the war, and counteracting the military operations of the other. Such assistance is manifestly inconsistent with the assumption of neutrality, and the consequent obligation of strict impartiality. And if this obligation be not observed, the nations at war become entitled to enforce it, in two modes, either by the capture and confiscation of the goods, or by the seizure or interception, merely, of the goods, on payment of the value. The general recognized principles, we have seen, are thus given by M. Tetens. In the first place, all articles exclusively destined for armaments and military equipments, are absolutely contraband during war, and form contraband of the first order; of course, to be judged of according to their principal character and most common use; and whether the articles have been already fabricated or manufactured, and are of immediate application to military use, or are still raw or rude materials, which require a new manufacture to become such—this does not change their quality, seeing their destination for war is manifest. And, therefore, materials fit for making, or being made instruments of war, and of which the destination for this use is not doubtful, are also to be classed among the absolute articles of contraband. In the second place, there are goods, such as iron, leather, masts, horses, &c., of which the qualities do not afford sufficient evidence of their destination for war; but which destination may become evident by the very quantity of the articles transported; or, if there still remains any doubt, the places to which they are addressed, the time of their being sent, and other circumstances, may make sufficiently clear, whether the use, to which they are destined, is for war or not. And these may, therefore, be justly ranked among contraband articles of the second order, goods, which, although they are not absolutely such by their nature, become such by their number and their quantity.

In the third place, as the destination of the goods for war, forms the basis of the right of the belligerents, in this respect, the latter cannot be denied the right of confiscating, as illicit, whatever is destined to the military service of their enemy, not only contraband goods of the first and second order, but generally all things of which the destination for hostile armaments is manifest. When a fleet is to be equipped or fitted out, or an army to be supplied with provisions, and magazines or stores are prepared for these purposes, from that time all conveyances of goods, to such places by neutrals, are justly considered contraband, although they should not be so from their nature. They become illicit by circumstances alone, and may be called contraband, par accident, or from circumstances. Even grain and money are prohibited articles in this case, as they are in the case of blockade. And there is, then, ground for the confiscation of the ships, as well as of the cargoes, saving, however, the modifications and the exceptions, to which the proved ignorance of the neutral furnisher, or the constraint of the enemy, may give right.

Goods, then, which are contraband during war, are such, not so much because they are useful or necessary for military service, as by their destination for the enemy, whether indicated by their nature or qualities, or by their quantity or number being inconsistent with any other purpose, or by their being directly shipped for naval arsenals, or ports of military equipment, or for the immediate supply of land or marine forces.

But when the destination of the goods does not appear, from the direct shipment, for the supply of fleets and armies, and is not indicated by the nature or qualities of the goods, natural or artificial, or by the quantity or number of the goods, as inconsistent with their application to any other use, (which may happen with linen and woollen cloths, sail cloth, &c.,) if no preponderating cause can justly determine the judgment, it is no longer permitted to rank these articles among contraband, either of the first or second order. The right of belligerents, with regard to contraband, is no longer applicable to them; and neither the cargoes nor the vessels can be justly condemned. Nevertheless, these articles being of great utility for war, often even requisites of the first necessity for armaments, belligerents preserve the right of preventing them from passing to their enemies. It follows, then, that, when the destination of the goods is not manifestly for war, but that they may, nevertheless, be important or necessary for military use, the right of war is limited to that of preventing their importation into the country of the enemy. They may be taken by the belligerent nation for itself, by paying their just value; they may be sent to other countries; or they may be diverted in some other manner from falling into the hands of the enemy. In this case, neither the neutral merchant who ships them, nor the ship-master who conveys them, can be considered as aiding the enemy; and, therefore, neither the cargo nor the vessel are liable to confiscation.

Such appears to be the origin and foundation of the limited right of interception of neutral goods going to the country of the enemy, on payment of a fair valuation. And if, in reason or law, the destination of goods for the military purposes of the enemy, as appearing from express and direct shipment for the supply of armies or fleets, or as indicated by the nature or qualities of the goods, as actual instruments, or as capable of being made instruments of war, or by their quantity or number, as being inapplicable to any other than warlike or military purposes, has been held sufficient to infer and warrant confiscation and appropriation, the obvious utility of the goods so shipped for the country of the enemy, as subservient to the purposes of war, offensive or defensive, must afford sufficient ground, in reason and in law, for the much milder measure,—the simple interception of these goods, upon condition of restitution, or payment of the price or market value.

This mitigated right of interception and pre-emption, as applicable to goods not strictly contraband, but of utility for war, we have seen, in our first volume, has also been directly, or indirectly, recognized by various preceding jurists, such as, by Grotius, vol. I., pp. 112–116, by Heineccius, p. 210, and pp. 312, 313, note, by Bynkershoek, pp. 218, 219, by Vattel, p. 237, by Rutherforth, pp. 277–280, by Bouchaud, p. 346. But our author here labours strenuously to show, that this comparatively harmless, or innoxious right, as recognized by Grotius, Bynkershoek, and Vattel, exists or emerges, only in cases of extreme necessity, as of blockade. And in pointing out the omission or error of Grotius, in not noticing the shipment of the goods, as indicating a design to do damage, and as therefore giving, at least, a right[1] to guard against it, or to take security against any future similar attempt, Rutherforth seems to put the same construction upon the expressions of Grotius, understanding the degree of necessity, which Grotius deemed requisite to justify the interception as not existing, "unless the exigency of affairs be such, that we cannot possibly do without them." But we cannot agree either with our author, or Dr. Rutherforth, that either Grotius or Vattel, by the expressions they used, really intended to limit the emergence of the right of interception and pre-emption of goods, on their passage to the enemy, to cases of blockade, or to cases of such extreme necessity, as when a belligerent cannot possibly do without the goods. The breach of blockade, and the consequent confiscation of the goods, rests on an entirely different principle, the military occupation by the enemy of the port blockaded, and the illegal interference by the neutral with this military operation, which has in all countries and ages been held sufficient to warrant, not merely the interception and pre-emption, but the confiscation and appropriation of the vessel and cargo, and required no other extreme necessity to justify it. Such, therefore, could not be the necessity contemplated either by Grotius or Vattel. And the argument, that the case referred to in illustration by Grotius, must also, although not even alluded to by Vattel, have been the very case which Vattel had in view, to the effect of limiting his general observation to the mere case of blockade, is certainly far-fetched, (récherché,) and but little calculated to produce conviction. Nor does the question of an extreme necessity, such as the disappointment otherwise of the reduction of a blockaded place by famine, appear to be at all requisite to support such a comparatively

[1] See Vol. I. pp. 278, 279.

mild measure, as the mere interception of goods, under the onerous condition of paying their value. And if it has been found consistent with the principles of justice and general expediency, that the industry of neutrals, in casting cannon, or manufacturing firelocks and musket barrels, and in compounding the ingredients of gunpowder, should be forfeited by their simple destination to a belligerent, it must surely be equally consistent, or less inconsistent with the principles of justice and general expediency, merely to require or compel the neutral proprietor, or farmer, or grain merchant, to sell for a price, or to take a less price than he might perhaps obtain, by actually conveying the grain to a country threatened with famine. So far as the diplomatic papers of the British government at that time, (here rather ostentatiously quoted by our author,) attempted to justify the orders in council of 1793 or 1795, upon the ground of the probability of reducing the French nation, in their revolutionary state, to peace, by famine, or of the internal convulsions of that nation having altered the common consuetudinary international law of Europe, the able diplomatic answer of Count Bernstorff was well founded. But the mere interception of the cargoes of neutral Danish grain, on their passage to supply with subsistence the armies of France, in their invasion of the adjacent peaceful countries, was founded in international justice, and required no such futile arguments, as those before alluded to, to support it.

Our author proceeds, § 6, to the discussion between the French and American governments, with regard to the principle of "free ships, free goods." In 1793, the French government complained of goods, belonging to Frenchmen, having been seized on board American vessels by English cruizers. And, to this remonstrance, we shall here quote a part of the able answer given by

Mr. Jefferson, as extracted by our author, from the American state papers;[1] because, on the point referred to, it appears to us to contain a more correct statement of the common consuetudinary maritime law of nations at that period, than that given by the author, from M. Portalis, to whose merits, however, we have not failed, formerly, to do justice. "Mr. Jefferson laid it down as a principle, that, according to the universal law of nations, the goods of a friend, found on board the vessel of an enemy are free, and the goods of an enemy on board a friendly vessel, are good prize. Agreeably to this principle, he supposed, the English cruizers had, in the cases specified, seized the property of French citizens found on board American vessels; and he avowed he knew not any principle, by which this seizure could be objected to, or impugned. It was true, that several nations, desiring to avoid the inconveniences of subjecting their vessels to be stopped at sea, visited, and carried into foreign ports, to be there judged of, under the pretence that they were loaded with hostile goods, had, on some occasions introduced, by special treaties, another principle between themselves, namely, that hostile vessels should render their cargoes hostile, and friendly vessels should render their cargoes friendly,—a principle less embarrassing for commerce, and equally advantageous for all parties, for gain and for loss. But this was entirely the effect of particular treaties, modifying, in these special cases, the general principle of the law of nations, and being applicable only to nations, who had consented to this modification. England had, in general, adhered to the rigorous principle, not having granted, as far as could be remembered, the modification of permitting the property of the goods to follow that of the vessel, with the single exception of her

[1] Vol. I p. 184.

treaty with France.[1] The United States had adopted this modification in their treaties with France, Holland, and Prussia; and, consequently, so far as regarded these powers, the American vessels covered the goods of their enemies, while the Americans lost their own goods on board the vessels of these enemies. With England, Spain, Portugal, and Austria, they had no convention to oppose to these powers acting agreeably to the common law of nations, by considering hostile merchandise as good prize, even on board friendly vessels" * * * "Although they should have succeeded in establishing the rule of 'free ships, free goods,' with all nations, they would neither gain nor lose by it; but they would be less exposed to vexatious visits at sea. They were making efforts to arrive at this state of things; but the result depended on the will of other nations, as well as on their will; they could not accomplish it, until these other nations should be ready to concur in it."

About this time, our author observes, § 6, the French government likewise complained of the United States having, by their treaty with England in 1794, violated their anterior engagements with France, by which the principles of the armed neutrality of 1780 were recognized. And we shall also quote the answer to this French remonstrance, as given by our author, from Waités' state papers.[2] "At the date of the signature of the treaty of 1778, the armed neutrality was not yet formed; and, consequently, the state of things upon which this treaty behoved to operate or bear, could be regulated only by the pre-existing law of nations, and

[1] Unwilling, apparently, to allow England the benefit of an error, committed by an American statesman, our author takes care to point out, in a note, that when Mr. Jefferson wrote, there were other two treaties in force, by which England had conceded the maxim, (granted the favour,) of "free ships, free goods," that of 1654 with Portugal, and that of 1674 with Holland!

[2] Vol. IV. pp. 38-47.

independently of the principles of the armed neutrality. According to this pre-existing law, free vessels did not render the goods free; and hostile vessels did not render the goods hostile. The stipulation, then, contained in the treaty of 1778, formed an exception to a general rule, still obligatory in all the cases, in which it was not modified by particular conventions. If the treaty between England and the United States had never been concluded, or if this treaty had contained no stipulation applicable to this matter, the right of the belligerent states would not have the less existed. The treaty has not established *a* new right; it has merely modified and regulated the exercise of a right already existing. The desire of establishing the new principle universally, was not more sensibly felt by any other nation, than it was by the United States. The latter did not lose sight of this object; and they pursued it by the means which they deemed most suitable. But the desire to establish a principle, must not be confounded with the assertion, that this principle was already established; and they had never imagined they were bound to seek to establish it by force, against the will of any of the maritime powers."

Our author next shortly notices the decree of the French directory in March 1796, by which "it declared, that the United States had renounced the privileges granted by the treaty of 1778; and the law passed by the two councils of the republic in January 1797, by which it was declared, that all neutral vessels loaded with merchandise belonging to the enemy should be seized, and confiscated as good prize." "These decrees," continues our author, "and other similar ordinances, promulgated under the government of the directory, encouraged the license of French cruizers against the commerce of neutrals; and this state of things was still more aggravated, by the abuses in the exercise of the jurisdiction of the tribunals, judging of the validity of captures, until the establishment of the Conseil des Prises in 1800." The stipulations of the treaty of 1778 with the United States were then renewed, by the convention of September 1800; and the ordonnance of that year, (1778) says our Author, "recognizing the principles, which, subsequently, became the basis of the armed neutrality, was established as the general rule, according to which the French cruizers and tribunals were to be guided, with regard to neutral nations, between whom and France there existed no special conventions." "As long as this wise and moderate administration, and as long, also, as the decision of the new council of prizes were directed by the learned and virtuous magistrate, whose name is identified with the formation of the Code Civil of Napoleon, there was no reason for complaint on the part of neutrals, of the application of the Code des Prises by the French tribunals." "But, to this system of modern law," continues our Author, "there soon, unfortunately, succeeded measures of violence, sanctioned by the imperial decrees of France, and the orders in council of England, by which these two powers, returning to the usages of war, in the ages of barbarism, prohibited all neutral commerce, under the pretext of reprisals against their mutual injustice, by establishing blockades not recognized by the true principles of maritime law." In illustration of these principles, our Author concludes this section, by quoting some passages from the speech of M. Portalis, at the installation of the Council of Prizes in 1800, which we formerly noticed.[1] And we shall also quote the paragraph, in which the views of Portalis, referred to, appear to be condensed, and in which we quite agree.

[1] Vol. I. pp. 434-436

"Since civilization has, to use the expression, added new nations to the human race, there are always, among the numerous nations who cover the surface of the globe, some having an interest, from their situation, to preserve neutrality; and this neutrality, which is, in time of war, the sole bond of social relations, and of useful communication among men, ought to be religiously respected as a real public benefit. The belligerent powers are, undoubtedly, entitled to prevent and to watch the frauds of a pretended neutrality. If the open enemy is always known, the neutral may conceal a real enemy under the garb of a friend; he is then struck by the right of war, and he deserves to be so. But let us be on our guard, in the application of this formidable right, against mistaking or misunderstanding (méconnaitre) the treaties, the customs consecrated by the constant and uniform practice of nations, and the principles which guarantee their sovereignty and independence."[1]

Of the events of the French Imperial war, here merely alluded to by our Author, we have already given a sufficiently full account, and have no wish here to revert to them. And, in courtesy, we can easily excuse this brief notice of French continental and maritime aggression from 1803 to 1814, in a treatise, of which the author was a competitor for literary honours, in a question, proposed by the learned Institute of France. But while we quite excuse the elegant brevity of the notice, we cannot acquiesce in the indiscriminate censure it conveys, and must correct the erroneous impression it is obviously calculated to make. It implies, that, by the adoption of a new system of blockade, Britain was the aggressor, and provoked the outrageous decrees of Berlin and Milan. But this is not true; for,

[1] pp. 301–4.

prior to those decrees, Britain had not adopted any new system of blockade, or, as it has been called, the paper blockade, or blocus de cabinet. The orders for blockade, prior to these decrees, uniformly directed the naval preparations requisite to maintain an actual blockade by a sufficient force. And her prize tribunals had, several years prior to the peace of Amiens, declared by their judgments, that there could be no breach of blockade, unless an actual and efficient blockade was maintained by an adequate force; and, consequently, that otherwise there could be no confiscation or condemnation as prize for breach of blockade. It was not till after the Berlin decree had proclaimed the continental blockade, and the victories of Napoleon at Austerlitz and Friedland, had rendered that blockade actual and efficient, through the compulsory alliances which these victories enabled him to make with the other continental powers, for the exclusion of Britain from all European commerce, that the British government issued the subsequent Orders of January and November 1807, which were merely retaliatory and conditional, dependent entirely on the recal of the French decrees. It is to be regretted this merely retaliatory measure was resorted to. It does not appear, that it was really calculated to attain the object in view, that of putting an end to the continental blockade. And we do not maintain its legality, so far as it tended indirectly to affect the properly national commerce of real and bonâ fide neutral nations. But, after the peace of Tilsit, it was difficult to discover any government, which, whatever might be its disposition, was really and bonâ fide neutral in relation to Britain. And so far as directed against the enemy, and those other continental governments or nations, who joined with Napoleon, in carrying into effect his blockade of Britain, the justice of the Orders in council is indisputable. For such orders, however, the British government and nation have no partiality. They were resorted to merely pro tempore and conditionally, in an extreme case, in order to resist an unparalleled system of aggression. And it is to be trusted, such an extreme case of necessity will never again occur among nations;—and, at all events, that such a remedy will never be resorted to.

Returning to the close of the French revolutionary war, terminated by the peace of Amiens, our Author, in § 7, gives a rather detailed account of the discussion between Britain and the powers of the north, with regard to the right of visiting merchant vessels under the convoy of armed neutral vessels. In the case of the capture, in 1798, of the fleet of Swedish merchant vessels, carrying naval stores from Sweden to the Mediterranean ports, under the power of France, he states the grounds of the judgment given by Sir William Scott.[1] He next notices the case of a Danish frigate escorting, in December 1799, a fleet of merchant vessels, and refusing to submit to the right of visit on the part of English ships of war; and gives, of course, pretty fully, the answer of Count Bernstorff to the British remonstrance. The Author next notices the case of the Danish frigate le Freya, which, in July 1800, says he, "in wishing to defend the convoy of merchant vessels, which she escorted, against an English squadron in the Channel, provoked a combat, with the loss of lives on both sides." And here it is impossible to avoid noticing the meaning which these expressions are calculated, indirectly, to convey, as different from the actual truth. The English squadron did not attack, as enemies, either the Danish merchant vessels, or the frigate that convoyed them; it merely requested to be quietly allowed to visit

[1] Rob. Adm. Rep. Vol. I. p. 340.

and search the merchant vessels, according to the ordinary exercise of that right. That a Danish frigate could maintain a combat with a British squadron, or that there could be any other result than a capture, is incredible. The Danish government demanded reparation; the British government replied, they had more reason to make such a demand; and charged a minister with a special mission to Copenhagen, for the settlement of the dispute. Our Author, of course, takes care to remark, that a British fleet was sent to the Sound to give greater weight to the representations of the ambassador—sending a fleet to support a legal claim, sanctioned by the usage of centuries, and to resist an attempt, at the enforcement upon Britain of a new rule of law—as if this was something infinitely worse, than Napoleon sending armies to Vienna, Berlin, and Moscow, to support his manifestly unjust pretensions, and to tyrannise over the other continental nations. Nay, so far as then depended on the British government, the dispatch of this fleet would not have led to any hostilities. For, as our Author states, the negociation was terminated by a convention, signed at Copenhagen, the 29th August 1800, by which the question of right was reserved for ulterior examination; the Danish frigate, and the vessels under her convoy, were restored; and it was agreed, that, to avoid similar disputes, the Danish government should suspend her convoys, until the question was decided by a definitive convention.

In § 8, our Author proceeds to give an account of the armed neutrality of 1800, commenced by the Russian Emperor Paul; recites the terms of this new northern confederacy; and seems to attach to it more importance than it deserves, calling it a quadruple alliance. As it did not survive its originator, and did not last a year, we did not formerly consider this transient combination, as requiring much detail in our historical sketch. But we may here, with our Author, briefly resume the narrative of these proceedings of the northern powers at the conclusion of the last century, as showing, that, however to be lamented, the battle of Copenhagen was unavoidable on the part of Britain. Separating himself from his alliances with Austria and Britain, and in violation of his own positive engagements by treaties with Britain in the course of that war; the Russian Emperor Paul, from what motive or influence, has not distinctly appeared, suddenly resolved on reviving the scheme of the armed neutrality of 1780; made proposals to that effect to Sweden, Denmark, and Prussia; and, without any other provocation, on the part of the British government, than sending a fleet to the Sound, first directed the sequestration of all British property in Russia, and afterwards laid an embargo on all the British vessels in his ports, upon the untrue and absurd pretence of the British government having failed to perform an alleged promise, to put him in possession of the island of Malta. As the Danish government was bound, by the convention of the 20th August 1800, not to grant any escort to their merchant vessels, until the question should be settled in a definitive manner between the two powers, it might have been expected, it would have abode by that so recent convention, and not have entered into a new confederacy with Russia, directed against Britain. And the British minister, at Copenhagen, accordingly demanded a full, open, and satisfactory answer, upon the nature, object, and extent of the obligations which Denmark might have contracted, or of the negociations, which she was prosecuting.

On this occasion, Count Bernstorff, apparently dazzled by the prospect of forcing England to admit the favourite neutral pretension of "free ship, free goods," through the united efforts of Russia, Sweden, and Prussia, seems to have laid aside his ordinary caution and prudence; and returned an evasive answer, which could not fail to lead to war; namely, that the engagements which Denmark was on the eve of contracting, were not hostile to England, or contrary to those which she had undertaken by the convention of August; that the provisional and temporary abandonment, not of a principle, as to which the question remained undecided, but of a measure, the right to adopt which, never had been, and never could be contested, was by no means in opposition to the general and permanent principles, with regard to which the powers of the north were on the point of re-establishing a concert, which, far from compromising their neutrality, was destined only to confirm it. To this answer the British government replied, by an Order in council in January 1801, laying an embargo on Russian, Swedish, and Danish vessels, and a declaration, that the new code of maritime law, which it had been wished to establish in 1780, and which it was now sought to revive, was an innovation, injurious to the dearest interests of England,—an innovation which Russia had renounced, by her alliance with England, at the commencement of the then existing war. Having thus resolved to join with Russia, in extorting, by force, from Britain, that pretension and privilege, which, in former ages, it had sought to obtain by treaty, and which, in consequence of the neutrality, it had from its caution and prudence, contrived almost uniformly to maintain, it had found so profitable and advantageous, the Danish government co-operated with Russia, in shutting the mouths of the Elbe and the Weser, against British commerce; and the Danish troops occupied the Hanseatic cities of Hamburgh and Lubec, while the Prussian troops occupied the Electorate of Hanover and Bremen. The war was commenced, and terminated by the battle of Copenhagen in April 1801, followed by an armistice with Denmark, to which Russia and Sweden afterwards acceded. The death of the Emperor Paul dissolved the confederacy, of which he was the founder. And the matters in dispute were settled by the British convention of 1801, with the Russian Emperor Alexander, to which Denmark and Sweden likewise afterwards acceded.

From his pretty long account of the maritime convention of 1801, between Britain and Russia, in § 9, our Author passes at once, in § 10, to the congress of Vienna. He thus, to all appearance, designedly omits any history of the temporary Imperial government of France, or of the practice of continental or maritime warfare during that period. It would have been difficult for a citizen of the United States of America, or for any impartial international jurist, to have justified or supported the groundless pretexts, upon which Napoleon, invaded, overcame by his military skill, all patriotic, but ill concerted resistance, traversed with his victorious armies, the territories of almost all the continental nations, and for a time subjected them, either directly to his dominion, or indirectly to his baneful influence. It would have been a difficult task, even with the aid, which the abuse of the British Orders in council might have afforded, to have justified the Berlin and Milan decrees, or the subsequent imperial ordonnances relative to maritime commerce.

And, perhaps, it would not have been quite courteous, to have expressed an independent and impartial opinion on these subjects, as an international jurist or historian, in a work addressed to the Institute of France. We shall willingly, therefore, here pass over, with our

Author, this portion of the history of maritime law, especially, as we have, perhaps, already dwelt more than enough on that period. And as our Author treats no more of navigation, except in § 22, of the liberty of the navigation of the Rhine and other German rivers, we shall return to his discussion, in § 9, of the maritime convention of 1801, between Britain and Russia.

CHAPTER XIX.

(CONTINUED.)

Review of part of Dr. Wheaton's History of the Law of Nations in Europe.

SECTION II.

UPON the first perusal, we were surprised, our Author should have allotted so much space to his account of the armed neutrality of 1780; which was never absolutely and unconditionally recognized, or acted upon, either by France or Spain, any more than by Britain, and which was not only contrary to the practice of Russia, the ostensible prime mover in the scheme, in her former maritime wars, as testified by the Russian Admiral Greig, but was, in a few years, departed from, by that very power, both in her own marine regulations, and in successive treaties with Britain and other states. We were still more surprised, to observe, the vast importance attached by our Author to the resuscitation of the scheme of the armed neutrality by the Russian Emperor Paul, in 1800, which did not last a year, and to the convention of June 1801, between Britain and the Russian Emperor Alexander, by which that second confederacy was dissolved. This last was, no doubt, an important convention for Britain, inasmuch as it was a complete abandonment by Russia, and also by Sweden and Denmark, who were provisionally admitted, and afterwards acceded to that convention, of the lately strongly urged pretension of the neutral flag to protect at sea, the property of the enemy, from capture by the opposite belligerent. But this treaty between Britain and the three Northern powers, could not, and did not, alter the general Common consuetudinary maritime law of nations. As Conventional law, it was adopted only by a portion of the maritime Powers. And we have now to inquire, what was really the state of the maritime international law of Europe, at this period, whether Conventional, or Common consuetudinary.

With regard to the Conventional maritime law of nations, properly so called, as constituted by existing treaties, the privileges stipulated by various treaties, in favour of neutrals during war, in the latter part of the seventeenth century, and in the earlier part of the eighteenth century, had all, we have seen, ceased and expired, by the express annulment of these treaties, as well as by their violation otherwise, as on the part of the republican government of France; or by the infringement of the counter-stipulations in these treaties, as in the case of Holland; or by the intervention of hostilities, and by the omission, obviously intentional, to renew these stipulations and engagements, at the peace of Amiens in 1801, or in the treaties of Paris and Ghent in 1814, or in the general definitive treaties in 1815. And the Russian scheme of the armed neutrality in 1800, had also, upon a second trial, proved abortive, except with regard to privateers, not being allowed to search merchant vessels under convoy.

With regard, again, to the Common consuetudinary maritime law of nations, the legal fiction, so strongly urged, if not invented by Hübner, in support of the rule of "free ship, free goods," namely, that the neutral vessel in the open seas, is a part of the territory of the neutral state, had been refuted by Rutherforth and Lampredi; was considered by Schmalz in 1816, to be too much of a gratuitous hypothesis, to be admitted as the foundation of a compulsory right; and was abandoned as untenable by Rayneval, who substituted for it, the right of national independence, as implying, by a rather singular extension of the hitherto recognized meaning of the term, a right to go upon the high seas, and to protect, by force, the property of one belligerent nation from seizure by another belligerent. The rule itself, of "free ship, free goods," was admitted by B. S. Nau, in 1803, to be extremely favourable and advantageous for neutrals; and a rule of such an import was considered by Tetens, in 1805, as not exigible by one independent nation from another, and as not likely ever to be conceded by Maritime, any more than by Continental belligerents. The rule, too, by which the belligerent is held entitled to capture the property of the enemy on the open sea, although on board a neutral vessel, had been sanctioned by the opinions of all the eminent international jurists, from Grotius to Vattel, had, independently of special treaty, been uniformly recognized in the individual legislation and judicial practice of nations, and was, in 1814, after mature deliberation, declared by the learned, intelligent, and independent lawyer, Jacobsen, to be the only rule consistent with justice, and the common law of nations.

There still remained the ingenious scheme, apparently first suggested, in 1780, by Totze, the reputed author of La Liberté de la Navigation, and of un Essai sur un Code Maritime Européen, and followed out by Martens and Klüber, of carving out of the similar or equipollent clauses of treaties, a system of the law of nations, that was to be binding, not merely on the contracting parties, and while the treaties lasted, but after their termination, in perpetuity, upon all the contracting parties, not merely in relation to the opposite contracting parties, but in relation to all other nations, and even upon nations, who had not entered into any such treaties, upon the ground of the majority of the maritime states of Europe having entered into various such treaties, in the course of the last two centuries. But even this ingenious theory, though certainly plausible, did not appear likely to stand the test of more rigid investigation, or to afford a very stable basis for a new system of compulsory international law. And its validity for such a purpose was, as we have seen, abandoned by Martens himself, in the last edition of his Droit des Gens Moderne de l'Europe, which he published at Göttingen in 1821, a short time before his death. For, in his introduction, § 7, note c, he thus expresses himself:—"Although the system of the armed neutrality, adopted in its time by so many powers, approaches the nearest to this idea, (a general convention) it could not be held as received, even between, or among, the maritime powers solely, for the relations of each with each reciprocally, even not speaking of England." And at the close of the work, § 344, note a, "Wherefore the question, whether Great Britain ought to adopt, as a general rule, the principle frequently introduced in Europe, since the seventeenth century, that the 'ship covers the cargo,' rests upon another question, doubtful, and disputed, namely, which of the two principles is conformable to the natural law."

In these circumstances, our Author appears to have found it requisite, to endeavour to make the most of the situation, in which the events before alluded to, had left the Conventional maritime law of nations; the principles of the recent theories of the Positive natural. or Common consuetudinary law of nations, having been found insufficient to support the deductions or conclusions of their authors. And, our surprise at the importance ascribed by our Author, to the two transient armed neutralities ceased, upon reading the following paragraph:—"We have believed it necessary, to enter into these details of the circumstances, which accompanied the formation of the convention of 1801, because, according to us, (suivant nous) it ought to be regarded, not solely as forming a new conventional law between the contracting parties, but as containing a recognition of the universal pre-existing rights, which they could not justly refuse to grant to other powers. The object of the treaty was to determine, and to declare, the law of nations, upon the different points, which had been so much contested; the three powers of the North conceding the principle of 'free ship, free goods,' and that of the right of search, with a modification; and England recognizing the principles of the armed neutrality, with reference to the commerce of the colonies, and upon the coasts of an enemy, with reference to the right of blockade, and with reference to the mode of exercising the right of visit; and conceding, besides, to Russia, the limitation of contraband to warlike stores alone. With regard to the question of convoys—a question, which was not comprehended in the armed neutrality of 1780, a modification, to the satisfaction of the powers of the North, was conceded by England."[1]

Now this is, really, a very curious paragraph. The mode of argument is new, and certainly very convenient. And our author's own phrase "according to us," (suivant nous) warrants us in considering Dr. Wheaton, as here,

[1] § 9, pp. 320, 321

not the independent, just, and impartial historian of maritime international law, but as the advocate, like Hübner, of the interests of neutral nations, willing to support the cause of his clients at any hazard. We must, therefore, examine this reasoning more minutely; which is manifestly an attempt to derive some benefit from the convention, which the British government concluded with the Russian Emperor Alexander, in June 1801, by confounding and mixing it up, with the articles of the Russian declarations and conventions of the Empress Catherine in 1780, and of the Emperor Paul in 1800, so as to give the convention of 1801, a meaning or signification, which it was never intended to bear, and which it can never, in fair and sound construction, be made to bear.

It might be questioned, whether this convention of 1801, be still in force, or whether it was not annulled by the Russian declaration of war, in November 1808, and subsequent acts of hostility; without being specially renewed in 1812 or 1815. But supposing it to be now in full force, upon what principle of law or reason, we would ask, can any of the other nations, who were not parties to the convention between Britain and Russia in 1801, be held entitled in any way, to found upon, or to avail themselves of that convention? Article eighth of this convention, declares, "that the stipulations contained in it, shall be regarded as permanent, and shall serve as a constant rule" (not for all other nations, which would have been absurdly presumptuous, but) "for the *contracting parties, in the matter of commerce and navigation.*" The other nations, just alluded to, France, Spain, Holland, Austria, Prussia, the Neapolitan Kingdom, and the United States of America, had no concern, or connection whatever, in the formation of this convention. With regard to them, it was completely, Res inter alios acta. The governments of Britain and Russia, were not then pretending to establish a maritime international code for Europe. It was not likely, they would insert in their particular convention, any stipulations in favour of France, just after Buonaparte had returned from Egypt, and had become First Consul. And it is still more improbable, the British government would be disposed, or intended to do so, since within a few months of the date of this convention, that government would not, and did not, even agree, according to the usual practice, to renew by the treaty of peace of Amiens, the treaties, which had, in former times, been concluded between the parties to that treaty. The convention of 1801, itself, contains no stipulations in favour of any third party, except Denmark and Sweden, who by article IX. are invited to accede; and this very exception confirms the intention to exclude all other nations. On the other hand, supposing the convention had contained, instead of what seem to be considered beneficial clauses, provisions injurious to the interests of these other nations, that were not parties to it, who would have been so hardy, or so foolish, as to maintain, that these provisions were binding upon these other nations, either France or the United States of America?

Not content, with maintaining, that all the nations of the world are entitled to found upon the British convention with Russia in June 1801, against Great Britain, although these other nations were not parties to, and had no connection with that treaty, our Author next endeavours to show, by his construction of that treaty, that it amounted to a recognition by Great Britain of the principles of the armed neutrality, with regard to the coasting and colonial trade of the enemy, with regard to the right of blockade, and with regard to the mode of exercising the right of visitation and search. And as the question is important, and our Author's ingenious, but fallacious, representation, may have considerable effect, in misleading the ignorant, on the European continent, as well as in his own country, it becomes necessary to examine more minutely, the accuracy of his statement and argument.

"That such," continues our Author, "is the true construction of the convention of 1801, was rendered evident by the discussion which took place in the House of Peers, on the 12th November 1801, at the time of the production of the documents connected with this negociation. On this occasion, Lord Grenville, who had already retired from the ministry, with his friend Mr. Pitt, leaving to their successors, the charge of making peace with France, and with the powers of the North, as they might deem best, (comme ils l'entendraient) expressed his entire conviction, that the convention had essentially weakened the system of maritime law supported by the English government, and declared that the inadmissible pretensions of the powers of the Baltic had been favoured by the feeble and temporising policy, which England had followed towards these powers, during the last years of the war of American independence." * * * "The principal objection," continues our Author, "urged by Lord Grenville to the convention of 1801, was, that, in its composition, (rédaction) the two offensive conventions of the armed neutrality had been followed, with a scrupulous and servile exactness, as far as they could be applied. England had then negociated, and concluded this treaty, upon the basis of these same inadmissible conventions, which she had wished to put down by war. She placed herself, then, in the face of Europe, not as resisting, but as acceding to the treaties of the armed neutrality; with modifications, it is true, and changes in certain essential points; but sanctioning, by this concession, the weight and the authority of the transactions, which she had formerly regarded as flagrant violations of public law, and so justifying on her part even the extremities of war. Whatever may be the principles of the maritime law, which may be contested in future, they must be discussed with some regard for the treaties of the armed neutrality. Whatever expressions there may be of a doubtful meaning, that were transferred from these treaties to the convention, and there were many, they must, according to the best rules of interpretation, be explained by reference to the original act, by which they were at first incorporated into the code of the public law. It was under the influence of this impression, that it was necessary to proceed to the examination of the convention of 1801, and to compare it with those pretensions, for which England had last year determined, it was necessary, even amidst all the embarrassments of the moment, to incur the additional dangers of a war with the powers of the North."

Before going on, with our Author, to make the comparison, here proposed, we must premise a few observations. Although, perhaps, the talented and patriotic Lord Grenville little suspected, that any of his speeches would be used to limit and restrict the maritime rights of his country, we admit, that Dr. Wheaton, as a foreign jurist, or historian, is entitled to avail himself of the popular nature of the British constitution, and to urge the arguments, employed by the party in Parliament, in opposition to the ministry of the day, so far as regards legal principle, the natural, or Common consuetudinary law of nations, or in the language of Grotius, the rectae rationis dictamina. But to contend, that the construction, which a British Peer, or other Member of

Parliament in opposition to the ministry, puts, in the fervour of argument, upon a treaty with a foreign power, is to be held, by inference, to have been the meaning and intention of the British government, in opposition to the express declaration of their meaning by the ministers themselves who made it, is quite unwarranted. So far as other nations are concerned, the import of a treaty, concluded by the British government, as binding the nation, must be what the terms of the treaty itself, in ordinary, fair, and sound construction bear, confirmed by the public declaration of the government at the time, that such was its intention in this its own act; not the conjectural construction, of which an opposition Member of Parliament may, from extraneous sources, argue it is susceptible, and may urge, perhaps, chiefly in support of the politics of his party in the state. Besides, the adduction of Lord Grenville as an authority, is rather unfortunate. For that statesman admitted none of the imperial dogmas of the armed neutrality. On the other hand, he claimed for England no rights, which he did not admit to be competent to every other independent maritime state. He claimed, indeed, for England, all those rights, which had been recognized as the Common consuetudinary law of nations, by the practice of all the maritime European states for centuries, and by all the international jurists, from Grotius to Vattel. And his complaint against his successors in office, was merely, that, by the convention with Russia, in June 1801, they had conceded to the Northern powers too much of their rights, under the Common law of nations. But he never admitted, that this convention with Russia, Denmark, and Sweden, was binding on Britain, in relation to all the other maritime states of Europe, or was a concession in their favour of any part of the Common consuetudinary international rights, competent to every maritime state. As little did either the British ministry, at the time, or Lord Grenville, ever admit so absurd a construction, as, that this convention must be held to be an absolute surrender of every maritime right, ever exercised or claimed by Great Britain, which was not specially stipulated for, in that treaty, or that the non-insertion in this convention of provisions against, or at least, negative of, the other points, which had been proposed or demanded in the Russian declarations of 1780 and 1800, was an admission or recognition of these points against Britain, and in favour, not only of the opposite contracting parties, who had made no stipulations regarding these matters, but in favour, also, even of those other maritime states, who were not, in any shape, parties to that treaty.

In the ordinary mode of interpreting treaties, it has been the practice to search for their true import and meaning, at least, first in their contents, not in what is not contained in them. But, it seems, those other Powers, who were merely third parties to the transaction, have a right, not only to found upon the terms of the convention between the British government, and the Emperor Alexander, in 1801, but also to have taken into consideration, as parts or illustrations of it, all the state papers for twenty years preceding, at all connected with the subject; from the declaration of the Empress Catherine in 1780, prepared by her minister, Count Panin, apparently to please King Frederic II. of Prussia, to the provisions of the convention, which, in 1800, the Emperor Paul thought fit to conclude with Sweden and Denmark, so much to the detriment of the latter. That the true interpretation of a treaty is to be obtained by going out of its own terms, and mixing up with it, not merely other treaties between the same

Powers, but also ex-parte declarations, invitations to accede, and vague and indefinite answers for twenty years preceding, is a singular doctrine. And, that a treaty is to be held to embrace, not merely the stipulations and provisions which it actually contains, but also by its silence, or by the absence from it, of provisions expressly negative of all the other claims, which have been urged and discussed under these different state papers for so long a period, to imply a settlement of all these points in favour of the claimants, is a still more astounding proposition. Great Britain, it is contended, must, by this convention, be held, not only to have undertaken all the engagements or obligations contained in it, with regard to all other nations, although not parties to it, but must also be held to have admitted all the assertions and claims, which these other nations, not parties to it, have made or urged, since 1780, because they are not positively contradicted in that treaty. It was not enough, it seems, that Great Britain, in 1780, and in 1800, resisted the rather presumptuous attempt of the Northern powers to compel her, by force, to adopt, for their advantage, a rule, contrary to the principles of universal justice, and contrary to the Common consuetudinary law and practice for centuries, of all the European nations. She must be held, it should seem, by this convention, to have admitted, not only what she did concede, but likewise all the pretensions which her adversaries had brought forward, since the middle of the eighteenth century. It is curious this argument did not occur to the Emperor Napoleon and his ministers, so fertile in pretexts, to justify acts of aggression, and the undue constraint of other nations.

With regard to our Author's so often repeated representations of the right of visit and search, and of the capture of hostile goods at sea, although on board neutral vessels, as if they were mere pretensions, and as being a new system peculiar to Britain, it is not easy, altogether, to acquit him of the charge of attempting to mislead the ignorant. So far is the English administration of the law of nations, in this department, from being either new or peculiar, or a mere pretension, that, as we have seen, and our Author must have known, it is neither more nor less than what has been the common consuetudinary law of Europe for upwards of five centuries,—of all the maritime European states, sanctioned by the approval of the most eminent international jurists of the southern, central, and northern countries of Europe, from Grotius to Vattel, Lampredi, and Jacobsen; and uniformly observed in the practice of all these nations, as evinced by their statutes, ordinances, proclamations, and judicial determinations; excepting only where express paction and special stipulations have, for a time, authorized a deviation from the common law.

Such special stipulations, in particular treaties, could only bind the contracting parties, and cannot be held available, in perpetuity, in favour of all and sundry nations. The number and frequency of such stipulations in treaties, cannot establish, as a part of the common law of nations, a rule, which allows a neutral state to protect the property, and carry on for its behoof, the trade of a belligerent nation, and thereby to deprive the opposed belligerent of the means, which the Author of Nature affords it, of obtaining justice; or which, in other words, allows a pretended friend, by such a war in disguise, to do greater mischief to the opposed belligerent, than his open, actual hostility, could effect.

Besides, any treaties, containing stipulations of this description, in the seventeenth and eighteenth centuries, such as those of 1666 and 1674, and as that of Utrecht, in 1713, had all expired, or been annulled, or had otherwise ceased to exist, before the termination of the eighteenth century. The treaty of Amiens in 1801, did not, any more than the treaties of peace in 1814 and 1815, renew any such stipulations and engagements. And the famous scheme of the armed neutrality of 1780, our Author has been forced to admit, had been completely departed from, and actually abandoned. Thus he says, "The principles in question, had, in effect, soon after the armed neutrality of 1780, been abjured or renounced by almost all the parties, who ever entered into that league; by Russia in her war with the Porte in 1787; by Sweden in her war with Russia in 1789; by Russia, Prussia, Austria, Spain, Portugal, and America, in their treaties with England during the first war of the French Revolution; by Denmark and Sweden in their ordinances promulgated in 1793; these powers being neutral; and in their mutual treaty of 1794; and also by Russia in her treaty with the United States of America in 1799. In the official papers, published by the Empress Catherine and her successor, during the war with France, pretensions were put forth by the Russian Cabinet, quite as extensive as the ancient maritime law of Europe."

We thus approach the examination of the convention of June and October 1801, between Great Britain and Russia, confessedly in the absence, and after the cessation of all conventional law, on the points we are now contemplating. By the third article of this convention, His Imperial Russian Majesty, and His Britannic Majesty, having resolved to place under a sufficient safeguard the liberty of the commerce and navigation of their subjects, in the event that either of them should be at war, while the other should remain at peace, agreed, &c., upon five propositions. And in examining our Author's representation of the import of these, in order to guard against the influence of national bias, we shall keep in view the commentary of M. Schoell, the very intelligent and impartial German historian.

The first proposition is, "that the vessels of the neutral power may navigate freely to the ports, and upon the coasts of the nations at war." And Great Britain, our Author maintains, "thereby conceded the rule, according to which, the belligerent powers, refused to neutrals the liberty of prosecuting, in time of war, the branches of the commerce of the enemy, from which they are excluded in time of peace. This rule had been principally applied by England to the commerce of the coasts, and of the colonies of France—a commerce exclusively appropriated, in time of peace, to national vessels. This monopoly had been mitigated solely in time of war, in consequence of the superiority of the naval power of England, which rendered the French navigation too dangerous to be continued. In these circumstances, France had admitted neutral vessels to participate in the commerce of her coasts and her colonies. And the powers of the North had insisted in the league of the armed neutrality of 1780 and of 1800, upon the right of prosecuting these two branches of commerce."

Now, independently of France pretending to found a right to have her coasting and colonial trade carried on for her behoof, by convenient neutrals, when she may have been disabled from doing so herself, upon a treaty, entered into more than forty years ago, between Britain on the one side, and Russia, Sweden, and Denmark on the other, to which neither France, nor any of the other maritime powers of Europe were parties—the whole of this paragraph is very fallacious. The rule, by which the accustomed trade of neutrals during peace, that is, the trade open to them, during peace, was assumed as an equitable limitation and measure of the extent of the commerce, to which they are entitled, during war, we have already seen, was not first introduced by the English, or for the first time, in the war of 1756; but was recognized by the elder Baron de Cocceii, towards the close of the seventeenth century, and by other subsequent international lawyers,[1] and practised by France herself, during the war of the succession.

In agreeing, by the clause before quoted, that Russian, and also Danish and Swedish vessels, when neutral, might freely trade to the ports of the nations at war, Britain did no more than recognize the Common consuetudinary law of nations, which she had observed for centuries, under the ordinary restrictions likewise observed in practice, of the seizure and confiscation of goods, the property of the enemy, when found at sea, on board neutral vessels, on payment of the freight, and of goods contraband of war, from their natural fitness, or artificial adaptation for war, or from their direct and special destination for military purposes. For, at common law, agreeably to the distinction noticed by Mr. Ward, neutrals are entitled to trade—to carry on their own trade *with* either belligerent, but not to trade, or to carry on their trade, *for* the behoof of either belligerent. By agreeing, that Russian, Danish, and Swedish vessels, when neutral, might navigate freely upon the coasts of the nations at war, Britain appears to have given up, with regard to the nations, who were parties to this treaty, and so long as it lasted, the right at common law of confiscating neutral vessels engaged in the coasting trade of the enemy, from which they are excluded during peace; for, navigating freely upon the coasts of the nations at war, may imply navigating from

[1] Vol. I. p. 140.

hostile port to hostile port. It might, perhaps, be questioned, whether the terms, before quoted, do not merely authorize the vessels, before-mentioned, to carry on their own proper trade with the enemy, in their own vessels, and by means of their own capitals, and do not authorize such neutrals to carry on, for the enemy, their proper trade by means of hostile capitals. We shall here adopt the more extensive and liberal interpretation, holding the terms to embrace both descriptions of trade, until more definitely expressed. And, we have only to add, that, with regard to the other European nations, this treaty had, and could have no effect whatever; and that the broad principle of the common law remains entire, namely, that neutrals are entitled, during war, to have intercourse with the ports of the enemy which are not efficiently blockaded, and so to carry on their own accustomed trade, but not to trade *for* the enemy, or to carry on his trade for his behoof, such as carrying on for him his coasting trade, from which foreigners are uniformly excluded, and which the naval operations of his antagonist alone have disabled him from carrying on himself.

It is here amusing to observe, the rather inappropriate application made by our Author of the term "monopoly," to the conduct or practice of a great nation, in excluding foreigners, during peace, from its own proper coasting trade! And, we suspect, the French government will be disposed to continue this so called monopoly, in its colonial, as well as coasting trade, if it follows the advice given in the able brochure, published in 1779, under the title of "Considérations sur l'Admission des Navires Neutres aux Colonies Françoises de l'Amérique en tems de Guerre," and stated to have been fouud among the papers of a French Judge, well known for his love of literature.

With regard to the terms of the first proposition of the third article of the convention of 1801, as affecting the question of neutrals carrying on the colonial trade of the enemy, although it did not, for the first time, emerge just in the war of 1756, it is plain, it could not emerge, till considerable progress had been made in the art of distant navigation; and, if not till after the discovery of the American islands and continent, at least, not till after the European nations had acquired distant colonies. And, as these colonies, though distant, may be viewed as part of the territory of the mother country, though not usually, if ever called so, it seems to have been apprehended, the terms of this article of the convention of June 1801, "to navigate freely upon the coasts of the nations at war," might, perhaps, in the absence of better argument, be construed to mean, upon the coasts of the mother country and its colonial territory as a whole, so as to imply, from a port in the mother country, to a port in the colony. And, to anticipate any such interpretation, and to prevent any such misconstruction, an explanatory article, as our Author is forced to admit, in a note, although passed over in silence in the text, was added to the convention of June, in the month of October 1801, by which it is expressly declared, "That the liberty of commerce and navigation, granted by the said article third, to the subjects of the neutral powers, does not authorize them to transport, directly, in time of war, the merchandise and produce of the colonies of the belligerent powers into the continental possessions, nor vice versâ, from the mother country into the colonies of the enemy; but that the said subjects are, nevertheless, to enjoy, for this commerce, the same advantages and facilities, which the most favoured nations enjoy, particularly the United States of America."[1]

[1] Martens' Recueil Supp. Tom III. p. 192.

And this declaration was subsequently explained by the British instructions of June 1803, to be the liberty of trading directly between the colonies of the enemy, and the neutral country to which the vessel belongs, and laden with the property of the inhabitants of such neutral country. So far, it thus appears, was the British government from consenting by the convention of June and October 1801, as alleged, to the interposition of neutrals, in general, between the hostile or belligerent mother country and its colonies, that it did not make any such concession even in favour of the Northern nations, parties to that treaty. Still less did the British government make any such concession to the other European nations, who were not parties to, and have not the shadow of a right to found upon that treaty, of which the terms relate solely and exclusively to the eventual neutrality of the contracting nations. And the circumstance of the later confederacy in 1800, having found it necessary to rest contented with a less concession, than what the confederacy of 1780 had presumed to demand, but had not obtained, affords but a lame and impotent argument, for holding that these governments, who did not succeed in 1780 and 1782, in obtaining any concession, and who were not parties to the second brief confederacy, have, strange to tell, actually obtained a greater concession, by doing nothing, than those who were parties to the second confederacy, and really obtained the limited conventional concession, before specified.

The second section of this third article of the convention of 1801, provides, "that the goods loaded on board the neutral vessels, shall be free, with the exception of articles contraband of war, and goods the property of the enemy; and it is agreed not to comprehend in the number of the latter, merchandise of the produce, growth, or manufacture of the countries at war, which should have been acquired by the subjects of the neutral power, and should have been transported on their account; which merchandise cannot be excepted, in any case, from the liberty granted to the flag of the said power."

Our Author is here obliged to admit, "that the seizure and confiscation of hostile property, on board neutral vessels at sea, were fully confirmed by the third article, section second, of this convention of 1801, bearing the concession of the opposite principle of 'free ship, free goods,' on the part of the powers of the North." But he obviously makes this admission unwillingly and ungraciously. To make the convention appear more harsh and severe, he omits the limiting expletives, or to mention that, to warrant the seizure, the goods must be the property of the enemy, voluntarily exposed in the open seas. He talks of the two rules, as if they were equally founded, or equally unfounded, in reason, law, and justice; as if the rule agreed to by this convention, had not been approved, as founded in justice, by all the more eminent international jurists of Europe, from Grotius to Vattel; and apparently forgetful of the observation made by his distinguished countryman, Mr. Chancellor Kent, "no civilized nation, which does not arrogantly set all ordinary law and justice at defiance, will venture to disregard the uniform sense of established writers on international law."

Farther, our Author here continues to designate the rule, recognized by this treaty, "the pretensions of England;" as if it had not been justified by the uniform opinions of all the jurists just alluded to; as if it had not been the uniform practice of all the nations of Europe, in their administration of maritime international law, for five centuries, except in cases of special paction, by which the contracting governments consented reciprocally to concede the right, and created a privilege in favour of each other, contingently for an indefinite, or more frequently for a definite period, as in the case of the treaty of Utrecht in 1713, between France and Holland.

Finally, our Author takes care to conclude the paragraph, with the remark, that this convention bears the concession of the opposite principle of "free ship, free goods" on the part of the powers of the North, as if this last rule had ever been recognized by any of the more eminent jurists, as justly or universally expedient; thereby insinuating, that this rule was merely then abandoned by the Northern powers, and inferentially, not by the Southern powers of Europe; not quite in consistency with the doctrine, he seems to have all along here maintained, that the Southern powers are entitled to take advantage of this convention, but are not bound by it, Indeed, the truth is, that all the governments, whether northern or southern, who composed either of the confederacies of 1780 or 1800, are chargeable, at least, with unparalleled inconsistency, in combining to demand, and in threatening to exact by force, from another nation, the observance of a rule, which none of themselves had ever observed, except under special paction, and reciprocal stipulation, and which almost all of them in a few years afterwards, by their conduct, publicly renounced, and egregiously infringed and contravened.

The third section of this same article relates to contraband of war, and contains an enumeration of the articles agreed upon, to be held as such. And in his commentary, our Author, not content with the terms of this section of the convention of 1801, remarks, that it renewed the temporary treaty of commerce between

Great Britain and Russia, of February 1797; that by the latter treaty the subjects of Russia, when neutral, were declared entitled to carry naval stores in Russian vessels to the enemy; and that by the convention of June and October 1801, this temporary treaty of commerce was not merely renewed, but transferred into the perpetual convention of 1801, not only in favour of, or against the contracting parties, but in favour of all other maritime states. Now, we have perused this treaty of commerce of February 1797, between Great Britain and Russia,[1] and we cannot discover in it, any express terms bearing precisely that Russian subjects, when neutral, were thereby specially authorized to carry naval stores, in Russian vessels, to the enemy, or more than the usual general declaration, that when neutral, they might carry the produce of their country, innocent goods, not contraband of war, to the ports of other countries, although at war with Britain.

But whether, as alleged by our Author, this treaty of commerce of 1797, contained, or did not contain, a clause, permitting Russian subjects, in express terms, to carry naval stores to hostile ports in their own vessels, is here of little consequence. For, it is plain, such a special permission could not be taken advantage of, or made available, in their favour, by the subjects of any other maritime state than Russia. And it seems, little less than absurd, to argue, that, by merely confirming, of new, the commercial treaty of 1797, by the convention of 1801, the contracting parties intended to make, or did declare perpetual, a temporary treaty of commerce for eight years only, contrary to the uniform established usage, recognized in that treaty itself, article twenty-sixth, of fixing, in all treaties of commerce, a certain period of duration. All treaties of peace, it is

[1] Martens' Recueil, Tom. VI. p. 722.

well known, proceed upon the assumption of perpetual amity,—of no future differences, disputes, or wars. But, to argue from such a practice, that all engagements undertaken, in such treaties, are to be held perpetually and unconditionally binding on the parties, not only in favour of the contracting parties themselves, but in favour of all other states, whether parties to the treaty or not, seems really puerile.

Nevertheless, our author thus proceeds with his argument, which we shall quote, in literal translation, to preclude any charge of not doing it justice. "The third and fourth sections of this article, relative to contraband, and to blockaded ports, did not contain a concession of particular privileges in favour of the contracting parties solely, but a recognition of universal and pre-existing rights, which they could not refuse to concede to any other independent state." But of what avail is all this? What were the universal and pre-existing rights, here stated to have been recognized, in contradistinction to particular privileges conceded in favour of contracting parties? Have we not seen, from the history of the legal practice of the European nations, that the right to capture the property of the enemy in the open seas, although carried by neutrals, is as much an universal and pre-existing right, as any limitation of the particular right of blockade, or any specification of articles to be held contraband of war? Are not the latter, if not concessions of privileges, rather special stipulations, than recognitions of universal pre-existing rights? No person, who has merely glanced over the various collections of international treaties, can fail to be aware, that these treaties contain not merely stipulations and concessions, which are deviations from the Common consuetudinary law of nations, but also conventional recognitions of what are truly principles of the common law. Accordingly, the British government could have no hesitation, in recognizing, by this convention, the rule of blockade, recognized by her international tribunals in their general practice, that to be effectual in law, to infer confiscation from a breach of it, a maritime blockade must be maintained by an adequate naval force. But while they did so, as to blockade, they did otherwise with regard to contraband. They, by this convention, agreed to restrict articles contraband of war, such as to infer confiscation to the mere instruments of war, in favour of Russia, and of Denmark and Sweden, should the latter accede to the convention. But no special surrender appears to have been made, even in favour of the contracting parties, of the Common law right of mere interception and preemption at the market value, when the articles are not, from their nature or adaptation, instruments of war, but calculated to afford material aid to one of the belligerents, from their direct destination, and being, in course, to supply the wants of armies or fleets, actually engaged in, or preparing for military operations.

Our Author proceeds, "The third section was introduced by a separate preamble, declaring, that the intention of the contracting parties was, to avoid all ambiguity and misunderstanding about what was to be distinguished as contraband of war. Conformably to this intention, they then declared, what are the objects they recognize as being such; and this declaration was followed by a special reservation, 'that what is stipulated in the present article, shall not prejudice the particular stipulations of either Crown with other Powers, by which objects of the like kind might be reserved, prohibited, or permitted.'" "If the intention," continues our Author, "of the contracting parties, had been to treat this question solely with regard to their conduct towards each other, and to leave it upon the same footing, as before the league of 1800, all mention of contraband in this part of the convention, would have been superfluous. In that case, it was merely necessary to renew the ancient treaties, which had enumerated the objects of contraband; and as this renewal was expressly stipulated in another article of the convention, the third section behoved to be considered as having in view some distinct object. This object was to prescribe a general rule for all future discussions, with whatever Power it might be, upon the question of naval or military stores, and as establishing a principle of universal law for determining the interpretation of the technical term of contraband of war. The reservation of particular treaties with other Powers, could not be reconciled with a more limited interpretation. It would have been superfluous to declare, that a stipulation, with the Powers of the Baltic alone, should not prejudice subsisting treaties between England and other nations. But, the reservation was not only prudent, but necessary, when she wished to lay down an universal principle, applicable to her transactions with every other independent state. In recognizing a pre-existing right, and in establishing a new interpretation of the law of nations, it was of great importance to reserve, expressly, the exception in favour of her already established claims, by some particular treaties with other Powers."

Now, the introductory terms, at the commencement of this third section, are just the expressions with which almost every attempt, by treaty, to enumerate the articles of contraband of war, and thereby to prevent all disputes, commences. And the preamble of article third, under which this section is comprehended, is, that the contracting parties, "having resolved to put under a sufficient safe-guard, the liberty of the *commerce*, and of the *navigation* of *their subjects*, in the event of one of them being at war, while the other is neutral, have agreed," &c., showing clearly the intention, or object of the parties, was merely to regulate the conduct, and preserve the rights of their respective subjects, in maritime commerce and navigation, not presumptuously to prescribe a code for the other maritime nations of Europe. Nor can the reservation, before quoted, be in fair and sound reasoning founded on, to prove, in opposition to such an explicit preamble, that the lately belligerent, now peace contracting states, Britain on the one side, and Russia, with Denmark and Sweden, on the other, intended something more, than a treaty between, or among themselves; namely, that they intended to go out of their own concerns, and beyond their powers, and to become so benevolent and philanthropic, as to clear up all ambiguities, and settle all differences, not merely for themselves, but for all other nations indiscriminately, whether they chose or not. Such a presumptuous and preposterous intention and arrangement, cannot, in reason, be deduced as a necessary consequence of the reservation founded on. The reservation was necessary and proper, as well as usual, in such cases; and it was necessary and proper, just for the opposite purposes of that, for which our Author contends. Both the contracting parties appear to have previously entered into, or might enter into treaties with other third parties, fixing the description of contraband goods. And while these treaties lasted, or might be entered into, and lasted, it was necessary to stipulate, that the convention of 1801 should not bring the contracting parties under any obligation to violate existing treaties, or preclude them from making other stipulations with other states. And this reservation was put in, not because the parties conceived they had, by this treaty, established, or could establish, any universal law of contraband, but that they might still be at liberty to fulfil any special engagements they might have entered into, or might still enter into, with other nations, relative to that matter.

Our Author thus proceeds, "The interpretation given to the contraband of war by the convention, was derived exclusively from the treaties of the armed neutrality. In the league of 1780, the Empress of Russia had declared, that her engagements with England, relative to contraband, behoved to be henceforth considered as an invariable rule of natural and universal law. The convention of 1801 had adopted the same rule, and agreeably to the same principle, in enumerating all the articles mentioned in the treaty of 1797, between England and Russia, and in declaring, conformably to this treaty, that the two sovereigns recognized these articles only, as being contraband. England, in all her future (subsequent?) discussions with neutral powers, behoved to submit to the consequences of this new rule of public law, which she had herself proclaimed. She had publicly renounced her ancient pretensions, and she had conceded, that naval stores should not be considered as contraband of war, and that she no longer considered them as such. She had expressed this concession, even in the same terms which were employed at first, to render it universal; and she had inserted it in her treaty with these same Powers, who had entered into a confederacy, with the sole view, or object, of compelling her to observe this new law."

Now, this paragraph is very incorrect and fallacious. The interpretation given to the terms contraband of war, by the convention of 1801, was not derived exclusively from the treaties of the armed neutrality. They are almost identical with, and obviously derived from the terms of the treaty of commerce, concluded between Britain and Russia, so far back as 1766, which was continued by the convention of 1793, and still farther continued by the treaty of commerce of February 1797. No treaty was entered into between these powers, at the time the Empress Catherine propounded her scheme of the armed neutrality. There was no league at that time, to which either France or Spain, any more than Great Britain, acceded, or were parties. The convention of June 1801, of new, confirmed the treaty of February 1797, which was soon to expire. And the simple truth is, that, in 1766, in 1793, in 1797, and in 1801, the British government chose, by special treaty, to concede to Russia, for a time, a limitation of contraband of war, to certain specified articles, all mere instruments of war. But, because Britain chose to make this concession to Russia, in consideration of the native produce of the latter, or otherwise, is it to be maintained, she must make the same concession to France, Spain, Prussia, or Holland, or any other nations, not parties to these treaties? It has become almost a proverbial observation, that Britain loses as much by her negociations, as she gains by her arms. If such interpretations, as that here contended for, are to be given to treaties, namely, that what she concedes by treaty to one Power, she must be held to have conceded to all others, she had better not treat, or negociate, at all. And the series of assertions which our Author here parades, are a series of unfounded assumptions, and unwarranted gratuitous inferences. England certainly entered into the treaties with Russia, before enumerated, in 1766, 1793, 1797, and 1801; and, in these treaties, she agreed to limit the description of contraband, to certain specified articles which are instruments of war, or warlike stores. But she did not make any such concession, or allowance, to any other of the nations of the world, who were not parties to these treaties. And, that she neither extended, nor meant to extend, this concession, to all and sundry other nations, is manifest, from the special provision in the convention of June 1801, namely, article ninth, which was deemed necessary to admit Denmark and Sweden, (the former of which nations had chiefly suffered in fighting the battle of neutral pretensions) to the benefit of this convention. England never proclaimed, nor consented to the proclamation of any new rule of public law, either in 1780, or 1800, or 1801; and therefore, cannot be bound to submit to the consequences of an act, which she never performed, or consented to. She had never publicly renounced her ancient claim of right, under the Common law of nations, or conceded, generally, that naval stores should not be considered as contraband of war, or that she recognized them no longer as such. She had not, as alleged, expressed this concession, in the terms which had been employed, at first, to render it universal. For, upon examination of these treaties with Russia,[1] it will be found, that articles tenth and eleventh in the treaty of 1766, are almost entirely identical in expression, with articles tenth and eleventh, in the treaty of 1797, obviously copied, the one from the other; and that the convention of 1801, separate article second, merely confirms, of new, the treaty of commerce of 1797.

The fact, then, again, is simply this. The British government conceded to the Emperor Alexander, the same specification of the articles of contraband, which they had voluntarily conceded to the Empress Catherine in 1766, and to the Emperor Paul in 1797. And how the circumstance of the British government having ad-

[1] Mart. Recueil, I. 144, VI. 746, and Supp. II. 476.

mitted the accession to this last treaty, of the other two Northern powers, who had been induced to combine against Britain, with the Emperor Paul, in the inconsistent scheme he so suddenly adopted in 1800, can be held to imply an extension of the treaty to all other powers, in addition to those specially admitted, it is not easy to comprehend. Denmark and Sweden, indeed, rather unwisely, entered into a confederacy with Paul, to compel Great Britain, by force, to give up the Common law right, which had been exercised not only by Britain, but, independently of special paction, by all the other maritime states of Europe, for five hundred years, and to adopt another one-sided rule, all in favour of neutrals, and all against one, at least, of the opposed belligerents; and to concede to them a special privilege, which no one nation is entitled to exact from another. In this attempt the Northern powers failed, as the Hanse towns had done in former ages, when they endeavoured to enforce the same unequal rule, against Denmark, or Sweden, or England, or France. But while the British government resisted, and wisely resisted, such tyrannical dictation, they agreed, in consideration of the very uncertain state, in which the French revolution had still, at that time, placed the other continental nations; and in consideration, also, as in former times, of the nature of a great part of the produce of the Northern states, to concede for an indefinite time, to the Emperor Alexander, the same limitation in the enumeration of contraband of war, as they had formerly done, for limited periods, to the Empress Catherine, and the Emperor Paul. And this, in truth, and when discharged of false colouring, is all that Britain, in this matter, really did.

The 4th section of the third article of the convention of 1801, defines what is to be deemed a blockaded port.

And our Author's first argument is founded on the allegation, "that the stipulation, with regard to blockaded ports in the convention of 1801, was also transcribed, with the exception of a single word, from the corresponding articles of the two conventions of the armed neutrality. The articles had declared, that to determine what characterizes a blockaded port, this denomination be given only to that port where there is by the disposition of the power who attacks it, with vessels stationed and sufficiently near, an evident danger in entering. In the convention of 1801, instead of the expressions, "et suffisamment proches," the contracting parties had substituted, "ou suffisamment proches." There was not the least doubt, that by this change of a single word, minute as it was, they wished to establish in all their extent, the principles supported by England, upon this grand question of maritime blockades, and against which the article had been framed in the two conventions. But what Lord Grenville complained of, was, the want of foresight in leaving a principle, so important, to depend upon the minute and scarcely perceptible variation of a single particle." But, really, this renewal, by a foreigner, after the lapse of more than forty years, of the argumentation of a British Peer, in opposition, against the ministers who had succeeded him, is rather puerile. The clause, defining a legal blockade, in the convention of 1801, it is true, does not appear to have been transcribed, like the preceding clauses regarding contraband goods, and trade in innocent goods, from the previous British and Russian treaties of 1766 and 1797. But, from whatever source or quarter, this clause was derived, is immaterial. It was, of course, proposed, and urged by the neutral powers, who naturally enough expressed it in the same terms, as had been used by them in their treaties with each other, in

1780 and 1800, when the neutral pretensions went a great deal farther, than the convention of 1801 sanctioned. And the British government could not have any reasonable objection to this clause, except as being superfluous. For Britain had admitted the substance of this clause, as being the rule of the Common consuetudinary law of nations from the year 1689, when she was induced by Holland, to join in declaring the coasts of France in a state of blockade, but, on remonstrance, recalled the proclamation;—to a period, subsequent to the date of the convention we are now considering, namely, 1807, when the French Berlin decree, declaring Great Britain in a state of blockade, provoked the British orders in council of January and November 1807, interdicting reciprocally all commerce with France, erroneously denominated a blockade. Indeed, the British government could not, with any propriety, object to such a clause, when, within a few years preceding, the British Prize Court of Appeal had held, "Although Admiral Jervis had declared the West India Islands under blockade, yet, that as the fact did not support the declaration, a blockade could not be deemed legally to exist;" and when the then very eminent Judge of the High Court of Admiralty had repeatedly delivered the same doctrine.

The other two objections, which our Author here also borrows from Lord Grenville's anti-ministerial speech, do not seem to require much answer. It is, manifestly, a far-fetched and feeble argument, to say, that the use of the terms in this clause, "la puissance qui l'attaque," implies a dereliction of the right to blockade a sea-port, for the purpose merely of intercepting supplies of provisions to a country, or adjacent district.[1] The other objection is founded on the nature

[1] Rob. Adm. Rep. Vol. I. p. 83

of naval warlike operations depending on variations in seasons and weather, in consequence of which a squadron, employed in the blockade of a port, and of sufficient force for this service, yet cannot always remain stationary before the port, or even near enough to render the entrance evidently dangerous. Now, the general observation is unquestionably true. But to any one who has perused the judgments of Sir William Scott, in cases of blockade, it will be manifest, that, even under this clause, which scarcely appears to make any modification of the Common law of nations, and does not at all vary that law, except with reference to the contracting parties, the right of actual legal blockade may be exercised, to as great an extent and effect, as is consistent with justice.

The fourth article of the convention of June 1801, under the concession made by Great Britain to Russia, Denmark, and Sweden, confines and limits the exercise of the right of visitation and search of merchant vessels, sailing under their neutral national convoy, to the state or government ships of war of the belligerents, detailing, in five sections, the mode in which the procedure is to take place. And, again indebted to the antiministerial speech of Lord Grenville, in November 1801, our Author here attempts to show, that, by the convention of 1801, the British government, in a great measure, admitted the doctrine of the armed neutrality, and conceded the right of search in the case of neutral vessels under convoy. Thus, "The pretension of the neutral league of 1800, limited the visit to a simple reading of the papers, which were to be communicated, to the officer of the belligerent power, on board the neutral ship of war. The same form of procedure had been stipulated by the convention of 1801; and it was added in the two treaties, that if the papers were recognized as regular, there should not be room for any other visit. An exception was, nevertheless, still added in the convention of 1801, which formed the only real distinction between the two treaties. It was not declared, in an absolute manner, as formerly, that there should not be any other visit in any case; but only in the case in which there existed, "aucun motif valable de suspicion." Bona fides behoved necessarily, to preclude the belligerent power from pretending that the right of which the exercise behoved to be suspended, except in the case in which there existed some valid ground of suspicion, could, nevertheless, be exercised in all cases, at its discretion."

Even supposing, however, the mode of procedure agreed to, by the convention of 1801, to have amounted to a relinquishment, in some measure, of the right of search, this concession was in favour only of Russia, Denmark and Sweden; and cannot, consistently with legal principle, be taken advantage of, by the other maritime states, who took no share in, and had no connection with, this convention; with reference to whom it was truly, res inter alios acta. And with regard to the limitation, alleged to arise from the insertion in the fourth section of the words, "motif valable de suspicion," these terms, are by the convention only applicable to the search of merchant vessels actually sailing under convoy; and, although they were applicable to the search of merchant vessels, not able, or not willing to place themselves under convoy, the terms are sufficiently comprehensive, to include all cases, where there is reasonable ground for suspicion,—where such suspicion can be entertained bonâ fide. And beyond that point, the British government and nation, can have no wish to exercise such a right.

After the preceding commentary on the convention

of 1801, our Author subjoins, that the stipulation inserted in the treaty of Utrecht in favour of the rule, that the flag ought to cover the cargo, was not renewed by the treaty of Amiens in 1801–2, between Britain and France. The fact is, that, at that time, neither of the governments either practised the rule, or wished it to be renewed. And, we may add, that, as little was it renewed by the treaty of Ghent in 1814, or by the treaty of Paris in 1815.

Our Author concludes his account of the discussions concerning the armed neutrality scheme, contained in § 9, of the fourth and last period of his history, by noticing the declaration of the Russian Emperor Alexander in 1807, "proclaiming of new, the principles of the armed neutrality, that monument of the wisdom of the Empress Catherine; and engaging never to derogate from that system." He notices also the answer of the British government in 1807; and adds, "The subsequent treaties of peace and commerce between England and Russia observe silence on the point in dispute." In the preceding commentary, our Author argued most stoutly, that all the other maritime states have a right to be admitted to the benefit of the convention of June and October 1801, between Britain on the one side, and Russia, Denmark and Sweden on the other, upon the pretence of Britain having thereby, contrary to its express declarations, and actual conduct, adopted, ex propri motu, and gratuitously, the doctrines of the armed neutrality, and of her having thereby established rules of law, inconsistent with the principles of equal justice, injurious to nations, who may be forced into war, and unduly favourable to nations, who pretend neutrality, that they may profit by the unfortunate disputes of their neighbours. And it is rather amusing to find our Author, here, ultimately raising a doubt, whether this very convention be still in force, or rather, whether it was not annulled by the Russian declaration of 1807, and subsequent war between Russia and Britain, and is not now binding, in consequence of the silence of the subsequent treaties. The treaty of peace of Oerebro, 18th July 1812, was hurriedly entered into: and makes provision only for the re-establishment of friendship and commerce generally, upon the footing of the most favoured nations. But it is here quite unnecessary, to examine minutely, the other subsequent treaties of alliance, between Great Britain and Russia, in order to find an express and special renewal of the convention of 1801. For no other government or nation, has any right to enquire, whether it be now in force or not, except those, who were actually parties to it; and the latter will, no doubt, attend to their own interests.

Before concluding this our too long review of Dr. Wheaton's History of the Law of Nations, so far as regards matters maritime, we must acknowledge our obligation to him, for enabling us to transcribe from his additional notes b, the argument maintained by the minister of the United States, in the negociation in 1798 with the Prussian government, for the renewal of the treaty of 1785. For, with reference to the pretension of the neutral flag covering the hostile cargo at sea, the averments then made on the part of the American government, contain and exhibit, a perspicuous and concise, and what is of still greater importance, a correct and true view, of the real and actual state and condition of the Common consuetudinary maritime law of nations, as existing at the close of the eighteenth century, and as liable to be affected and modified by special conventions; besides suggesting the only mode, in which, by treaty, such a stipulation, so contrary to fact and legal principle, can be made, so far to operate, practically, with equality or justice.

"We have," says our Author, in note b, p. 314, "already explained, that, by the treaty of 1785, between the United States of America and Prussia, the rights of neutral navigation and commerce, in time of war, had been recognized upon the basis of the armed neutrality of 1780. At the time of the negociation, commenced in 1798, for the renewal of the treaty of 1785, the American government had given instructions to its plenipotentiary, Mr. John Quincy Adams, to propose to the Prussian cabinet, to suppress these stipulations of the old treaty, and to substitute the rules of the ordinary law of nations. This instruction was founded upon the fact, alleged by the American government, that the principle of 'free ships, free goods,' had not been respected by any of the belligerent Powers during the then existing war, not even by those who had formerly armed themselves to defend it. The American government admitted, that the mutual interest of the two nations, as well as that of all neutral states, ought to lead them to recognize the principle, that the 'flag covers the cargo,' provided the principle was generally recognized and respected by the belligerent powers. But, that the experience of the present war, had shown too clearly, that the most formal stipulations to that effect, were not observed; while the neutral state, in case of its becoming belligerent, would be bound by its engagements, and would thus be a loser, in all cases, as a neutral power, and as a belligerent. War between the United States and France, then, appeared to be imminent; and in that case, the commerce of the latter would be protected by the neutral flag, while the American commerce would be exposed, as it was already, to the depredations of the French privateers. If, at the end of the war, all the great maritime powers should unite to recognize the principles of the armed neutrality, the United States would be desirous to accede to such an engagement, and to observe it, as a general rule. But if the maritime war in Europe were to continue, and especially if the United States were to take part in it, it would be in the last degree impolitic to fetter the operations of their privateers by such like engagements."

"In acknowledging the receipt of these instructions, Mr. Adams expressed to his government, doubts, whether the proposed changes in the treaty of 1785 with Prussia would be opportune. He observed, that the principle of the 'flag covering the cargo,' continued to be supported by the maritime powers of the north of Europe, although the stipulations in favour of the principle had been too little observed, in all the wars. In the present war, the principle had been less than ever respected; the maritime power of England having received so great an extension; and France believing herself liberated by the example of her enemy, from the ordinary obligations of the law of nations. But that France still recognized, in principle, the rules of the armed neutrality, and, above all, desired to constrain England to recognize them. Such was also the policy of Prussia, and of the other powers of the Baltic. They had even maintained, on several occasions, that the principle, that 'the flag covers the cargo,' formed a rule of the *ordinary law of nations*, independently of particular conventions. This doctrine was supported by the Danish publicist, Hübner, in his Traité de la Saisie des Batimens Neutres; who laid down as a principle, that, according to the natural law of nations, 'free ships rendered the goods free.' The question had been recently discussed profoundly, by Lampredi, a highly esteemed Italian publicist, who insists, that in this case, there is, by the law of nature, a collision between two rights equally incontestable;—that the belligerent Power has the right to visit, and that the neutral has the right to withdraw himself from the visit. The question put, in this manner, depends, then, on the right of the strongest; and, the belligerent Power being armed, the neutral master and crew are constrained to submit to the visit. Mr. Adams was of opinion, that this reasoning was of great weight, and that Lampredi had presented the question in its true point of view. At the same time, he admitted, there would be great inconveniences, when two maritime Powers were at war, if the neutral state should be held bound, by the principle, that 'free ships render goods free,' towards one of the Powers, and by the opposite principle towards the other; and, in these circumstances, it was not to be expected the principle of 'free navigation' would be scrupulously respected by either of the belligerent Powers. He was, therefore, of opinion, that the stipulation should be made contingent, and that the contracting parties might stipulate, that, in all the cases, in which the one of the parties should be at war, with a third Power, while the other should remain neuter, the neutral vessel should render the cargo free, provided the enemy of the Power at war, recognized the same principle, and caused it to be respected in their prize courts; and that, in the opposite case, the rigorous rule of the *ordinary* law of nations should be observed."

"Notwithstanding his doubts with regard to the reception the proposal would meet with, the American negociator, following out the instructions of his government, proposed to the Prussian plenipotentiaries, to substitute for the twelfth article of the old treaty, stipulating that "free vessels render the goods free," the rule of the *ordinary* law of nations, that all hostile property, on board neutral vessels, should remain subject to capture, and that all neutral property, on board hostile vessels, should remain free." To this proposal, the Prussian Plenipotentiaries made long objections. To their communication, the American minister, Mr. Adams, replied, "That the principle on which his government founded, in proposing the change, relative to the security of hostile property, on board neutral vessels, is, that, by the ordinary law of nations, in time of maritime war, hostile goods, on board neutral vessels, are liable to capture, and neutral goods, on board hostile vessels, are free. That this rule cannot be changed, but by the general consent of all the maritime powers, or by particular treaties, of which the engagements can only extend to the contracting parties. That the contrary principle, of which the establishment was to be one of the principal objects of the armed neutrality, during the war of American independence, had not been universally recognized, even at that epoch; and has not been maintained during the present war, by any of the powers, who acceded to that system at the time. That even Prussia herself, so far as she was a belligerent party, in her last war, did not admit it; and that, at the present moment, the ancient principle of the law of nations subsists still, in all its force, among all the Powers, except in the cases, when the opposite rule is stipulated by the engagements of a positive treaty."

"In proposing, then, to recognize the liberty of neutral goods, on board hostile vessels, and to recognize as subject to capture, hostile goods, on board neutral vessels, the wish has merely been to *confirm*, by the treaty, the *principles* which *exist* at this moment, even independently of all treaty; the wish has been, not to make, but to *avoid* a *change* in the existing order of things."

These discussions were protracted to a considerable length, and led Mr. Adams to remark to his government, the tenacity with which the Prussian government adhered to the principle, "that the neutral flag should cover the merchandise belonging to the enemy." Indeed, it appears, that, when he acceded to the armed neutrality in 1780, Frederic II. having no treaty of commerce with any of the belligerent powers, adopted this new rule, as well as the very restricted list of contraband goods, as being the most favourable to neutral interest, agreeably to his usual sagacious policy, and without, perhaps, examining very minutely, the competing rights of nations, who are forced, by aggression, to go to war.

But, it is here unnecessary to detail this negociation any farther, especially as it terminated, merely, in the reservation of the question, till a more convenient opportunity should occur. The preceding quotations show, sufficiently, what was the view entertained by the American government and its ablest jurists, in 1798, of the *Ordinary*, or Common consuetudinary law of nations, as then existing. And we have only farther to observe, that Mr. Adams, or our Author, have not, by any means, done Lampredi justice, in representing, that, according to his mode of putting the question, it depended on the right of the strongest. It was scarcely to be supposed, that any man, who could write such a work, as Juris Publici Universalis, sive Juris Naturae, et Gentium Theoremata, would exhibit any right as depending merely on the possession of superior physical force. And, on reverting to the passages, which, to prevent any misunderstanding, we quoted literally from his work, Del Commercio dei Popoli Neutrali in tempo di Guerra, in our first volume,[1] it will be found, Lampredi points out, how frequently in human affairs, in jurisprudence, or internal municipal law, as well as in

[1] Pp. 382-389

international law, collisions of rights take place; and solves the difficulty, not by resting the preference on the possession of greater physical power, but by considerations of equity and general expediency, particularly by showing, that the right, of which the suspension or non-exercise, admits of nearly adequate reparation, or compensation, ought to be postponed to the right, of which the suspension, or non-exercise, does not physically admit of such reparation or compensation.

CHAPTER XX.

Conclusion.

We have now concluded our historical review; and we venture to hope we have been able to afford our readers some assistance and facility, not only in tracing historically, through successive ages, the progress of Maritime international law, but also in forming for themselves pretty correct notions of the leading doctrines of this branch of law, as at present recognized. After such a tedious narrative, interspersed with long argumentative discussions, we certainly have no wish or intention, to add to the length of the work, by any full recapitulation of the leading doctrines just alluded to. Indeed, any necessity for such a farther detailed statement of principles, appears to us to be superseded, by the abridgement we have given of the work of M. Tetens. This work was composed by an impartial and enlightened neutral, possessed of all the talent and practical knowledge requisite for enabling him to do so with success; and after almost all the great leading questions in dispute, had emerged, and been discussed, excepting the Continental system of Napoleon, and the British Retaliatory Orders in Council of 1807, which, it is to be hoped, after astounding mankind for a while, have both, like comets, passed from the planetary system of international law, never to return.

The work of M. Tetens, is, of course, free from all British bias, national partiality, or prejudice. And, so far as there is any leaning, it is obviously to the neutral side,—to the full extent of what are really neutral rights. For this reason, we recommend this short work, as the fairest foreign specimen we have met with, of maritime international law during war, now generally recognized and observed. And, in doing so, we do not conceive we are at all deficient in patriotism, or attachment to our native country. For Britain has no peculiar and exclusive system of maritime international law, as falsely represented. She has no occasion to ask, and asks nothing but truth, justice, and reciprocity; Nil sibi postulat, quod non aliis tribuit. And, upon this footing, we shall merely notice briefly, how the more important disputed questions appear, from the preceding historical deduction, to have been settled, or to have stood, at the general peace of 1815, or stand at present; alluding also to the means, by which any farther alleviation of the evils of maritime war, may probably be effected.

I.

CONVENTIONAL MARITIME INTERNATIONAL LAW.

Beginning, of course, with the conventional branch of maritime international law during war, we have not found any treaties, containing stipulations relative to neutral commerce and navigation, and entered into prior to the peace of Amiens, to be now obligatory and in force, except the convention of June and October 1801, between Britain and Russia, to which Denmark and Sweden acceded, under an express provision in the treaty to that effect. And, supposing that treaty to be still in force, we may refer to it, as constituting Conventional law, between Britain and the maritime Powers of the Baltic; but not between any of these Powers, and the other maritime Powers of Europe, or America. Any farther detailed account, however, of that convention, would be here superfluous, as we have already discussed its import and provisions, at more than sufficient length.

The other treaties among the different European Powers, prior to the peace of Amiens, which contained special stipulations with regard to neutral commerce and navigation, particularly with regard to the neutral flag covering the hostile cargo, such as those of 1713, 1763, and 1783, we have seen, have all expired, or been formally declared null, or been forfeited by the non-fulfilment of counter-stipulations, or been passed from, as unjust and unequal in execution, or otherwise, tacitly, from mutual consent. And these prior treaties were neither renewed at the close of the French revolutionary war in 1801, nor at the close of the French imperial war in 1815.

Since the general peace, in 1815, certain treaties of commerce and navigation have been concluded among the different maritime states; such as the treaties of Britain in 1815, with the United States of America, in 1824 with the Low Countries, in 1825 with Denmark and the Hanse towns, in 1826 with France, in 1827 with the United States of America, in 1837 with Holland, in 1829 and 1838 with Austria. And these treaties, so far as they have not expired, from being limited, according to the usual practice in such cases, to definite periods, without a renewal, are, of course, to be first consulted, as constituting the existing Conventional maritime law of nations between these states. But these treaties, we have seen, chiefly regulate the intercourse of the contracting parties during peace; and, with reference to war, embrace only a very few points, such as fixing the period, within which foreigners may depart, upon a rupture; enumerating certain articles as contraband; and declaring, according to the common law, that, to be legally effectual, the blockade must be actual, without stipulating "free ship, free goods," or any of the other dogmas of the armed neutrality.

II.

COMMON CONSUETUDINARY MARITIME LAW OF NATIONS DURING WAR.

In the preceding historical deduction, we have seen, that the chief disputed claims of belligerents and neutrals in their collision, have been thus regulated in practice, where there was no special compact.

Principal Rights of Belligerents in Maritime War.

1. In maritime war, or the use of physical power, at sea, by nation against nation, for the enforcement of legal rights, belligerent nations may lawfully capture and confiscate, not only the ships of the enemy, but also the goods of the enemy on board these ships, in the open seas.

2. Belligerents may lawfully capture and confiscate the goods of the enemy at sea, although on board neutral vessels, on payment to the neutral of the stipulated freight; but not goods belonging to neutrals on board hostile vessels; the national character of the cargo, as well as that of the vessel, being determined, by that of the proprietors, to whom they respectively belong; and hostile goods on board a neutral vessel, not inferring

any forfeiture of the vessel, or of other goods on board, belonging to neutrals.

3. Belligerents may lawfully capture and confiscate, in the open seas, even the goods of neutrals, which are contraband of war, or which are, from their natural qualities, construction, or composition, quantity, or number, directly subservient to the purposes of war, and destined for the enemy; without any payment of freight, or allowance for detention. But the neutral vessel is not liable to confiscation, in consequence of the carriage of such contraband goods, unless they both belong to the same person, or persons, or are disguised by false papers.

4. Belligerents may lawfully intercept and retain, upon payment of the market value, in other words, under the right of pre-emption, goods, which are not, from their nature, construction, composition, quantity or number, and destination, instruments of, or directly subservient to the purposes of war, but may, in the particular state and circumstances of the war, afford the requisite supplies for the armies or fleets of the enemy, or are destined to the naval arsenals, or ports of equipment, of the enemy.

5. Belligerents may blockade the sea-ports, and adjacent parts of the coasts, and mouths of rivers belonging to the enemy, and may lawfully confiscate vessels and cargoes, for breach of blockade. But, to warrant such confiscation, the blockade must have been actual, and constantly maintained, so far as the weather permitted, by an adequate naval force. And the penalty of confiscation does not extend beyond the current voyage, unless the outward and homeward voyage be proved to form one and the same adventure and transaction.

6. For the effectual exercise of the preceding rights, belligerent nations are entitled, by their national ships

of war, and their duly commissioned privateers, to stop, visit, and search merchant vessels, so as to ascertain, to whom the vessels and cargoes belong, and whether the goods on board be contraband of war, or belong to the enemy, agreeably to the mode fixed, by the long established usage of nations.

7. Belligerents are entitled to adjudicate vessels and cargoes, captured as prize, in the open sea, in their Admiralty and other Prize Courts, established in the country of the captor, or in its colonies or other dependencies, but deciding according to the maritime law of nations.

Principal Rights of Neutrals in Maritime War.

1. Neutrals are entitled, during war, as during peace, to carry on their own trade, from the ports of their own, and other neutral countries, to and from, the ports of the enemy, or opposed belligerent, whether parent state or colony. But they are not entitled, under the penalty of confiscation, to trade directly between the ports of the parent state, and those of its colonies, or to carry the goods of the enemy from the ports of the parent state to those of its colonies, and from the ports of the colonies to those of the parent state; partly, because this would be carrying on for the enemy, his colonial trade, from which all neutrals are excluded during peace, but chiefly, because such an interposition would be lending a material assistance to the enemy, inconsistent with the impartiality, which is the essence of neutrality; especially if the enemy had been compelled to *throw* open this exclusive trade, and to admit neutrals, in consequence of the military operations of his antagonist.

Neutrals, however, although not entitled to aid the

enemy, by carrying on for him the trade, which his adversary has disabled him from carrying on himself, may carry on their own proper trade, by importing the goods purchased by them, in the colonies of the enemy, into their own country, and afterwards exporting these goods to the mother country; provided they act bonâ fide,—provided the importation and exportation of the colonial produce be not simulate, or pretended,—provided there has been a real exchange of property and tran-shipment,—in short, provided it be the proper trade of the neutral, not of the enemy.

2. Upon the same principle, neutrals are not entitled to trade, or carry the goods of the enemy, from port to port, on the coasts of the hostile country; or, in other words, to carry on for him, the coasting trade of the enemy, formerly, under the like penalty of confiscation, now softened into loss of freight.

3. Neutrals are entitled to the stipulated freight for goods belonging to the enemy, when captured by the belligerents, and to indemnification for undue detention. But neutrals are not entitled to freight for the carriage of goods, which are clearly contraband of war, by treaty, or from their natural quality, construction, composition, quantity, number, and direct destination to the enemy.

4. Neutral goods are not liable to confiscation from being on board a hostile vessel, or from being loaded or shipped along with hostile goods. Nor is a neutral vessel liable to confiscation from having on board hostile goods.

5. Although not entitled to freight, neutral vessels are not liable to confiscation, from the carriage of goods contraband of war; unless both ship and cargo belong to the same persons and the goods are attempted to be covered by false papers.

6. Neutral states are entitled to adjudicate in their

prize courts, when the capture has been made within their territorial seas, or when the capture has been made from the subjects of these neutral states, and the captured vessel and cargo have been brought into their ports.

Meliorations to be expected in Maritime warfare.

Such seem to be the leading general rules of the Common consuetudinary maritime law of nations, which have been disputed, but are at present recognized. And deeming it superfluous to enumerate those other various co-ordinate general rules, of this department of international law, which have not been disputed, but have all along been tacitly acquiesced in, or to recapitulate those subordinate and more minute questions and rules, most of which have been noticed, if not discussed, in the course of our review of the works of the more eminent international jurists, we shall conclude with reverting, shortly, to the interesting question, whether, and how far the abuses, which have occurred in maritime wars, if such wars cannot be altogether avoided, may be alleviated, and reduced within the range of operations, necessary for the attainment of the legitimate end of all wars.

And here, we cannot but consider, as a very inadequate remedy, although it were practicable, the boasted maxim of "free ship, free goods;"—the unilateral rule, originally invented and introduced, and, from obviously interested motives, so earnestly urged by the neutral states in possession of the carrying trade,—the commerce de fret,—and latterly supported, for a time, by the great Continental maritime states, who, while they, either voluntarily, or from compulsion, persevered in warfare themselves, found it convenient, at little or no cost, to counteract, or defeat, the military operations of their enemies, by obtaining, under this fictitious rule, a safe conveyance by sea, during war, for the various commodities which they might desire to export *or* import, and particularly, a mode of carrying on, at little more expense, and with complete security from the enemy, their coasting and colonial trade.

For, the observance of this rule, founded on fiction, so inconsistent with fact and the natural feelings of justice, cannot, de jure, be exacted by any one independent nation from another; and, as maintained by the Spanish government in 1780, and by the government of the United States, in its negociation with Prussia in 1798, cannot, except under a contingent condition, become the subject of an equal and fair contract or convention. Indeed, this rule, as a remedy for the abuses that occur in maritime war, seems tantamount to a proposal to remedy excessive litigation in a country, by shutting up all the Courts of justice. The chief, if not the only reasons, which have been assigned, or which perhaps can be assigned, other than uni-lateral interest, for the adoption of this rule, are the great difficulties encountered in discriminating neutral from hostile property; chiefly occasioned, it cannot be denied, by the frauds of neutrals, acting in collusion with the enemy. And the plan proposed for obviating these difficulties, is a screen, a cloak, a cover, which conceals from the Judge the illicit as well as the lawful commodities, so that having no opportunity of seeing any difference in the goods in point of legal right, he has fewer disputes to decide. Such an uni-lateral rule as this, introduced solely by paction, was justly exploded at the end of the eighteenth century; and was excluded from treaties, as it had all along been, from the practice of the Common law of nations. And there is little or no reason to expect, it will again be introduced, even in special conventions.

But, it is to be hoped, there are other less clumsy and more efficient modes of, at least, alleviating the evils which have occurred in maritime warfare, beyond those which unavoidably result from the use of physical force, by nation against nation, although resorted to only in self-defence, or in the prosecution of undoubted rights. M. Tetens has distinctly shown, that, by far the greatest part of the abuses complained of, do not necessarily arise from the application of the rules of justice between belligerents and neutrals; and that other means, quite practicable, may be adopted, for checking these abuses. And, to avoid repetition, we beg to refer to our quotations, from the excellent work of that jurist, contained in this volume.[1]

The measures, to be effectual, must, of course, be adopted by both the parties interested in the suppression of the abuses. The belligerents, as resorting to war, in vindication of their rights, and as thereby the originators of the relative state of nations in which these abuses take place, are bound, in the first instance, to apply all practicable remedies. In modern Europe, the belligerent governments, in general, have already done a great deal to prevent unwarranted captures at sea, and any severe treatment on the part of their privateers, of the masters, officers, and crews of neutral merchant vessels. But they might still do more. They might abolish their privateers, and carry on their operations against the maritime trade of the enemy by their regular navies; as we have, again and again, earnestly recommended, for reasons, which it is here unnecessary to repeat. Unfortunately however, this, perhaps the most important of all the remedies which belligerents

[1] pp. 164–184.

can adopt, is the most difficult of accomplishment; since the abolition of privateers cannot take place, or be expected, except by the universal consent of all the maritime states; because no single nation can, with a due regard to its own safety, give up this mode of warfare, while other nations continue it.

In the meantime therefore, it remains to be considered, what other and farther measures, can be adopted by belligerent governments, for preventing unwarranted captures, and the undue treatment of the masters and mariners of neutral vessels. For centuries past, security has been taken by the maritime governments of Europe, from the owners and commanders of privateers, for their correct conduct in their cruizes. And, for a long period, special instructions have also been issued by them, to the Commanders of their cruizers, whether national ships of war, or privateers, at the commencement, and in the course of the war. But these instructions might be made still more special and distinct,—might be more effectually brought home to the knowledge of every commander or subordinate officer of a privateer, as well as of the officers of the regular navy,—and might be enforced, under more severe penalties for non-observance, regularly inflicted, so as to deter others from similar offences or delinquencies. Indeed, it might be made a condition, of every grant of a commission, to a privateer, that, during all its cruizes, there should be on board two persons, properly qualified, in the employment of government, to see that the commander and subordinate officers of the privateer acted in conformity with their instructions, and treated the master and crew of the merchant vessel, when stopped and visited, with all the lenity which the accomplishment of a legal capture admits.

On the other hand, it is equally a duty incumbent on

the governments of neutral nations, and it is, perhaps, still more in their power, to prevent the abuses complained of, than in that of even the belligerent governments themselves. For experience proves, that the difficulties encountered in distinguishing hostile from neutral goods, arise chiefly from the physical facility of giving, to the former, the semblance and ostensible appearance of the latter, and from the fraudulent ingenuity, exerted and exhibited, in such a variety of ways, for the accomplishment of this object. These fraudulent devices are well exposed by M. Tetens. And it is abundantly obvious, that it is not the belligerent, but the neutral governments themselves, who have the power, and whose duty it is, to detect, check, and repress such frauds. It is a duty which they owe to their own honest subjects, who act and trade bonâ fide. For, although a neutral vessel, carrying a really neutral cargo, has nothing to fear, and a neutral vessel, though carrying a hostile cargo, if not contraband, receives her stipulated freight, and suffers merely the detention, which may possibly disappoint her master, in obtaining another freight so soon as he might otherwise have done, the bonâ fide neutral trader is frequently subjected to a more narrow search and examination, and to a longer detention, than he would otherwise incur, in consequence of the frauds committed by his fellow-countrymen, and the suspicions thereby unavoidably excited.

Now, all these frauds are committed for the purpose of concealing and disguising the property of the enemy, and necessarily imply collusion with the subjects of the hostile government. But such fraudulent collusion, it is surely in the power of neutral governments to check and suppress, by a set of prohibitory regulations, enforced by adequate penalties for infringement, and by maintaining merely such a surveillance over their foreign trade, and the portion of their subjects engaged in that trade, as they actually do at present, for the prevention of smuggling and for ensuring the payment of their own internal taxes, on the importation or exportation of commodities, as part of the revenue of the state.

It has been alleged, that instead of checking fraudulent neutralizations of hostile property and interests, some neutral governments have, from favour to one of the belligerent nations, or other more interested considerations, rather encouraged, or at least connived at such practices in their subjects. And, if such has been the conduct of any neutral government, it would certainly furnish a more than sufficient answer to its complaints, of the abuses committed by belligerent cruizers. But we cannot believe, that such conduct would be adopted by any government, that deserved the appellation of civilized. And the support of justice and of the genuine law of nations, happily requires no aid from untrue, and still less from false allegations or representations. Magna Vis Veritatis.

Finally, besides taking the necessary preliminary measures, for preventing, as far as practicable, unwarranted captures by privateers, and the undue treatment of the masters and crews of neutral merchant vessels, and with a view to the ascertainment of the legality of the capture when made, it becomes the duty of belligerent governments, to have well organized prize tribunals, composed of judges appointed for life, ad vitam aut culpam, with suitable salaries—of individuals, not only highly talented, and profoundly learned in that department of the law, but also, on the one hand, so clear sighted and of such practical sagacity, as to unravel the plots and detect the fraudulent schemes and devices of neutrals and enemies acting in collusion; and, on the other hand, of such unspotted integrity, as to be above all suspicion of partiality, and of such firmness and independence of mind, as to support and protect, as far as practicable, the honest bonâ fide neutral trader, against any act of arrogance or oppression, on the part of any of his own countrymen.

It is likewise most desirable, that the Bar, as well as the Judges of these international courts, should be not only learned, but highly talented and of independent mind; and, that all reasonable allowances should be made for full freedom of debate. So far as can be done, consistently with the attainment of this object, the expenses of the judicial procedure ought to be made moderate. And, in the event of the pecuniary means requisite for obtaining a full investigation and fair trial, being, in any case, deficient, aid ought to be afforded by the belligerent government, for that purpose.

Printed in Dunstable, United Kingdom

91222341R00338